시원스쿨
토익
실전 1500제

RC READING

시원스쿨 토익
실전 1500제 RC

초판 1쇄 발행 2021년 1월 8일
초판 7쇄 발행 2024년 4월 30일

지은이 정상 시원스쿨어학연구소
펴낸곳 (주)에스제이더블유인터내셔널
펴낸이 양홍걸 이시원

홈페이지 www.siwonschool.com
주소 서울시 영등포구 영신로 166 시원스쿨
교재 구입 문의 02)2014-8151
고객센터 02)6409-0878

ISBN 979-11-6150-436-0 13740
Number 1-110201-02020400-02

시원스쿨 토익

토익

1500

실전 제

RC READING

최소의 비용으로 초고속 고득점 달성
시원스쿨 토익 실전 1500제

본 저자는 토익 강의만 10년 이상, 토익 교재를 20권 이상 저술한 사람으로, 이 분야 최고 전문가라는 자부심이 있습니다. 하지만, 완벽한 사람은 없기에 새 교재를 선보일 때마다 두근두근하는 걱정과 기대가 함께 있어왔습니다. 그런데 「시원스쿨 토익 실전 1500제」를 내놓으면서는 오로지 확신만 듭니다. '시원스쿨어학연구소'라는 시험영어 분야 최고 전문가들과 함께 문제를 개발했기 때문입니다.

「시원스쿨 토익 실전 1500제」는 최근 10년간 토익 기출 빅데이터를 완벽하게 분석한 결과를 토대로 최빈출 고난도 문제 유형들을 총 망라하여 900점 이상을 보장하는 실전 모의고사 문제집입니다. 이 교재를 선택한 여러분의 성적 향상은 저와 시원스쿨어학연구소가 책임지겠습니다. 대신, 여러분께서는 다음 세 가지 약속을 반드시 이행해 주셔야 합니다.

첫째, 반드시 TEST 한 회를 실제 시험을 보듯이 집중하고 풀어야 합니다. 중간에 멈추거나 여러 번 나누어 풀면 그 효과가 급격히 떨어진다는 것을 명심하세요.

둘째, 동영상 강의 혹은 교재 해설을 반복해 보면서 가능한 한 완벽하게 이해하려 애써야 합니다. 오답 이유 뿐 아니라 정답 이유까지 말입니다. 맞힌 문제라고 대충 넘겨버리면 결코 원하는 성적을 얻을 수 없습니다.

셋째, 교재 속 어휘/표현은 파트를 막론하고 모두 암기하려 노력합시다. 그 과정에서 어휘 문제 뿐 아니라 독해와 LC 직청직해 능력까지 모두 좋아집니다.

저는 여러분이 시원스쿨랩과 저에게 보여주시는 기대와 사랑을 10배, 100배로 돌려드리겠다는 각오로 게시판의 모든 학습 질문에 명쾌하게 답변드릴 것을 약속 드립니다.

기출 빅데이터를 토대로 한 문제 한 문제 엄선한 「시원스쿨 토익 실전 1500제」는 토익의 빈출 유형들을 총망라하고 있으므로, 15회를 전부 풀고 모든 문제를 철저히 소화한다면, 반드시 900점 이상의 고득점을 달성할 수 있을 것입니다. 「시원스쿨 토익 실전 1500제」를 파트너 삼아 최단 시간 안에 목표 점수를 성취하고, 여러분의 오랜 꿈을 이루시기를 진심으로 바랍니다.

정 상, 시원스쿨어학연구소

목차

왜 「시원스쿨 토익 실전 1500제」인가?

01 영어시험 연구 전문 조직이 개발

토익 베스트셀러 집필진, 토익 990점 수십 회 만점자, 토익 콘텐츠 개발 경력 10년의 원어민 연구원, 미국/호주/영국의 명문대학원 석사 출신 영어 테스트 전문가들이 포진한 영어시험 연구 조직인 시원스쿨어학연구소가 직접 개발하였습니다.

개발 과정 모든 연구원이 시험 응시 ➡ 해당 시험 정밀 분석 ➡ 10년 기출 빅데이터 비교 분석 ➡ 적중 문제 유형 예측 ➡ 문항 개발 ➡ 문제/해설 파일럿 테스트 ➡ 피드백 적용 ➡ 최종 검수

02 빅데이터 정밀 분석에 기초하여 가장 많이 나오는 것만 수록

최신 기출 문제들을 빠짐 없이 분석하여 자주 출제되는 문제 유형과 문장 구조, 어휘와 구문을 모든 문항에 적용하였습니다. 시험에 가장 많이 나오는 것들만 빠르게 공부하여 시간과 에너지 낭비 없이 단기간에 900점 이상을 이룰 수 있습니다.

분석 과정
다음과 같은 심층 분석으로 모든 문항에 출제빈도 및 중요도를 반영

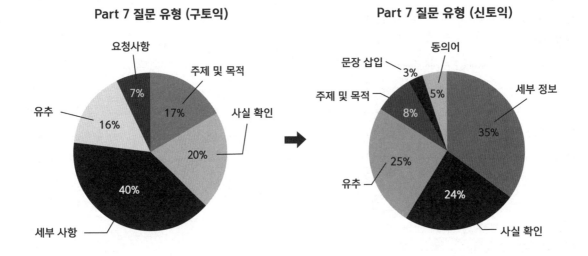

Part 7 질문 유형 (구토익)

Part 7 질문 유형 (신토익)

03 토익 실전 모의고사 15회분! 압도적 분량의 최다 실전 문제

최신의 기출 트렌드를 반영한 실전 문제집으로서, 실전 모의고사 총 15회분이라는 압도적으로 많은 양의 실전문제를 실었습니다.

- 최신 기출 트렌드 반영
- 실전 모의고사 15회
  (1회 100문제 X 15회 = 1500문제)

04 900점+ 고득점 직행 보장 문제

지난 10년간의 토익 기출 빅데이터 분석을 통해 고득점을 방해하는 다음과 같은 세 가지 문제 유형을 뽑아 충분히 연습할 수 있게 배치하여 본서를 풀면 고득점으로 직행할 수 있습니다.

- 고수도 틀리는 어려운 문제 유형
- 토익 수험자들이 거의 매번 실수하는 문제 유형
- 기존의 유형과는 달라 당혹스러운 새로운 문제 유형

05 필수 학습 콘텐츠 무료 제공

토익 학습자들의 경제적 부담을 최소화하기 위해 필수 학습 콘텐츠인 **문제 해설**, **오답노트**, **Answer Sheet**를 무료로 제공합니다.
시원스쿨랩 홈페이지(lab.siwonschool.com)에서 다운로드 할 수 있습니다.

- TEST 15회 해설 전부 무료 제공
- 시원스쿨 토익 오답노트 무료 제공

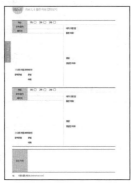

TOEIC이란?

TOEIC은 ETS(Educational Testing Service)가 출제하는 국제 커뮤니케이션 영어 능력 평가 시험(Test Of English for International Communication)입니다. 즉, 토익은 영어로 업무적인 소통을 할 수 있는 능력을 평가하는 시험으로서, 다음과 같은 비즈니스 실무 상황들을 다룹니다.

기업일반	계약, 협상, 홍보, 영업, 비즈니스 계획, 회의, 행사, 장소 예약
제조	공장 관리, 조립라인, 품질관리
금융과 예산	은행, 투자, 세금, 회계, 청구
개발	연구, 제품개발
사무실	회의, 서신 교환(편지, 메모, 전화, 팩스, E-mail 등), 사무용품/가구 주문과 사용
인사	입사지원, 채용, 승진, 급여, 퇴직
부동산	건축, 설계서, 부동산 매매 및 임대, 전기/가스/수도 설비
여가	교통수단, 티켓팅, 여행 일정, 역/공항, 자동차/호텔 예약 및 연기와 취소, 영화, 공연, 전시

토익 파트별 문항 구성

구성	파트	내용	문항 수 및 문항 번호		시간	배점
Listening Test	Part 1	사진 묘사	6	1~6	45분	495점
	Part 2	질의 응답	25	7~31		
	Part 3	짧은 대화	39 (13지문)	32~70		
	Part 4	짧은 담화	30 (10지문)	71~100		
Reading Test	Part 5	단문 빈칸 채우기 (문법, 어휘)	30	101~130	75분	495점
	Part 6	장문 빈칸 채우기 (문법, 문맥에 맞는 어휘)	16 (4지문)	131~146		
	Part 7	독해 단일 지문	29	147~175		
		이중 지문	10	176~185		
		삼중 지문	15	186~200		
합계			200문제		120분	990 점

접수부터 성적 확인까지

01 접수

- TOEIC 위원회 인터넷 사이트(www.toeic.co.kr)에서 접수 일정을 확인하고 접수합니다.
- 접수 시 최근 6개월 이내 촬영한 jpg 형식의 사진이 필요하므로 미리 준비합니다.
- 토익 응시료는 (2024년 6월 기준) 정기 접수 시 52,500원입니다.
- 시험 30일 전부터는 특별추가접수에 해당하여 추가 비용이 발생하니 잊지 말고 정기 접수 기간에 접수하도록 합니다.

02 시험 당일 할 일

- 아침을 적당히 챙겨 먹습니다. 빈속은 집중력 저하의 주범이고 과식은 졸음을 유발합니다.
- 고사장을 반드시 확인합니다.
- 시험 준비물을 챙깁니다.
  - 신분증 (주민등록증, 운전면허증, 기간 만료 전 여권, 공무원증만 인정. 학생증 안됨. 단, 중고등학생은 국내 학생증 인정)
  - B연필과 깨끗하게 잘 지워지는 지우개 (볼펜이나 사인펜은 안됨. 연필은 뭉툭하게 깎아서 여러 자루 준비)
  - 아날로그 시계 (전자시계는 안됨)
  - 수험표 (필수 준비물은 아님. 수험번호는 시험장에서 감독관이 답안지에 부착해주는 라벨을 보고 적으면 됨)
- 고사장으로 이동하는 동안에는 「시원스쿨 토익 실전 1500제」 LC 음원을 들으며 귀를 예열합니다.
- 최소 30분 전에 입실을 마치고(오전 시험은 오전 9:20까지, 오후 시험은 오후 2:20까지) 지시에 따라 답안지에 기본 정보를 기입한 뒤, 「시원스쿨 토익 실전 1500제」를 풀고나서 정리한 「시원스쿨 토익 오답노트」를 훑어봅니다.
- 안내 방송이 끝나고 시험 시작 전 5분의 휴식시간이 주어지는데, 이때 화장실에 꼭 다녀옵니다.

03 시험 진행

오전 시험	오후 시험	내용
9:30 - 9:45	2:30 - 2:45	답안지 작성 오리엔테이션
9:45 - 9:50	2:45 - 2:50	수험자 휴식시간
9:50 - 10:10	2:50 - 3:10	신분증 확인, 문제지 배부
10:10 - 10:55	3:10 - 3:55	듣기 평가
10:55 - 12:10	3:55 - 5:10	독해 평가

04 성적 확인

- 시험일로부터 9일 후 낮 12시에 한국 TOEIC 위원회 사이트(www.toeic.co.kr)에서 성적이 발표됩니다.

「시원스쿨 토익 실전 1500제」고득점 보장 학습법

학습 단계	학습 방법	유의 사항
1	시험 문제 풀기	1. 반드시 **실제 시험을 보는 것과 똑같이** 해야 합니다. 2. 휴대폰 전원을 끄고 책상 위에는 연필/지우기/답안지만 놓고, 제한 시간을 지켜 문제를 풉니다. 제한 시간 내에 답안 마킹까지 끝내야 합니다. 3. 200번 문제가 끝날 때까지 중간에 멈추지 않습니다.
2	채점 틀린 문제 다시 풀기	채점 후 바로 틀린 문제의 해설을 보지 말고, 다시 한 번 내 힘으로 풀어봅니다.
3	틀린 문제 완전히 이해하기	1. 틀린 문제는 물론이고, 찍어서 맞은 문제, 맞았지만 헷갈렸던 문제까지 모두 표시해서 **완벽하게 이해**해야 합니다. 2. 해설을 천천히 읽고도 이해가 잘 안된다면 **시원스쿨랩 (lab.siwonschool.com) 홈페이지의 공부 질문하기** 게시판에 질문을 올려주세요. 저자가 직접 답변해 드립니다. 3. 기초가 부족하다고 느끼거나 다양한 실전 전략을 익히고 싶다면 강의 수강을 권장합니다.
4	오답노트 작성하기	1. 시원스쿨랩 홈페이지 교재자료실에서 **시원스쿨 토익 오답노트**를 다운로드 받아 출력해 여러 장 복사해 둡니다. 2. 샘플 예시대로 오답노트를 작성합니다. 3. **[시원스쿨 토익 실전 1500제] 오답노트 전용 파일**에 오답노트지를 보관합니다.
5	추가 복습	1. **오답노트**에 정리한 내용을 확인합니다. 2. 해설지에 정리되어 있는 **어휘/표현**을 외웁니다.

「시원스쿨 토익 실전 1500제」 초단기 학습 플랜

실전 문제집은 오랫동안 공부하기 보다는 단기간에 집중적으로 공부하는 것이 효과가 좋습니다. 따라서 15일 동안은 하루에 최소 3시간 이상 할애하여 매일 학습하도록 합니다. 특히 RC는 시일이 지난 후 다시 풀어보는 것이 좋기 때문에 교재를 끝낸 후 반드시 다시 풀어 보세요.

1차 학습_15일 완성

Day 1	Day 2	Day 3	Day 4	Day 5
- TEST 1 풀기 - 채점 및 복습 - 오답노트 정리 - 추가 복습	- TEST 2 풀기 - 채점 및 복습 - 오답노트 정리 - 추가 복습	- TEST 3 풀기 - 채점 및 복습 - 오답노트 정리 - 추가 복습	- TEST 4 풀기 - 채점 및 복습 - 오답노트 정리 - 추가 복습	- TEST 5 풀기 - 채점 및 복습 - 오답노트 정리 - 추가 복습
Day 6	**Day 7**	**Day 8**	**Day 9**	**Day 10**
- TEST 6 풀기 - 채점 및 복습 - 오답노트 정리 - 추가 복습	- TEST 7 풀기 - 채점 및 복습 - 오답노트 정리 - 추가 복습	- TEST 8 풀기 - 채점 및 복습 - 오답노트 정리 - 추가 복습	- TEST 9 풀기 - 채점 및 복습 - 오답노트 정리 - 추가 복습	- TEST 10 풀기 - 채점 및 복습 - 오답노트 정리 - 추가 복습
Day 11	**Day 12**	**Day 13**	**Day 14**	**Day 15**
- TEST 11 풀기 - 채점 및 복습 - 오답노트 정리 - 추가 복습	- TEST 12 풀기 - 채점 및 복습 - 오답노트 정리 - 추가 복습	- TEST 13 풀기 - 채점 및 복습 - 오답노트 정리 - 추가 복습	- TEST 14 풀기 - 채점 및 복습 - 오답노트 정리 - 추가 복습	- TEST 15 풀기 - 채점 및 복습 - 오답노트 정리 - 추가 복습

2차 학습_5일 완성

Day 1	Day 2	Day 3	Day 4	Day 5

- TEST 1~3
  다시 풀기
- 채점 및 복습
- 오답노트 정리
- 추가 복습
	- TEST 4~6
	  다시 풀기
	- 채점 및 복습
	- 오답노트 정리
	- 추가 복습
		- TEST 7~9
		  다시 풀기
		- 채점 및 복습
		- 오답노트 정리
		- 추가 복습
			- TEST 10~12 다시
			  풀기
			- 채점 및 복습
			- 오답노트 정리
			- 추가 복습
				- TEST 13~15 다시
				  풀기
				- 채점 및 복습
				- 오답노트 정리
				- 추가 복습

시원스쿨랩이 제안하는 RC 학습법

📍 Part 5_단문 빈칸 채우기

• Part 5는 이렇다!

> * 총 30문항
> * 문법과 어휘는 3:2의 비율로 출제
> * 복잡한 문법이나 어려운 어휘는 나오지 않는 추세

복잡한 문법은 거의 나오지 않고 기본적인 문장 구조와 품사에 대한 이해만 있다면 수월하게 풀 수 있는 수준이다. 어휘도 지나치게 어려운 단어는 거의 찾아 볼 수 없다.

• Part 5는 이렇게 대비하자!

1. LC시간에 최소 10개는 풀어두자.

Part 1과 2가 시작되기 전 direction시간에 최소 10개는 반드시 풀어야만 한다. 상대적으로 RC에서 시간이 부족하기 때문이다. 고수라면 같은 시간에 20개 이상 푸는 것도 가능하다.

2. 문장 구조를 빨리 볼 수 있는 눈을 키우자.

명사, 동사, 형용사, 부사, 전치사, 접속사 이렇게 딱 6가지 품사가 각기 어떤 역할을 하며, 문장의 어느 위치에 와야 하는지만 잘 이해하면 충분하다. 이걸 문장 구조와 품사라고 하는데, 이것만 빨리 파악할 수 있다면 토익에서 문법 부분은 충분하다. 이 부분이 잘 학습된 사람이라면 Part 7이나 LC까지도 큰 도움을 얻을 수 있다.

3. 어휘는 기출 빈도대로 정리하자.

토익에 잘 나오는 어휘가 따로 있다. 따라서 토익 기출 문제들을 전문적으로 분석하여 빅데이터를 활용한 어휘집을 선택하는 것이 스마트한 학습자가 되는 지름길이다.

4. 5초안에 모르면 패스!

딱 봐서 무슨 문제인지 모르겠다 하면 과감히 넘기고 다음 문제를 풀어야 한다. 5초안에 모르겠다면 사실 그 문제는 더 시간을 많이 가져도 풀기 어렵다. 따라서 아는 문제부터 해서 끝까지 일단 풀고 그래도 시간이 남으면 못 푼 문제를 다시 보는 것이 옳은 전략이다.

📍 Part 6_장문 빈칸 채우기

• Part 6는 이렇다!

* 총 16문항
* 4문제는 문맥상 적절한 문장 고르기
* 나머지 12문제는 어휘 8문항, 문법 4문항 정도 출제

Part 6는 이메일이나 기사글 등 하나의 글이 주어지고, 그 안에서 4문제를 연속해서 푸는 형태이다. 이 중 3문제는 Part 5와 마찬가지로 문법과 어휘를 묻는다. 나머지 한 문제는 학생들이 힘들어 하는 '문맥상 적절한 문장 고르기' 유형이다.

문법은 Part 5와 마찬가지로 간단한 문장구조와 품사에 대한 이해만 있으면 해결이 가능하다. 어휘의 경우는 Part 6라는 특성에 맞추어 전체 맥락에 맞게 답을 선택하여야 한다. 다시 말해, 그 한 문장에만 어울린다고 답을 하면 안 된다는 뜻이다.

Part 6는 4문제가 늘어난 대신 전체 지문의 길이는 과거보다 짧아진 편이므로 무리하게 앞뒤만 보고 풀려 하지 말고 전체적으로 차분히 읽어 나가면서 정답을 찾기로 하자. 그래야 '문맥상 문장 고르기' 유형도 해결이 가능하다.

• Part 6는 이렇게 대비하자!

1. 문법과 어휘는 Part 5와 유사하게 푼다.

문법은 기본적인 구조와 품사에 대한 이해만 있으면 수월하게 풀린다. 어휘는 기본적으로 보기의 단어를 다 알아야 하겠지만, 문맥을 파악하면서 적절한 어휘를 선택하는 것이 관건이다.

2. 반드시 전체 본문을 다 읽는다.

괜히 빨리 푼답시고 빈칸의 앞뒤만 보고 하려 들지 말자. Part 6는 Part 5와 달리 문맥 파악이 관건이다. 따라서 반드시 앞에서부터 차분히 보면서 한 문제씩 해결해 나가야 한다.

3. 문맥상 문장 선택, 신유형

문맥에 어울리는 문장 선택 문제의 경우, 주어진 보기의 각 문장들에 단서들이 있다. 주로 접속(부)사, 지시어, 관사 등이 그 단서 역할을 한다. 따라서 본문의 해당부분의 앞이나 뒤가 보기 문장의 단서와 맞물리는 지점을 찾아 답으로 골라야 한다.

4. Part 7 → 6 → 5의 순서로 푼다.

시간적 여유가 있을 때 독해를 먼저 하고 그 다음 Part 6를, 마지막으로 가장 여유가 없는 종료 전에 Part 5를 하는 것이 좋다. 시간은 Part 7에 60분, Part 6에 8분, Part 5에 7분을 할애하는 것이 가장 합리적이다. 물론 마킹 시간 포함이다.

📍 Part 7_독해

• Part 7은 이렇다!

* 총 54문항 출제
* 신유형 1) 문자 메시지/온라인 채팅 유형 – 화자 의도 파악 유형 (2문항)
* 신유형 2) 주어진 문장의 적절한 위치 찾기 (2문항)
* 신유형 3) 삼중지문 3세트 (15문항) - 삼중지문 대조 유형

Part 7에서 가장 부담스러운 것은 아무래도 삼중지문일 것이다. 5문제가 한 세트를 이루어 총 3세트, 즉 15문제나 출제되고 읽어야 할 지문의 양도 가장 많다. 그뿐인가? 정답의 단서가 한 지문에서만 주어지는 문제도 있지만, 문제에 따라서는 두 지문, 혹은 세 지문을 멀티 체크해야 답을 찾을 수 있는 고난도 문제도 출제되고 있다. '주어진 문장의 적절한 위치 찾기' 문제 역시 부담스러운 유형이다. 화자 의도 파악 유형은 크게 어렵진 않다.

< 문제 수에 따른 분류 >
* 단일지문 29문항 (지문 10개 / 지문당 2~4문항)
* 이중지문 10문항 (지문 2개 / 지문당 5문항)
* 삼중지문 15문항 (지문 3개 / 지문당 5문항)

< 문제 유형에 따른 분류 >
* 주제/목적 찾기 유형 → 두 번째로 자주 묻는 유형
* 사실 관계 확인 유형 (이중지문 대조 포함) → 가장 많이 출제됨
* 추론/암시 유형 → 사실관계 확인 유형의 심화 버전
* 동의어 찾기 유형 → 어휘 능력 필요
* 문장 위치 삽입 유형 → 지시어, 접속(부)사, 관사 등에 유의
* 화자의 의도 파악 유형 → 문자 메시지, 온라인 채팅에서 등장

• Part 7은 이렇게 대비하자!

1. 이중지문/삼중지문 → 단일 지문의 순서로 풀어라.

심리적 압박이 덜 할 때 이중지문/삼중지문을 먼저 풀어 두는 것이 좋다. 시간에 쫓기게 되면 긴 지문은 눈에 잘 들어오지 않기 때문이다. 물론 무한정 풀고 있으면 안 된다. 이중지문/삼중지문에 약 30분, 단일 지문에 약 30분을 쓰는 것이 적절하다.

2. 이중지문 대조 유형에 유의하라.

176번~200번 사이에 이중지문/삼중지문 대조 유형들이 나온다. 이는 한 지문만 보고 푸는 것이 아니라, 두 지문 혹은 세 지문을 보고 단서를 조합하여 답을 결정해야 하는 형태이다. 질문이나 보기에 고유명사, 날짜, 요일, 숫자 등이 나오면 이중지문 대조 유형이라 생각하고 지문간 연결 고리를 재빨리 찾도록 한다.

3. 문장 위치 삽입 유형은 지시어 등 단서를 활용하라.

우선 주어진 문장을 정확히 파악하자. 이후에 다른 문제들을 풀면서 동시에 중간중간 만나게 되는 4군데 위치에 주어진 문장을 한번씩 넣어 보아 논리적 흐름에 잘 어울리는지를 확인한다. 이때 접속(부)사나 대명사, 지시어 등은 좋은 단서가 되니 적극 활용하자.

• Part 7 문제 풀이 노하우

1. 본문보다 질문부터 읽어라!

질문을 미리 읽으면 그 유형에 따라, 지문의 어느 부분을 읽어야 할 지 정할 수 있으므로 질문을 미리 읽고 그에 맞는 전략을 활용하는 것이 좋다.

2. 질문 유형에 따른 해법대로 접근한다.

상당수의 학생들은 질문을 미리 읽으라니까 한 단어, 한 단어 읽으면서 해석을 한다. 절대로 토익의 질문은 해석하는 게 아니다. 한눈에 탁 보고, '아, 무슨 질문 유형!'이라고 바로 파악해야 하는 거다. 예를 들어, "What does this article mainly discuss?"라고 쓰여 있으면 질문을 해석하는 게 아니라, '아, 주제 문제!'라고 즉각적으로 파악해야 하는 것이다.

3. 보기는 미리 읽지 않아도 좋다.

보기는 미리 읽어도 본문 읽을 때 보기 내용이 기억 나지 않아서 다시 읽어야 하는 불편함이 있기 때문에, 질문만 미리 읽고 그 유형에 따라 본문 중에 읽어야 할 곳을 짚어서 읽은 후 질문으로 돌아와서 보기를 읽는 것이 시간을 절약하는 방법이다. 단, 사실 관계 확인 유형은 보기도 읽는 것이 좋다. (A)~(D)를 하나씩 본문과 대조해야 하는데, (A)~(D) 순서대로 본문에 나오지 않는 경우도 꽤 있기 때문에 미리 읽어 두어야 시간이 절약된다.

4. 본문의 내용이 보기의 어떤 단어로 바뀌었는지 반드시 확인한다.

본문의 말이 정답에 그대로 나오는 경우는 거의 없다. 오히려 그대로 나온 보기라면 오답일 가능성이 높다. 따라서 본문은 잘 해석하는데, 답을 자꾸 틀리는 학생들의 경우는, 본문의 말이 바뀌어 있는 보기를 이해하지 못하는 것이 원인이라 볼 수 있다. 이것을 패러프레이즈(paraphrase)라고 하는데, 이걸 잘 이해하기 위해서는 단어 실력이 뒷받침 되어야 하는 것은 기본이고, 많은 글을 읽어 영어 문장의 이해 능력을 높여야 한다.

5. 한 세트씩 가마킹, 그리고 4회로 나누어 본마킹을 한다.

사람마다 자신만의 방법을 가지고 있겠지만, 나만의 방법을 소개한다. 지문 하나에 대해서 문제가 세 개라면 세 개 모두 시험지에 풀고 'A, C, B'와 같이 잠시 답을 기억하여 답안지에 살짝 표시를 한다. 완전한 마킹을 하는 것이 아니라 살짝 표시만 하는 것이다. 이것을 '가마킹'이라고 한다. 시험지에 싹 풀고 한꺼번에 마킹하는 사람도 있는데, 나중에 시간이 부족하여 미처 마킹을 다 못 하거나, 시간에 쫓겨 마킹하다 실수하여 밀려 쓰는 경우도 있을 수 있다. 때문에 한 세트씩 푸는 대로 마킹하는 방법을 권한다.

또한 나는 가마킹 해둔 것을 중간 중간 정식 마킹을 한다. 삼중지문 끝나고 한번, 이중지문 끝나고 한번, 그리고 단일지문 10개 중 다섯 지문당 한 번씩 마킹하는 식이다. 이렇게 하는 이유는 나중에 혹시라도 마킹을 못할 수 있는 경우에 대비하기 위해서이기도 하고, 다음 단계를 들어가기 전에 잠시 머리를 식히는 기분 전환 효과도 있기 때문이다.

실전모의고사
TEST 1

TEST 1 해설

바로 보기

시작 시간 _____시 _____분

종료 시간 _____시 _____분

▸ 중간에 멈추지 말고 처음부터 끝까지 풀어보세요. 문제를 풀 때는 실전처럼 답안지에 마킹하세요.

▸ Part 7 고난도 문제에 대한 수험자들의 요청에 따라 TEST 1에서는 특별히 '문장 삽입' 유형을 1지문 더
추가하여 3지문을 집중 훈련하도록 하였습니다.

READING TEST

In the Reading test, you will read a variety of texts and answer several different types of reading comprehension questions. The entire Reading test will last 75 minutes. There are three parts, and directions are given for each part. You are encouraged to answer as many questions as possible within the time allowed. You must mark your answers on the separate answer sheet. Do not write your answers in your test book.

PART 5

Directions: A word or phrase is missing in each of the sentences below. Four answer choices are given below each sentence. Select the best answer to complete the sentence. Then mark the letter (A), (B), (C), or (D) on your answer sheet.

101. Ms. Keane will give each of the new recruits a company handbook before ------- trains them on Tuesday.

(A) she
(B) her
(C) hers
(D) herself

102. Mr. Tanaka is retiring from his role as CEO so that he can ------- on his new business venture.

(A) focus
(B) focuses
(C) focusing
(D) to focus

103. Before attaching the television screen to the display stand, make sure the base is completely -------.

(A) stable
(B) stably
(C) stabler
(D) stabilize

104. Those attending the medical convention can be reimbursed for all ------- if receipts are kept and presented to the accounting manager.

(A) expenses
(B) expensive
(C) expense
(D) expensively

105. Over the past six months, Mr. Nevin ------- rapidly through the company's ranks, and will soon be promoted to manager.

(A) rise
(B) rising
(C) has risen
(D) will rise

106. The refreshments in the third-floor storeroom are available only ------- staff training sessions.

(A) at
(B) to
(C) for
(D) in

107. Litewire Technologies hopes to sell its headquarters building for ------- $5 million before the end of this year.

(A) approximates
(B) approximation
(C) approximately
(D) approximate

108. Ursula Rice's ------- for speaking at the annual Young Inventor's Convention is obvious to all audience members.

(A) enthusiasm
(B) likeness
(C) entitlement
(D) reservation

109. A training session for all new recruits will be held ------- the weekly staff meeting.

    (A) only
    (B) following
    (C) where
    (D) since

110. The budget for the company trip was ------- expected due to the company's recent poor sales performance.

    (A) little more
    (B) slightly less
    (C) now that
    (D) less than

111. Mr. Davis wants all sales representatives to attend the upcoming training session ------- how experienced they may be.

    (A) regardless of
    (B) aside from
    (C) instead of
    (D) prior to

112. The maintenance manager, Mr. Snow, will ------- the recycled materials into three bins.

    (A) separate
    (B) choose
    (C) assess
    (D) provide

113. Dranich Textiles is seeking an assembly line ------- with experience in managing employees.

    (A) operational
    (B) operating
    (C) operator
    (D) operate

114. ------- some of our new rides proved to be unpopular, the past year was a highly profitable one for our amusement park.

    (A) Despite
    (B) Moreover
    (C) Even though
    (D) On the contrary

115. Customers may check the status of any ------- orders by clicking on the "My Orders" tab on our Web site.

    (A) dependent
    (B) efficient
    (C) pending
    (D) sustained

116. Many firms have publicly announced plans to reduce waste products ------- promote an image of environmental awareness.

    (A) towards
    (B) in order to
    (C) so that
    (D) in advance of

117. All guests should be seated five minutes ------- the first course of the banquet is scheduled to be served.

    (A) among
    (B) over
    (C) from
    (D) before

118. The music concert on Sandy Beach will probably be canceled tomorrow because heavy rain -------.

    (A) predicts
    (B) prediction
    (C) is predicted
    (D) was predicting

119. Pintex Pharmaceuticals will keep its research laboratories ------- by installing fingerprint scanners at each entrance.

    (A) secure
    (B) security
    (C) securely
    (D) securing

120. The president of Aeon Computers is expected to make a ------- surprising announcement regarding the future of the company.

(A) regularly
(B) potentially
(C) formally
(D) diligently

121. Economists are certain that the construction of the waterpark in Gleneagles Valley will boost tourism in the ------- region.

(A) surround
(B) surrounds
(C) surrounded
(D) surrounding

122. ------- robotics technology is helping factories to increase production levels and efficiency.

(A) Allowed
(B) Promoted
(C) Experienced
(D) Improved

123. Rexan Pharmaceuticals ------- advertises job vacancies in its company magazine, so current employees can apply internally.

(A) recently
(B) regularly
(C) previously
(D) greatly

124. Last week, Mr. Spencer started figuring out ways to ------- his trip around the world.

(A) exchange
(B) travel
(C) invest
(D) finance

125. King Sub offers more than 100 types of sandwiches, ------- with a side order of French fries.

(A) much
(B) most
(C) nearly
(D) very

126. Mizuno Art Gallery's sculpture competition restricts ------- to one per contestant.

(A) circumstances
(B) applicants
(C) locations
(D) entries

127. The curator has emphasized that the art gallery ------- a food- and drink-free building.

(A) should remain
(B) that remains
(C) to remain
(D) remaining

128. Due to a software error, the graphic design department is not finished ------- the flyers for the store's grand opening.

(A) with
(B) out
(C) from
(D) of

129. The keynote speaker's address finished so ------- that most members of the audience did not realize it was over.

(A) limitedly
(B) continuously
(C) previously
(D) abruptly

130. When decorating the patients' waiting room, the doctor sought ------- from three different painting companies.

(A) requests
(B) replacements
(C) estimates
(D) conclusions

PART 6

Directions: Read the texts that follow. A word, phrase, or sentence is missing in parts of each text. Four answer choices for each question are given below the text. Select the best answer to complete the text. Then mark the letter (A), (B), (C) or (D) on your answer sheet.

Questions 131-134 refer to the following announcement.

Sharon Gutierrez's Face-to-Face Sales Workshops

Sharon Gutierrez is a world-renowned ------- on the topic of face-to-face sales approaches. Ms.
                                         131.

Gutierrez ------- as International Sales Director at Renegade Software for almost three decades.
          132.

Drawing on her many years of sales and negotiation experience at Renegade, Ms. Gutierrez will

deliver a series of comprehensive workshops incorporating several unique techniques. -------. As
                                                                                     133.

a result, attendees will understand how to sell items even to the most unwilling consumers. Please

be advised that there are no spaces left for the workshops scheduled for May 7 and 8. -------, the
                                                                                      134.

sessions being held on May 9 and 10 still have several spots available. If you are interested in

attending, call the personnel office at Extension 102.

---

131. (A) authority
    (B) authorized
    (C) authorizing
    (D) authorization

132. (A) is serving
    (B) will serve
    (C) has served
    (D) had been serving

133. (A) During her time at Renegade, she broke
      several sales records.
    (B) One is an approach that uses reverse
      psychology to close a sale.
    (C) She has worked at numerous prestigious
      companies throughout her career.
    (D) Participants should inform the event
      coordinator of their desire to attend.

134. (A) For instance
    (B) However
    (C) Thus
    (D) Unfortunately

GO ON TO THE NEXT PAGE

Questions 135-138 refer to the following e-mail.

To:	Alana Myles <amyles@serve4all.com.au>
From:	Raymond Boyle <rboyle@nsccallcenter.com.au>
Date:	5 September
Subject:	Assembly Line System

Hi Alana,

Thanks for taking the time to chat with me at the technology conference. I enjoyed hearing about the new assembly line system you recently installed at your manufacturing plant. You mentioned that the system ------- an advanced conveyor belt, as well as an automated error detection device.
135.
I was surprised by how much the system improved ------- and efficiency. It certainly seems -------
136. **137.**
an effective way to easily meet monthly quotas and deadlines. -------. Would you mind sending me
138.
more detailed information about the costs and benefits?

I hope to hear back from you soon regarding this matter.

Best wishes,

Raymond

135. (A) will involve
(B) to involve
(C) involving
(D) involved

136. (A) preference
(B) productivity
(C) relocation
(D) recruitment

137. (A) as though
(B) instead of
(C) around
(D) like

138. (A) I'm considering recruiting more workers.
(B) I'm afraid I had to leave the conference earlier than planned.
(C) I'd like to install a similar system at my plant.
(D) I'd be grateful if you could offer us an extension.

UPCOMING QUALITY ANALYSIS AT HEXAM CHEMICALS INC.

The quality analysis is the first ------- of the factory's production efficiency evaluation. It is a
139.
comprehensive analysis of the company's quality control procedures and practices. A grade will be

assigned to our factory based on the findings of the quality assurance inspector. -------. It also helps
140.

------- ways in which specific processes may be improved.
141.

This yearly production efficiency evaluation is considered ------- for maintaining efficient production
142.
levels at our manufacturing plant. We appreciate the cooperation of all staff during this time.

---

139. (A) index
(B) edition
(C) phase
(D) participant

140. (A) The primary aim of the analysis is to
determine weaknesses in quality control.
(B) Several factories have raised concerns
about employee productivity.
(C) Assembly line operators are satisfied with
the installation of new equipment.
(D) Inspectors will spend approximately three
days investigating the malfunction.

141. (A) accomplish
(B) identify
(C) know
(D) distribute

142. (A) necessarily
(B) necessitating
(C) necessity
(D) necessary

GO ON TO THE NEXT PAGE

Questions 143-146 refer to the following e-mail.

To:	ebenjani@mailtwo.com
From:	noreply@evergreenclub.com
Date:	January 8
Subject:	New Parking Permit

Dear Ms. Benjani,

This e-mail has been sent to you because you ------- a new parking permit for Evergreen Country
                                              143.
Club's VIP parking lot. Your old permit has been canceled, and your new one is ready for you to pick

up at the reception desk. Please be aware that it will ------- in 6 months. This permit has a special
                                                        144.
barcode that should be scanned using the machine at the entrance to the parking lot. To use the

permit, enter it into the machine ------- prompted.
                                  145.

Evergreen Country Club strives to give our members the best experience possible. ------- .
                                                                                 146.

Regards,

Evergreen Country Club

---

143. (A) request
    (B) requested
    (C) requesting
    (D) requests

144. (A) modify
    (B) expire
    (C) activate
    (D) apply

145. (A) since
    (B) when
    (C) then
    (D) before

146. (A) We allow all members to bring up to two
        guests once per month.
    (B) As a new member of the country club,
        you will be given a tour of the premises.
    (C) Visit the member services department to
        sign up for this event.
    (D) If you did not request a permit change,
        please inform us straight away.

PART 7

Directions: In this part you will read a selection of texts, such as magazine and newspaper articles, e-mails, and instant messages. Each text or set of texts is followed by several questions. Select the best answer for each question and mark the letter (A), (B), (C), or (D) on your answer sheet.

Questions 147-148 refer to the following e-mail.

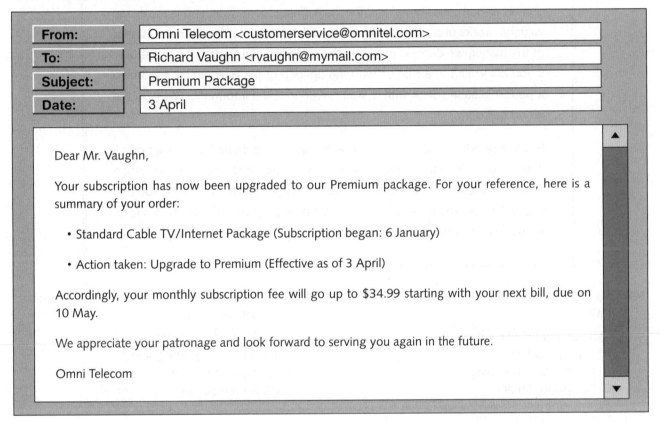

From:	Omni Telecom <customerservice@omnitel.com>
To:	Richard Vaughn <rvaughn@mymail.com>
Subject:	Premium Package
Date:	3 April

Dear Mr. Vaughn,

Your subscription has now been upgraded to our Premium package. For your reference, here is a summary of your order:

- Standard Cable TV/Internet Package (Subscription began: 6 January)

- Action taken: Upgrade to Premium (Effective as of 3 April)

Accordingly, your monthly subscription fee will go up to $34.99 starting with your next bill, due on 10 May.

We appreciate your patronage and look forward to serving you again in the future.

Omni Telecom

147. Why was the e-mail sent?

(A) To promote a new TV/Internet package
(B) To request more information about a service
(C) To notify a customer of a payment policy
(D) To confirm a change to a subscription

148. What information is given to Mr. Vaughn about payment?

(A) He will receive a refund for an overpayment.
(B) He must pay a service fee by the end of April.
(C) He will pay a higher amount per month.
(D) He sent a payment of $34.99 in January.

GO ON TO THE NEXT PAGE

We are always happy to receive donations!

Norwood Country Manor & Gardens is committed to ensuring that visitors are able to access all of the rooms in the manor at no cost, including the grand ballroom, the library, and the main dining room, which houses several valuable works of art. In order to continually restore and maintain the interior of the manor, we depend partly on the generous donations of our patrons. If you are willing to assist us with the upkeep of the building by becoming a patron, please speak with a staff member at the information desk in the grand ballroom.

Patronage brings you a variety of perks, such as substantial savings on all items in our gift shop, a special book of historical photographs of Norwood Manor, and an invitation to the gala held each year in the gardens. You can find out more about the benefits of patronage by visiting our Web site at www.norwoodmanor.co.uk.

149. Where would the flyer most likely be handed out?

(A) In an academic institute
(B) In an art gallery
(C) In a historical building
(D) In a public library

150. What is stated about the interior of the building?

(A) It is free to enter.
(B) It was recently renovated.
(C) It contains antique furniture.
(D) Some rooms are inaccessible.

151. What is NOT mentioned as a benefit received by patrons?

(A) An event invitation
(B) A book of photography
(C) A gift shop discount
(D) A Web site user account

Questions 152-153 refer to the following text-message chain.

Steve Tudyk [3:05 P.M.]
Hi, Anna. I just heard that Michael Crawford won't be able to lead the staff orientation this month because of an urgent work deadline.

Anna Acosta [3:08 P.M.]
Do you want me to tell the Personnel Department to choose someone to take his place?

Steve Tudyk [3:10 P.M.]
Well, I'd suggest asking Caroline Ford from our Bridge End branch. She has training experience, but I'm not sure if she'll be free on such short notice.

Anna Acosta [3:11 P.M.]
I'll look into it.

Steve Tudyk [3:12 P.M.]
Thanks. And if she's too busy to cover for Michael, I'll try to think of someone else.

Anna Acosta [3:13 P.M.]
Okay, I'll get back to you.

152. Why did Mr. Tudyk send the message?

(A) To ask about a work deadline
(B) To announce a cancelation
(C) To confirm a training session
(D) To suggest rescheduling an event

153. At 3:11 P.M., what does Ms. Acosta mean when she writes, "I'll look into it"?

(A) She will check what time the orientation begins.
(B) She will review a list of training session attendees.
(C) She will inquire about Ms. Ford's schedule.
(D) She will obtain directions to the Bridge End branch.

GO ON TO THE NEXT PAGE

Questions 154-155 refer to the following e-mail.

To:	Bryan Carnegie
From:	Wati Prakoso
Date:	June 19
Subject:	Shopping mall design
Attachment:	📎 Building_Blueprint

Good morning,

During our previous consultation, we talked about some ways to reduce the construction cost of the Rickfield Shopping Mall by removing some unnecessary features. I went ahead and made some amendments to the original design, and I have attached the modified blueprint for you to review. Please consider each modification carefully and then let me know whether you are satisfied with everything. Once I have received your confirmation, I'll arrange the first meeting with the construction team.

Regards,

Wati Prakoso
Lead Architect
Rickfield Shopping Mall Project

154. What is the purpose of the e-mail?

(A) To suggest reducing a construction budget
(B) To follow up on a previously discussed issue
(C) To provide a list of features of a new shopping mall
(D) To arrange a consultation with a client

155. What does Mr. Prakoso ask Mr. Carnegie to do with the attached blueprint?

(A) Evaluate changes and approve them
(B) Modify specific features and highlight them
(C) Discuss it with the construction team
(D) Bring a copy to an upcoming meeting

Questions 156-157 refer to the following form.

Tellman Manufacturing Inc.

Equipment Malfunction/Worker Accident Report Form

1. **Reason for Report**
   ● Equipment Malfunction   ○ Worker Accident

2. **Report Submitted By:**
   Name: *Jacob Kiwombo*   Position: *Assembly Line Supervisor*
   Work Location: Production Plant 2   ○ Day Shift   ● Evening Shift   ○ Night Shift

3. **Please give details of the malfunction or accident that you are reporting.**
   When I was leaving work on Tuesday, 16 October, at around 11 P.M., I noticed that the conveyor belt of the assembly line was running slower than usual. I mentioned it to the night shift manager before I left, but he was unable to fix the problem. However, this evening, when I arrived at the factory to begin my shift, I tested the production efficiency of the equipment and confirmed a reduction of almost 40%.

4. **Action taken to resolve the issue:**
   After running further tests and checking all parts, I came to the conclusion that the motor needed to be replaced. Fortunately, we had a spare one in the warehouse, so the repair work was completed within one hour and production was only slightly delayed.

   Report Submitter's Signature : *Jacob Kiwombo*   Date: 17 October

5. **Verification of receipt by the Personnel Department**
   Report received by: *Lisa Kohler*
   Report logged on: 17 October (Copy e-mailed to report submitter)

156. What is suggested about Mr. Kiwombo?

(A) He had an accident while working in a factory.
(B) He normally leaves Production Plant 2 at night.
(C) He used to work as the night shift manager.
(D) He tried to contact a repair specialist.

157. What did NOT happen on 17 October?

(A) A mechanical part was replaced.
(B) Mr. Kiwombo tested some machinery.
(C) A malfunction was first detected.
(D) A copy of a report was sent to Mr. Kiwombo.

GO ON TO THE NEXT PAGE

A Healthy Body Leads to a Productive Mind

5 April – Esurance Online, a vehicle insurance company based in Boulder, Montana, is offering its workers a financial incentive to get more exercise. Employees will be paid an extra $150 per month if they attend at least three 1-hour fitness sessions in the company's conference rooms per week.

— [1] —. Considering the rising cost of gym memberships, this is a tremendously generous policy for the company to implement. Esurance Online has hired a personal fitness instructor who will lead a variety of classes such as yoga, spinning, and aerobics.

According to Esurance Online's personnel manager, Peter Selby, enrollment in fitness sessions is by no means mandatory, but the vast majority of workers are expected to take advantage of the opportunity, and the extra money. — [2] —. This new policy is based on a recent study that shows how a healthy physical condition can positively affect one's ability to focus well in the workplace. According to the scientist who led the study, workers who exercise regularly and maintain a healthy physical condition can get their work done more quickly and to a higher standard.— [3] —.

Furthermore, the study claims that a worker who rarely exercises and is in poor physical condition works at only 50% of his or her potential efficiency. — [4] —. Esurance Online's new policy on staff fitness aims to benefit both its workforce and its overall business performance.

158. What is the purpose of the article?

(A) To announce a joint venture with a local gym

(B) To advise employees to attend a workshop

(C) To explain a company's recent success

(D) To describe a company's new policy

159. What does the article state about encouraging staff to exercise more regularly?

(A) It can make people feel more tired in the workplace.

(B) It encourages more communication between staff members.

(C) It helps people to accomplish tasks more efficiently.

(D) It prevents staff from meeting important deadlines.

160. In which of the positions marked [1], [2], [3], and [4] does the following sentence best belong?

"This can result in a significant reduction in productivity for a company."

(A) [1]

(B) [2]

(C) [3]

(D) [4]

Questions 161-163 refer to the following e-mail.

To:	The Ferny Times <inquiries@thefernytimes.com>
From:	Maria Erdinger<mariaerdinger@anomail.net >
Subject:	Recent article
Date:	August 10

To the editor:

I really enjoyed the article titled "Hometown Bands of Ferny: The Jazz Wizards" which you recently included in the August 7 edition of *The Ferny Times*. As a big fan of local bands, and our town's musical heritage, I was pleased to see such a large article about one of our most famous groups. However, I feel that I need to mention an inaccuracy in the piece.
— [1] —.

According to the article, the original saxophone player in The Jazz Wizards was Serge Duplass. Actually, Serge started off as a member of the road crew, tuning instruments and setting up the stage. — [2] —. Marek Kozlowski was the saxophonist when the band first formed, but later retired with a hand injury. I remember those days clearly as I interviewed the members several times when I was writing for a local music magazine. — [3] —.

I understand that this was only one aspect of the article, but Mr. Kozlowski was a very inspirational and innovative musician, and he was instrumental in the success of The Jazz Wizards. However, it seems he rarely gets the credit he deserves. — [4] —. It would be nice if you could acknowledge his contributions in any similar articles in the future.

Sincerely,

Maria Erdinger

161. What is the main purpose of the e-mail?

(A) To correct some information
(B) To announce an upcoming concert
(C) To seek new musicians for a band
(D) To praise a writer's work

162. Who most likely is Ms. Erdinger?

(A) A musician
(B) A concert promoter
(C) A record store owner
(D) A journalist

163. In which of the positions marked [1], [2], [3], and [4] does the following sentence best belong?

"He did not properly join the band until a few years later."

(A) [1]
(B) [2]
(C) [3]
(D) [4]

GO ON TO THE NEXT PAGE

Questions 164-167 refer to the following letter.

15 November

Mr. Samuel Torrance
3109 Riverview Road
San Jose, CA 95110

Dear Mr. Torrance,

We at Global Fitness are pleased to see that you have been enjoying our weekly yoga classes for the past 18 months. I am contacting you to let you know that our class fees will undergo some changes. — [1] —. Starting from December 1, the price of a 12-month yoga membership (52 classes per year) will increase from $520.00 to $624.00. This rate ($12 per class) still enables you to make considerable savings compared with the standard non-member price of $15 for each session. — [2] —.

We also want to remind you that members of our gym get to enjoy a free subscription to our monthly magazine, which is full of helpful articles about keeping fit and eating healthily. The magazine also contains discount coupons for a wider variety of health foods and supplements. — [3] —.

Although your current membership is set to expire at the end of November, you can easily renew it either in person or over the phone. Simply call our member services center at 555-2878 between the hours of 9 A.M. and 6 P.M. — [4] —.

For more information about our full class schedule and rates, visit www.globalfitnessonline.com.

Regards,

Roy Lippman
Member Services Manager
Global Fitness

---

164. What is implied about Mr. Torrance?

(A) He often contributes articles to the Global Fitness magazine.
(B) He teaches weekly yoga classes at Global Fitness.
(C) He has been going to Global Fitness for more than one year.
(D) He recently complained to Global Fitness about class fees.

165. How much will a yoga class at Global Fitness cost next year for members of the gym?

(A) $10.00
(B) $12.00
(C) $15.00
(D) $20.00

166. In which of the positions marked [1], [2], [3], and [4] does the following sentence best belong?

"Our operators will only need to ask you for a few details to complete the process."

(A) [1]
(B) [2]
(C) [3]
(D) [4]

167. According to Mr. Lippman, what information is available on the Web site?

(A) Discount coupons
(B) Business locations
(C) Fitness tips
(D) Class fees

Argo Solutions Reaches Target

Detroit (September 7) – Argo Solutions has achieved its target of establishing a series of computer programming workshops for those hoping to learn skills required for jobs in the technology sector. The target was first announced when the company became a part of the Classes for the Masses initiative one year ago. Argo specializes in creating business spreadsheet and database programs.

With the financial assistance of local governments in Detroit, Chicago, and St. Louis, members of the initiative set up various professional development workshops or seminars to provide opportunities for individuals to learn useful new skills. In the case of Argo Solutions, its workshops are held every Monday at its headquarters in Detroit.

"According to the terms set out by the founder of the initiative, we had to provide a comprehensive learning experience that runs regularly throughout the year," said Argo Solutions CEO Leon Dolenz. "We are proud of the workshops that we now offer, which are led by some of our most experienced and skilled programmers."

In addition to joining the education initiative, the company is planning to hire around 100 new workers at its headquarters later this year, as demand for the company's products is rising sharply.

Argo Solutions currently has five offices throughout the United States and employs more than 5,000 individuals.

168. What is the main topic of the article?

(A) Argo Solutions intends to construct a new office in the United States.
(B) Argo Solutions is committed to providing education opportunities.
(C) Argo Solutions is providing materials to a local technical college.
(D) Argo Solutions has developed a new system for recruiting employees.

169. What does Argo Solutions produce?

(A) Software for business use
(B) University textbooks
(C) Laptops for local schools
(D) Market research reports

170. The word "terms" in paragraph 3, line 1, is closest in meaning to

(A) ideas
(B) durations
(C) labels
(D) conditions

171. What is indicated about the Classes for the Masses Initiative?

(A) It was launched five years ago.
(B) It requires members to be located in Detroit.
(C) It is partially funded by local governments.
(D) It has allowed Argo Solutions to expand its workforce.

GO ON TO THE NEXT PAGE

Questions 172-175 refer to the following online chat discussion.

Lacey Bingham [2:24 P.M.]

Hello, fellow hiking fans. I'm looking for some suggestions. I'm taking a trip to Peak Valley for a week, stopping at Gilly Forest, Brann Springs, and Morley Glen.

Kyle North [2:28 P.M.]

I just returned from a camping expedition at Peak Valley National Park. It's such a picturesque region.

Lacey Bingham [2:32 P.M.]

That's what I read online. Local accommodation is supposed to be good, so I'm trying to decide whether to book a hotel or take tents. What do you think?

Teresa Jackson [2:37 P.M.]

We took tents and used the campgrounds when we visited. There's a campground at the start of most trails.

Lacey Bingham [2:40 P.M.]

Do Peak Valley campgrounds have any amenities, Teresa?

Kyle North [2:43 P.M.]

Hotel rooms wouldn't be too expensive if there is a group of you traveling together.

Teresa Jackson [2:48 P.M.]

Some of them have a small store and some washrooms, but they're pretty empty overall.

Walter Killian [2:51 P.M.]

But if the weather forecast looks bad, you might regret sleeping in a tent.

Lacey Bingham [2:55 P.M.]

Even those things would be nice, Teresa. The places around here should try to follow Peak Valley's example. And Walter, you have a good point. We'd better just book rooms.

Walter Killian [2:59 P.M.]

You'll find a great hotel called The Holly Inn next to the visitor information center. The owner will even prepare a complimentary lunch for you before you set off for the mountain in the morning. That's where I always stay.

Lacey Bingham [3:04 P.M.]

Great. Then I think I'm all set. Thanks, everyone.

172. With whom was Ms. Bingham most likely chatting?

(A) People who live in Peak Valley
(B) People who will accompany her on her trip
(C) People who hike on a regular basis
(D) People who work at a national park

173. Why has Ms. Bingham decided to book a hotel room?

(A) Because the campgrounds will be too busy
(B) Because she thinks sleeping in a tent is uncomfortable
(C) Because she thinks the room rate is quite reasonable
(D) Because she is concerned about the weather

174. At 2:55 P.M., what does Ms. Bingham most likely mean when she writes, "The places around here should try to follow Peak Valley's example"?

(A) The hotels in her region are not affordably priced.
(B) The campgrounds in her area have poor amenities.
(C) The hiking trails in her area are poorly maintained.
(D) The mountains near her home are not scenic.

175. What does Mr. Killian indicate about The Holly Inn?

(A) Trail entrances are located nearby.
(B) The proprietor is an experienced hiking guide.
(C) Hikers can receive complimentary food.
(D) Information pamphlets can be obtained by guests.

GO ON TO THE NEXT PAGE

Pederson Paintbrush Company

Pederson Paintbrush Company has been designing and manufacturing paintbrushes for more than fifty years. Suitable for a wide variety of painting techniques, our brushes combine the finest quality of handles and bristles and are commonly used by renowned artists as well as those who merely paint as a hobby.

<u>Cleaning and Maintenance Tips</u>
When you plan to put your Pederson brushes away after use, they should first be cleaned using brush soap and cool water. Make sure to clean the base of the bristles thoroughly. Afterwards, store your brushes horizontally or vertically (brush-end facing up) to prevent bristles from becoming deformed. Never store brushes in water, as this can bend the bristles and cause the handles to swell and crack.

In order to prolong the lifespan of your brushes, it is important to keep your brushes clean. How quickly you need to clean your brushes will depend on the style of painting you enjoy. If you paint with oils, you may clean your brushes within twenty minutes after use. If you prefer using watercolors, clean your brushes within ten minutes after use, and if you use acrylic paints, always clean your brushes immediately after use.

We also provide an affordably priced repair service (with a modest fee for return shipping) for damaged brushes that need some extra care and attention. Make sure you clean your brushes prior to sending them, and roll them up individually in paper. Then, place them in a box bearing your return address and send them to our workshop location listed below:

Pederson Paintbrush Company
43 Knox Road
Norwich, UK
NR1 4LU

We charge a standard fee of five pounds per brush, and repairs will be completed within one month. If you require an express service, the fee will be ten pounds per brush and the repairs will be completed within two weeks.

We look forward to serving you!

To:	Pederson Paintbrush Company <inquiry@pedersonbrushes.co.uk>
From:	Toby Galbraith <tgalbraith@artcentral.co.uk>
Date:	January 22
Re:	Brush repairs

Dear sir/madam,

On January 2, I sent two of my Pederson paintbrushes in for repairs and requested the express service. As such, I included a payment of twenty pounds in the package. However, I have yet to receive my brushes, and I'm wondering what could be taking so long. Please let me know whether the repairs have been carried out yet. The package was sent to your Oxford Road location, and I wrapped the brushes in paper as recommended in your flyer.

Regards,

Toby Galbraith

176. What is suggested about Pederson brushes?

(A) They are popular with professional artists.
(B) They are guaranteed to last for fifty years.
(C) They can be purchased by mail.
(D) They should be used only for oil painting.

177. According to the pamphlet, what will damage Pederson brushes?

(A) Placing them horizontally
(B) Keeping them in a box
(C) Leaving them out to dry
(D) Storing them in water

178. What is indicated about painting with oils?

(A) It requires brushes to be replaced more regularly.
(B) It needs more cleaning time than painting with watercolors.
(C) It affects when brushes should be cleaned.
(D) It allows artists to clean their brushes only with water.

179. Why did Mr. Galbraith send the e-mail?

(A) To inquire about the cost of paintbrush repairs
(B) To find out details about a new range of Pederson brushes
(C) To confirm that he is satisfied with some products
(D) To request a progress update on a service

180. What did Mr. Galbraith fail to do?

(A) Use the correct packaging technique
(B) Send an accurate payment for a service
(C) Include a minimum number of brushes
(D) Write down the correct shipping address

GO ON TO THE NEXT PAGE

To:	customerservice@eztech.com
From:	ablume@santo.net
Date:	May 9
Subject:	Gift voucher

Dear Customer Service Manager,

I tried to use the printable EZ Tech gift voucher that came with my new color printer that I bought from your Web site, but it has been rejected in two major electronics stores: Digizone and Nixon Electronics. I'm trying to use it to buy an EZ Tech monitor, but the store clerks have told me that their payment systems aren't set up to process this particular type of voucher. I tried calling your helpline, but the person I spoke to couldn't understand why the voucher isn't being accepted. It's a $50 one and it has the serial number 48739720 printed along the bottom. Please let me know what I should do.

Thanks,

Annabelle Blume

E-Mail Message

To:	Annabelle Blume <ablume@santo.net >
From:	EZ Tech Customer Service <customerservice@eztech.com>
Date:	May 10
Subject:	Re: Gift voucher

Dear Ms. Blume,

Thanks for e-mailing EZ Tech Customer Services with your recent query. I ran your e-mail address through our system and verified that you did indeed receive a valid $50 voucher bearing the number 48739720. This voucher will remain valid until December 31, and you can redeem it at several different locations.

However, the stores you visited are not on the list of stores that will accept the particular voucher you possess. I'm very sorry for the inconvenience. If you look on the front of your voucher, in the small print at the bottom, you'll see a list of all the store chains that will accept your EZ Tech voucher.

By the way, if you need to speak with our customer service team again in the future, the best way is by visiting www.eztech.com/livehelp and speaking to a representative in real time via online chatting. This will ensure that your questions are answered quickly and effectively every time.

Regards,

Ryan Fitzpatrick

EZ Tech Customer Service

181. What did Ms. Blume do before writing her May 9 e-mail?

(A) She compared different EZ Tech monitors.

(B) She telephoned for customer support.

(C) She visited the Nixon Electronics Web site.

(D) She returned an EZ Tech product to a store.

182. How did Mr. Fitzpatrick verify Ms. Blume's purchase?

(A) By checking a purchase date and delivery information

(B) By contacting the manager of an electronics store

(C) By referencing the number on her credit card

(D) By checking the customer database for a purchase record

183. Why was the voucher not able to be processed?

(A) The EZ Tech database shows the serial numbers do not match.

(B) Ms. Blume's voucher expired and was not valid.

(C) The store payment systems experienced a malfunction.

(D) Digizone and Nixon Electronics are not participating.

184. In the second e-mail, the word "ran" in paragraph 1, line 1, is closest in meaning to

(A) expedited

(B) managed

(C) entered

(D) repeated

185. How does Mr. Fitzpatrick recommend that Ms. Blume contact a representative if she has a question?

(A) By responding to his e-mail

(B) By calling a special number

(C) By visiting a service center

(D) By using a chat program

GO ON TO THE NEXT PAGE

Questions 186-190 refer to the following Web page, article, and review.

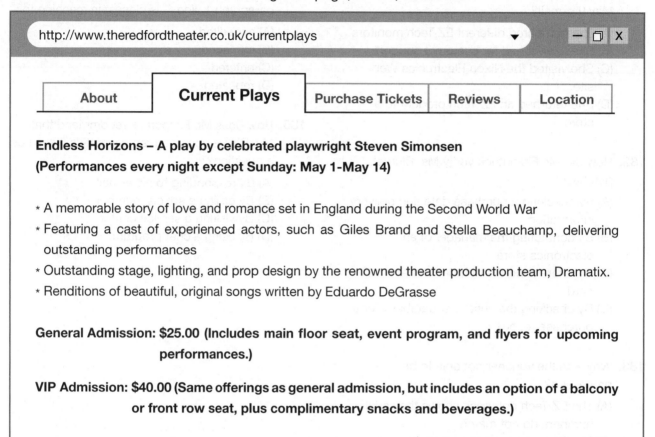

http://www.theredfordtheater.co.uk/currentplays

| About | **Current Plays** | Purchase Tickets | Reviews | Location |

Endless Horizons – A play by celebrated playwright Steven Simonsen
(Performances every night except Sunday: May 1-May 14)

* A memorable story of love and romance set in England during the Second World War
* Featuring a cast of experienced actors, such as Giles Brand and Stella Beauchamp, delivering outstanding performances
* Outstanding stage, lighting, and prop design by the renowned theater production team, Dramatix.
* Renditions of beautiful, original songs written by Eduardo DeGrasse

General Admission: $25.00 (Includes main floor seat, event program, and flyers for upcoming performances.)

VIP Admission: $40.00 (Same offerings as general admission, but includes an option of a balcony or front row seat, plus complimentary snacks and beverages.)

Empty Seats at The Redford Theater

Seattle (May 7) – One of the most anticipated plays on the theater circuit, Endless Horizons, has suffered poor audience numbers in its opening week due to an issue with the theater's Web site.

According to many disappointed theater fans, they thought that they had bought tickets for a performance of Endless Horizons, but the tickets were never mailed to them. It is thought that the theater's Web site malfunctioned due to the high demand for tickets, resulting in numerous cases where, even though payment was taken, seats were never assigned nor tickets sent out.

http://www.theaterlovers.com/reviews/0386   ▼   — □ X

Title of Play: Endless Horizons
Venue: The Redford Theater
Date: May 3

I caught a performance of Endless Horizons on May 3 and I thoroughly enjoyed the show. I've always been a big fan of plays written by Steve Simonsen, and this one was no exception. Stella Beuchamp and Giles Brand did an especially fantastic job in this one! I thought the songs could have been a bit better, as there weren't many memorable ones, but that didn't affect my overall enjoyment of the play. I did find it strange that there were many empty seats, and I was confused to hear about the problems that some people experienced. Fortunately, everything went smoothly for me.

Loretta Mancini

Date Posted: May 11

186. What is NOT included in the general admission price for the play at The Redford Theater?

(A) A main floor seat
(B) Refreshments
(C) A program
(D) Promotional materials

187. Why was the article written?

(A) To publicize a Web site problem
(B) To discuss poor reviews of a play
(C) To recommend purchasing tickets early
(D) To apologize for a lack of tickets

188. In the article, the word "taken" in paragraph 2, line 5, is the closest in meaning to

(A) erased
(B) brought
(C) received
(D) deducted

189. What does Ms. Mancini confirm about Endless Horizons?

(A) The stage design was impressive.
(B) The actors performed well.
(C) The songs were well written.
(D) The cast of performers was large.

190. What does Ms. Mancini suggest about her trip to the theater?

(A) She was upgraded from general admission to VIP.
(B) She requested to move to a different seat.
(C) She was able to locate The Redford Theater easily.
(D) She had no difficulty purchasing tickets online.

GO ON TO THE NEXT PAGE

Questions 191-195 refer to the following e-mails and meeting minutes.

To:	Rachel Mulholland
From:	Liz Dillon
Date:	Monday, November 16
Subject:	How to take notes at the meeting

Hi Rachel,

I'm very happy that you don't mind helping out at the residents' association meeting this evening. As you know, it's normally my job to do that, but since I've been promoted to chairwoman of the committee, I simply won't have enough time to do it. So, I'd like to give you a few tips so that you don't miss anything. When the meeting begins, I'll take attendance and then briefly outline all of the topics on this week's agenda. You don't need to list these in your notes, but I would like you to provide a summary of each point we discuss. Also, take a note of which members are present, and which ones were unable to attend. Tomorrow, you should add the notes to our association's Web site. It's pretty straight forward. If you have any other questions, feel free to stop by my apartment or reply by e-mail.

See you this evening!

Thanks again,

Liz

Notes From Dearborn Condominiums Residents' Association Meeting
Monday, November 16
7:30 ~ 8:30 P.M.

In Attendance: Adela Murray, Adam Moore, Rachel Mulholland, Liz Dillon, Gillian Jacobson, Liam Cunningham, Gregor Faraday, Polly Jenkins

Unable to Attend: Caroline Stern, Allan Grogan

Liz noted that some of the lights in the parking lot are broken. This is a matter of safety and security, she said, so she has contacted the city council to have them deal with the repairs immediately.

Adela spoke in detail about the changes to the garbage collection. Starting next week, garbage should be placed at the back door of the condo building every Tuesday and Friday by 8 A.M.

Liam and Gregor discussed the completion of the clean-up project they were working on. Over the past week, they've been tidying the communal area around the swimming pool. Everyone agreed that their efforts should be commended.

The annual residents' dinner will take place on Friday, November 27. Because Adam Moore will be on vacation in the Philippines at that time, Gillian will be responsible for arranging this year's event.

Notes taken by Rachel Mulholland

E-Mail Message

To:	Rachel Mulholland
From:	Allan Grogan
Date:	Tuesday, November 17
Subject:	Notes from the meeting

Hi Rachel,

As you know, I was out of town on business and unable to make it to yesterday's meeting. I checked the notes you took and posted to our Web site. I wanted to thank you for putting them up so quickly and for doing such a thorough job.

However, there were a couple of issues that I wanted to bring to your attention. First, you probably should've included Caroline Stern in the notes about the swimming pool. I know she was involved and that she put in a lot of effort. Also, I think it would be a good idea to list the agenda topics at the beginning of the notes so that it's easy to skim through them.

Thanks again,

Allan

---

191. What is suggested about Ms. Dillon?

(A) She will be unable to attend this week's meeting.
(B) She will introduce an agenda at the meeting.
(C) She recently moved out of Dearborn Condominiums.
(D) She is the building manager at Dearborn Condominiums.

192. In the second e-mail, the word "issues" in paragraph 2, line 1 is closest in meaning to

(A) matters
(B) publications
(C) provisions
(D) requests

193. What is Mr. Moore usually responsible for?

(A) Making a garbage collection schedule
(B) Taking notes at residents' meetings
(C) Organizing an annual meal
(D) Guarding a parking lot

194. What did Ms. Stern do recently?

(A) Cleaned a common area
(B) Contacted the city council
(C) Repaired some lights
(D) Traveled overseas on vacation

195. What recommendation for taking meeting notes do Ms. Dillon and Mr. Grogan disagree on?

(A) Summarizing each discussion
(B) Posting notes online
(C) Taking attendance
(D) Listing discussion topics

GO ON TO THE NEXT PAGE

(EDINBURGH, SCOTLAND) - According to a recent study, sales of bubble tea are increasing exponentially throughout Scotland and the rest of the United Kingdom, although it still has a long way to go to catch up with carbonated soft drinks.

As with many other food and beverage trends, part of the appeal of bubble tea is that it is seen as a uniquely foreign and exotic product. Someone who was at the forefront of the new craze was local entrepreneur Alex Wong, the founder of Edinburgh-based bubble tea company Eastern Pearl. Around 8 years ago, Wong relocated to Taiwan to pursue a career in teaching, and he noticed that locals spent a lot of their free time frequenting tea shops. "I was working as an English teacher, and I spent a lot of time at a local tea shop," he said. "I couldn't get enough of the bubble tea and the various ways it can be customized with pearls and ice."

After spending five years at First Star English Academy in Taipei, he returned to Edinburgh and began selling bubble tea from a mobile stall on the street. Now, two years after his return to Edinburgh, Wong's delicious bubble tea (which comes in many delicious flavors, such as oolong, Earl Grey, and green tea, plus differently flavored pearls) can be found in almost every supermarket in the United Kingdom - and his company will soon be attempting to expand into the mainland-European market by distributing products in Germany, France and The Netherlands. Based on his success in the UK, we expect to see a continued rise in popularity of Eastern Pearl.

To:	Alex Wong <alexwong@easternpearl.com>
From:	Polly Liu <pollyliu@scotedu.com>
Date:	April 28
Subject:	Well done!

Hi Alex,

I'm so pleased to see that your business was recently covered in The Edinburgh Times! I was very impressed with the feature and amazed by how well you've done since we last met at the Young Entrepreneurs Convention last year. I was wondering whether you'd be interested in coming to talk to the students at my academy about your experience in the business world. Would you be able to find some free time to have a meal together and discuss it? I'd be available to meet next week on Monday at 6 P.M., Tuesday at 7 P.M., Wednesday at 12 P.M., or Thursday at 9 A.M. By the way, our old coworker from First Star, Jasper Munro, is also interested in catching up with you. Perhaps he could join us.

Best wishes,

Polly Liu

To:	Polly Liu <pollyliu@scotedu.com>
From:	Alex Wong <alexwong@easternpearl.com>
Date:	April 29
Subject:	RE: Well done!

Hi Polly,

It's nice to hear from you! I'm afraid I'll be extremely busy next week, but I'd still like to meet you for a quick bite to eat. How about meeting at 12 for lunch? If that suits you, we can discuss a suitable place to meet. Regarding your request for me to talk to your students... I would love to! I could tell them all about Eastern Pearl's plans to break into other European markets and expand our consumer base and market share. Let's go over the details during lunch next week.

Regards,

Alex Wong

196. What is indicated about the bubble tea market in Scotland?

(A) It mainly attempts to target young consumers.
(B) It has overtaken the carbonated soft drinks market in sales.
(C) It was inspired by beverages from overseas.
(D) It is struggling to reach consumers in Edinburgh.

197. What is most likely true about both Mr. Wong and Ms. Liu?

(A) They developed a range of bubble teas.
(B) They plan to attend a convention together.
(C) They worked together in Taipei.
(D) They co-founded a business in Edinburgh.

198. In the first e-mail, the word "feature" in paragraph 1, line 2, is closest in meaning to

(A) aspect
(B) topic
(C) characteristic
(D) article

199. When most likely will Mr. Wong and Ms. Liu meet?

(A) On Monday
(B) On Tuesday
(C) On Wednesday
(D) On Thursday

200. What does Mr. Wong offer to do?

(A) Discuss his company's expansion
(B) Offer employment opportunities to students
(C) Make a reservation at a restaurant
(D) Give Ms. Liu a tour of his workplace

Stop! This is the end of the test. If you finish before time is called, you may go back to Parts 5, 6, and 7 and check your work.

정답 p.468 / 점수 환산표 p.476

실전모의고사
TEST 2

TEST 2 해설

바로 보기

시작 시간 _____시 _____분

종료 시간 _____시 _____분

▶ 중간에 멈추지 말고 처음부터 끝까지 풀어보세요. 문제를 풀 때는 실전처럼 답안지에 마킹하세요.

READING TEST

In the Reading test, you will read a variety of texts and answer several different types of reading comprehension questions. The entire Reading test will last 75 minutes. There are three parts, and directions are given for each part. You are encouraged to answer as many questions as possible within the time allowed. You must mark your answers on the separate answer sheet. Do not write your answers in your test book.

PART 5

Directions: A word or phrase is missing in each of the sentences below. Four answer choices are given below each sentence. Select the best answer to complete the sentence. Then mark the letter (A), (B), (C), or (D) on your answer sheet.

101. A colleague of ------- will assist me in showing the Japanese clients around our manufacturing plant.
(A) my
(B) me
(C) mine
(D) I

102. Ms. Henchy ------- any queries regarding the plan to renovate the staff cafeteria.
(A) answering
(B) answer
(C) will answer
(D) to answer

103. The department store manager ------- explained the reason for the extended opening hours this week.
(A) clears
(B) clearing
(C) clear
(D) clearly

104. Based on the data, the snowfall is heaviest in Manford County ------- January 1 and March 1.
(A) onto
(B) under
(C) between
(D) among

105. The number of vehicle owners who ------- satellite navigation systems is steadily rising.
(A) use
(B) reach
(C) spend
(D) achieve

106. ------- our factories in India and Taiwan have shut down, the plant in China is still in operation.
(A) Before
(B) Rather than
(C) Although
(D) Depending on

107. Even though we have sent several e-mail notifications, many of our members ------- have not returned their overdue library books.
(A) ever
(B) still
(C) soon
(D) nearly

108. We would like to remind staff that monitors, projectors, and other conference center ------- must not be removed from the premises.
(A) guidelines
(B) productivity
(C) property
(D) substance

109. Many of the wines offered at our restaurant are imported ------- from our supplier in France.

(A) directly
(B) directed
(C) direction
(D) directing

110. The board members are gathering next Wednesday to discuss ------- to cut expenses at our company.

(A) so
(B) expected
(C) how
(D) after

111. A professor skilled in the ------- of infectious diseases will give the keynote speech at the MRD Medical Conference.

(A) renewal
(B) treatment
(C) allocation
(D) involvement

112. Goldstein Jewelry is proud to work with a vast network of ------- retail outlets throughout Europe.

(A) affiliate
(B) affiliated
(C) affiliation
(D) affiliations

113. When beginning an architectural project, it is common to start with a ------- drawing of the structure.

(A) sturdy
(B) basic
(C) concerned
(D) punctual

114. We invited Mr. Collins to lead the workshop because Ms. Benson spoke so ------- of his leadership qualities.

(A) highly
(B) higher
(C) high
(D) highest

115. Make sure that you give yourself a ------- amount of time to reach the conference venue during rush hour.

(A) reasonably
(B) reasonable
(C) reasoning
(D) reason

116. Many entrepreneurs specializing ------- technology start-ups have been invited to speak at this year's convention.

(A) for
(B) of
(C) in
(D) to

117. For a ------- description of our organization's goals and vision, visit our Web site at www.outreachafrica.ca.

(A) detailed
(B) reported
(C) listed
(D) contracted

118. Marty McInnes has withdrawn his ------- after deciding to remain in his role as the CEO of Belltower Industries.

(A) resign
(B) resigning
(C) resigned
(D) resignation

119. Employee bonuses will ------- based on the overall performance of each individual staff member over the past year.

(A) differ
(B) convene
(C) include
(D) calculate

GO ON TO THE NEXT PAGE

120. Because the redecorated conference room still smells of fresh paint, the sales team will hold its meeting ------- this week.

(A) only
(B) previously
(C) seldom
(D) elsewhere

121. Social media advertising has ------- Strike Energy Beverages to almost triple its consumer base.

(A) emerged
(B) approved
(C) improved
(D) enabled

122. ------- the flyers have been printed, Ms. Jenner will begin distributing them to shoppers downtown.

(A) Other than
(B) As soon as
(C) In addition to
(D) So that

123. Several architects noted that the new City Hall's exterior appearance is ------- similar to that of the Montero Museum in Bilbao.

(A) slight
(B) slightest
(C) slightly
(D) slightness

124. Mr. Hodges hired a moving consultant to ------- all stages of the company's relocation to Pearce Industrial Park.

(A) prefer
(B) demand
(C) oversee
(D) alert

125. At the banquet this evening, Mr. DeBoer will be recognized for his three decades of ------- service to Brunton Investment Group.

(A) value
(B) values
(C) valuing
(D) valuable

126. This year's Canadian Jazz Festival will be held in Montreal ------- the city's long history of jazz music.

(A) because of
(B) prior to
(C) plus
(D) besides

127. ------- reviewing numerous potential venues, Mr. Heard chose to hold the product launch at the Huxley Convention Center.

(A) If
(B) Beside
(C) After
(D) Meanwhile

128. To ensure that the drug testing procedure is as ------- as possible, we will allow an inspector to observe each stage.

(A) profitable
(B) exuberant
(C) transparent
(D) remarkable

129. Meeting minutes are ------- taken by the CEO's personal assistant and then published online.

(A) timely
(B) gradually
(C) highly
(D) typically

130. If any manager misplaces a company credit card, the accounting manager will cancel it and send -------.

(A) other
(B) other one
(C) one another
(D) another

PART 6

Directions: Read the texts that follow. A word, phrase, or sentence is missing in parts of each text. Four answer choices for each question are given below the text. Select the best answer to complete the text. Then mark the letter (A), (B), (C) or (D) on your answer sheet.

Questions 131-134 refer to the following e-mail.

To: tsweeney@seamail.net
From: lvelosi@roughneck.com
Subject: Tool Rental
Date: March 14

Dear Mr. Sweeney,

I am contacting you regarding the circular saw you rented, ------- due to be returned on March 13.
131.

If you wish to ------- an extension to the rental period, please contact me at your earliest possible
132.

convenience. ------- workplace is open from 9 A.M. until 6 P.M., Monday through Friday, and you can
133.

reach me there at 555-4989.

If you still require the tool, I can change the return date and let you know how much extra you will

need to pay. -------.
134.

As you are a long-time customer, I will not charge you a late return fee this time. But, I hope to hear

from you soon regarding this matter.

Sincerely,

Linda Velosi
Roughneck Equipment Rental

---

131. (A) which was
(B) this had
(C) when is
(D) that being

132. (A) cancel
(B) inquire
(C) request
(D) install

133. (A) Its
(B) My
(C) Any
(D) Their

134. (A) The renovations should be complete by next Friday.
(B) The rental period is typically seven days.
(C) We have several similar tools that may interest you.
(D) Please let me know what you would prefer to do.

GO ON TO THE NEXT PAGE

Questions 135-138 refer to the following e-mail.

To: Fergus Murphy <fmurphy@homemail.com>

From: Edward Rushford <erushford@worldhistorymag.com>

Subject: Subscription

Date: November 4

Dear Mr. Murphy,

We hope you are satisfied with your subscription to *World History Magazine*. This e-mail is to advise

you that your monthly subscription ------- on 30 November. If you choose to extend your subscription
                                       135.

before it ends, you will receive a 20 percent discount on your next 12 issues of our magazine. This

special offer is available only ------- the end of this month. Respond directly to this e-mail or call our
                                  136.

hotline at 555-1918 to renew your subscription. At *World History Magazine*, we appreciate each and

every one of our subscribers and we want them to continue receiving our publication every month

without -------. And don't forget that our subscribers receive a discount on our annual book, The Year
         137.

in Review, which normally retails at $25.99. The next edition of this book will be released on January

25. -------.
    138.

Sincerely,

Edward Rushford
Subscriber Services
World History Magazine

135. (A) to be expiring
     (B) must have expired
     (C) has expired
     (D) will expire

136. (A) during
     (B) until
     (C) inside
     (D) between

137. (A) disrupts
     (B) disrupted
     (C) disruptive
     (D) disruption

138. (A) Our subscription fees will decrease
         starting next year.
     (B) As a subscriber, you can purchase it for
         only $9.99.
     (C) Instead, this will be launched later this
         month.
     (D) Thank you for your feedback about our
         publication.

Questions 139-142 refer to the following excerpt from a brochure.

Animal Defense Foundation

The goal of the Animal Defense Foundation is to ensure that no local wildlife is wrongfully harmed through illegal hunting. We ------- patrol the woodland areas and streams in Berkshire County.
139.

-------. We then report their presence to the local authorities.
140.

------- a locally-founded group, the Animal Defense Foundation depends on the assistance of local
141.
residents. We need your support to ------- our local wildlife. If you believe that illegal hunting may be
142.
occurring in your area, please contact us at 555-3878.

---

139. (A) continue
(B) continuous
(C) continued
(D) continuously

140. (A) A water conservation law has been passed recently.
(B) Finally, we offer environmental education opportunities.
(C) This enables us to stop hunters from entering the area.
(D) Our organization is the largest in the region dedicated to public health.

141. (A) As
(B) At
(C) Through
(D) Including

142. (A) control
(B) protect
(C) obtain
(D) deliver

Questions 143-146 refer to the following advertisement.

Private Dining Rooms Available for Hire

Bonetti's Restaurant is celebrating the opening of its new private dining rooms! A spectacular lakeside dining experience could be ------! All private dining rooms ------ picturesque views of
143.   144.
Bennett Lake. You can enjoy a variety of freshly-caught seafood and our locally-sourced ingredients in total privacy. We also have a mouth-watering selection of desserts. ------, you may not have any
145.
room left to try them! Bonetti's Restaurant prides itself on its very generous portion sizes, so you might be full after your main course! Our private dining rooms can be booked for groups of up to 25 people. ------. We hope to serve you soon at Bonetti's Restaurant!
146.

Andrew Bonnetti (555-0097), Restaurant Manager

---

143. (A) many
(B) yours
(C) mine
(D) others

144. (A) featured
(B) featuring
(C) feature
(D) have featured

145. (A) However
(B) Therefore
(C) Similarly
(D) Consequently

146. (A) All of them praised our impressive selection of dishes.
(B) We expect the renovation to be finished by the end of the month.
(C) These can be customized to meet your dietary requirements.
(D) Larger parties may be accommodated in special circumstances.

PART 7

Directions: In this part you will read a selection of texts, such as magazine and newspaper articles, e-mails, and instant messages. Each text or set of texts is followed by several questions. Select the best answer for each question and mark the letter (A), (B), (C), or (D) on your answer sheet.

Questions 147-148 refer to the following form.

Horseshoe Bay: Island Hopping Adventure
July 17 – July 18
Exotica Tours, Silver Beach, San Fernando

Name: *Brittany Lawler*
Nationality: *Canadian*
Hotel: *Angel Wave Hotel*
Address: *151 Sunset Road, San Fernando*
E-mail: *blawler@globetel.ca*

I will participate on:

_____ July 17 - Morning session: includes scuba diving lesson, buffet lunch by the pool, and water safety talk (8:30 A.M. - 12:30 P.M.)

__X__ July 18 - Full-day adventure: five destinations (Coral Island, Palm Island, Blue Moon Island, Lagoon Island, Dolphin Island)

Fee:
__X__ One Day ($65 USD)
_____ Both Days ($100 USD)

---

147. What is the purpose of the form?

(A) To change a travel itinerary
(B) To schedule a training session
(C) To make a hotel reservation
(D) To sign up for a tour

148. According to the form, what will Ms. Lawler most likely do?

(A) Learn how to scuba dive
(B) Provide transportation
(C) Enjoy an outdoor lunch
(D) Visit several locations

GO ON TO THE NEXT PAGE

Questions 149-150 refer to the following e-mail.

To:	Adam Montoya <amontoya@hornerealty.com>
From:	Lisa Tarley <ltarley@hornerealty.com>
Subject:	Apartment Info
Date:	February 23

Dear Adam,

Just like you asked, I have changed our Horne Real Estate Web site to reflect the following details about the furnishings and appliances that will be installed in the apartments in the Greenfield Building. The apartments will not be fully-furnished until April, but buyers can choose specific furnishings and appliances in advance when they sign a lease. These items will be installed prior to their move-in date. Also, our agents will be available to give viewings to potential buyers on Tuesdays, Thursdays, and Saturdays.

If you need me to add anything to the site, please do not hesitate to let me know.

Regards,

Lisa

149. Why was the e-mail sent?

(A) To confirm the availability of some apartments
(B) To point out an error in a housing lease
(C) To recommend a new apartment building
(D) To report on some property information

150. What is suggested about Horne Real Estate?

(A) Its agents sometimes work on weekends.
(B) Its headquarters are in the Greenfield Building.
(C) It typically sells unfurnished apartments.
(D) It allows customers to view properties online.

Questions 151-152 refer to the following text-message chain.

Philip Halliday [3:15 P.M.]
Iris, are you still at the main stage area?

Iris Metzger [3:16 P.M.]
Yes. The band is almost finished with its performance.

Philip Halliday [3:18 P.M.]
Do you still want to go and see The Haymakers next? They're playing on the second stage.

Iris Metzger [3:19 P.M.]
I can't wait to see them. They always put on a great show.

Philip Halliday [3:20 P.M.]
Oh, for sure. They know how to get the crowd dancing.

Iris Metzger [3:22 P.M.]
Will you be near the front of the crowd?

Philip Halliday [3:23 P.M.]
Yes, I'll be right up in front. See you there!

151. At 3:20 P.M., what does Mr. Halliday most likely mean when he writes, "Oh, for sure"?

(A) He is certain Ms. Metzger will find the second stage.
(B) The band playing on the main stage was enjoyable.
(C) He recommends that Ms. Metzger purchase a ticket.
(D) He shares Ms. Metzger's opinion of The Haymakers.

152. What is probably true about Ms. Metzger?

(A) She wants Mr. Halliday to check a performance schedule.
(B) She is scheduled to give a performance later today.
(C) She thinks Mr. Halliday will be at the second stage before her.
(D) She would prefer to stand at the back of the crowd.

GO ON TO THE NEXT PAGE

Questions 153-154 refer to the following e-mail.

From:	Brian Croll <bcroll@crollproduce.ca>
To:	Dave Costanza <dconstanza@costanzas.ca>
Subject:	Fruit/Veg Delivery
Date:	August 19

Dear Mr. Costanza,

With regret, we are sending this e-mail to inform you that free delivery will no longer be offered to our clients. In an effort to reduce our expenses and continue offering the highest quality of fresh fruits and vegetables, we feel that it is necessary to charge clients a minimal fee for shipping. This will become effective on October 1. If you would like to discuss this issue in more detail, please respond directly to this message. Shipping charges vary depending on our clients' proximity to our distribution warehouse. We are sorry for this slight inconvenience, and we hope it will not affect our business relationship with your restaurant.

Regards,

Brian Croll
Owner
Croll Produce

153. What is the purpose of the e-mail?

(A) To apologize for a late delivery
(B) To confirm an order of produce
(C) To announce a change to a service
(D) To request additional information

154. What is Mr. Costanza asked to do?

(A) Send an e-mail
(B) Make a phone call
(C) Visit a warehouse
(D) Confirm his address

Questions 155-157 refer to the following information.

The Butland Theater Group, based at Butland Theater in the city of Havenbrook, is an independently-operated acting group that performs for audiences throughout the southern states of the U.S. Originally founded by amateur drama students who wanted to produce unique plays and musicals, the Butland Theater Group is committed to bringing audiences the highest standard of acting and stage production.

— [1] —. The vast majority of our 85 members reside in Havenbrook and are very community-oriented. — [2] —. Furthermore, most of our shows are held right here in town at the Butland Theater. — [3] —. At a performance by the Butland Theater Group, you will have the pleasure of watching a dedicated group of individuals that has built a strong reputation by entertaining the people of Havenbrook for three decades. — [4] —.

155. Where would the information most likely appear?

(A) In a pamphlet for potential theatergoers
(B) In a historical book about Havenbrook
(C) In an advertisement for an acting audition
(D) In a newsletter for Butland Theater staff

156. How long has the theater group been active?

(A) For 3 months
(B) For 3 years
(C) For 30 years
(D) For 300 years

157. In which of the positions marked [1], [2], [3], and [4] does the following sentence best belong?

"There's a good chance that you have seen them working in your own neighborhood."

(A) [1]
(B) [2]
(C) [3]
(D) [4]

GO ON TO THE NEXT PAGE

Blazecom Cable & Internet Service Subscription Renewal

Make sure you continue to receive uninterrupted service!

Customer Name: Mr. Jordan Cranston

Home Address: 552 Spalding Drive, Orlando, FL, 32803

Tel. Number: 301-555-3907

E-mail Address: jcranston@blazecom.net

Customer Signature: Jordan Cranston

First Payment Due Upon Renewal: $99.99

Standard Package: $89.99 per month

This 12-month package includes 96 cable TV channels and our fastest Internet.

Subscribers can enjoy the following:

- HD Channels at no extra charge
- Free Roam TV on your mobile devices
- Up to 150 Mbps download speed
- $100 credit on Blazecom merchandise

Premium Package: $109.99 per month

This 18-month package includes 122 cable TV channels and our fastest Internet.

In addition to the standard package's offerings, you will receive access to our full library of Box Office movies at no extra charge.

Technical support hotline: Our technical support team is available to all customers 24 hours a day, seven days a week. Call 555-3892.

Box Office movies: Charges for movies that are purchased through our Box Office service will be added to each monthly bill for those without a Premium Package.

---

158. What is implied about Mr. Cranston?

(A) He inquired about a new cable TV package.

(B) He has experienced problems with an Internet connection.

(C) He currently has a subscription with Blazecom.

(D) He has recently moved to a new home address.

159. What is NOT part of the Standard Package?

(A) The option to watch TV on a cell phone

(B) Access to more than 100 television channels

(C) A maximum download speed of 150 Mbps

(D) Credit on Blazecom products

160. What additional benefit can a customer receive by upgrading from Standard to Premium?

(A) A faster Internet speed

(B) Free Box Office movies

(C) Online technical support

(D) A warranty on hardware

Questions 161-163 refer to the following article.

Business Weekly

BURKVILLE (March 9) – After months of negotiations, Atraxo Chemicals has finalized its acquisition of Tirion Corporation. This will come as good news to local residents, as it means that Atraxo will take over and continue the construction of the Tirion factory in Burkville, which was left half-finished due to budget problems.

The manufacturing plant was supposed to create more than 250 new jobs in Burkville, but as a result of Tirion's financial difficulties, construction ceased approximately one year ago. According to Amy Jarecki, a spokeswoman for Atraxo, work on the plant will restart immediately and last for three or four months, with production set to begin later this year.

"We will be fully operational in mid-August," stated Jarecki. "So, we will begin advertising job vacancies approximately two months prior to that."

The factory will handle the manufacturing of several popular Tirion products as well as Atraxo's forthcoming Meadow Fresh range of household cleansers.

Atraxo Chemicals is currently headquartered in Winnipeg and distributes its products throughout North America, Europe, and Asia.

161. What is the purpose of the article?

(A) To describe competition in the chemicals industry
(B) To announce the resumption of a project
(C) To promote the launch of a new product range
(D) To explain why a company is downsizing

162. According to Ms. Jarecki, what will happen in August?

(A) A building will be renovated.
(B) A company will begin recruiting workers.
(C) A factory will commence production.
(D) A new manager will be introduced.

163. What is indicated about Atraxo Chemicals?

(A) It will close its Winnipeg headquarters.
(B) It manufactures cleaning products.
(C) It has been purchased by a global corporation.
(D) It operates several factories in Burkville.

GO ON TO THE NEXT PAGE

E-Mail Message

To:	Moira Paterson <mpaterson@alcatek.com>
From:	Desmond Davis <ddavis@alcatek.com>
Subject:	Overseas Assignment
Date:	March 24

Hi Moira,

I am delighted that you have agreed to work in Hyderabad, India, from April 15 to June 15. — [1] —. I will go ahead and begin organizing your flights, accommodations, and transportation on your behalf. Of course, this will all be covered by Alcatek. Additional expenses such as meals and gas will be reimbursed to you upon your return, assuming you save receipts. — [2] —.

You will be working alongside Sanjit Gupta, the quality control manager at our new manufacturing plant in Hyderabad, and your role will be to evaluate the efficiency and effectiveness of all production processes within the facility. Mr. Gupta mentioned to me that you had a brief discussion last year during our company workshop, and he was impressed with your knowledge of quality assurance. — [3] —.

Please review the attached list of potential apartments thoroughly. Once you decide on which one you like the most, please let me know and I will arrange for the deposit and rent to be paid up front. All of them are situated just a short distance from the factory and come fully furnished. Please note that this should be taken care of without delay, as these are highly desirable places. — [4] —.

Best wishes,

Desmond Davis
Human Resources Manager
Alcatek Corporation

---

164. What aspect of Ms. Paterson's overseas assignment is NOT mentioned?

(A) The work she will carry out
(B) The payment she will receive
(C) The name of her supervisor
(D) The duration of the project

165. What does the e-mail indicate about Mr. Gupta?

(A) He conducted an interview with Ms. Paterson.
(B) He teaches a workshop on quality assurance.
(C) He supervises Mr. Davis's department.
(D) He met Ms. Paterson at a company event.

166. What will Ms. Paterson most likely do next?

(A) Submit her payment information
(B) Choose her preferred property
(C) Change her travel itinerary
(D) Schedule a meeting with Mr. Gupta

167. In which of the positions marked [1], [2], [3], and [4] does the following sentence best belong?

"I'm sure you'll prove to be a valuable asset to his workforce."

(A) [1]
(B) [2]
(C) [3]
(D) [4]

Questions 168-171 refer to the following online chat discussion.

Betty Cheng [1:31 P.M.]
Karl, has Edison Print Shop finished the flyers yet?

Karl Steiner [1:33 P.M.]
I just got off the phone with the shop manager, and they've had a bit of a delay. They originally hoped to deliver all our promotional materials by Tuesday. But, because of a technical glitch, it looks like we'll receive them on Thursday morning instead.

Betty Cheng [1:34 P.M.]
Does that leave us enough time to distribute them?

Pete Dickov [1:37 P.M.]
I think we had better get the flyers out as quickly as possible. I wanted to take some to the city fair on Friday as well.

Karl Steiner [1:40 P.M.]
It won't be a problem. Once we receive them on Thursday, we will still have enough time to hand them out to shoppers downtown and tell them about Saturday's event. Pete, I'll set aside a batch that you can take to the fair.

Betty Cheng [1:42 P.M.]
Okay, just let me know if there's any change with the print shop's schedule. Oh... I just remembered... did you organize the music for Saturday?

Karl Steiner [1:44 P.M.]
I'm just about to do it. I need to call the band's guitarist back to finalize the payment for their performance. I met with him last Friday and discussed the type of music we'd like them to play.

Pete Dickov [1:45 P.M.]
Great work. Thanks, Karl. I'm certain the grand opening is going to be a great success!

168. What is the purpose of the discussion?

(A) To schedule a team meeting
(B) To confirm the completion of a project
(C) To go over some event details
(D) To discuss marketing options

169. According to the discussion, when will the flyers most likely be ready?

(A) On Tuesday
(B) On Thursday
(C) On Friday
(D) On Saturday

170. At 1:40 P.M., what does Mr. Steiner most likely mean when he writes, "It won't be a problem"?

(A) The flyers have a professional appearance.
(B) There will be plenty of time available.
(C) A city fair will go ahead as planned.
(D) The print shop is conveniently located.

171. What will Mr. Steiner most likely do next?

(A) Distribute materials
(B) Update a Web site
(C) Call the print shop manager
(D) Contact a band member

GO ON TO THE NEXT PAGE

August 2
Mr. Vernon Ayers
Ayers Systems Inc.
Wyatt Technology Park,
Denver

Dear Mr. Ayers,

I am delighted that you have agreed to lead a product design workshop at one of our upcoming TKS Technology Conferences. In accordance with the policies of our event, you will be reimbursed for your expenses via your online account in addition to receiving $55 per hour for the duration of your participation.

As previously discussed, we would like you to lead the workshop at our final summer conference on Saturday, August 15. You may confirm your participation by calling our HR Department manager, Les Selleck, at 555-3674. If you are unable to participate in the summer conference, please inform Mr. Selleck as soon as possible. We will then make alternative arrangements for you to lead a workshop at our first fall conference on Saturday, September 5.

You should submit the reimbursement form to our accounting team no more than three days after your appearance at the conference. At that time, you must also include all relevant receipts for accommodation and travel. Meals are not covered under our reimbursement policy.

To assist you with your preparations for your role at the conference, we would like to put you in touch with the individual who performed the same role at each of our spring conferences. As such, you are advised to contact Ms. Gillian Bowers, who will be happy to provide you with advice and share some workshop materials with you. You may reach her at gbowers@livetek.com. Please be aware that finalized conference schedules for both of the aforementioned events will be sent to you on August 8, at which time you may decide whether or not you can participate in the summer event, as we hope.

If you have any questions, please direct them to our HR manager.

Best regards,

Angela Baker
Head Organizer, TKS Technology Conference

172. What is NOT indicated about the TKS Technology Conference?

(A) It will be held several times this year.
(B) It offers an hourly payment to workshop leaders.
(C) It provides complimentary meals to participants.
(D) It covers hotel and transportation costs.

173. What is true about Ms. Bowers?

(A) She has led a product design workshop in the past.
(B) She will give a talk at the upcoming TKS Technology Conference.
(C) She is currently employed at Ayers Systems Inc.
(D) She works in a human resources department.

174. When will Mr. Ayers officially be informed of the full conference schedules?

(A) On August 2
(B) On August 8
(C) On August 15
(D) On September 2

175. What is suggested about Mr. Ayers?

(A) He will be reimbursed for his expenses in cash.
(B) He might not necessarily appear at a summer workshop.
(C) He is likely to contact the accounting team before participating in the conference.
(D) He will get assistance from Angela Baker with workshop materials.

GO ON TO THE NEXT PAGE

Deeney Corporation - February Newsletter

On February 19, board members discussed several issues that most employees will be interested to learn more about. The main topic of the discussion was what to do with the empty fourth floor of our office building at 1046 Millbrook Avenue. It was last occupied by the Marketing Department before the decision to merge those employees with the advertising team on the third floor.

The company's personnel director, Leon Ramsay, called for a plan to convert the floor into a cafeteria for staff. He cited a recent scientific study that backs up his belief that good nutrition leads to higher productivity.

"There have been numerous complaints about the lack of good, affordable places to eat in this area. This results in many workers opting for fast food, which has a negative impact on their health and productivity. A staff cafeteria would provide nutritious food at reasonable prices."

Michael McKean, sales director, had a different proposal. He believes that the space should be utilized for staff training workshops and new-hire orientations.

Advertising director Tom Lautner said, "We don't need more space for training. We need more storage space for all of our records and office supplies."

Our CEO, Cindy Alvarez, suggested giving the employees a gym. She mentioned that workers at Deeney Corporation work long hours and rarely have time to work out once they leave the office.

Howerer, the CFO, Lisa Riggins, disagreed. "The floor isn't spacious enough for a cafeteria or exercise facilities. It's not like our headquarters on Stenson Street. That place has easily accommodated both for several years."

Deeney Corporation's president, Donald Trammel will consider these suggestions and make a final decision at the next board meeting on March 4.

Lasker Equipment

Invoice

Order from: Deeney Corporation
Headquarters, 223 Stenson Street, Pittsburgh

Send to: 1046 Millbrook Avenue

Product ID	Product Name/Quantity	Price
#3989	Bonner Treadmill (5)	$ 2,495.00
#4625	Archer Bicycle (5)	$ 1,995.00
#1765	Medium Yoga Mat (25)	$ 174.75
Total		$4,664.75

176. What does the article mainly discuss?

(A) Potential uses for part of a building
(B) Common complaints made by employees
(C) New work policies affecting board members
(D) Methods for reducing renovation expenses

177. What is indicated about the Marketing Department?

(A) It is based in a building on Stenson Street.
(B) It was relocated to a different floor.
(C) It held a meeting on February 19.
(D) It plans to hire new employees.

178. In the article, the phrase "backs up" in paragraph 2, line 4, is closest in meaning to

(A) delays
(B) blocks
(C) supports
(D) copies

179. What is suggested about Deeney Corporation's headquarters?

(A) It was recently renovated.
(B) It contains a cafeteria.
(C) It will move to a different building.
(D) It has experienced problems with productivity.

180. Whose proposal was most likely accepted on March 4?

(A) Ms. Alvarez's
(B) Mr. Ramsay's
(C) Mr. McKean's
(D) Mr. Lautner's

GO ON TO THE NEXT PAGE

E-Melody Music Streaming Service

Subscription Options

	Unlimited	Pro	Free
Monthly Fee	$15	$7.50	Free
Invitation Required	No	No	Yes
Access to Full Music Library	Yes	Yes	Yes
E-Melody Chat Room Access	Yes	Yes	No
No Advertisements	Yes	Yes	No
Play E-Melody Files on Mobile	Yes	No	No
Exclusive Content/Discounts*	Yes	No	No
Free Trials for Friends	Yes	No	No

Please be advised that a processing fee of $25 should be paid regardless of which subscription option is chosen. However, this fee can be avoided if you pay for a full 6 months of service in advance.

* **This information will be sent exclusively to subscribers by e-mail on a weekly basis.**

E-Mail Message

From:	evakrinkel@emelody.com
To:	rkeating@alphamail.com
Subject:	Re: Free trials for friends
Date:	November 16
Attachment:	Payment Confirmation

Dear Mr. Keating,

Thank you for subscribing to our music streaming service. I can confirm that we received your full payment of $45, which covers 6 months of fees at $7.50 per month, and your subscription was activated on November 14.

In your e-mail, you asked whether you were entitled to give free trials to your friends or family members. I'm afraid that your Pro subscription does not include free trials for our services. You would need to upgrade your subscription to the 'unlimited' level in order to qualify for this perk. If that is something you would be interested in doing, you would need to submit an additional payment of $45 to cover 6 months of unlimited access. However, please take note that individuals who sign up for free trials cannot use our chatrooms, turn off advertisements, or enjoy exclusive content.

Best wishes,

Eva Krinkel
Customer Service Representative
E-Melody Music Streaming

---

181. What is indicated about music streamed by E-Melody?

(A) It is updated on a daily basis.
(B) It does not include new releases.
(C) It is accessible by invitation only.
(D) It can be played on cell phones.

182. In the notice, the word "advised" in paragraph 2, line 1, is closest in meaning to

(A) suggested
(B) considered
(C) informed
(D) assisted

183. What can Mr. Keating NOT do through his E-Melody subscription?

(A) Enjoy services free of advertisements
(B) Use chat rooms provided by E-Melody
(C) Access a full selection of music files
(D) Get weekly updates about discounts

184. What can be inferred about Mr. Keating?

(A) He subscribed to E-Melody on November 16.
(B) He did not need to pay an additional charge.
(C) He submitted an incorrect sum of money to E-Melody.
(D) He decided against upgrading his subscription.

185. What is indicated about the friends of individuals who have unlimited subscriptions?

(A) They have only limited access to services.
(B) They must pay a fee in order to stream music.
(C) They will be issued a temporary chatroom password.
(D) They can receive details about exclusive content.

GO ON TO THE NEXT PAGE

Fresh Start at Huntsville's

Eden Valley Tours

By Leila Mahmoud

HUNTSVILLE (May 14) – Bernie Veitch, a long-serving tour guide at Eden Valley Tours who was hired by the company's founder Richard Stratton over twenty years ago, has taken over as owner and chairman. "When Richard announced that he wanted to move to Langston to concentrate on his career as a novelist," said Mr. Veitch, "I immediately put myself forward as his replacement."

Mr. Stratton added, "Bernie has been with the tour company since day one and nobody is more knowledgeable than he is when it comes to local sights and activities. I can't think of a better person to take over the reins." Veitch formally took control on May 5 and immediately introduced several new activity choices for tour members to enjoy, including a chocolate factory tour that Travel Pro Magazine columnist Frida Kohl described as "incredibly fun." To find out more about tour offerings, call 555-1087 or visit www. edenvalleytours.com.

EDEN VALLEY TOURS

ALL-DAY PACKAGE ($125 per person)

MORNING ACTIVITY

Chocolate Factory Tour at Kenmore Confectionary Inc.
OR Historical Walk through the streets of Huntsville

AFTERNOON ACTIVITY

Farmers Market Tour in Huntsville, Fredericktown, and Langston
OR Kayaking Tour at Indigo Lake, Red River, and Sawyer's Creek

EVENING ACTIVITY

Stargazing at Dark-Sky Preserve at Beaver Lake
OR Night Cruise on Sparrow River

http://www.travelwizard.com/reviews/tours/edenvalley/018 ▼ — ▢ X

My husband and I recently signed up for the all-day package with Eden Valley Tours. The tour was very well organized and the guide was informative and helpful. When we booked the tour one week in advance, the guide gave us the option to customize our tour package by choosing from various options. He was also happy to slightly adjust the locations for the afternoon activities so that some local friends could join us, even though it took more time for us to reach our destinations. In the end, the afternoon activity was not that exciting, although I must admit that Sawyer's Creek was beautiful. The tour of the chocolate factory was the high point of the day, especially with all the free samples. I'd love to go back there someday.

Overall Satisfaction Rating: 7/10
Posted by Martina Corman, May 28

186. What is the purpose of the article?

(A) To discuss a local business owner's career
(B) To congratulate a tour company on its recent success
(C) To recommend specific activities in Eden Valley
(D) To describe an ownership change at a business

187. Why is Mr. Stratton going to Langston?

(A) To focus on writing books
(B) To establish a new business
(C) To begin his retirement
(D) To lead a special tour

188. What detail from the article does Ms. Corman agree with?

(A) The all-day tour is the most reasonably priced in the area.
(B) The evening activity can be customized for tour groups.
(C) The activity that was reviewed in a magazine is enjoyable.
(D) The tour guide should be more knowledgeable about the area.

189. In the review, the word "took" in paragraph 1, line 5, is closest in meaning to

(A) carried
(B) required
(C) grasped
(D) arrived

190. What activity did Ms. Corman ask to make changes to?

(A) Historical Walk
(B) Farmers Market Tour
(C) Kayaking Tour
(D) Night Cruise

GO ON TO THE NEXT PAGE

Questions 191-195 refer to the following e-mail, notice, and article.

To:	tpontius@fabrichub.com
From:	bwelch@globalmaterials.com
Date:	September 7
Subject:	September Pickup

Dear Mr. Pontius,

I'm contacting you to let you know that a Global Materials employee, Isman Ali, will arrive at Fabric Hub between the hours of 8:30 A.M. and 10:30 A.M. on September 25. He will assess the materials you have collected and pay you a mutually agreeable price before taking them away.

As always, the price per item is greatly dependent on current global pricing trends in the textiles market. For example, the demand for recycled cotton has continued to fall, and prices have dropped accordingly. The same is true of wool and silk due to the abundance of each that is readily available. The good news, however, is that the demand for leather has skyrocketed, resulting in significant increases in the value of reclaimed leather. In fact, a fashion designer in France has contacted us requesting our full supply as soon as possible.

We look forward to doing business with you once again.

Regards,

Brianna Welch
Global Materials

Fabric Hub

At Fabric Hub, we pride ourselves on being the nation's busiest recycling point for all sorts of textiles. When donating your old, unwanted clothing or bed linens, make sure that you put the items in the specially marked bins. Our workers will then categorize the items as natural or synthetic textiles and further separate them into specific types.

Bin A: *Pants, jeans, skirts, dresses, shorts, etc.*
Bin B: *Jackets, sweaters, shirts, T-shirts, etc.*
Bin C: *Hats, socks, underwear, and footwear*
Bin D: *Bed sheets, pillow cases, curtains, etc.*

Due to a current high demand for certain textiles, we will also be accepting accessories such as belts, purses, and wallets through September 24.

If you have any questions, or if we can be of service in any way, please speak with one of our workers in the administration office.

PARIS (December 3) – Granduciel Couture just launched a new ad campaign for its upcoming clothing range, called Sophisticana. The new clothing range is made from high-quality materials and will include women's skirts, pants, and hats. The fashion label is keen to point out in the advertisements that these garments have been manufactured using recycled materials, and that the company is attempting to take a more environmentally-conscious direction. Only a few special items from the Sophisticana range will be on sale tomorrow at the French company's biggest store, which is situated in the heart of Paris. Fans of the fashion brand who live in other countries will need to remain patient until December 29. Granduciel Couture intends to make the full clothing range available in hundreds of stores throughout France by December 18.

191. What does Mr. Pontius most likely do for a living?

(A) Repair secondhand goods
(B) Create clothes for a fashion designer
(C) Purchase rare goods for collectors
(D) Run a textiles recycling facility

192. According to the notice, where should shoes be placed?

(A) In Bin A
(B) In Bin B
(C) In Bin C
(D) In Bin D

193. Why did Fabric Hub request that accessories be dropped off by September 24?

(A) Because the business will be closing temporarily
(B) Because the items will be picked up the following day
(C) Because a special offer will come to an end soon
(D) Because the business is running out of storage space

194. What is Granduciel Couture most likely using to produce its new clothing range?

(A) Cotton
(B) Silk
(C) Leather
(D) Wool

195. When will the new clothing range be available outside of France?

(A) On December 3
(B) On December 4
(C) On December 18
(D) On December 29

GO ON TO THE NEXT PAGE

Questions 196-200 refer to the following brochure, course description, and phone message.

Grange Business Institute Launches New Course
Business Management Course
Course Coordinator: Allan Nisbet
Cost: $2,600

This intensive course lasts for six months, with approximately ten evening classes held per month. The course is scheduled to begin on March 1. Only those with a prior degree related to business are eligible to enroll.

The aim of this course is to provide supplemental knowledge and instruction to individuals pursuing a career in business management. Topics to be covered include accounting, negotiating, marketing, and human resources management. Students will be graded based on written exams and regular coursework such as essays.

Each section of the course includes one textbook that is required reading. These textbooks can be purchased directly from the on-site bookstore at our institute. They may also be borrowed from the Grange Public Library, but please be aware that the lending period is rather short and requests for extensions are rarely granted. We recommend that you purchase your own copies to ensure you are fully equipped for each part of the course.

Business Management Course

Month	Course Section	Required Reading
1	Management Accounting	Principles of Managerial Accounting – 12th Edition (Author: Giles Sloan)
2	Managerial Negotiations	Essentials of Business Negotiation – 3rd Edition (Author: Joseph Kahn)
3	Human Resources Management	HR Management: A Strategic Approach – 10th Edition (Author: Theresa Phillips)
4	E-Business Strategies	Using the Web to Grow Your Business – 4th Edition (Author: Bryan Lowe)
5	Business Marketing	Business-to-Business Marketing – 5th Edition (Author: Kenneth Simms)
6	Operations Management	Production Processes and Supply Chains – 11th Edition (Author: Marek Petrovski)

Grange Business Institute is typically closed over the weekend, but our administration office opens briefly on Saturdays between 1 P.M. and 4 P.M. Course coordinators are occasionally present during that time, and we welcome any students who wish to drop by with questions about course schedules and materials.

WHILE YOU WERE OUT...

FOR: Allan Nisbet
MESSAGE RECEIVED: Saturday, 3:20 P.M.
Fax _____ In person ✓ Telephone _____

MESSAGE:
Ronald Barr dropped by the office earlier. He is taking your business management course, but he had a question about the required reading. He already has his own copy of the textbook, but it's the 3rd Edition, not the 4th Edition as listed in the course description. He'd like you to give him an e-mail at rbarr@citymail.net and let him know whether that edition is still suitable for the course.

196. What is suggested about the textbooks used during the Business Management course?

(A) They can be purchased at a discounted price.
(B) They are not carried by the institute's bookstore.
(C) They may only be borrowed for a limited time.
(D) They may not be necessary for some sections of the course.

197. In the brochure, the word "covered" in paragraph 2, line 2, is the closest in meaning to

(A) concealed
(B) protected
(C) discussed
(D) paid

198. What does the course description imply?

(A) The institute opens for a short time on Sundays.
(B) Instructors hold weekly meetings with students.
(C) Students can personalize their class schedules.
(D) Classes at the institute are held on weekdays.

199. What is suggested about Mr. Barr?

(A) He is unable to attend one section of the course.
(B) He has taken a course at Grange Business Institute before.
(C) He has obtained a business-related qualification.
(D) He is having difficulty purchasing a textbook.

200. Which section of the course was Mr. Barr's query related to?

(A) Management Accounting
(B) Managerial Negotiations
(C) Human Resources Management
(D) E-Business Strategies

Stop! This is the end of the test. If you finish before time is called, you may go back to Parts 5, 6, and 7 and check your work.

실전모의고사
TEST 3

TEST 3 해설

바로 보기

▶ 중간에 멈추지 말고 처음부터 끝까지 풀어보세요. 문제를 풀 때는 실전처럼 답안지에 마킹하세요.

READING TEST

In the Reading test, you will read a variety of texts and answer several different types of reading comprehension questions. The entire Reading test will last 75 minutes. There are three parts, and directions are given for each part. You are encouraged to answer as many questions as possible within the time allowed. You must mark your answers on the separate answer sheet. Do not write your answers in your test book.

PART 5

Directions: A word or phrase is missing in each of the sentences below. Four answer choices are given below each sentence. Select the best answer to complete the sentence. Then mark the letter (A), (B), (C), or (D) on your answer sheet.

101. The full payment will be sent to Burnside Construction upon the ------- of renovations.

(A) complete
(B) completes
(C) completing
(D) completion

102. The Arnhem Hotel trains its front desk workers to respond to guests' complaints as ------- as possible.

(A) quicker
(B) quickly
(C) quicken
(D) quickest

103. When visiting the newly opened branch of Crusty's Bakery, do not forget to help ------- to a free sample of our cookies.

(A) you
(B) your
(C) yourself
(D) yours

104. Because traffic jams are ------- to happen this weekend, motorists are advised to set off earlier than planned to avoid delays.

(A) liking
(B) likeness
(C) likely
(D) likes

105. In his new book, experienced accountant Vernon Clarke outlines ------- to ensure your future is financially secure.

(A) strategies
(B) strategize
(C) strategic
(D) strategically

106. Because Ms. Shilton is highly regarded as a journalist, ------- newspaper column is read by hundreds of thousands of people.

(A) she
(B) her
(C) hers
(D) herself

107. Kris Choi and Vivian Liu are expected to reach the final group stage at the global Internet marketing -------.

(A) competes
(B) competing
(C) competed
(D) competition

108. Turn off ------- electronic device in the office before leaving at the end of the day.

(A) all
(B) each
(C) whole
(D) complete

109. Miranda Chambers was awarded the Bettany Prize ------- her contributions to the field of journalism.
(A) about
(B) for
(C) when
(D) since

110. The bicycle chain on your Explorer MTB should ------- after each ride to prevent a buildup of dirt and grit.
(A) be cleaned
(B) cleaning
(C) have cleaned
(D) clean

111. Ms. Hudgens ------- her acceptance speech at the awards ceremony because she left her notes at home.
(A) accomplished
(B) improvised
(C) announced
(D) nominated

112. Packaging experts at Royale Deluxe Goods are collaborating to design special boxes for ------- its merchandise.
(A) transportation
(B) transport
(C) transporting
(D) transporter

113. At the fundraising event, the names of donors will be kept ------- and will only be known by the event organizers.
(A) cautious
(B) secret
(C) curious
(D) sturdy

114. According to the construction manager, there is a slight ------- that the new baseball stadium will be completed ahead of schedule.
(A) possible
(B) possibility
(C) possibly
(D) possibilities

115. Thousands of commuters have benefited ------- the construction of the Marlin Island Expressway.
(A) from
(B) when
(C) above
(D) it

116. For just an additional $20, you can have any name or message you like ------- on the back of your Nautilus G50 watch.
(A) installed
(B) engraved
(C) reserved
(D) progressed

117. While the stairways in the building are being painted, ------- to the third-floor cafeteria is by elevator only.
(A) direction
(B) reservation
(C) access
(D) order

118. Mr. Lacey will be in a board meeting all morning, but he will be available to speak with you ------- that.
(A) after
(B) into
(C) over
(D) behind

119. ------- Ms. Dawson will be overseas on business this week, Mr. Long will lead the management meeting on Thursday.
(A) Either
(B) Rather
(C) Unless
(D) Because

GO ON TO THE NEXT PAGE

120. The publishing deadline is set for 11 A.M. tomorrow, so it is ------- that he complete the revisions to the article by the end of today.

(A) authoritative
(B) imperative
(C) affirmative
(D) disruptive

121. The sales figures for the first quarter ------- the regional manager's earlier prediction.

(A) surpassed
(B) surpassing
(C) to surpass
(D) having surpassed

122. At Horizon Energy, we do ------- we can to assist customers who have queries about their monthly bills.

(A) neither
(B) that
(C) everything
(D) whichever

123. Ettien Corporation's financial ------- of staff performance has been praised by leading management experts.

(A) respect
(B) default
(C) omission
(D) recognition

124. The scratches on the dining table's surface are ------- visible now that the item has been polished using a special solution.

(A) barely
(B) precisely
(C) additionally
(D) carefully

125. The special guest speaker will discuss the financial problems ------- the healthcare industry in the UK.

(A) have faced
(B) facing
(C) are facing
(D) face

126. If consumers dislike the TV commercial for our curry-flavored instant noodles, it will affect not only that product ------- our entire range.

(A) such as
(B) even if
(C) as for
(D) but also

127. By signing up for a membership to the British Medical Association online, you can gain access to journal articles one week ------- non-members.

(A) between
(B) during
(C) ahead of
(D) away from

128. Eight sports venues, five of ------- are located in California, have been chosen to host the West Coast Soccer Tournament.

(A) them
(B) what
(C) those
(D) which

129. Because of her fear of public speaking, Ms. Petrie was ------- to address the staff at the year-end banquet.

(A) reluctance
(B) more reluctantly
(C) reluctantly
(D) reluctant

130. Ms. Bushell will make sure that the next sale event will be held during a week that ------- the town's peak tourism period.

(A) coincides with
(B) transfers to
(C) requests that
(D) responds to

PART 6

Directions: Read the texts that follow. A word, phrase, or sentence is missing in parts of each text. Four answer choices for each question are given below the text. Select the best answer to complete the text. Then mark the letter (A), (B), (C) or (D) on your answer sheet.

Questions 131-134 refer to the following letter.

Price Rite Food Supplies

9 November

Chuck Mulgrew

Chuck's Sandwich Shop

West Finch Avenue

Toronto, ON M1B 5K7

Dear Mr. Mulgrew,

As you requested over the phone on 5 November, we checked the monthly order of food supplies you submitted through our Web site on 2 November. As you had noted, the order did indeed include ten jars of mayonnaise more than you had specified. -------, on 8 November, we addressed this
131.
issue, which we acknowledge was our fault. On that date, we ------- ten units from your order. Your
132.
invoice has been modified ------- the change to this month's order, and this has been enclosed with
133.
this letter. -------. Your items should arrive by 15 November as you requested.
134.

Best regards,

Price Rite Food Supplies

131. (A) Furthermore
(B) In addition
(C) As a result
(D) On the contrary

132. (A) deduct
(B) deducted
(C) will deduct
(D) are deducting

133. (A) to reflect
(B) reflecting in
(C) a reflection of
(D) that reflect on

134. (A) All of our items can be viewed in our online catalog.
(B) By ordering in bulk, you can make further savings.
(C) We are not responsible for damage caused during shipping.
(D) Please accept our apologies for the error.

GO ON TO THE NEXT PAGE

Questions 135-138 refer to the following e-mail.

To: Customer Inquiries <inquiries@kpfurnishings.com>
From: Maxine Black <maxineblack@maillingo.com>
Date: Tuesday, May 11
Subject: Recent order

Dear sir/madam,

I visited the KP Furnishings store on Mayfair Road on May 5 and purchased an Amora Oak Computer Desk. When the desk was delivered two days later, I was very happy with it. -------, after closer **135.** inspection, I saw that there is a large scratch on the side of the item, which must've happened during shipping. According to your store's policy, refunds for ------- items are only available with a valid **136.** store receipt. -------. The store clerk ------- to hand me a proof of purchase when I paid for the item. **137.** **138.**

Please let me know how I can return the item and obtain a refund.

Thank you,

Maxine Black

---

135. (A) In fact
(B) Moreover
(C) Therefore
(D) However

136. (A) discounted
(B) defective
(C) unavailable
(D) returned

137. (A) In addition, the upper shelf is not attached firmly to the desk.
(B) Accordingly, I returned the item within five days of the purchase date.
(C) This policy applies to any item purchased through your online store.
(D) Regardless, I hope you can make an exception in this case.

138. (A) forgot
(B) will forget
(C) is forgetting
(D) has been forgotten

Questions 139-142 refer to the following information.

Checking In With Asiatic Airlines

At Asiatic Airlines, we strive to make sure our passengers can check in quickly and effortlessly. ------- is possible as a result of our well-organized check-in procedure. To help us ------- it, passengers
   139.   **140.**
should try to follow our check-in guidelines and tips. For example, always make sure you arrive at the airport three hours prior to your scheduled departure time. Although we always try to avoid long lines at our check-in counters, delays can still occur. -------. In such circumstances, we are truly grateful
                                                141.
to you for your -------.
            142.

Please remember that you may check in online 24 hours before your flight to speed up the process even further. Visit www.asiaticairlines.com for more details.

---

139. (A) What
     (B) There
     (C) This
     (D) Theirs

140. (A) change
     (B) issue
     (C) maintain
     (D) review

141. (A) Occasionally, we offer discounts on international destinations.
     (B) Sometimes, we have an extraordinarily high number of passengers.
     (C) You can select your seat when booking your flight in advance.
     (D) Our airplanes are known for their efficiency and safety.

142. (A) reluctance
     (B) advice
     (C) concern
     (D) patience

GO ON TO THE NEXT PAGE

Questions 143-146 refer to the following comment card.

The Alpha G5 is a smartphone that I would recommend to everyone. Its powerful processor allows me to browse the Internet and use applications quickly. It's a lot ------- than any other cell phone
143.
on the market. In fact, it lets me move from one Web page to another in less than a second! The Alpha G5 includes several innovative features that are simple to -------. For instance, it has a very
144.
convenient menu system that is easy to navigate. -------. And my favorite thing of all is that the
145.
battery only needs to be charged for approximately one hour ------- use.
146.

143. (A) faster
(B) brighter
(C) heavier
(D) cheaper

144. (A) order
(B) call
(C) operate
(D) assemble

145. (A) I normally use my cell phone while I'm relaxing at home.
(B) Alpha has been a leader in the market for five years.
(C) I was able to find the product in the store without any problems.
(D) To save energy, it turns to stand-by mode when left idle.

146. (A) once
(B) when
(C) so
(D) after

PART 7

Directions: In this part you will read a selection of texts, such as magazine and newspaper articles, e-mails, and instant messages. Each text or set of texts is followed by several questions. Select the best answer for each question and mark the letter (A), (B), (C), or (D) on your answer sheet.

Questions 147-148 refer to the following job advertisement.

Join our team at "Kristano's"

**Many vacancies are yet to be filled at our new location,
opening May 21.**

Now Hiring:

Servers, Dishwashers, Cooks, Cleaners

Morning, afternoon, and evening shifts available

Pick up an application form at our main location at 138 Naysmith Avenue.

Interviews will be held May 1 to May 17.

References from previous employers required.

---

147. What type of business is Kristano's?

(A) An appliance store
(B) A restaurant
(C) A cleaning company
(D) A food factory

148. What are job seekers asked to do?

(A) Submit a résumé by mail
(B) Choose a preferred interview date
(C) Visit the business in person
(D) Attend an event on May 21

Questions 149-150 refer to the following text-message chain.

[7:23 A.M.] Ray Simpson

Are you already in the laboratory?

[7:24 A.M.] Diana Mooney

Yes, I came in early to run some experiments on my samples.

[7:26 A.M.] Ray Simpson

Great! I'm standing outside the research facility, but my security keycard isn't working. I thought a security guard would be here already, but I was wrong. Would you mind coming down to open the door for me?

[7:28 A.M.] Diana Mooney

Sure, no problem. Which entrance are you at?

[7:31 A.M.] Ray Simpson

Oh, the one at the north parking lot. Sorry, I know it's pretty far from your lab.

[7:33 A.M.] Diana Mooney

Don't worry about it. I'll be down right away.

[7:35 A.M.] Ray Simpson

Thanks! I was worried I'd be stuck out here till 9!

---

149. What problem does Mr. Simpson mention?

(A) He is late for a meeting with Ms. Mooney.
(B) A security guard has not arrived yet.
(C) He has misplaced his door access card.
(D) An experiment is running behind schedule.

150. At 7:33 A.M., what does Ms. Mooney agree to do when she writes, "I'll be down right away"?

(A) Let Mr. Simpson into a building
(B) Visit a security office
(C) Help Mr. Simpson with his work
(D) Issue a replacement keycard

Questions 151-152 refer to the following notice.

Notice for Our Guests

Renovation work at White Cove Hotel will be ongoing from September 2 until October 5. The lobby and front desk will remain open to all guests during renovations, but the lounge area will not be open until the work concludes. Also, guests must leave their vehicles in the area behind the building because the underground lot will be off-limits.

Further improvements will be made in November. The restaurant on the second floor will be closed from November 12 to November 28. The restaurant renovation will be the final phase of our remodeling project.

---

151. What is the purpose of the notice?

(A) To attract guests to a newly-opened hotel
(B) To announce the completion of building renovations
(C) To recommend local tourist attractions
(D) To describe modifications at a business

152. What are guests asked to do?

(A) Avoid the lobby
(B) Obtain information at the front desk
(C) Use a specific parking lot
(D) Use the second-floor restaurant

GO ON TO THE NEXT PAGE

Questions 153-155 refer to the following notice.

Gravesend Manor Auction

An auction will be held on July 5, with numerous pieces of furniture and artwork from the abandoned Gravesend Manor up for sale. This historical building, situated on the outskirts of the city of Gravesend, has been vacant for several months ever since its original owner passed away. The owner of the manor, Ms. Glenda Howe, had requested that all furnishings be put up for auction at the National History Museum across the road from City Hall. Many antique collectors are expected to attend the event.

According to Ms. Howe's wishes, proceeds from the auction will go towards the renovation of Gravesend Manor, whose condition has declined over the years. With no family members, Ms. Howe left the building to the city of Gravesend with the hope that it will be converted into an orphanage. The city council has announced that it plans to honor Ms. Howe's wishes.

The city council is responsible for organizing the auction, so you should contact Graeme Bostwick at gbostwick@gravesend.co.uk if you wish to attend the event. Space is limited to 300 individuals, as the museum's exhibition hall is currently housing some fairly large exhibits.

153. Where will the auction be held?

(A) At a historical home
(B) At a museum
(C) At an antiques store
(D) At City Hall

154. According to the notice, how will some of the money from the sales be used?

(A) To restore a building
(B) To organize a community event
(C) To construct a monument
(D) To clean up a local park

155. Who most likely is Mr. Bostwick?

(A) A museum curator
(B) An art exhibitor
(C) A local historian
(D) An event organizer

Questions 156-157 refer to the following text message.

To: Kevin Hull
From: Natalie Pohler
Sent: Tue, 3:44 P.M.

Just finished the kitchen inspection at Raffles Restaurant. I won't have time to head back to headquarters. Heading straight to the Fiori Chemicals factory to evaluate the effectiveness of their new evacuation procedure. Please call ahead and ask them where would be the best spot for me to park. I know the building has several parking lots and entrances. Thanks.

156. In what industry does Ms. Pohler most likely work?

(A) Appliance repairs
(B) Health and safety
(C) Corporate catering
(D) Chemicals manufacturing

157. What does Ms. Pohler ask Mr. Hull to do?

(A) Open an entrance
(B) Send a building layout
(C) Meet in a parking lot
(D) Contact a factory

GO ON TO THE NEXT PAGE

Questions 158-159 refer to the following Web page.

http://www.portalscotland.com ▼ — ⟳ X

Portal Scotland aims to assist recent college or university graduates and other individuals looking to start or change their careers by compiling comprehensive lists of employment opportunities every month. Our experienced team searches for vacancies in an extensive variety of fields, from computing, science, and technology to retail, customer service, and manufacturing. Become a member of Portal Scotland and you can log in on a weekly basis to view both our job list and newsletter. Alternatively, you can simply add your name and address to our mailing list to receive a paper copy of each every week.

Name : _Sheila Van Buren_
Address : _497 Duntrune Terrace, Dundee, Scotland, DD5 R6T_

(Add)

158. For whom is the Web page mainly intended?

(A) Recruiters
(B) University staff
(C) Business owners
(D) Job seekers

159. What is implied about Ms. Van Buren?

(A) Her business will be listed on a Web site.
(B) She will receive newsletters by mail.
(C) Her details will be forwarded to potential employers.
(D) She has applied for a Portal Scotland membership.

Questions 160-162 refer to the following Web page.

http://www.zanzibarbistro.com/cocktailmenu/pineapplesunburst ▼   — ☐ X

Pineapple Sunburst

While the creation of some cocktails remains a mystery, the origin of the Pineapple Sunburst is well-known to all staff and patrons of Zanzibar Bistro. — [1] —. This cocktail has become increasingly popular since it was first created by the restaurant's founder, Olivia Castro, back in 2008. — [2] —. The creation of this cocktail occurred by accident when Castro picked up a bottle of pineapple juice instead of orange juice. — [3] —. Zanzibar Bistro manager Christopher Malika, who started off as Castro's trainee bar manager and later purchased the establishment from her when she retired, has never altered the recipe that was taught to him many years ago.

The ingredients are added in sequence: tequila, then ice, followed by the juice, and then the syrup. It gets its signature layered appearance as a result of adding each ingredient without stirring. — [4] —. When the steps are followed correctly, the beverage looks as good as it tastes!

160. What is indicated about the cocktail?

(A) It is always served unstirred.
(B) It has changed many times over the years.
(C) It is sold in establishments nationwide.
(D) It is Zanzibar Bistro's newest drink.

161. What is suggested about Olivia Castro?

(A) She was hired by Christopher Malika.
(B) She wrote a cocktail recipe book.
(C) She no longer runs a restaurant.
(D) She owns several dining locations.

162. In which of the positions marked [1], [2], [3], and [4] does the following sentence best belong?

"That error fortunately resulted in Zanzibar Bistro's signature cocktail."

(A) [1]
(B) [2]
(C) [3]
(D) [4]

Questions 163-165 refer to the following memo.

To: Sherman Trading Staff
From: Bruno Lesnar, CEO
Subject: News Announcement
Date: July 3

As you may already know, our new director of marketing, Rachel Munez, will soon be joining us at our headquarters. We will have a welcome luncheon at Mercedes Bistro on Monday, July 23, for Ms. Munez's first day at Sherman Trading. You are all welcome to join.

On a similar note, our current director of marketing will be moving to California once he leaves his position on the board here at Sherman Trading. Timothy Hilton will be officially stepping down on July 20. Mr. Hilton has served our company for 26 years and played a significant role in its success and prosperity. After such a distinguished career, he plans to leave the field for good and move to Orange County with his wife, a former real estate agent.

Mr. Hilton will be presented with a farewell gift by the company president, Jim Lange, at a meeting on July 20. Following the meeting, he will visit each department to say goodbye in person to all staff. Please try to be available at your workstations between 11 A.M. and 12 P.M. to bid him a fond farewell.

163. What is the memo announcing?

(A) An employment opportunity
(B) A company relocation
(C) A corporate merger
(D) A personnel change

164. According to the memo, what will happen on July 23?

(A) Mr. Lesnar will interview candidates.
(B) Ms. Munez will attend a special meal.
(C) Mr. Hilton will lead a training session.
(D) Mr. Lange will receive a gift.

165. Who is Mr. Hilton?

(A) A retiring board member
(B) A new marketing manager
(C) A real estate agent
(D) A recruitment expert

Questions 166-168 refer to the following information on a Web Page.

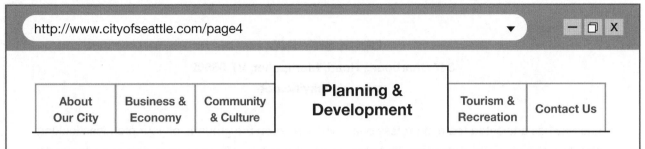

http://www.cityofseattle.com/page4

| About Our City | Business & Economy | Community & Culture | **Planning & Development** | Tourism & Recreation | Contact Us |

The City of Seattle's Planning & Development team oversees all aspects of the city's development and improvement. The team is involved in several projects, with the overall aim of improving our great city's infrastructure. This includes aspects such as urban renewal and construction, improved transportation networks, and development of vacant or dilapidated areas.

Current Work & Initiatives

- Maple Park: The gardens and walking paths in the eastern section of the park will be closed to the public from Saturday, May 13, to Saturday, May 20. This is to allow for the maintenance of existing plants and flowers, the planting of new ones, and the installation of features such as water fountains and hedges.

- As a result of budget restructuring, the resurfacing of the tennis courts in Valenwood Park, which was supposed to commence on May 23, will now begin on June 3. The tennis courts will remain open until that date.

A proposal to build a brand-new shopping mall in the downtown core has been tentatively accepted by the city council. A public forum will be held on May 10 which will give local residents an opportunity to hear more about the plan and ask questions. Directions to the forum venue can be viewed at www.cityhallseattle.gov. If you have any difficulties using our Web site, please contact our technical support team at 555-9287.

166. What is one purpose of the information?

(A) To announce employment opportunities in Seattle
(B) To provide information about a city's founding
(C) To describe some Seattle tourist attractions
(D) To provide details about some urban projects

167. Why will part of Maple Park be closed to the public for one week?

(A) It will host a special event.
(B) It will undergo landscaping.
(C) Its tennis courts will be repaired.
(D) It is experiencing budget problems.

168. According to the Web page, how can people obtain information about a construction plan?

(A) By visiting a Web site
(B) By sending an e-mail
(C) By attending a meeting
(D) By calling a phone number

GO ON TO THE NEXT PAGE

Questions 169-171 refer to the following brochure.

BLUE SKY INC.
347 Charbourg Road, Montpelier, VT 05602
www.blueskyinc.net

Blue Sky has a talented team of professionals who can keep the grounds of your premises looking attractive and neat. We understand that each of our clients has different needs, so we are happy to customize our services to ensure full satisfaction. Our general services include:

- Lawn maintenance: mowing, weeding, reseeding, etc.
- Flowerbed care: planting, watering, adding new soil
- Sweeping of all paved surfaces and steps
- Installation of decorative features (fountains, statues, etc.)
- Application of pesticides

An initial site evaluation is performed free of charge. One of our project supervisors will visit you at your location, evaluate the amount of work involved, and discuss various approaches. He or she will be able to tell you the amount of time a project will take from beginning to end. In some cases, weather may affect the project schedule, but we do our utmost to stick to it closely. Following this evaluation, you can decide whether you are happy with our plan. Evaluations can be arranged by sending an e-mail to customerservices@bluesky.net.

Blue Sky makes an effort to provide the best services at affordable rates. No other company can match the standard of service we provide at such low prices. We accomplish this even though we use the same tools and products as our rivals.

To find out more about our company's services, visit our Web site at www.blueskyinc.net.

---

169. What type of business is Blue Sky?

(A) An event planning agency
(B) A construction firm
(C) A landscaping service
(D) A painting company

170. How can potential customers receive scheduling information?

(A) By visiting the Blue Sky Web site
(B) By meeting with a Blue Sky manager
(C) By reading a Blue Sky pamphlet
(D) By calling Blue Sky customer services

171. How do Blue Sky's services differ from those of its competitors?

(A) They are a better value for the price.
(B) They require more powerful tools.
(C) They are performed more quickly.
(D) They are available seven days a week.

Questions 172-175 refer to the following e-mail.

To:	Rachel Brown, Luke Redgrave, Simon Mooney, Rita Lonegan
From:	Caroline Wickens
Date:	March 14
Subject:	Marketing campaign
Attachments:	Advertisement_design; Social_media_sites; Product_packaging_designs

Greetings everyone,

I appreciate your willingness to help with the marketing campaign for our new laptop computer, the Razor 800X, which will be launched in stores around the country on June 25.
— [1] —. As we discussed last week, we intend to advertise this new laptop aggressively. — [2] —. I'd like each of you to take responsibility for the tasks listed below, and please bear in mind that we expect you to give these tasks your maximum effort. — [3] —.

Rachel Brown: Create newspaper and magazine advertisements by April 20
                     (Using attached design)

Rita Lonegan: Conduct a survey of consumers over the next two weeks
                     (Attach the results in a group e-mail and send to all team members)

Simon Mooney: Contact social media Web sites to negotiate advertising space by May 18
                     (List of sites attached)

Luke Redgrave: Collaborate with the graphic design team on the attached product packaging designs
                     (Finished design due May 25)

— [4] —. On March 25, we will meet again to review how you are getting on. Prior to the meeting, make sure you write a report detailing your progress to that point.

Caroline Wickens
Director of Marketing
Razor Electronics

172. When are the print advertisements due?

(A) On March 25
(B) On April 20
(C) On May 18
(D) On June 25

173. Who does NOT need to open one of the attached files?

(A) Ms. Brown
(B) Ms. Lonegan
(C) Mr. Mooney
(D) Mr. Redgrave

174. What does Ms. Wickens ask the e-mail recipients to do before the next meeting?

(A) Create a schedule
(B) Prepare a report
(C) Send some designs
(D) Place advertisements

175. In which of the positions marked [1], [2], [3], and [4] does the following sentence best belong?

"We have several tasks to accomplish before then."

(A) [1]
(B) [2]
(C) [3]
(D) [4]

GO ON TO THE NEXT PAGE

E-Mail Message

From:	Ursula Gilman, Marketing Director
To:	Tristan Fleck, Chief Financial Officer
Subject:	Department Expenses
Date:	May 2
Attachment:	𝒪 Marketing Expenses (Jan.-Apr.)

Dear Mr. Fleck,

I'm writing to ask you to allocate additional budget resources for the Marketing Department. Please find attached a breakdown of marketing expenses for the period of January through April. As you will see, our expenses have steadily risen over the past few months due to an increased focus on advertising. For example, when we began advertising our current GX3 speakers on social media sites to prepare for releasing a new model in March, our expenses went up to $12,000. We have still managed to maintain our monthly budget of $45,000, but our expenses will continue rising over the next three months, as we will be hiring temporary staff during that period. Therefore, I would be grateful if you could give us a sum of $50,000 per month for the May-August period, which will ensure that we have ample funds to cover all additional expenses.

If you would like to speak about the expenses or my request for extra funds, please don't hesitate to contact me. I have meetings all day today and tomorrow, but I'll be free on Thursday and Friday.

Regards,

Ursula Gilman
Marketing Director
Browning Electronics

Marketing Department – Expenses (Jan. 1 – April 30)
Ursula Gilman

	January	February	March	April	Total
Print Media Advertising	$5,000	$8,000	$8,000	$8,000	$29,000
Social Media Advertising	$3,000	$10,000	$12,000	$12,000	$37,000
Research & Surveys	$10,000	$0	$0	$0	$10,000
Employee Salaries	$18,000	$18,000	$20,000	$22,000	$78,000
Total	$36,000	$36,000	$40,000	$42,000	$154,000

TEST 3

176. What is the purpose of the e-mail?

(A) To discuss a meeting schedule
(B) To explain an overspending problem
(C) To recommend ways to reduce expenses
(D) To request a budget increase

177. Why did Ms. Gilman concentrate on online advertising recently?

(A) To clear inventory
(B) To promote a new product
(C) To reduce marketing expenses
(D) To respond to customer demand

178. In the e-mail, the word " maintain" in paragraph 1, line 6, is closest in meaning to

(A) deliver
(B) keep
(C) repair
(D) insist

179. What is suggested about Ms. Gilman?

(A) She is requesting more personnel.
(B) She is trying to reduce office expenses.
(C) She will not be available until Thursday.
(D) She is planning a trip during the months of June through August.

180. What is one kind of expense that is likely to increase in the chart?

(A) Product development
(B) Employee training
(C) Building renovations
(D) Staff wages

GO ON TO THE NEXT PAGE

Questions 181-185 refer to the following e-mails.

To:	Simon Garner <sgarner@garnersecurity.ca>
From:	Allan McCain <amccain@quickmail.net>
Subject:	Apprenticeship
Date:	March 11

Dear Mr. Garner,

I'm very grateful that you have offered me a place in your apprenticeship program as a trainee security technician at Garner Security. It would be a great honor to work at your prestigious company. At the end of my apprenticeship period, I hope you decide that I can continue as a full-time employee.

I have a minor problem in that I am yet to finish my two-year course on electronics systems engineering at Mitchum Technical College. It is scheduled to end on Friday, April 27.
You mentioned in your apprenticeship offer that you would like me to begin work at the beginning of April, but I'm wondering if you would mind if I started on the first day of May instead. I have put a lot of effort into this course and I firmly believe that it will help me to perform better in my role at your firm.

Please consider this and let me know whether you approve.

Best regards,

Allan McCain

E-Mail Message

To:	Allan McCain <amccain@quickmail.net>
From:	Simon Garner <sgarner@garnersecurity.ca>
Date:	RE: Apprenticeship
Subject:	March 12

Hi Allan,

I appreciate your letting me know about your situation. I read an Internet article about the course you are taking, and it seems like it certainly will help you excel in my company. So, I'd be happy to move your first day as you requested. By the way, due to increasing demand for our services, we have decided to offer three year-long apprenticeships this year instead of two. All three of our new apprentices will be required to attend a one-day orientation session prior to officially starting the apprenticeship. Yours will be held on Saturday, April 21. As it is on a weekend, I assume you will be able to attend.

Please note that as our policy for new apprentices, you will undergo regular performance evaluations every three months. Therefore, your first one has been scheduled for August 1.

Please let me know if you have any further questions.

Best wishes,

Simon Garner

---

181. What is one purpose of the first e-mail?

(A) To inquire about the job duties of a position
(B) To list some academic qualifications
(C) To announce the completion of a college course
(D) To request the rescheduling of a start date

182. What is mentioned about the course on electronics systems engineering?

(A) It can be studied online.
(B) It is a requirement for all apprentices.
(C) It is discounted for Garner Security employees.
(D) It is beneficial to security technicians.

183. For how long will Mr. McCain's apprenticeship last?

(A) Three months
(B) One year
(C) Two years
(D) Three years

184. When will Mr. McCain officially begin his apprenticeship at Garner Security?

(A) On April 1
(B) On April 21
(C) On April 27
(D) On May 1

185. According to the second e-mail, what will Mr. McCain most likely do on August 1?

(A) Join a training session
(B) Take a written test
(C) Meet with other apprentices
(D) Attend a performance review

GO ON TO THE NEXT PAGE

Heaven Scent Under New Ownership

BIRMINGHAM (7 January) – After months of negotiation, UK-based Harmon Home Furnishings has finally purchased New Zealand candle manufacturer Heaven Scent and announced a few changes that will be implemented over the coming months. The first thing Harmon intends to do is alter the candles' labels so that they more closely resemble other Harmon labels.

Heaven Scent is the top-selling brand of candles in New Zealand and Australia, with almost 25,000 candles sold per month. The company is known for its "Sensational Scents to Spice Up Your Life!" slogan and its large, 15-centimeter tall, pyramid-shaped candles that burn and give off fragrance for an impressive 80 to 100 hours. However, Harmon has indicated that it may also make changes to the actual products in order to appeal to British consumers.

"Although we are big fans of the current Heaven Scent products, we might make our own changes in the UK," said Harmon's CEO, Clinton Maxwell. "We have discussed changing the appearance of the products, and maybe even the slogan and product name itself."

Harmon plans to begin selling Heaven Scent candles in stores throughout the UK at the beginning of February.

Heaven Scent
Fragranced Candles
"Sensational scents to spice up your life!"

Our Best-selling Fragrance
Coconut Hibiscus
- Distinctive square candles
- 80 to 100 hours of fragrance
- 15 centimeters tall

Check out our other fragrances:
French Vanilla
Apple Blossom

Coming Soon:
Tropical Breeze
Special 10th Anniversary Fragranced Candle

Produced by Heaven Scent Inc.
A Harmon Home Furnishings Company
Birmingham, UK

http://www.heavenscentcandles.co.uk/review02898   ▼   — ▢ X

Last month, I moved to the UK from New Zealand in order to start a new career, and I was delighted to see Heaven Scent candles in the local home furnishings stores! I bought one of each of the best-selling fragrances and found them all to be wonderful, especially the Coconut Hibiscus. The next one I want to get is the upcoming anniversary one!

The only problem is the lack of variety in the UK compared to back home in New Zealand. Although I've seen some of the original fragrances, like Summer Meadow, there are countless others that the stores don't carry. For example, where is Cinnamon Surprise? That one has been my favorite ever since I was a university student. Heaven Scent candles may not be the cheapest brand, but they're still the best. I don't mind spending a little extra for good quality!

Lola Abruzzi
5 March

---

186. What is the purpose of the article?

(A) To promote a new manufacturer of candles
(B) To announce the closure of a candle factory
(C) To provide details of a business deal
(D) To describe the rise in popularity of candles

187. What change to Heaven Scent candles is reflected in the product label?

(A) The candle height
(B) The candle shape
(C) The fragrance duration
(D) The product slogan

188. What is suggested about Ms. Abruzzi?

(A) She recently started a new job.
(B) She works in a home furnishings store.
(C) She prefers candles over electrical lighting.
(D) She has received free samples from Heaven Scent.

189. According to the review, why is Ms. Abruzzi disappointed?

(A) She thinks the quality of Heaven Scent products has declined.
(B) She cannot locate her preferred Heaven Scent candle fragrance.
(C) She is unable to order Heaven Scent candles from New Zealand.
(D) She has moved to a country that does not import Heaven Scent candles.

190. What fragrance is Ms. Abruzzi looking forward to trying?

(A) Cinnamon Surprise
(B) Coconut Hibiscus
(C) Tropical Breeze
(D) Summer Meadow

GO ON TO THE NEXT PAGE

Questions 191-195 refer to the following e-mails and invoice.

E-Mail Message

From:	lhaines@fyrefly.com
To:	ahayat@winfieldhotel.com
Date:	April 16
Subject:	Reservation #458278
Attachment :	Booking_confirmation.docx

Dear Ms. Hayat,

The booking confirmation for our hotel reservation (#458278) arrived today and it includes a room with multiple queen beds, which we did not reserve. We only need three rooms while we are in Denver for the upcoming conference. I checked my company credit card balance, and it appears that we have been charged for four rooms. I assume you will cancel this part of our reservation, which one of your colleagues must have made in error. However, I'd like to know what must be done in order to remove the wrong charge from the credit card.

Regards,

Lincoln Haines
Fyrefly Corporation

Booking Confirmation

From: Winfield Hotel
     208 Sawyer Street
     Denver, CO
     80217

To: Fyrefly Corporation
     1117 Watts Avenue
     Boulder, CO
     80309

Hotel Manager: Afshan Hayat

Booking Made By: Lincoln Haines

Reservation number: #458278

Booking date: April 15

Room	Room details	Rate per night	No.of Nights	Total Cost
Room 212	Standard Room, 1 Queen Bed	$210	2	$420
Room 301	Superior Room, 1 King Bed	$240	2	$480
Room 425	Deluxe Room, 2 King Beds	$260	3	$780
Room 508	Twin Room, 2 Queen Beds	$230	3	$690

Balance due $2,370

We look forward to making your stay pleasurable!

From:	ahayat@winfieldhotel.com
To:	lhaines@fyrefly.com
Date:	April 16
Subject:	RE: Reservation #458278

Please note: This is an automated response. Please do not reply to this e-mail.

I am sorry that I am not able to respond to your e-mail personally at this time. I am undergoing minor surgery and will be off work from April 15 to April 17. If your inquiry requires immediate attention, please contact one of my colleagues listed below by calling 555-3354 followed by the appropriate extension.

For inquiries about room availability: Call Dave Shatner at Extension 103
For inquiries about holding an event at our hotel: Call Elizabeth Milne at Extension 105
For inquiries about reservations: Call Shaheena Singh at Extension 108
For inquiries about payment issues: Call Miles McDonald at Extension 110

Best regards,

Afshan Hayat,
Hotel Manager
Winfield Hotel

191. What information does Mr. Haines request?

(A) How to extend a booking
(B) How to obtain a refund
(C) How to cancel a reservation
(D) How to make a payment

192. In the first e-mail, the word "assume" in paragraph 1, line 4, is closest in meaning to

(A) collect
(B) suppose
(C) handle
(D) accept

193. Which room was reserved by mistake?

(A) Room 212
(B) Room 301
(C) Room 425
(D) Room 508

194. Why is Ms. Hayat unable to help Mr. Haines?

(A) She is currently overseas on vacation.
(B) She is not authorized to deal with his inquiry.
(C) She is receiving medical treatment.
(D) She is participating in a training program.

195. Which extension number should Mr. Haines call?

(A) Extension 103
(B) Extension 105
(C) Extension 108
(D) Extension 110

GO ON TO THE NEXT PAGE

Questions 196-200 refer to the following advertisement, e-mail, and online review.

Marylebone Theater

509 Devonshire Street, London

Phone: (020) 555-9389

Regular Box Office Hours: Tuesday Through Sunday, 10:30 A.M. to 8:30 P.M.

CHECK OUT OUR ANNUAL SPRING FILM SERIES.

Each day will feature four films by a well-known special guest director, each of whom will give an introductory talk and take questions from the audience at the end of the film showings.

Saturday, March 23: The Films of Susan Dempsey
Saturday, March 30: The Films of Oleg Kasparov
Saturday, April 6: The Films of Giorgio Zanetti
Saturday, April 13: The Films of Gregory Ridley

Tickets may only be purchased on the day of each film series and will be sold on a first come, first served basis. Please note that the box office will open at 8:30 A.M. on Saturdays in order to accommodate the expected high demand for tickets.

Visit www.marylebonetheater.co.uk/springseries for a full schedule of film showings.

To:	All Movie Max Magazine Staff
From:	Lorraine Kessler
Subject:	Schedule
Date:	29 March

To all employees,

As previously discussed, I will be going to the Marylebone Theater tomorrow to interview the special guest for our magazine. I'd like some of you to come along and issue brief questionnaires to people exiting the theater at the end of the day. I will arrange transportation through Smithson Van Rental so that we can all get there together nice and early and enjoy all of the movies. Please notify me by 3 P.M. today if you're interested in helping out.

Thanks,

Lorraine Kessler
Senior Editor

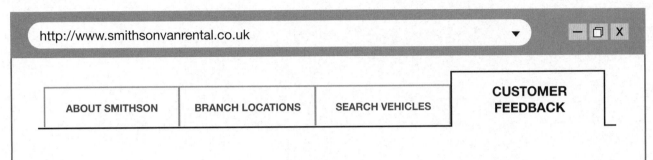

May 2

I had heard good things about renting through Smithson, and I wasn't disappointed. The vehicle was very modern, and spotless inside and out. Also, I thought it was relatively cheap compared to the quotes I received from other businesses. Lastly, the van I rented had an incredible stereo. At the end of March this year, I took 10 people to an event in London, and they were all very impressed with the sound from the speakers. I certainly wouldn't think twice about renting another Smithson van in the future.

Lorraine Kessler

196. According to the advertisement, what will happen on Saturdays?

(A) A movie audition will be held.
(B) An awards ceremony will take place.
(C) Actors will address an audience.
(D) Tickets will go on sale early.

197. What does Ms. Kessler ask employees to do?

(A) Interview film directors
(B) Work in a box office
(C) Survey event attendees
(D) Write a film review

198. Who did Ms. Kessler interview at Marylebone Theater?

(A) Susan Dempsey
(B) Oleg Kasparov
(C) Giorgio Zanetti
(D) Gregory Ridley

199. How many employees responded to Ms. Kessler's request?

(A) 5
(B) 10
(C) 15
(D) 20

200. What is NOT mentioned in the online review?

(A) The cleanliness of the vehicle
(B) The quality of the audio system
(C) The spaciousness of the vehicle
(D) The competitiveness of the price

Stop! This is the end of the test. If you finish before time is called, you may go back to Parts 5, 6, and 7 and check your work.

정답 p.469 / 점수 환산표 p.476

실전모의고사
TEST 4

TEST 4 해설

바로 보기

시작 시간 _____시 _____분

종료 시간 _____시 _____분

READING TEST

In the Reading test, you will read a variety of texts and answer several different types of reading comprehension questions. The entire Reading test will last 75 minutes. There are three parts, and directions are given for each part. You are encouraged to answer as many questions as possible within the time allowed. You must mark your answers on the separate answer sheet. Do not write your answers in your test book.

PART 5

Directions: A word or phrase is missing in each of the sentences below. Four answer choices are given below each sentence. Select the best answer to complete the sentence. Then mark the letter (A), (B), (C), or (D) on your answer sheet.

101. Greta Troy, an entry level worker at Cinema Showtime, has the ------- necessary to succeed in a management role.

(A) qualities
(B) duties
(C) varieties
(D) formalities

102. ------- the software development team put in extra hours for several weeks, they were able to meet the tight deadline.

(A) Because
(B) Although
(C) Despite
(D) Until

103. Beginning next month, the only ------- forms of payment will be cash and credit in our North York branch.

(A) acceptable
(B) accept
(C) accepts
(D) accepting

104. The company headquarters is ------- located in the middle of London's Richmond district, within walking distance of several major subway stations.

(A) exclusively
(B) conveniently
(C) awkwardly
(D) normally

105. The company president is extremely ------- to introduce new programs that she believes will boost sales.

(A) beneficial
(B) eager
(C) steady
(D) regular

106. Mr. Jones advised his client that he ------- the contract in order to keep it in a safe place for future reference.

(A) printed
(B) prints
(C) printing
(D) print

107. If many customers express dissatisfaction with a product, a company should ------- give refunds and reconsider the product design.

(A) either
(B) neither
(C) both
(D) between

108. The person who interviewed Mr. Kelli for the clerk position was very friendly and thoroughly answered ------- question he asked.

(A) many
(B) all
(C) some
(D) every

109. ------- the low number of attendees, the conference was deemed a success by the organizing team.

(A) Although
(B) Despite
(C) Regardless
(D) Nevertheless

110. The company will be closely examining its workflow system and making any needed changes once the third quarter reports are -------.

(A) finish
(B) finished
(C) finishing
(D) to finish

111. Repeat business typically ------- for more than half of Bluestone Education Inc.'s total revenue in an average year.

(A) highlights
(B) represents
(C) accounts
(D) introduces

112. The costs associated with training a staff member to use new technology are roughly ------- to finding and hiring a new worker.

(A) equal
(B) equalled
(C) equaling
(D) equality

113. We are ------- updating our Web site, so please call us at the office instead of filling out our online contact form.

(A) currently
(B) recently
(C) eventually
(D) plainly

114. Please take note that in order to prevent losses, all equipment borrowed from the audio-visual room must be returned ------- 4:30 P.M.

(A) until
(B) by
(C) in
(D) to

115. According to Mr. Kato, his package ------- a full five days after the promised delivery date of September 24.

(A) arrive
(B) arriving
(C) arrived
(D) arrival

116. Thanks to a large contract secured with the NCH Group last month, our firm was able to meet its third-quarter sales -------.

(A) purposes
(B) goals
(C) sources
(D) conceptions

117. Considering the present situation, ------- the future holds for our company and its shareholders remains to be seen.

(A) that
(B) which
(C) what
(D) so

118. The company president finally agreed to discuss merging with Allman Financial after ------- the idea for several years.

(A) dismiss
(B) dismissal
(C) dismissing
(D) dismissed

119. ------- all workers at CY Corporation say they are satisfied with the layout of the office and the availability of resources.

(A) Partly
(B) Somewhat
(C) Fully
(D) Almost

GO ON TO THE NEXT PAGE

120. A dramatic change in the company's rates
------- caused a flood of calls to account
managers from surprised clients looking for
an explanation.

(A) predictable
(B) predictably
(C) prediction
(D) predict

121. Between the two computer monitors we are
considering, the ------- one is more suitable
for our company's needs.

(A) wider
(B) widest
(C) widely
(D) widening

122. The ideal candidate is someone with an
excellent academic record, relevant work
experience, and steady ------- to their job
duties.

(A) dedicate
(B) dedicating
(C) dedicated
(D) dedication

123. In order to proceed to the next stage of the
selection process, applicants must -------
several education-related requirements.

(A) do
(B) meet
(C) employ
(D) desire

124. ------- chief financial officer, Ms. Berno must
keep track of all money spent and received in
the company.

(A) As
(B) At
(C) Throughout
(D) Except

125. The young female customer returned the
merchandise shortly after the purchase,
saying it was -------.

(A) defect
(B) defected
(C) defective
(D) defecting

126. Please be informed that no new employees
are to be hired ------- prior permission has
been granted by the head office.

(A) furthermore
(B) without
(C) excluding
(D) unless

127. While the value of the dollar has been rising
-------, economists predict a sharp decline in
the currency's value at the beginning of next
month.

(A) steady
(B) steadied
(C) steadies
(D) steadily

128. ------- measures to limit annual expenditure,
a plan is being considered to reduce the
workforce by 15 percent next year.

(A) Therefore
(B) In addition to
(C) Since
(D) Such as

129. We thank you in advance for your ------- in
rearranging your itinerary for your upcoming
business trip to Shanghai.

(A) cooperation
(B) adaptation
(C) organization
(D) information

130. The client asked the customer service
representative ------- her account information
and correct a mistake that had appeared on
her last bill.

(A) to modify
(B) modifying
(C) modification
(D) modify

PART 6

Directions: Read the texts that follow. A word, phrase, or sentence is missing in parts of each text. Four answer choices for each question are given below the text. Select the best answer to complete the text. Then mark the letter (A), (B), (C) or (D) on your answer sheet.

Questions 131-134 refer to the following article.

While many people travel to work every day in cars, health experts say this may not actually be the best choice for transportation.

Numerous studies have shown that people who get regular exercise, compared with those who do not, are ------- overall. One great way to get exercise each day is to walk or ride a bike to work.
131.

------- using public transportation can be preferable to driving, as many bus and subway riders
132.
have to walk for at least part of their journey to work.

------- to work can also be a great way to save money, and can be more relaxing. While drivers
133.
sit in traffic jams, passengers on buses and trains can read a newspaper, play a video game or

otherwise rest. ------- .
134.

131. (A) health
(B) healthful
(C) healthier
(D) healthily

132. (A) Even
(B) Although
(C) Because
(D) For

133. (A) Not that driving
(B) Not drives
(C) Not drive
(D) Not driving

134. (A) Therefore, using a car can be useful on certain occasions.
(B) This is why it is important to consider your posture while commuting to work.
(C) In short, choosing not to drive can be great for your body and your mind.
(D) Bus passes go on sale next week and can be purchased online.

GO ON TO THE NEXT PAGE

To: IT Department Employees

From: Penny Rahey, Lead Recruiter

Date: June 7

RE: Upcoming Opportunities

As many of you are well aware, our company has seen tremendous growth over the past number of years. ------- . In the coming weeks, we will be ------- several management positions. These are:
135. **136.**
senior database manager, senior security manager, and senior networking manager.

Because our policy is to hire ------- , those who are currently employed with our company will
137.
be considered first. We will only advertise to the public if there are no applications from qualified candidates.

If you are interested in one or more of these opportunities, please submit your application directly to me. ------- a résumé, I'd like a two-page essay describing your work with us and how you feel it
138.
would allow you to succeed in a management role. The deadline for applications is next Friday at 4 P.M. I look forward to reviewing all of them.

Sincerely,

Penny Rahey

Lead Recruiter

135. (A) Thank you for doing business with us throughout the years.
(B) Because of this, we will be temporarily halting production.
(C) I have received your request and will take it under consideration.
(D) As a result, we are continuously adding more IT personnel to our staff.

136. (A) fill
(B) filled
(C) filling
(D) fills

137. (A) internally
(B) exceptionally
(C) annually
(D) intently

138. (A) Furthermore
(B) Also
(C) In addition
(D) Instead of

Questions 139-142 refer to the following e-mail.

From:	tstubbert@abcweb.com
To:	manager@sunshineforless.com
Subject:	Advertisement in Last Saturday's Paper
Date:	February 1

To Whom It May Concern:

My friends and I travel every winter. We have always used your travel service because of the huge ------- of packages you offer and your great prices. I'm sorry to say, however, that this year we may
  139.
end up booking through someone else.

We are very upset about the advertisement that appeared in the travel section of our local paper this past Saturday. You advertised an all-inclusive package to Negril, Jamaica, for $687 a person. We were so excited that we called your office to purchase our tickets that day!

At that time, we found out about the many conditions and ------- fees. The final cost is actually closer
  140.
to $962 a person. Travelers must leave on Tuesday to get this deal, and it's only valid until February 10. I feel that these things should ------- initially. -------.
  141.   142.

I think the right thing to do would be to give us the package at the advertised price.

Sincerely,

Tracey Stubbert

---

139. (A) dimension
(B) selection
(C) adaptability
(D) possibility

140. (A) introductory
(B) overdue
(C) reasonable
(D) hidden

141. (A) have been mentioning
(B) have mentioned
(C) have been mentioned
(D) be mentioning

142. (A) In the future, you may want to be more direct in your promotional material.
(B) We do appreciate the offer of a discount on our next trip.
(C) Traveling in February is not preferred because of the cold weather.
(D) I would like to be refunded for the entire amount of the travel package.

GO ON TO THE NEXT PAGE

Questions 143-146 refer to the following advertisement.

With cold and flu season just around the corner, now is the time to get your bottle of concentrated vitamin C drops. We all know that vitamin C can provide a ------- to the immune system, but did
143.
you know it can be hard to get enough just by consuming citrus fruits and juices?

Our drops have a pleasantly mild orange flavour, and they can easily be added to water, juice, or even your favorite hot beverage!

What's the best part? A single drop ------- the same amount of vitamin C as an entire orange or
144.
a half a cup of juice. Just five drops will give your body all the vitamin C it needs for the day.

Don't spend the entire day peeling oranges or drinking juice in an effort to lessen your ------- of
145.
getting sick!

Purchase your bottle of Vitamin Pro Drops today. You can literally take them anywhere, and we guarantee you'll love the taste. ------- . No questions asked!
146.

---

143. (A) step
(B) boost
(C) plunge
(D) blow

144. (A) contain
(B) contains
(C) contained
(D) containing

145. (A) chances
(B) burdens
(C) effects
(D) thoughts

146. (A) If not, we'll give you a full refund.
(B) Please note that this product is not suitable for children.
(C) Feel free to ask a customer representative about our product.
(D) So pick up a bottle of Vitamin Pro Drops now.

PART 7

Directions: In this part you will read a selection of texts, such as magazine and newspaper articles, e-mails, and instant messages. Each text or set of texts is followed by several questions. Select the best answer for each question and mark the letter (A), (B), (C), or (D) on your answer sheet.

Questions 147–148 refer to the following information.

Thank you for choosing Walter Homes. Our remodeling team is ready to make the kitchen or bathroom in your home match the one in your dreams. However, before we begin, we will need you to prepare for our arrival. First of all, while renovations are in progress, you will not be able to stay in your home. This is for your safety. So please make sure that you have packed enough belongings for about a week. In addition, any pets should be removed from the house, and as a courtesy to your neighbors, please warn them that it might be a bit noisy over the next several days. Finally, please leave a spare key with the site manager to ensure ease of access for the workers. Once again, thank you for choosing Walter Homes. You can be sure that the home of your dreams will soon be a reality.

147. What kind of company is Walter Homes?

(A) A cleaning company
(B) A moving company
(C) A real estate company
(D) A construction company

148. What is the client NOT advised to do?

(A) Find a temporary accommodation
(B) Turn off electronic products
(C) Remove pets from the house
(D) Notify their neighbors

Questions 149-150 refer to the following text-message chain.

Janet [7:43 P.M.]
Are you both going to attend the annual holiday dinner?

Pedro [7:58 P.M.]
Yes, I will be there with my wife. How about you, Olivia?

Olivia [8:07 P.M.]
We will be there, too.

Janet [8:12 P.M.]
Great!

Olivia [8:15 P.M.]
Thank you for organizing it, Janet. It was a wonderful event last year. The meal was incredible and I loved the classical music that played throughout the evening.

Janet [8:18 P.M.]
Everyone was talking about the French onion soup and chicken dish for months. This year, the party will be Latin-themed.

Pedro [8:21 P.M.]
Are most of our colleagues going, too?

Janet [8:25 P.M.]
It looks that way. I still need to touch base with a few more people, but I expect it will be a full house like last year.

149. What is indicated about Janet?

(A) She comes from a Latin American country.
(B) She will play classical music at the dinner.
(C) She arranged last year's event.
(D) She recently started working for the company.

150. At 8:25 P.M., what does Janet mean when she says, "It looks that way"?

(A) She hasn't received many RSVPs to the party.
(B) Many colleagues will probably attend the dinner.
(C) Some decorations will be hung in the restaurant.
(D) The event will start later than planned.

Questions 151–152 refer to the following advertisement.

Have you considered a new career in the world of computer programming? Almost every business in the world today relies on software. So why not become a part of this incredible industry? Our fifteen-week computer programming course will give you the fundamental skills to get started in software development. You will work hands-on with professors who will get you ready to start work immediately. This course is specifically designed for eager students who are serious about their future. At the end of the course, each student will complete an internship so that they can hone their skills in a real-world environment. Students from any department can choose to take the course. There are no special requirements. However, students majoring in computer science will be given preference. Classes are filling up fast. Registration ends March 19. Visit Room 208 for more details.

151. Where would this advertisement most likely be found?

(A) At a software company
(B) At a computer store
(C) At a college campus
(D) At a bus station

152. How can interested individuals get additional information?

(A) By sending an e-mail
(B) By visiting a Web page
(C) By going to a specific room
(D) By attending a career fair

GO ON TO THE NEXT PAGE

Questions 153-154 refer to the following e-mail.

E-Mail Message

From: Sanjay Patel <spatel@staffordshire.com>
To: Joe Walsh <jwalsh@bestmail.com>
Subject: Your Complaint
Date: July 21

Dear Mr. Walsh,

I am writing in response to your e-mail about your experience at the Waldorf Hotel. We have reviewed your e-mail and forwarded a copy to the CEO. We always appreciate customer feedback.

At the Waldorf Hotel, we aspire to treat all of our customers with respect, which is why we were very disappointed to hear about your experience on Saturday, July 17.

As a token of our sincere apologies, we have chosen to refund the cost of your stay. It has been credited to your bank account. In addition, we would like to demonstrate to you that we have made improvements based on your experiences. Enclosed is a certificate for two free nights in any of our hotels worldwide.

Feedback from our customers is important, and we take it very seriously. I personally guarantee that if you stay with us in the future, you will not be disappointed.

Sincerely Yours,

Sanjay Patel
Vice President
Staffordshire Enterprises

---

153. Who most likely is Mr. Walsh?

(A) An employee of Waldorf Hotel
(B) An executive of a company
(C) A customer of Waldorf Hotel
(D) A personnel director

154. What is NOT something Mr. Patel has done for Mr. Walsh?

(A) Booked him a hotel room
(B) Given him an apology
(C) Offered him a free hotel room
(D) Refunded his money

Questions 155-157 refer to the following letter.

Living Interiors Magazine Ltd.
Private Bag 4590
Los Angeles, California

Dear Dr. Fraser,

This is to inform you that your subscription to Living Interiors will expire next month. We will remind you of this by e-mail and call you when we send your final issue in early December.

If you send in the renewal form below by the end of November, your subscription will continue without any delays and you will be able to enjoy our bumper Christmas edition filled with even more fabulous home living ideas than usual.

We offer discounts for subscriptions of one year or more and you'll receive a free Christmas basket when you renew your subscription.

Jennifer Golding

Jennifer Golding
Publisher

---

1 year (12 issues)	2 years (24 issues)	3 years (36 issues)
$67.00	$105.00	$140.00
SAVE $5.00	SAVE $39.00	SAVE $76.00

NAME _____

ADDRESS _____

ACCOUNT NUMBER _____   Living Interiors

* Please call us if you are unsure of your account number

155. Why should Dr. Fraser contact the magazine?

(A) To receive a complimentary gift
(B) To confirm a discount
(C) To complain about his Christmas gift
(D) To avoid an interruption in service

156. What will Living Interiors do for its Christmas issue?

(A) Renew all subscriptions
(B) Send holiday e-cards to subscribers
(C) Include additional contents
(D) Offer discounts to subscribers

157. How can customers save money on a Living Interiors subscription?

(A) By writing a letter to the editor
(B) By subscribing for a year or more
(C) By calling the office
(D) By referring a friend

GO ON TO THE NEXT PAGE

Questions 158-161 refer to the following online chat discussion.

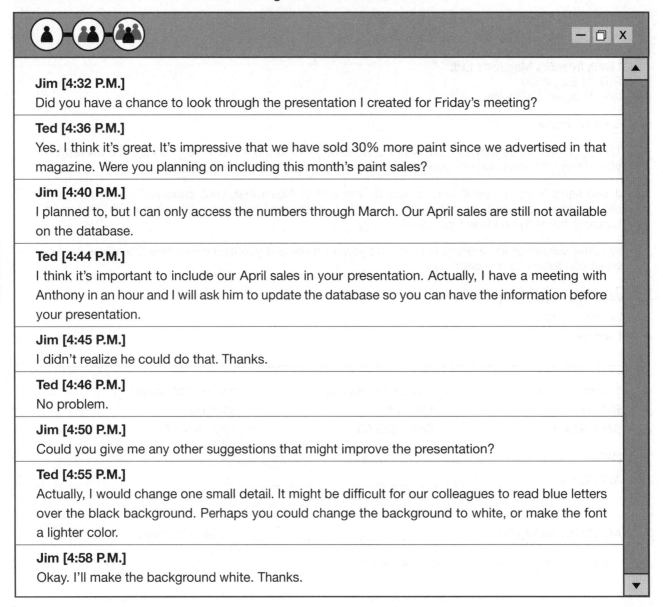

Jim [4:32 P.M.]
Did you have a chance to look through the presentation I created for Friday's meeting?

Ted [4:36 P.M.]
Yes. I think it's great. It's impressive that we have sold 30% more paint since we advertised in that magazine. Were you planning on including this month's paint sales?

Jim [4:40 P.M.]
I planned to, but I can only access the numbers through March. Our April sales are still not available on the database.

Ted [4:44 P.M.]
I think it's important to include our April sales in your presentation. Actually, I have a meeting with Anthony in an hour and I will ask him to update the database so you can have the information before your presentation.

Jim [4:45 P.M.]
I didn't realize he could do that. Thanks.

Ted [4:46 P.M.]
No problem.

Jim [4:50 P.M.]
Could you give me any other suggestions that might improve the presentation?

Ted [4:55 P.M.]
Actually, I would change one small detail. It might be difficult for our colleagues to read blue letters over the black background. Perhaps you could change the background to white, or make the font a lighter color.

Jim [4:58 P.M.]
Okay. I'll make the background white. Thanks.

158. What does Ted and Jim's company sell?

(A) Magazines
(B) Paints
(C) Commercials
(D) Calendars

159. What will Anthony most likely be asked to do?

(A) E-mail Jim the information
(B) Edit Jim's presentation
(C) Discuss the database
(D) Update the sales information

160. At 4:45 P.M., what does Jim mean when he writes, "I didn't realize he could do that"?

(A) He misunderstood Anthony's role.
(B) He forgot Ted had a meeting.
(C) He thought Anthony couldn't log in.
(D) He hadn't heard of the database.

161. What does Ted say about the presentation's design?

(A) The font is too small.
(B) It is impressively designed.
(C) It includes all the facts and figures.
(D) The color selection is problematic.

Questions 162-164 refer to the following memorandum.

To: All staff
Re: New building entry cards

We have decided to enhance our security by restricting building access to employees carrying official identification only. — [1] —. This policy change is due to the recent thefts of company property. Please note that it will also prevent staff from entering the office after hours and members of the public from entering the lobby during the day.

All employees will be issued with a new ID card that will list their exact position within the company. — [2] —. Members of the public will be required to obtain a visitor's card. To get this card, they will need to report to the front desk, where they will fill in a form and provide two forms of identification to the security guard. — [3] —. Friends and family of staff who are not here for business matters will be asked to wait in the foyer and will not be able to proceed to the upstairs offices.

With the new card, you will still be able to gain access to all common staff areas such as the staff lunch room, fitness center, library and meeting rooms.

We are also introducing a fingerprint identification system, so staff will be required to press their fingers onto a keypad before they can gain access to restricted areas. — [4] —.

Please contact Sally Webster at the front desk to make an appointment to get your photo taken for your new card. Cards will be issued to all employees on April 1, so please ensure that you have your photograph taken and forms filled in by March 10 to allow time for processing. You should make a booking during the following times:

Monday to Wednesday: 11:00 A.M. - 4:00 P.M.
Friday: 12:00 P.M. - 4:00 P.M.

Old identification cards should be handed in when you apply for your new card as these will be destroyed.

162. Why are employees receiving new identification cards?

(A) The old cards are out of date.
(B) The new cards have more details on them.
(C) The company has recently changed its name.
(D) Some company items were stolen.

163. What is the company introducing to upgrade security in addition to the new ID?

(A) A fingerprint identification system
(B) A new staff security training program
(C) More guards at the reception area
(D) Security cameras in common areas

164. In which of the positions marked [1], [2], [3], and [4] does the following sentence best belong?

"Only authorized employees will be able to enter these areas."

(A) [1]
(B) [2]
(C) [3]
(D) [4]

GO ON TO THE NEXT PAGE

Researcher Required

E-Training Plus has a vacancy for a researcher who will assist our sales and marketing manager with producing online advertising strategies. The role will involve researching the latest trends in the online education market and writing reports with detailed figures and graphics.

The successful applicant will have a university degree and two to three years' experience in a similar role. Excellent written communication skills are required, and the candidate must be able to multi-task and work well under pressure. As some presentations may be needed, familiarity with such software would be a plus.

The position is full time at 40 hours a week, with possible overtime. Evening hours will be required on Mondays and Fridays, though the candidate may request to work fewer hours on other workdays to compensate for that time, given the manager's permission. The salary for the position will reflect the candidate's skills and experience.

If you are interested in the position, please send your résumé, samples of your written work and two references to HR manager David Williams at david.w@trainingplus.com and CEO Frank Fisher at frank.f@trainingplus.com. Please do not contact the company by phone, and we would prefer applications not to be sent by mail.

165. Who would the position most likely suit?

(A) A market analyst
(B) A political journalist
(C) A science teacher
(D) An investment counsellor

166. What is NOT required for the position?

(A) Reference letters
(B) A few years of experience
(C) Good writing skills
(D) An outgoing personality

167. What is able to be negotiated?

(A) Working hours
(B) The salary
(C) The position title
(D) Lunch breaks

Memorandum

To: All Staff
From: Jasmine Liao
Date: August 27

Dear staff,

As we approach the end of the year, please remember that all holidays must be taken before the end of December. Unfortunately, we cannot allow staff to carry over holiday time to the next year, so if you do not use up all your holidays, you will lose them.

A reminder also that time off must be received by senior management, in writing, one month in advance. Requests should be made on the proper form, a copy of which has been attached to this memorandum. In special circumstances, a last-minute holiday may be granted. Speak to me in person for such requests.

And finally, remember that holidays are scheduled on a first-come, first-served basis. A lot of you have several days, even weeks, of holiday time remaining. Make sure you get your holiday request in to your manager well in advance to avoid disappointment.

Here's to a great last four months this year. Keep up the good work, and don't forget to reward yourselves with some well-deserved time off!

Jasmine

168. What is the main purpose of the memorandum?

(A) To express gratitude to staff for their hard work
(B) To announce public holidays for the coming year
(C) To explain how to transfer holiday time to next year
(D) To remind staff to request vacation time

169. What is NOT listed as a holiday policy?

(A) Holidays must be used up before the end of the year.
(B) Holiday time is granted first to employees with seniority.
(C) Holiday time must be approved by management.
(D) Holiday requests must be made one month in advance.

170. Why might a staff member speak with Jasmine in person?

(A) To extend a vacation
(B) To request a holiday at short notice
(C) To get approval for a holiday
(D) To receive the vacation form

171. What is implied in the memorandum?

(A) Many employees have holiday time left over.
(B) Employees are not filling out the proper form.
(C) Managers have updated the vacation request form.
(D) New employees are eligible for holidays in the new year.

GO ON TO THE NEXT PAGE

10th Anniversary Concert Production of Cleopatra

After a continuous run of 10 years, Cleopatra is now the world's highest-grossing musical theater production of all time. Translated into over 30 languages worldwide, the musical has enchanted audiences from America and Argentina to Ireland and Indonesia.

Now, producer Sarah Gambi is using the production's 10th anniversary to put together a "dream cast," hand-chosen from leading cast members from the last decade. — [1] —. This star-studded iteration of Cleopatra will celebrate the incredible success of the musical by immortalizing it in a once-in-a-lifetime production that brings together some of theater's most talented actors. "This production will live on in the hearts and minds of the audience and everyone involved," she said. "A cast like this will never be duplicated."

The work, the second piece from the partnership of writer Rosemary Kozak and composer Al Johnson, will be staged as a concert-version, with no set pieces or props, but will be sung in full costume at microphones set up across the front of the stage. A chorus of over 300 singers, who will represent performances from all around the world, will support the lead characters.

The $25 million USD production will be a limited engagement. — [2] —. It will be performed over two nights, April 24 and 25, at the Royal Palace Hall in London, England, where the musical originally opened to rave reviews.

The show promises to be a sensation. — [3] —. However, a quick search on the Internet shows that many are for sale online — if you are willing to drop a thousand dollars on one ticket! If you do not have an extra thousand dollars lying around, the show will be broadcast on cable television in May. The airdate was not available at the time of printing.

Cleopatra has already broken several records in the musical theater world. — [4] —. No doubt this concert production will go down in history as one of the most spectacular live performances of all time.

172. What is unique about the 10th anniversary performance?

(A) It will be available on the Internet.
(B) It will be translated into 30 languages.
(C) It will feature new music by Al Johnson.
(D) It will be performed in a concert style.

173. What is Sarah Gambi doing to make her production rememberable?

(A) She is having all the characters wear the same costume.
(B) She is uniting some of the world's greatest actors.
(C) She is launching a series of aggressive promotional events.
(D) She is hiring a team of professional chorus singers.

174. What is implied about the latest Cleopatra?

(A) It will be performed the same place where it opened.
(B) It is expected to break a musical record for the first time.
(C) It will be broadcast live by a local television network.
(D) It is the only work written by Kozak and Johnson.

175. In which of the positions marked [1], [2], [3], and [4] does the following sentence best belong?

"Tickets sold out within 10 minutes of being open for sales!"

(A) [1]
(B) [2]
(C) [3]
(D) [4]

GO ON TO THE NEXT PAGE

Questions 176-180 refer to the following e-mail and memorandum.

To:	Terry Fitzgerald <tfitzgerald@zcorpinc.com>
From:	Tanya Halliday <thalliday@zcorpinc.com>
Subject:	Audio Visual Room Use
Date:	March 7

Hi Terry,

I don't want to get any fellow staff members in trouble, but I thought you should know that some workers are leaving the audio-visual room in an unacceptable condition.

This past Wednesday I made a presentation to the New York firm. When I entered the room to set up my slide show, I found papers on the floor, several half-empty cups of coffee on the tables, and even some food crumbs on the chairs. Thankfully I had time to clean up before the clients came in. It would have been quite embarrassing to have them observe the space in such a poor state.

I know that the rules regarding the use and upkeep of corporate property are quite clear. However, it seems that some team members are not following them. Maybe it might be worth mentioning them again in your next memorandum.

Thank you.

Tanya

MEMO

TO: All Staff
FROM: Terry Fitzgerald
SUBJECT: Policies for Employees
DATE: March 9

Dear Staff:

First, I really appreciate the complaints I've recently received about careless work practices. Upon reviewing them, I have become deeply concerned about the work ethics of some employees and harmful effects they might have on the rest of us. Please be advised that the company rules and regulations are very straightforward and that from this date on, they will be implemented by the book, with virtually no exceptions. In the hope that such issues that were reported to me will never happen again, I would like to remind you of these excerpts from our policies:

Section 1, Clause 3: All employees will keep areas used by staff members and/or clients neat and tidy. This includes putting waste into the garbage cans provided and removing any food or beverages brought into rooms.

Section 2, Clause 5: Employees are permitted to use the designated parking spaces at the back of the building only. The spaces in front of the building are strictly reserved for management.

Section 3, Clause 6: Those who wish to borrow equipment such as overhead projectors must sign it out with Tracey in the Technical Department. Unless otherwise arranged, all equipment must be returned by the end of the business day.

Section 4, Clause 1: Any employee missing more than three consecutive days due to illness is expected to produce a doctor's note upon returning. Otherwise, a formal note regarding the employee's unexcused absence will be placed in his or her file.

If you have any questions regarding these policies or others, please refer to the Employee Company Handbook that was given to you by the personnel manager at the time you were hired. If for some reason you do not have a copy, please e-mail me. I will see to it personally that you receive one.

176. What is the purpose of the e-mail?

(A) To encourage employees to handle equipment properly

(B) To warn an employee who was poorly prepared for a presentation

(C) To report the misuse of a shared office space

(D) To propose a renovation at the company's technical facility

177. In the e-mail, the word "following" in paragraph 3, line 2, is closest in meaning to

(A) seeking

(B) succeeding

(C) tracing

(D) observing

178. According to the memo, why might a formal note be placed in an employee's file?

(A) An employee was neglectful in maintaining office cleanliness.

(B) An employee parked at the front of the building and not the back.

(C) An employee had a prolonged absence and did not provide an acceptable excuse.

(D) An employee failed to return equipment by the end of the day.

179. What part of the Employee Company handbook specifically addresses the concerns expressed in the e-mail?

(A) Section 1, Clause 3

(B) Section 2, Clause 5

(C) Section 3, Clause 6

(D) Section 4, Clause 1

180. What can be inferred about Terry?

(A) He believes Tanya should have kept the issue to herself.

(B) He is the person who hands out the employee handbook.

(C) He received complaints other than the one from Tanya.

(D) He feels that some of the company's policies are confusing.

GO ON TO THE NEXT PAGE

Industrial Foods Monthly
Special Survey

We are asking our subscribers what they would like to see in future issues of Industrial Foods Monthly. Your input will help us select the right content for our publication.

1. What types of articles would you like to see in future issues?
   A. More informational articles
   B. More problem-solving narratives
   C. I am satisfied with the current content.

2. How much editorial comment do you like?
   A. The current amount is just right
   B. Less would be better
   C. More would be better

3. Do you want more articles on innovations from other countries?
   A. Yes
   B. No

4. Should the magazine have more vendor advertisements?
   A. Yes
   B. No
   C. It should have less.

Feel free to comment below and then mail this postcard. Postage will be paid by Industrial Foods Monthly.

Thank you for your suggestions!

Industrial Foods Monthly
Reader opinion survey results

A survey was conducted earlier this year to poll our readers on some specific topics that will affect our future direction. The results are now in.

We were pleased to find the responses to the second and fourth questions showed that most of our readership (over 85% in each case) is happy with the amount of vendor advertising and with the editorial material in our publication.

One thing that surprised us was that about 63% of the readers answered "yes" to the third question. Apparently, the growing global marketplace is causing them some concern.

Lastly, a huge 77% of our readers would like to see more problem-solving narratives. This means that writers need to shift their focus from informational and scientific research to interesting case histories of how specific companies and business owners solved their unique problems. Next month, we are planning a brainstorming workshop with our contributors on how to get started on this.

181. What is the purpose of the survey?

    (A) To help determine future content
    (B) To increase worldwide readership
    (C) To assess advertisers' needs
    (D) To rate the magazine's success

182. Who is the survey most likely intended for?

    (A) Managers of grocery store chains
    (B) Owners of restaurant franchises
    (C) Publishing company employees
    (D) Advertising account executives

183. What percentage of readers said they wanted to learn more about foreign innovations?

    (A) 40%
    (B) 63%
    (C) 77%
    (D) 85%

184. What is mentioned about the magazine's articles?

    (A) Most people complained about too much advertising.
    (B) A small number of readers are interested in the global market.
    (C) Readers typically like learning about other people's solutions.
    (D) A majority of subscribers do not agree with the writers' general opinions.

185. What will occur next month?

    (A) A new survey will be completed.
    (B) A meeting for investors will take place.
    (C) A new infomercial will be developed.
    (D) A workshop for writers will be held.

TEST 4

GO ON TO THE NEXT PAGE

Questions 186-190 refer to the following Web page, e-mail, and survey.

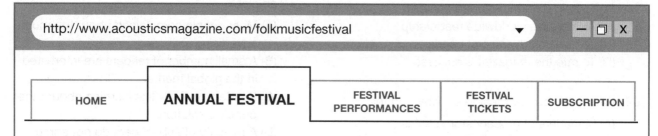

http://www.acousticsmagazine.com/folkmusicfestival

| HOME | **ANNUAL FESTIVAL** | FESTIVAL PERFORMANCES | FESTIVAL TICKETS | SUBSCRIPTION |

Don't miss the tenth annual Acoustics Folk Music Festival in Vancouver on Saturday, August 23.

The Acoustics Folk Music Festival brings together some of the most exciting musicians working within the genre of folk music. This year's festival will be held at Granville Concert Hall in Vancouver, and the headlining act is singer/songwriter Mark Foster. Foster, winner of numerous music industry awards, will play hits from all seven of his best-selling albums. Other notable performers include popular folk singers and musicians such as Edward Corrie, Elizabeth Jones, Sven Magnusson, and Rosita Munoz. More details about each performer and a full event schedule can be found on our Festival Performances page.

The first 250 *Acoustics Magazine* subscribers who arrive at the Granville Concert Hall will receive a gift bag containing CDs and other merchandise. Just bring along proof that you currently hold a subscription to our magazine. We recommend that you bring a printout or screenshot of your subscription information, which you can find by clicking the Subscription tab.

Tickets go on sale on July 1 at a discounted rate, but a price increase is scheduled for August 1, so act quickly to save some money! You can purchase tickets online by clicking the tab at the top of the page.

To:	Edward Corrie <ecorrie@dmusicnet.com>
From:	Wendy Moore <wmoore@acousticsmag.com>
Subject:	Festival performance
Date:	August 27
Attachment:	Survey.doc

Dear Edward,

I just wanted to thank you for taking the time to travel here to Vancouver to participate in the Acoustics Folk Music Festival. We really appreciated your participation and enjoyed your performance. The way you incorporated piano music into traditional folk music was very innovative. You were definitely one of the event's most unique performers. I am certain that everyone in attendance was impressed with the level of craftsmanship you must put into such beautiful, lush musical arrangements. We received a lot of positive feedback from attendees about your performance, and I've attached one of our survey forms, which was submitted by Sylvia Linney. Hers is just one of many surveys that specifically mentioned you and your performance.

Regards,

Wendy Moore
PR & Events Committee
Acoustics Magazine

Acoustics Folk Music Festival Audience Member Survey

	Excellent	Good	Okay	Poor
Venue Interior		X		
Venue Parking				X
Performances	X			
Refreshments		X		

Comments: While the inside of the venue is impressive, the parking facilities nearby are far from adequate. It took a long time to find a space for my car, and in the end, I had to park about six blocks from the venue. I had to walk quite a long distance, and this meant that I had to miss the headlining act on Saturday evening. The festival in general was excellent, as always. My personal highlight was the performance given by the pianist. I was surprised to see that instrument at a folk festival, but it really worked well.

Sylvia Linney

186. What is indicated about the festival?

(A) It will be hosted by multiple venues in Vancouver.
(B) It involves musicians from a wide variety of music genres.
(C) Some attendees will receive complimentary items.
(D) Tickets must be purchased before August 1.

187. What is a purpose of the e-mail?

(A) To propose a musical collaboration
(B) To organize a meeting to plan an event
(C) To inquire about a performance schedule
(D) To provide feedback on a concert

188. In the e-mail, the word "level" in paragraph 1, line 5, is closest in meaning to

(A) surface
(B) amount
(C) position
(D) rank

189. What is suggested about Ms. Linney?

(A) She found the venue to be in poor condition.
(B) She was satisfied with the parking facilities.
(C) She felt some of the performances were not impressive.
(D) She did not watch Mark Foster's performance.

190. Which musician did Ms. Linney particularly like?

(A) Edward Corrie
(B) Elizabeth Jones
(C) Sven Magnusson
(D) Rosita Munoz

GO ON TO THE NEXT PAGE

Heights Party Planning

Providing the best parties in Clayville, Champlain, and Milton,
as well as smaller towns outside the city limits

Prime Package

Suitable for indoor spaces up to 150 square meters. Includes seats and tables as well as buffet tables with catering from Beverly's Catering. At least one week of notice is required for reservations.

Celebrate Package

Suitable for indoor spaces of up to 200 square meters. Seats, tables, and buffet services from Beverly's Catering are included. This package also includes a DJ performance with an included area for dancing.

Aristocrats Package

Suitable for indoor or outdoor spaces up to 300 square meters. Seats, tables and buffet services from Beverly's Catering are included. This high-class package includes a performance by a string quartet and space for ballroom-style dancing.

All Out Package

Suitable for outdoor spaces of up to 400 square meters. Includes snack bar services from Beverly's Catering and seating, but no tables. This package is for big celebrations and includes performances by multiple musical artists.

We offer another 10% discount to repeat customers for all these packages. We also offer customized party packages. To find out information about prices and more,
go to www.heightspartyplanning.com or call Lisa Munro at 351-555-0188.

July 12 – Valley Mall celebrated its re-opening this past weekend with a party that was attended by many Champlain residents. DJ Spencer Clark kept attendees dancing and many praised the cuisine offered by Beverly's Catering. Of special note was the chicken tikka masala, which is a favored dish in Delhi, the hometown of the mall's owner, Sanjit Dalek.

Mr. Dalek gave a short speech to the crowd in the 180-square-meter space reserved for the celebration. "We are very thankful to the community of Champlain for supporting this mall and we are sorry to have kept it closed for so long. We hope that you find the restorations worth the wait. It was necessary to address some safety hazards even when our sales were high." He continued, "We have been able to add more stores for your shopping convenience as well. We'd also like to thank Lisa Munro at Heights Party Planning for putting together this celebration for us and Beverly's Catering for providing my favorite dish. We hope that you enjoy yourselves and that the restorations make your shopping experience more enjoyable."

Local author and friend of Mr. Dalek, Gail Ritchie, was in attendance for the celebrations. Concerning Valley Mall, Ms. Ritchie said, "The mall looks great. I'm sure the community will be happy about the mall reopening as it is a great gathering place for residents."

E-Mail Message

To: editor@champlaintimes.com
From: sanjitdalek@vmall.com
Subject: Recent article
Date: July 13

To the Editor,

I would like to start by thanking you for the coverage of the recent event at my mall. It was certainly a successful occasion, and everyone in attendance had a good time. However, the reporter who covered the event seemed to have been mistaken on a specific point. My acquaintance who was quoted in the article is actually the head chef at the local restaurant called Baywalk Bistro. I guess the reporter simply misunderstood. If you would consider running a correction, or an advertisement for Baywalk Bistro, it would mean a lot both to me and my friend.

Best regards,

Sanjit Dalek

191. What is indicated about the four party packages?

(A) They all include seats and tables.
(B) They are all suitable for outdoor spaces.
(C) They all include a musical performance.
(D) They all can be further discounted.

192. Which package was most likely selected by Mr. Dalek?

(A) Prime Package
(B) Celebrate Package
(C) Aristocrats Package
(D) All Out Package

193. Why was the article written?

(A) To review a local author's book
(B) To report on a grand reopening
(C) To promote a catering service
(D) To announce a mall's upcoming sale

194. Why did Valley Mall undergo renovations?

(A) The mall had some issues with safety.
(B) Its customers complained about the lack of parking.
(C) It was not attracting many shoppers.
(D) The owner wanted to add more retail space.

195. According to the e-mail, whose profession was described incorrectly in the article?

(A) Sanjit Dalek's
(B) Spencer Clark's
(C) Lisa Munro's
(D) Gail Ritchie's

GO ON TO THE NEXT PAGE

Questions 196-200 refer to following e-mails and attachment.

E-Mail Message

To:	MPV Mailing List
From:	Bill Carver <bcarver@tncoutfitters.com>
Subject:	Jacket deals
Date:	February 27
Attachment:	GoodsonJackets.doc

Dear sir/madam,

As a member of Medical Professionals of Vermont (MPV), you can receive special deals on specific Goodson jackets carried by Town & Country Outfitters. Goodson makes apparel for all seasons that will last for years. All products listed in the attachment come with the Town and Country Outfitters guarantee of the highest quality goods. Please note that the discounts are only available until the end of March.

We appreciate your continued patronage of Town & Country Outfitters!

Best Wishes,

Bill Carver

Proprietor, Town & Country Outfitters

Town and Country Outfitters
77 Moreland Road, Montpellier, Vermont

Deep Freeze Jacket: The thickest of the Goodson coats, this coat will ensure you stay warm even in the coldest winter weather. The jacket comes with six outer pockets, as well as two pockets inside the jacket. It closes with zipper and buttons. The attached hood has faux fur trimming. Comes in black or white. $149.99 → $109.99

True Adapt Jacket: This durable coat is perfect for cool and cold weather as it comes with a unique feature, a removable wool vest, making it perfect for both autumn and winter. The jacket has four outer pockets and one inner pocket. It closes with zippers and buttons and has an attached hood. Comes in blue, black, and red. $129.99 → $99.99

Action Pack Jacket: Perfect for autumn weather, this medium-weight jacket will protect you from the wind even in late autumn. This jacket is great for hiking and seeing the beautiful fall foliage. It even includes a small inner pocket perfect for smaller cameras, as well as three outer pockets. Comes in green, blue, black, and yellow. $109.99 → $79.99

Spring Loaded Jacket: This lightweight jacket will help protect you from the wind and rain during the spring months. The jacket also makes carrying your valuables easy with four outer pockets and two inner pockets. The removable hood snaps on easily and can be taken off just as easily. Comes in blue, green, purple, and white. $79.99 → $59.99

Dandy Downpour Jacket: Made especially for the wet summer months, this rain jacket will keep you dry in the pouring rain, but will help you stay cool with its ultra-lightweight material. It comes with an extra-large hood to keep your face dry even if you don't have an umbrella. Comes in yellow, blue, and red. $59.99 → $49.99

To purchase any of these discounted items, e-mail Bill Carver at bcarver@tncoutfitters.com.

To:	Bill Carver <bcarver@tncoutfitters.com>
From:	Benjamin Black <bblack@trutonclinic.com>
Subject:	Re: Jacket deals
Date:	February 28

Dear Mr. Carver,

I received the e-mail you sent out yesterday about the discounted Goodson jackets. We are having an outing with the workers at the clinic next month and I'd like to give everyone a jacket for all their hard work. Therefore, I'd like to order 10 blue jackets with removable hoods. If possible, I'd like our clinic name on the jacket, just like last time I ordered from you. Please let me know if this is possible and how much extra it would cost.

Thank you.

Benjamin Black, M.C.
Chief Physician, Truton Clinic

TEST 4

196. What is suggested about Town & Country Outfitters?

(A) It provides other companies' goods.
(B) It produces all-season outfits.
(C) It makes medical equipment.
(D) It provides special offers only to its premium members.

197. According to the attachment, how should a person place an order?

(A) By visiting the Town & Country Outfitters store
(B) By sending a payment to a Goodson employee
(C) By contacting a store owner by e-mail
(D) By filling out an electronic order form

198. How is the True Adapt Jacket different from other jackets?

(A) It has an inner pocket.
(B) It has a removable lining.
(C) It has both buttons and a zipper.
(D) It is stain-resistant.

199. What is implied about Mr. Black?

(A) He is a new customer of Town & Country Outfitters.
(B) He recently moved out of Vermont.
(C) He regularly purchases Goodson products.
(D) He belongs to the Medical Professionals of Vermont.

200. What type of jacket will Mr. Black most likely purchase?

(A) Deep Freeze Jacket
(B) Action Pack Jacket
(C) Spring Loaded Jacket
(D) Dandy Downpour Jacket

Stop! This is the end of the test. If you finish before time is called, you may go back to Parts 5, 6, and 7 and check your work.

정답 p.469 / 점수 환산표 p.476

실전모의고사
TEST 5

TEST 5 해설

바로 보기

- 시작 시간 _____시 _____분
- 종료 시간 _____시 _____분

▶ 중간에 멈추지 말고 처음부터 끝까지 풀어보세요. 문제를 풀 때는 실전처럼 답안지에 마킹하세요.

READING TEST

In the Reading test, you will read a variety of texts and answer several different types of reading comprehension questions. The entire Reading test will last 75 minutes. There are three parts, and directions are given for each part. You are encouraged to answer as many questions as possible within the time allowed. You must mark your answers on the separate answer sheet. Do not write your answers in your test book.

PART 5

Directions: A word or phrase is missing in each of the sentences below. Four answer choices are given below each sentence. Select the best answer to complete the sentence. Then mark the letter (A), (B), (C), or (D) on your answer sheet.

101. Among other ------- improvements to employee benefits, staff who have been with the company for five or more years will receive three extra vacation days this year.

(A) substance
(B) substantial
(C) substantially
(D) substantiate

102. Our supplier, KG Furnisher, was neither able to meet the order deadline, ------- provide all the products we needed.

(A) and
(B) or
(C) to
(D) nor

103. An increase in customers requesting a more spacious dining room forced the owner and the manager to consider ------- the whole restaurant.

(A) to renovate
(B) renovated
(C) renovating
(D) renovation

104. Although the company appeared to have been generating record profits, it was ------- facing bankruptcy.

(A) actually
(B) completely
(C) finally
(D) partially

105. The city's most prestigious research hospital is currently located ------- the university campus outside the town.

(A) of
(B) from
(C) with
(D) on

106. We ------- to inform you that your order has been delayed by two weeks as we currently do not have it in stock.

(A) react
(B) suggest
(C) regret
(D) accept

107. Weekly staff meetings are indispensable for monitoring the organization's performance and ------- problems before they actually arise.

(A) prevent
(B) prevented
(C) prevention
(D) preventing

108. The director advised the marketing team not to finalize the advertising strategy until the market survey ------- have been compiled.

(A) results
(B) participants
(C) purchases
(D) locations

109. The audience gave the keynote speaker a ------- reception on the opening day of the Advanced Education Seminar.

(A) warm
(B) high
(C) wide
(D) urgent

110. Written correspondence is not nearly as ------- as verbal communication when it comes to establishing and maintaining customer/client relationships.

(A) effect
(B) effecting
(C) effectively
(D) effective

111. The chief negotiator's presence will ------- that contract talks go smoothly and the best deal is obtained.

(A) ensure
(B) approve
(C) pledge
(D) hope

112. The path to success involves being able to recognize ------- weaknesses and capitalize on opportunities that present themselves.

(A) you
(B) yourself
(C) your
(D) yours

113. It is a proven fact that the ------- an employee stays at the same company, the more that employee is committed to the company's values and goals.

(A) long
(B) longer
(C) longs
(D) longing

114. Fluctuations in a company's stock prices are not always ------- on the firm's sales performance or popularity among customers.

(A) caused
(B) relevant
(C) indicative
(D) dependent

115. An ------- of the photo has been requested, which will be hung in the display case in the office lobby.

(A) enlarging
(B) enlargement
(C) enlarged
(D) enlarger

116. Our long-term financial forecast predicts a ------- decline in revenue over the third quarter, followed by a slow but steady recovery as we move into next year.

(A) bright
(B) fortunate
(C) profitable
(D) sharp

117. Please ensure that all printed materials ------- to our company branding standards, which were updated yesterday by our marketing department.

(A) adhere
(B) to adhere
(C) adhering
(D) having adhered

118. ------- having closed some overseas offices to cut costs, the company continued to run a deficit.

(A) Nonetheless
(B) However
(C) Despite
(D) Whether

119. Be sure to send out a memo before the conference to let the participants know where the conference center is -------.

(A) location
(B) locates
(C) locating
(D) located

120. The advertising team has made a decision to stop running the newspaper advertisements ------- they start to generate more sales.

(A) unless
(B) otherwise
(C) which
(D) thus

GO ON TO THE NEXT PAGE

121. The information given to us by our supplier was not only informative, but ------- was extremely thorough as well.

(A) none
(B) one
(C) he
(D) it

122. The IT team is quick to intervene in the event of a computer failure, allowing us all to ------- our work without delay.

(A) continue
(B) continued
(C) continues
(D) continuing

123. ------- we started donating money to help organizations in the local community, we have attracted more clients.

(A) Since
(B) Until
(C) When
(D) Before

124. Many delegates failed to recognize the importance of attending the conference because its scope was ------- to marketing and fundraising only.

(A) limited
(B) covered
(C) remained
(D) guided

125. Given increasing customer complaints about late deliveries, changes to the company's logistics system are a ------- rather than an option.

(A) necessity
(B) preference
(C) concern
(D) revision

126. Please consider the formality of the event you have been invited to and plan to dress -------.

(A) precisely
(B) affordably
(C) accordingly
(D) similarly

127. Making the wrong choice when choosing telecommunications providers can ------- in high monthly expenses.

(A) lead
(B) finish
(C) result
(D) cause

128. ------- further notice, all staff members must attend in-house professional development workshops once a month.

(A) Until
(B) Before
(C) For
(D) With

129. Management was unimpressed with the advertising campaign designed by Blue Creative, a company ------- work is often praised as being unique and ahead of its time.

(A) whose
(B) who
(C) that
(D) what

130. All new employees are encouraged to read the company history book, which ------- the philosophical foundation of the corporation.

(A) details
(B) detailed
(C) detail
(D) detailing

PART 6

Directions: Read the texts that follow. A word, phrase, or sentence is missing in parts of each text. Four answer choices for each question are given below the text. Select the best answer to complete the text. Then mark the letter (A), (B), (C) or (D) on your answer sheet.

Questions 131-134 refer to the following memo.

To: Maintenance Staff
From: Carissa Dempsey, Maintenance Manager
Date: February 21
RE: South Land Hospital Location

Dear Staff:

First of all, let me say that all of you are doing an ------- job at all of our locations. I regularly receive
131.
positive comments from the companies and organizations we work for.

In recent weeks, it has come to my attention that staff working at the South Land Hospital have
been asked to provide services that are outside what is offered in our Basic Bronze package. Such
requests have included taking the garbage to the dumpster, wiping off chairs in the waiting room, and
cleaning out coffee pots. In every case, our staff members performed these ------- tasks.
132.

While I understand your desire to please our clients, it's important to provide only what we agreed to
at the time the contract was signed. -------.
133.

If you have any concerns or questions about the services included in any of our packages, I am
------- to address them. Please feel free to stop by my office any time, and keep up the great work.
134.

Sincerely,

Carissa Dempsey, Maintenance Manager

---

131. (A) exemplary
(B) frequent
(C) accessible
(D) eventual

132. (A) addition
(B) additions
(C) additional
(D) additionally

133. (A) In this way, your assistance will be very
much appreciated.
(B) So, I want you all to sign the form at the
bottom of the page.
(C) This will help ensure we don't take time
away from our other valued clients.
(D) This addition to the service will be offered
to customers for a limited time only.

134. (A) plain
(B) hesitant
(C) willing
(D) possible

GO ON TO THE NEXT PAGE

Questions 135-138 refer to the following article.

East News Service — The top cell phone company in the eastern United States, Portable Phones Inc. ------- that its new application for business customers will make it possible to conduct a productive
135.

business meeting anytime, anywhere. After testing their offering with focus groups for the past six months and getting favorable responses, the company is finally ready to unveil "Meetings On The Go."

Available for a monthly fee, this application can support meetings involving up to eight people. Slide shows, graphs, and other information can be transferred to the cell phone memory and then displayed to everyone using "Meetings On The Go." A marketing representative described it as "the conference call ------- a new generation."
136.

While the cell phone company sees its new service as revolutionary, not everyone agrees. One business owner who wished to speak ------- explained: "This can all be done on a computer
137.

using free software. ------- . The screen is just too small."
138.

135. (A) believe
(B) believes
(C) believed
(D) believing

136. (A) toward
(B) onto
(C) during
(D) for

137. (A) anonymously
(B) cautiously
(C) preliminarily
(D) arbitrarily

138. (A) People will soon realize these new models of computers are nothing more than a temporary trend.
(B) In addition, most serious business people don't want to share presentations and charts using a cell phone.
(C) Consequently, mobile phone sales are likely to increase over the next quarter.
(D) However, using apps on handheld devices is a popular way to share content with coworkers.

From: hmin@beautycare.com
To: mkim@beautycare.com
Subject: Contract Details for Lifting Face Cream
Date: August 2

Dear Ms. Kim:

As you requested last week, I am providing an e-mail update on the status of our contract ------- **139.** with the developers of Lifting Face Cream.

I had a chance to meet with a representative from the company yesterday, and I'm happy to say we now have a better idea of the possible size of the order and how much they are willing to pay. The company would ------- **140.** order 3,000 15-mL tubes of cream, which would need to be produced and packaged within the next four months.

The representative felt our quote of $4.00 per tube was high, and said the most the company would pay is $2.75. I ran the numbers, and this ------- **141.** gives us a healthy profit margin. ------- **142.** .

I told him I would need to speak with you before I gave a definite answer. Please let me know how you would like to proceed.

Sincerely,

Hana Min

TEST 5

139. (A) intentions
     (B) negotiations
     (C) terminations
     (D) approaches

140. (A) initial
     (B) initials
     (C) initialed
     (D) initially

141. (A) still
     (B) soon
     (C) once
     (D) yet

142. (A) Please consider giving us a discount on
         your product pricing.
     (B) We can return the cream if it does not
         meet our expectations.
     (C) So, we will probably stick with our original
         offer to Lifting Face Cream.
     (D) We'll still make money, just not as much
         as we originally hoped.

GO ON TO THE NEXT PAGE

Questions 143-146 refer to the following advertisement.

Tired of ------- your home? Dreaming of one day having a bungalow or townhouse to call your own?
143.

Then read on!

With plenty of homes on the market and interest rates at historic lows, NOW is the best time to buy!

At No Worries Realty, we have a staff of twelve real estate agents, and ------- have at least 10 years
144.

of experience. Unlike some other companies, we won't try to convince you to purchase a home that's

not right for you just to make a sale.

Our process is designed to find you exactly the home you want at a price you can afford. First, you'll

fill out a detailed questionnaire that asks you about your preferred area, number of bathrooms, floor

space, and of course cost. -------.
145.

When you're ready to buy, we'll take care of all the paperwork and help you arrange a home -------.
146.

All you'll need to do is just pack and move in!

Call us at 633-435-4505 to begin the exciting process of searching for your first home!

143. (A) rent
(B) rents
(C) rented
(D) renting

144. (A) everyone
(B) all
(C) each
(D) any

145. (A) Then, your agent will take you to only
those homes that meet your criteria.
(B) Your order has been received and is now
being processed by an agent.
(C) Once we have this information, we will do
our best to find you a suitable job.
(D) We at No Worries Realty appreciate your
listing your home with us.

146. (A) inspect
(B) inspected
(C) inspecting
(D) inspection

PART 7

Directions: In this part you will read a selection of texts, such as magazine and newspaper articles, e-mails, and instant messages. Each text or set of texts is followed by several questions. Select the best answer for each question and mark the letter (A), (B), (C), or (D) on your answer sheet.

Questions 147-148 refer to the following notice.

NOTICE FOR ALL TOUR GUIDES

Beginning February 1, we will be adding a few interesting stops to our popular walking tour of the Haven Hills neighborhood. You would normally take your group directly from St. Luke's Cathedral to Netty's Coffee Shop, but we would like you to start taking a detour past Colman Bridge and Dunford Hotel. Both sites have rich histories, which we expect you to become knowledgeable about in advance.

Don't forget that we will not be open during January, which is typically the coldest month of the year and a time when demand for tours is exceedingly low. All guides will receive full pay during this time. We appreciate your service.

---

147. What is the notice mainly about?

(A) The history of a neighborhood
(B) Changes to a tour route
(C) The opening of a new business
(D) Showing gratitude to volunteer guides

148. What will most likely happen in January?

(A) New tour packages will be introduced.
(B) Some new guides will be hired.
(C) Employees will receive pay cuts.
(D) A business will close temporarily.

GO ON TO THE NEXT PAGE

Questions 149-150 refer to the following text-message chain.

Linda   **[8:03 P.M.]**

Malcolm, I wanted to let you know that we will be announcing your retirement to the rest of staff at our meeting tomorrow.

Malcolm   **[8:08 P.M.]**

Oh. Should I prepare a speech?

Linda   **[8:14 P.M.]**

That won't be necessary.

Malcolm   **[8:15 P.M.]**

Got it. I suppose most people already know by now anyway.

Linda   **[8:16 P.M.]**

I don't know how we are going to replace you, Malcolm.

Malcolm   **[8:17 P.M.]**

Thank you, Linda. That means a lot.

Linda   **[8:19 P.M.]**

We are going to miss seeing you around the office. What will you do with all of your new free time?

Malcolm   **[8:22 P.M.]**

I was going to travel, but I changed my mind after talking with a close friend. Instead, I am going to volunteer at a local food bank a few days a week.

---

149. At 8:16 p.m., what does Linda mean when she says, "I don't know how we are going to replace you, Malcom"?

(A) Malcolm left the company unexpectedly.
(B) She appreciates Malcolm's work effort.
(C) There are few qualified candidates.
(D) She plans to train a new staff member.

150. What can be inferred about Malcolm's new position?

(A) He will be in charge of finances.
(B) He will start in a few days.
(C) He will work every day.
(D) He will not be paid.

Questions 151-152 refer to the following e-mail.

To:	Jason Mirello <jmirello@electro.net>
From:	Natalie Portland <nportland@electro.net>
Subject:	Product launch
Date:	May 27

Dear Jason,

As you know, we are holding a special sales event in our Chicago branch to mark the launch of our new range of stovetop appliances. It would be really great if everybody involved with the project could be present in store to talk to customers. All the R&D personnel have confirmed their attendance, apart from Trevor Mitchell, who is away on vacation. All of the catalogs are being stored in your office at the moment - just a reminder that you are to bring them along to the store. I have arranged a celebratory dinner at the Italian restaurant Fortuna afterwards. I know the chef personally, and he has agreed to provide us with a discount.

See you at the store,

Natalie Portland
Project Manager

151. Who most likely is Trevor Mitchell?

(A) A reporter
(B) A customer
(C) A store owner
(D) A researcher

152. What does Ms. Portland expect Mr. Mirello to do?

(A) Search for an event venue
(B) Transport some documents
(C) Make a restaurant reservation
(D) Demonstrate a product

GO ON TO THE NEXT PAGE

Yaletown Gazette

Summer Celebration Planned

April 13

As the town approaches its 150th anniversary of its founding, newly elected mayor Percy Hammonds has announced an array of events to mark this historic occasion. Perhaps the highlight of the summer calendar is set to be a series of performances by visiting musicians held over Independence Day weekend. The event will be headlined by local band The Canadians, and supported by new sensation Peter Eagles. Gibble Convention Hall will host the event, and demand for seats is expected to be exceptionally high, with additional seating already installed at the venue. Customers are advised to book tickets early. To do so, please visit www.yaletown.com/summerevents and follow the instructions there.

153. What does the article mainly discuss?

(A) A music festival
(B) A sports competition
(C) A mayoral election
(D) A fundraising event

154. According to the article, what can people do on the town's Web site?

(A) View an itinerary
(B) Leave a comment
(C) Reserve tickets
(D) Make a donation

Questions 155-157 refer to the following e-mail.

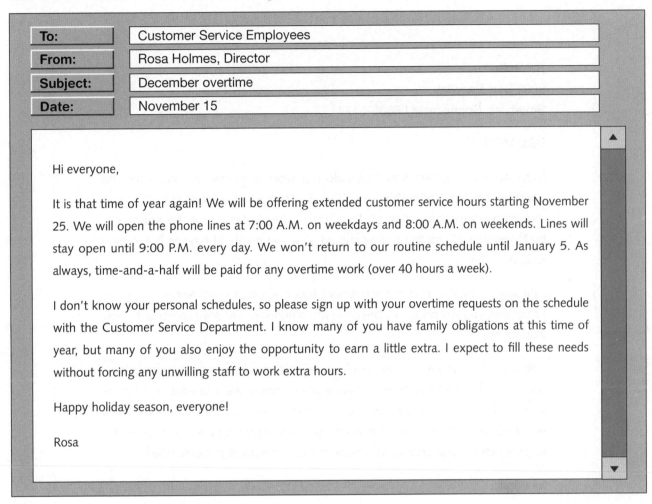

To:	Customer Service Employees
From:	Rosa Holmes, Director
Subject:	December overtime
Date:	November 15

Hi everyone,

It is that time of year again! We will be offering extended customer service hours starting November 25. We will open the phone lines at 7:00 A.M. on weekdays and 8:00 A.M. on weekends. Lines will stay open until 9:00 P.M. every day. We won't return to our routine schedule until January 5. As always, time-and-a-half will be paid for any overtime work (over 40 hours a week).

I don't know your personal schedules, so please sign up with your overtime requests on the schedule with the Customer Service Department. I know many of you have family obligations at this time of year, but many of you also enjoy the opportunity to earn a little extra. I expect to fill these needs without forcing any unwilling staff to work extra hours.

Happy holiday season, everyone!

Rosa

155. Why was the e-mail written?

(A) To describe a full-time vacancy
(B) To ask for people to volunteer
(C) To extend best wishes for the holiday
(D) To announce an opportunity to join a program

156. When will the Customer Service Department return to its regular work hours?

(A) November 25
(B) January 5
(C) January 15
(D) January 25

157. What is suggested about the overtime work?

(A) It will not include weekends.
(B) Extra money will be paid.
(C) It will only be required for one month.
(D) It is mandatory for all employees.

GO ON TO THE NEXT PAGE

Questions 158-160 refer to the following letter.

Ralph Griffin
8083 Blue Parkway
Smartville, Connecticut 06638-5174

Dear Mr. Griffin,

I am writing to inform you that I do not plan to renew our lease for the apartment at 856 Cedar Drive. — [1] —. The terms of the lease state that you require one month's notice of departure. I plan to be out of the apartment by November 30, so this notice should give you plenty of time to find a new tenant. — [2] —.

I think you will find that the apartment has been well maintained. — [3] —. I trust that you will provide a check in the amount of my down payment upon inspection.

I also want to thank you for being a reliable landlord over the past three years. You have always been available when repairs were needed and I have thoroughly enjoyed my stay on Cedar Drive. — [4] —. I think we have had a very positive relationship and wonder if you would provide me with a reference to prospective landlords in New York. It would be greatly appreciated.

Sincerely,

Heidi Cummings

158. What is the main purpose of the letter?

(A) To request repairs to a property
(B) To give notice of plans to vacate
(C) To give details about a potential tenant
(D) To ask for a letter of reference

159. What is Mr. Griffin NOT likely to do?

(A) Ask Ms. Cummings to pay for damages
(B) Return Ms. Cummings' damage deposit
(C) Inspect the apartment on Cedar Drive
(D) Write a letter of recommendation for the tenant

160. In which of the positions marked [1], [2], [3], and [4] does the following sentence best belong?

"It is clean and there has been no structural damage."

(A) [1]
(B) [2]
(C) [3]
(D) [4]

Questions 161-164 refer to the following online chat discussion.

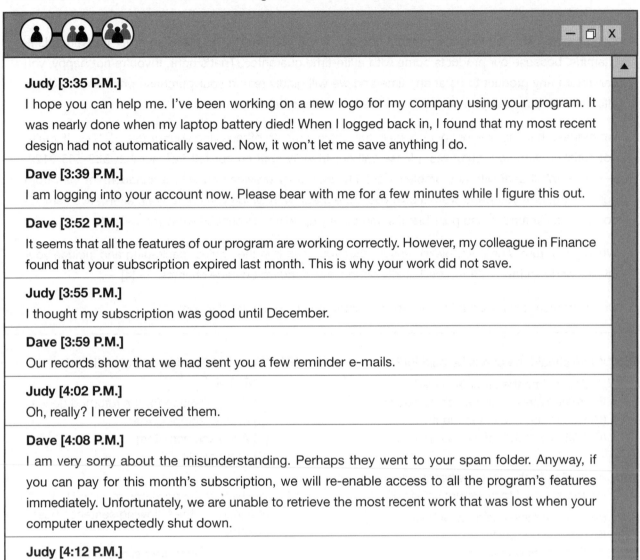

Judy [3:35 P.M.]

I hope you can help me. I've been working on a new logo for my company using your program. It was nearly done when my laptop battery died! When I logged back in, I found that my most recent design had not automatically saved. Now, it won't let me save anything I do.

Dave [3:39 P.M.]

I am logging into your account now. Please bear with me for a few minutes while I figure this out.

Dave [3:52 P.M.]

It seems that all the features of our program are working correctly. However, my colleague in Finance found that your subscription expired last month. This is why your work did not save.

Judy [3:55 P.M.]

I thought my subscription was good until December.

Dave [3:59 P.M.]

Our records show that we had sent you a few reminder e-mails.

Judy [4:02 P.M.]

Oh, really? I never received them.

Dave [4:08 P.M.]

I am very sorry about the misunderstanding. Perhaps they went to your spam folder. Anyway, if you can pay for this month's subscription, we will re-enable access to all the program's features immediately. Unfortunately, we are unable to retrieve the most recent work that was lost when your computer unexpectedly shut down.

Judy [4:12 P.M.]

I see. Thank you for your help.

161. What most likely is Judy's job title?

(A) Graphic Designer
(B) Customer Service Representative
(C) Financial Advisor
(D) IT Technician

162. What is indicated about Judy?

(A) She couldn't find a battery.
(B) She designed a program.
(C) She is now able to save her work.
(D) She lost the logo she was working on.

163. At 4:02 P.M., what does Judy mean when she writes, "I never received them"?

(A) She could not update her software.
(B) She did not use Dave's subscription.
(C) She did not record the information.
(D) She did not see any reminders.

164. What does Dave advise Judy to do?

(A) Back up her work frequently
(B) Renew a subscription
(C) Search for the deleted content
(D) E-mail some information

GO ON TO THE NEXT PAGE

Questions 165-168 refer to the following notice.

Congratulations! You made a wonderful decision when you decided to place an order for Nature Link vitamins, because our products come with a life-time guarantee. That's right, if you're not happy, you can return any product to us at any time and we will gladly refund your purchase price or provide an alternative product as long as you follow the instructions below.

We request that you pay for your goods in full within a month of receiving your order. — [1] —. If you're not satisfied with your purchase, please call our friendly staff on our toll-free number 569-555-0129. — [2] —. We'll deal with any problems quickly and either provide you with a replacement item from our catalog, or if you want, we will give you store credit with which you can buy an alternative item. Of course, a full refund is also possible. It's completely up to you to choose what you'd like to do.

When you return a product, please ensure that you send it in the original packaging and include your invoice and receipt. — [3] —. We'll gladly refund any standard postage charges. — [4] —.

Our customers are important to us and we guarantee customer satisfaction!

165. When should the goods be paid for?

(A) At the time the order is placed
(B) Immediately after the item is delivered
(C) Before the end of the month
(D) Within a month of receiving them

166. According to the notice, what should customers do if they are not satisfied?

(A) Leave a message on a Web site
(B) Call the company
(C) Read their guarantee
(D) Send the products back immediately

167. What is NOT offered to dissatisfied customers?

(A) Compensation for the returned goods
(B) Priority shipping fees
(C) A replacement item
(D) Store credit

168. In which of the positions marked [1], [2], [3], and [4] does the following sentence best belong?

"This is because we believe in the highest quality of customer service."

(A) [1]
(B) [2]
(C) [3]
(D) [4]

Questions 169-171 refer to the following e-mail message.

```
┌─────────────────────────────────────────────────────────────────┐
│                        E-Mail Message                             │
├─────────────────────────────────────────────────────────────────┤
│                                                                   │
│   From:          Aaron Blackmore                                  │
│   To:            Mary Engels                                      │
│   Date:          February 18                                      │
│   Subject:       Lunch meeting                                    │
│                                                                   │
├─────────────────────────────────────────────────────────────────┤
│                                                                   │
│   Do you think we can meet for lunch tomorrow? We need to go over │
│   the additions we should make to the slide presentation we are   │
│   giving later this week. You have worked on projects for Brown   │
│   & Sons longer than I have, and I want your input on the details.│
│                                                                   │
│   I understand that Blue Ridge Associates will be sending someone │
│   to the presentation, as well as Miranda Products, who are       │
│   already interested. Do you have any background information      │
│   about this new company?                                         │
│                                                                   │
│   I have booked a table at The Rib House for lunch tomorrow.      │
│   Expect it to be a long lunch. Please let me know if you cannot  │
│   make it.                                                        │
│                                                                   │
│   Thanks.                                                         │
│                                                                   │
└─────────────────────────────────────────────────────────────────┘
```

169. What is the reason for the lunch meeting?

(A) To design an office addition
(B) To edit a presentation
(C) To discuss a new project
(D) To write a proposal

170. What can be inferred about the presentation?

(A) Several companies will be attending it.
(B) Mary is willing to assist Aaron with it.
(C) It will take place at The Rib House.
(D) It needs to be made considerably longer.

171. Which organization does Mary have work experience with?

(A) The Rib House
(B) Blue Ridge Associates
(C) Miranda Products
(D) Brown & Sons

GO ON TO THE NEXT PAGE

Enjoy a week on the Gold Coast for only $299!

As a summer holiday bonus deal, Holiday Travel Direct Ltd. is cutting $100 off the price of our popular Gold Coast holiday package. To get these special deals, you must make a booking by July 10 and travel by July 31.

These prices won't be repeated, so call us now to avoid disappointment! You can depart from any of these cities:

- New York *
- Detroit
- Chicago
- Houston

All of the packages include 3-star accommodation and economy flights. Transfers and all lunches are also included. Please be aware that not all dates are available and that flight tax and other airline charges are not included. Children fly for half price.

We accept all major credit cards, but do not accept checks. Additional discounts are available for groups, corporate customers and those who join our loyalty program.

* There is a $50 surcharge for flights departing from New York.

Free gift: If you book and pay for your package by July 5, you will receive a complimentary breakfast and a travel bag.

172. What is suggested about the special package in the advertisement?

(A) The price will be raised after July 10.
(B) It is a brand-new package for the holiday season.
(C) First-class tickets can be purchased for an extra $50.
(D) Travelers can use any payment method.

173. What is special about flights departing from New York?

(A) There are limited seats available.
(B) They aren't direct flights.
(C) The aircraft is smaller.
(D) An extra charge is needed.

174. What is NOT included in the cost of the package?

(A) Flight taxes
(B) Accommodations
(C) Transfers
(D) Lunches

175. What will you receive if you book and pay by July 5?

(A) Free baggage handling
(B) A discount for children
(C) A free meal
(D) A special membership card

GO ON TO THE NEXT PAGE

Questions 176-180 refer to the following advertisement and review.

Business Masters Inc. - Latest Offering!
Empowering Employees
By Julia Lederstrom

In this day of the multi-national mega corporation, this book is a very timely examination of what it takes to get the most from your employees, especially within a large corporation. Respected author Julia Lederstrom examines the psychology and dynamics of extremely large work groups. She then applies her conclusions to the modern workplace. Her underlying theory that employees are a major key to the success or failure of a large corporation is supported by evidence from the global marketplace. Relying on a detailed analysis of many corporate case histories, she uncovers the corporate behaviors and patterns common to companies that succeed and fail. Her well-founded conclusions may surprise even the most experienced human resources manager or corporate executive. They will no doubt also provide immense benefit to these professionals.

Author biography: A professor at Harvard Business School, Julia Lederstrom has conducted extensive research into corporate dynamics and behavior. She holds advanced degrees in both business and psychology, and she serves on the board of directors for two multi-national corporations. Her previous book, *Motivating for Success*, was a bestseller.

Monthly Book Review
by Meghan Williams

Empowering Employees
By Julia Lederstrom
Business Masters Inc., $44.95

This book is a scholarly investigation into the subject of employee dynamics within a large corporation. The book is well organized. It is clear where the research descriptions and the author's conclusions can be found. However, the book is very difficult to read. Lederstrom's writing is both boring and extremely long-winded.

The title of the book indicates that there will be some suggestions that human resource managers may use on the job. In fact, the suggestions given are very vague and high-level. The readers are left to figure out for themselves how to implement them in an actual business environment.

As a graduate student who recently took Ms. Lederstrom's classes, I can see that this book may work well as a university textbook. However, I cannot see it being of much value to a corporate executive.

176. According to the advertisement, who will benefit from reading *Empowering Employees*?

(A) Corporate marketing professionals
(B) Human resource supervisors
(C) Business degree professors
(D) Corporate recruitment personnel

177. What is NOT mentioned about Julia Lederstrom?

(A) She has done business research.
(B) She has two university degrees.
(C) She has worked in human resources.
(D) She has published a previous book.

178. What did Julia Lederstrom use to reach her conclusions?

(A) Case studies from businesses
(B) Books about corporate practices
(C) Interviews with employees
(D) Personal work experience

179. What can be inferred about Meghan Williams?

(A) She works for a publishing company.
(B) She attends a business school.
(C) She runs a personnel department.
(D) She conducts research on corporate management.

180. What does Meghan Williams say about Julia Lederstrom?

(A) She lacks professional credentials.
(B) Her book provides useful on-site advice.
(C) She has written many business-related textbooks.
(D) Her writing style is uninteresting.

GO ON TO THE NEXT PAGE

Questions 181-185 refer to the following e-mails.

From:	Paul Sullivan <psullivan@htchemicals.com>
To:	Ernie Hobbs <ehobbs@htchemicals.com>
Subject:	Lost key
Date:	April 23

Hi Ernie,

Do you know anything about the key to the supply closet? My assistant, Christine, is putting together some materials for my meeting with clients this afternoon, and she needs some binders. Usually the key is kept in the receptionist's desk, but she says she hasn't seen it since yesterday morning.

I understand the need to lock the supply closet to discourage employees from taking products for their own personal use, but we do need to be able to get things for legitimate business uses. It is a waste of Christine's time and my time to have to run around the office looking for something as simple as a key. We are far too busy to waste time in this way.

Thank you,
Paul Sullivan

E-Mail Message

From: Ernie Hobbs <ehobbs@htchemicals.com>
To: Paul Sullivan <psullivan@htchemicals.com>
Subject: Re: Lost key
Date: April 23

Hi Paul,

I am sorry that you are having such trouble getting supplies. We haven't been able to find the missing key and no one knows who used it last. I always have a key, since I have the master key to all the rooms and offices in our building. I have now placed a back-up key in the drawer where you'd usually find it, so your assistant can pick up anything she needs at any time today.

We lock the room mainly because the late-night janitorial service staff had been taking things, not employees. I did not realize that locking the room would cause such a problem for people in the course of their job.

Would you like me to get a copy of the key made for each manager so that they can take care of their own needs? Or perhaps I should open it each morning and lock it up again at the end of the day so that it can be open all day.

Regards,

Ernie

181. To whom did Mr. Sullivan send the e-mail?

    (A) His client
    (B) His colleague
    (C) A locksmith
    (D) A supplier

182. What is Christine doing?

    (A) Compiling some materials
    (B) Taking a store room inventory
    (C) Arranging a meeting with some clients
    (D) Ordering new copies of keys

183. When was the key probably missing?

    (A) Early yesterday
    (B) Late last night
    (C) Early this morning
    (D) A few minutes ago

184. In the second e-mail, the word "pick up" in paragraph 1, line 4, is closest in meaning to

    (A) meet
    (B) harvest
    (C) get
    (D) deliver

185. How has Ernie solved the problem?

    (A) He gave each supervisor a key.
    (B) He found a new janitorial service.
    (C) He personally distributed supplies.
    (D) He put a key in the receptionist's desk.

GO ON TO THE NEXT PAGE

Questions 186-190 refer to the following advertisements and e-mail.

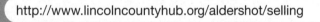http://www.lincolncountyhub.org/aldershot/buying

Aldershot Resident Seeking Used Car

Topic: Second-hand Vehicles
Date: July 25

I just received an employment offer from Rentona Corporation in Newhampton, which is too far for public transportation, so I'm looking to buy a used car before starting work on September 6. I'm seeking a sedan or a hatchback with ample space in the trunk, as my job requires me to transport various work materials. I'd prefer a modest color such as black, white, or silver rather than a bright color, but I'll consider any vehicle that looks attractive. Finally, the car should be less than five years old and have been driven fewer than 70,000 miles. My budget is a maximum of $2,500.

Posted by: Paul Shepard
E-mail: paul_shepard@allmail.net

http://www.lincolncountyhub.org/aldershot/selling

Selling a car in downtown Aldershot

Topic: Second-hand Vehicles
Date: July 26

I'm planning to move overseas on August 31 and would like to sell my car before I leave. The car is a Toshida sedan, which is a light red color, and it was purchased four years ago and has less than 50,000 miles on it. I also have a satellite navigation system and various charging cables that I could throw in for a low price, so please inquire if you're interested and make me an offer. The car may need a tune-up, so I'm willing to let it go for $2,300. I live on Main Street in Aldershot.

Posted by: Abigail Ritchie
E-mail: aritchie@eworld.com

To:	Abigail Ritchie <aritchie@eworld.com>
From:	Paul Shepard <paul_shepard@allmail.net>
Date:	July 26
Subject:	Car

Dear Ms. Ritchie,

I was browsing the second-hand vehicles section of lincolncountyhub.org today, and I noticed you're selling your car. Based on the details in your posting, I think your car is almost exactly what I'm looking for! I'd love to take it out for a test drive, and I don't live far from Main Street. I'm free on July 29, if that suits you. And, if I'm happy with the car, I'd like to purchase it and receive the keys the day before you leave the country. That would suit me perfectly!

I hope to hear from you soon.

Paul Shepard
555-1134

186. Why does Mr. Shepard need to purchase a car?

(A) His new workplace is relatively far.
(B) His current car has broken down.
(C) He wants to visit clients more easily.
(D) He plans to go on a road trip.

187. What aspect of the vehicle does NOT match Mr. Shepard's preferences?

(A) The mileage
(B) The color
(C) The age
(D) The price

188. For what situation does Ms. Ritchie encourage additional inquiries?

(A) When a person lives outside Aldershot
(B) When a person needs to change a purchase date
(C) When a person wants to pay by credit card
(D) When a person wants extra items

189. Why does Mr. Shepard send the e-mail?

(A) To confirm that he wishes to make a purchase
(B) To negotiate a price for a used car
(C) To inquire about a vehicle's specifications
(D) To make an arrangement to test a vehicle

190. When would Mr. Shepard prefer to take ownership of the car?

(A) On July 29
(B) On August 30
(C) On August 31
(D) On September 6

GO ON TO THE NEXT PAGE

Questions 191-195 refer to the following e-mails and article.

E-Mail Message

To: Fiona Trasker <ftrasker@bestaviation.com>
From: Martin Bianucci <mbianucci@vortexentertainment.com>
Date: June 18
Subject: Private Jet

Dear Fiona,

I appreciate your taking the time to speak with me over the phone yesterday. As I mentioned, I am looking for a new private jet that I can use to attend meetings and events around the world. I'm happy to consider used planes, as long as I can purchase them outright and receive full ownership. Ideally, I would prefer something that is less than ten years old and capable of long-haul trips. I'll consider anything in the price range of $12 million to $20 million. Of course, I would expect the interior of the jet to have an attractive, contemporary design, and it should be able to comfortably accommodate at least 15 passengers.

I'd like to secure my new plane relatively quickly, but I need to find a buyer for my current one first. If I can find a buyer for my current plane in early-July, I'd be willing to purchase my new plane on July 15 in preparation for an awards show in New York City at the end of the month. I know that a new used plane may require some modifications before I use it to visit a public event.

Sincerely,

Martin Bianucci

To:	Martin Bianucci <mbianucci@vortexentertainment.com>
From:	Fiona Trasker <ftrasker@bestaviation.com>
Date:	June 21
Subject:	Re: Private Jet

Dear Mr. Bianucci,

I've compiled a shortlist of some used private jets that match your specifications. I will schedule viewings for us once you let me know which days and times you would be available.

1. Private Jet: Air Wave 60
    Purchase Price: $20 million
    Details: Includes an advanced air circulation system that improves air flow and leaves passengers feeling refreshed at the end of their journey.

2. Private Jet: Slip Stream 500
    Purchase Price: $16 million
    Details: Includes satellite phone, wireless network, and entertainment system. Still has the logo of the original owner's company on each wing. These will need to be removed.

3. Private Jet: Canopy Flyer 55S
    Purchase price: $13 million
    Details: Features advanced sound suppression system that reduces noise by 20 percent. Spacious cabin with three separate living areas and four bathrooms.

Sincerely,

Fiona Trasker

Vortex Entertainment CEO Buys New Airplane

By Colin Morrow

LOS ANGELES (July 30)- Martin Bianucci, CEO of the music and film production company Vortex Entertainment, has purchased himself a Slip Stream 500 private jet, which he has named "Bianucci One." He boarded it for the first time yesterday when he flew into New York for an awards ceremony.

The "Bianucci One" boasts two Rankin Mark III engines that produce a total thrust power of 13,900 lbs. Although its powerful engine makes more noise than those of some other planes, you cannot hear it in the cabin at all because of the newly-equipped advanced sound-absorbing system. When the aircraft is full of crew and passengers, it can travel impressive distances of up to 8,065 kilometers.

Mr. Bianucci's new jet may not seat as many people as his old one, but it comes with a wide array of modern amenities and technologies. However, the cost of running the airplane will total approximately $1 million per year.

191. Who most likely is Ms. Trasker?

(A) An airline employee
(B) A sales representative
(C) A flying instructor
(D) An event planner

192. What is indicated about Mr. Bianucci?

(A) He would prefer to buy a brand-new jet.
(B) He spent more money than originally planned.
(C) He successfully sold his old jet.
(D) He met with Ms. Trasker at his business premises.

193. What is indicated about "Bianucci One"?

(A) It is a newly-built aircraft.
(B) Its original logos were removed.
(C) It was purchased in New York City.
(D) It was previously owned by a celebrity.

194. According to the article, how is Mr. Bianucci's new airplane different from his old one?

(A) It has more powerful engines.
(B) It produces more sound in the cabin.
(C) It can fly for longer durations.
(D) It accommodates fewer passengers.

195. In the article, the word "running" in paragraph 3, line 4, is closest in meaning to

(A) traveling
(B) boarding
(C) operating
(D) approving

GO ON TO THE NEXT PAGE

Questions 196–200 refer to the following e-mails and checklist.

E-Mail Message

To: employment@cartermuseum.org
From: Claire Potter <cpotter@artmail.com>
Date: February 3
Subject: Possible opening

To Whom It May Concern,

I was informed by your current curator that she will be leaving your museum as she is relocating to another city. So I would like to inquire about her position because I have extensive experience as a museum curator.

The museum I currently work at, Humes Gallery, can vouch for my qualifications and my extensive knowledge on paintings from all around the world, especially those from medieval Europe and 15th century Asia.

In addition to this, I have written many scholarly articles for arts journals including *The National Arts Quarterly* and *Arts International*. Most recently, I wrote an essay for *The International Journal of Arts* concerning arts education in public schools. You are welcome to contact any of these publications to verify the quality of my work.

Please tell me what would need to be done to officially apply for this position.

Regards,

Claire Potter

To:	Claire Potter <cpotter@artmail.com>
From:	Glen Insley <ginsley@cartermuseum.org>
Date:	February 4
Subject:	Re: Possible opening

Dear Ms. Potter,

Indeed, our current curator has informed us that she will be leaving our museum within a month. The Carter Museum will be searching for an individual who is knowledgeable about many kinds of art as he or she will need to cover information regarding exhibits in professional publications such as *The International Journal of Arts*, and give guided tours to visitors. Actually, I recognize your name, as I read your recent award-winning article on arts in public schools and found it to be very impressive.

The position of curator at our museum is highly sought-after because we have been the most respected museum since our opening 15 years ago. Therefore, all applicants must submit a formal application to the hiring manager, including a résumé and a cover letter. Additionally, a letter of reference as well as a copy of a scholarly article need to be submitted to our Personnel Office along with the other documents. All applications must also include a recent photograph of you, which will be used for our records, and for your ID card should you be hired. If your application is deemed successful, you will be contacted to schedule an interview.

Regards,

Glen Insley

Personnel director, Carter Museum

Claire Potter

Application Package

For the attention of the hiring manager at The Carter Museum

Documents included:

- ☑ **Current résumé**
- ☑ **Cover letter**
- ☑ **Letter from previous employer**
- ☑ **Copy of published journal article**

196. Why did Ms. Potter send the e-mail?

(A) To schedule a group trip to a museum
(B) To ask about the museum's policy changes
(C) To inquire about a job opportunity
(D) To request information about an art exhibit

197. In what publication did Mr. Insley most likely read Ms. Potter's work?

(A) The National Arts Quarterly
(B) Arts International
(C) The Carter Museum Newsletter
(D) The International Journal of Arts

198. In the second e-mail, the word "cover" in paragraph 1, line 3, is closest in meaning to

(A) protect
(B) verify
(C) include
(D) conceal

199. What is NOT indicated about The Carter Museum?

(A) It has been open for 15 years.
(B) It has won several awards.
(C) It offers tours to visitors.
(D) It contributes work to journals.

200. What required document did Ms. Potter most likely forget to include in her application package?

(A) A reference letter
(B) An ID card
(C) An article sample
(D) A photograph

Stop! This is the end of the test. If you finish before time is called, you may go back to Parts 5, 6, and 7 and check your work.

정답 p.470 / 점수 환산표 p.476

실전모의고사
TEST 6

TEST 6 해설

바로 보기

시작 시간 _____시 _____분

종료 시간 _____시 _____분

▶ 중간에 멈추지 말고 처음부터 끝까지 풀어보세요. 문제를 풀 때는 실전처럼 답안지에 마킹하세요.

READING TEST

In the Reading test, you will read a variety of texts and answer several different types of reading comprehension questions. The entire Reading test will last 75 minutes. There are three parts, and directions are given for each part. You are encouraged to answer as many questions as possible within the time allowed. You must mark your answers on the separate answer sheet. Do not write your answers in your test book.

PART 5

Directions: A word or phrase is missing in each of the sentences below. Four answer choices are given below each sentence. Select the best answer to complete the sentence. Then mark the letter (A), (B), (C), or (D) on your answer sheet.

101. Please ------- that due to unexpected problems with our computer system, you will be unable to access your account until further notice.

(A) note
(B) notes
(C) noted
(D) noting

102. The employees have been advised to issue payment ------- upon receiving an invoice from any of the company's regular suppliers.

(A) contemporarily
(B) moderately
(C) immediately
(D) periodically

103. Because of the recent service interruptions, Vita Tech has decided to ------- the subscription period for all customers free of charge by three months.

(A) extend
(B) promote
(C) evaluate
(D) subscribe

104. With the help from the strategic planning team, our director has been brainstorming ------- ways to increase revenue and cut costs.

(A) creatively
(B) creative
(C) creation
(D) create

105. We're pleased to introduce you to our new accountant, a highly ------- professional who will be joining our team as of next Monday.

(A) known
(B) succeeded
(C) required
(D) qualified

106. With 50 locations to serve you ------- the greater New York area, our customer service is far superior to our competitors'.

(A) to
(B) on
(C) at
(D) in

107. You'd better choose someone else to work on this project because I just can't imagine ------- working well with these tight deadlines.

(A) my
(B) me
(C) I
(D) myself

108. Our head engineer has announced she will be taking a position elsewhere, and as a result, we have begun the search for her -------.

(A) preservation
(B) recruitment
(C) recipient
(D) replacement

109. Most ambitious managers are likely to take ------- from the books and speeches of successful business leaders.

(A) inspire
(B) inspired
(C) inspiring
(D) inspiration

110. The accounting team is always very busy at this time of year as they ------- for the end-of-year rush to review all records and accounts.

(A) make
(B) prepare
(C) manage
(D) head

111. The board members hope to ------- a lot more customers with the launch of the new Web-based advertising campaign.

(A) attract
(B) attractive
(C) attracting
(D) attracted

112. The new safety warden will be responsible for implementing safety ------- and educating staff on how to respond in emergency situations.

(A) recognitions
(B) preferences
(C) inclinations
(D) procedures

113. ------- a significant rise in demand, the expansion of the production facilities has been delayed due to financial difficulties.

(A) Despite
(B) Although
(C) Since
(D) However

114. All staff-wide notices must be approved for circulation by management before being ------- to employees and posted on the bulletin board.

(A) distribute
(B) distributing
(C) distributes
(D) distributed

115. To recognize dedicated employees and ------- a culture of company loyalty, Cloe Inc. grants a special bonus and a month-long vacation to anyone with 10 years of service.

(A) indicate
(B) establish
(C) remain
(D) represent

116. Taking on a host of new clients all at once has benefited the business's finances, but it also has had a negative ------- on employees' work and personal relationships.

(A) effecting
(B) effectively
(C) effective
(D) effect

117. If First Moving hopes to stay ahead of our competition, we need to remain ------- of all new product developments in the market.

(A) aware
(B) timely
(C) current
(D) dated

118. As explained previously, parking fees will increase by $1 per day for all staff members, ------- on weekends and holidays.

(A) but
(B) except
(C) about
(D) yet

119. Rio Electronics Inc.'s Marketing Department is preparing to survey ------- users online on the level of satisfaction with the company's new products.

(A) they
(B) them
(C) theirs
(D) their

GO ON TO THE NEXT PAGE

120. The company president frequently updates all staff on the merger with the Star Entertainment Group, ------- will take place in a few weeks' time.

(A) who
(B) whose
(C) which
(D) how

121. All workers should be ------- of any changes to the work schedule well in advance to give them time to make alternative transportation arrangements.

(A) inform
(B) informing
(C) informs
(D) informed

122. Every six months, an independent company completes a ------- of each employee's sales, and department managers consult it when determining yearly raises.

(A) return
(B) relief
(C) review
(D) revisit

123. Having such a large staff means that in this company one will never have to perform tasks that are ------- their job description.

(A) toward
(B) outside
(C) for
(D) beside

124. To get the best results from your dishwasher, use only those detergents ------- mentioned in the product manual.

(A) courteously
(B) reflectively
(C) relatively
(D) specifically

125. The Finance Department is reminding all staff ------- of the requirements when filling out purchase orders.

(A) to mind
(B) will be mindful
(C) be mindful
(D) to be mindful

126. Attendance in the information technology workshops is encouraged, ------- staff members are limited to one free out-of-town session per year.

(A) such as
(B) nevertheless
(C) because
(D) although

127. Don't be afraid to ------- a change in our factory's work procedures if you think it would improve our efficiency.

(A) approach
(B) appoint
(C) initiate
(D) launch

128. To celebrate the store's 15th anniversary, all items will be discounted an extra 15% in ------- of our dedicated customers.

(A) appreciate
(B) appreciating
(C) appreciation
(D) appreciated

129. ------- managers and supervisors are invited to attend a conference on effective leadership where they will learn how to improve workplace morale and productivity.

(A) Every
(B) All
(C) Almost
(D) Each

130. The new logo represents our style well through its sharp lines, minimal color, and overall -------.

(A) simple
(B) simplify
(C) simplicity
(D) simply

PART 6

Directions: Read the texts that follow. A word, phrase, or sentence is missing in parts of each text. Four answer choices for each question are given below the text. Select the best answer to complete the text. Then mark the letter (A), (B), (C) or (D) on your answer sheet.

Questions 131-134 refer to the following notice.

All Springfield employees,

Friday, March 13, will be our fourth annual charity golf tournament. ------- from the tournament will
        131.

benefit the local homeless shelter. If you have not signed up to play in the tournament, you can speak

with Jim Brewer. Although Jim retired last month, he will remain the chief organizer of this year's

event. Even if you do not wish to participate in the tournament, you can still contribute. ------- . To
                                                                                   132.

help out, you can sign up with Cathy Corbin by calling at 555-3528.

The tournament will begin ------- at 8:00 A.M., and it will end by 3:00 P.M. All employees who -------
                       133.   **134.**

in the tournament will have a day off on Monday, March 16. We trust that the tournament will be

a fun recreational activity for golfers and non-golfers alike. More importantly, we hope we can raise

enough funds to make a difference in the lives of homeless people in our city.

131. (A) Successes
(B) Outcomes
(C) Proceeds
(D) Courses

132. (A) Volunteers will be asked to assist in the running of the tournament.
(B) We appreciate all of the hard work he put into organizing the event this year.
(C) Last year's event was won by Derek Bowman in the HR Department.
(D) Tickets are limited to three per person and may be purchased by the general public.

133. (A) promptly
(B) previously
(C) consequently
(D) urgently

134. (A) participating
(B) participate
(C) to participate
(D) participation

GO ON TO THE NEXT PAGE

Questions 135-138 refer to the following article.

You can now do most of your shopping without ever leaving the comfort of your own home. You can purchase appliances and furniture from various companies' online catalogues. You can order books online, or even download them ------- to your e-reader device.
135.

-------, while more and more vendors are adding online shopping to their Web sites, many are still
136.
reluctant to make the jump to cyberspace. For instance, while some might be willing to buy, say, a new sofa over the Internet, most people probably want to see it in person and try sitting in it before committing to buying it. For some businesses, offering online shopping involves incurring extra delivery expenses, which means either making less profit or charging customers more for online orders than they would pay in store.

The shift to online shopping has also been slowed by demographic realities. -------. In some, the
137.
majority of citizens are approaching or past retirement age. These people are often not very tech savvy, ------- they make up the bulk of many businesses' customer bases.
138.

135. (A) directed
(B) directing
(C) direction
(D) directly

136. (A) However
(B) Therefore
(C) In fact
(D) In addition

137. (A) For instance, high-speed Internet is not available in some areas.
(B) Western countries mostly have aging populations now.
(C) This makes it expensive for some of the customers.
(D) The number of new products released each year is increasing.

138. (A) otherwise
(B) still
(C) yet
(D) despite

Questions 139-142 refer to the following e-mail.

To: Gary Harlowe <gharlowe@denizen.com>
From: Tamara Jenner <tjenner@eazymail.net>
Subject: Computer Programmer Position
Date: October 16

Dear Mr. Harlowe,

-------. This is a role that I feel I would be ideally suited for, and I would be extremely proud to work
139.
at a company as well-established as Denizen Systems. However, I regret to inform you that, even if

you select me, I would be unable to ------- the position.
140.

Due to family commitments, I will be relocating to Rochester at the beginning of next year, and the

distance ------- my new hometown and Denizen's headquarters in Scottsdale would be too large.
141.
Commuting would take up too much of my time, especially ------- the rush hour traffic on
142.
Highway 42.

I hope you find an ideal candidate for the position, and I wish you and your company much success

in your future endeavors.

Regards,

Tamara Jenner

---

139. (A) I am writing to inquire about available positions.
(B) It has come to my attention that we need to hire new staff.
(C) We are delighted to make you an offer of employment.
(D) Thank you for giving me the opportunity to interview for the job.

140. (A) accept
(B) perform
(C) apply
(D) change

141. (A) among
(B) opposite
(C) between
(D) within

142. (A) considered
(B) consider
(C) consideration
(D) considering

GO ON TO THE NEXT PAGE

Questions 143-146 refer to the following memo.

MEMO

To: All Security Personnel
From: Greg Davidson, Chief Security Officer
Date: August 16
RE: New Security Measures

As many of you are undoubtedly already aware, we have recently suffered a series of security breaches. While most didn't lead to any serious problems, the last incident almost cost us blueprints ------- several million dollars. Fortunately, we were able to recover them before they fell into the
143.
hands of our competitors. ------- .
                     144.

First of all, you must now scan the ID cards of everyone coming into the facility. There will be no ------- . This is true even for our highest-ranking employees.
145.

Also, all computers must be checked to ensure that they have the proper security software installed on them and that they are fully protected.

Finally, after closing time, security must check the entire facility to make sure no one is staying late without ------- permission from their supervisors. Anyone found in the building without such
          146.
permission must provide a detailed written account of why he or she has remained on the premises.

Thank you in advance for your compliance.

Greg Davidson

---

143. (A) worth
     (B) expensive
     (C) valued
     (D) priced

144. (A) It will be extremely difficult to replace these documents.
     (B) Therefore, we are implementing a new set of security policies.
     (C) So, please think carefully before sharing information with other people.
     (D) Thank you for your attention on this serious matter.

145. (A) submissions
     (B) exceptions
     (C) transactions
     (D) correlations

146. (A) write
     (B) writing
     (C) wrote
     (D) written

Directions: In this part you will read a selection of texts, such as magazine and newspaper articles, e-mails, and instant messages. Each text or set of texts is followed by several questions. Select the best answer for each question and mark the letter (A), (B), (C), or (D) on your answer sheet.

Questions 147-148 refer to the following advertisement.

Vacancy: Friendly, Organized Individual Required

As one of the leading law firms in the state of Maine, Brown, Franklin & Maguire is delighted to announce an exciting opportunity for the ideal candidate.

Specializing in financial law, our law firm has been in existence for over 50 years. We are now searching for a new colleague to welcome customers at our front reception desk. Preferably, applicants will have at least five years of experience in a similar role and be well acquainted with the ManageMate IT software package. As well as a monthly salary, the successful candidate will also be eligible to take advantage of the travel coupons given to all employees.

Please note: The company car and use of our lakeside resort have been discontinued and are no longer included in our employment packages.

---

147. What position is being advertised?

(A) IT consultant
(B) Lawyer
(C) Financial director
(D) Receptionist

148. According to the advertisement, what do Brown, Franklin & Maguire employees receive?

(A) Travel vouchers
(B) Use of resort facilities
(C) A monthly bonus
(D) A company car

GO ON TO THE NEXT PAGE

Questions 149-150 refer to the following text-message chain.

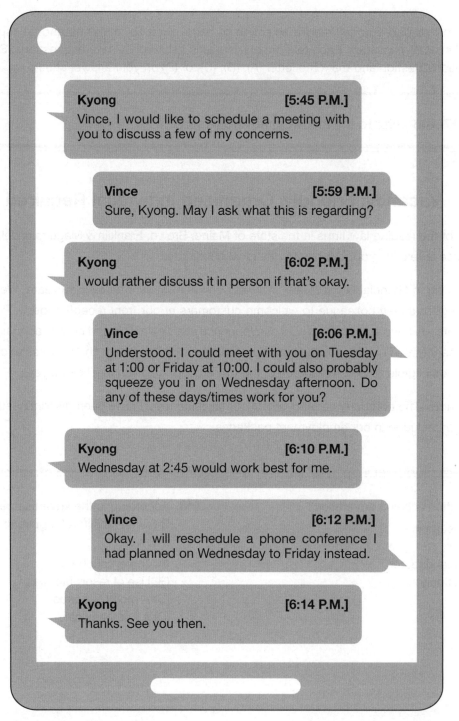

Kyong [5:45 P.M.]
Vince, I would like to schedule a meeting with you to discuss a few of my concerns.

Vince [5:59 P.M.]
Sure, Kyong. May I ask what this is regarding?

Kyong [6:02 P.M.]
I would rather discuss it in person if that's okay.

Vince [6:06 P.M.]
Understood. I could meet with you on Tuesday at 1:00 or Friday at 10:00. I could also probably squeeze you in on Wednesday afternoon. Do any of these days/times work for you?

Kyong [6:10 P.M.]
Wednesday at 2:45 would work best for me.

Vince [6:12 P.M.]
Okay. I will reschedule a phone conference I had planned on Wednesday to Friday instead.

Kyong [6:14 P.M.]
Thanks. See you then.

149. At 6:06 P.M., what does Vince mean when he says, "Understood"?

(A) He understands Kyong's problem.
(B) He acknowledges that a problem has been solved
(C) He already knows Kyong has a busy schedule.
(D) He believes that the issue is private.

150. What does Vince indicate he will do?

(A) He will change his plans for Wednesday.
(B) He will have a phone conference on Wednesday.
(C) He will meet with Kyong immediately.
(D) He will cancel his Friday meeting.

Questions **151-152** refer to the following memo.

To: Shop Floor Staff
Subject: Policy Changes
Date: September 26

As you all know, it's important that we look our best when serving customers. A professional appearance presents a professional image of our company. With this in mind, we have taken the decision to implement a staff uniform. The colors selected are green polo shirts with orange trousers to match our corporate logo. All employees are advised to come along to the team briefing next Monday morning at 9:00 A.M. This will allow you time to try on the garments before the policy goes into effect.

Thanks in advance,

Nick Rangle
Human Resources
Garden World Ltd.

151. What is the memo mainly about?
(A) Alterations to a hiring policy
(B) The redesign of a logo
(C) Changes to a schedule
(D) A new dress code

152. What does Mr. Rangle recommend that employees do?
(A) Attend a meeting
(B) Speak to a manager
(C) Purchase some clothes
(D) Serve customers quickly

GO ON TO THE NEXT PAGE

WORK REQUEST

Date: September 1
Employer: East Coast Products
Address: 2335 Cottonwood Road
City: Savannah
State: Georgia
Zip code: 31425

Nature of business: Pulp and Paper
Project Start Date: January 1
Project Completion Date: March 31

Project Summary: Installation of specialty paper machine – including installation of electrical, mechanical, control software, etc. The new machine is to be integrated into an existing paper plant, but in its own building. Regarding the installation process, Savannah-based companies will be given preference.

153. What is the purpose of the form?

(A) To report on a company's relocation
(B) To compare different factory machines
(C) To outline an upcoming project
(D) To request repairs at a paper plant

154. What is indicated about East Coast Products?

(A) It has several job vacancies at its facility.
(B) It will expand its range of manufactured products.
(C) It prefers to work with local companies.
(D) It plans to move one of its existing buildings.

Silver City Library

Summer Schedule and Changes

June 11

Please note that the Silver City Library

will commence its summer hours on June 15.

Monday – Wednesday	10 A.M. – 5 P.M.
Thursday – Friday	10 A.M. – 6 P.M.
Saturday	10 A.M. – 4 P.M.
Sunday	12 noon – 3 P.M.

Lending durations will also be different during the summer.

Books	3 weeks
Magazines	1 week
Videos/DVDs	2 days
CDs (music or talking books)	2 weeks

Regular library hours and services will resume on September 15.

155. On what day can library members check out a book after 5:00 P.M.?

(A) Monday
(B) Wednesday
(C) Friday
(D) Saturday

156. Which item would have the shortest lending duration?

(A) A mystery novel
(B) A medical research journal
(C) A popular movie
(D) A band's latest record

157. What will happen in September?

(A) The opening hours will change again.
(B) The library will be closed on the 15th.
(C) The library will cease offering movies.
(D) All library materials will be due back.

GO ON TO THE NEXT PAGE

TEST 6

Questions 158-160 refer to the following memo.

To: All Employees
From: Ron Sellers, Office Manager
Date: October 23
Subject: Office management

Over the last month we have been upgrading our computer systems, including both software and hardware. — [1] —. The upgrades include the following:

- A new high-end color laser printer in each work area of the office. — [2] —. The company will no longer be asking a print shop to create our promotional materials. If you need help getting started, ask the graphic designer to show you how to print the items you require. — [3] —.

- All employees now have laptops instead of desktop computer models. While in the office, please be sure to use the attached locks so that they cannot be easily removed. — [4] —.

- Please note that after this week, hand-written or e-mailed expense reports and timesheets will no longer be accepted. Our corporate software should be used at all times, especially now that everyone can take their computer home with them. We do not have anyone available to enter your information into the database, so if you do not do it, you will not receive your pay.

Thank you for your attention to these matters. Please discuss any questions with your immediate supervisor.

Ron

---

158. What is the main topic of the memo?

(A) Hiring a new manager
(B) How to design flyers
(C) Ordering laptop computers
(D) New office equipment

159. According to the memo, what should employees not do?

(A) Take their computers home
(B) E-mail their timesheets
(C) Print their own brochures
(D) Lock up their computers

160. In which of the positions marked [1], [2], [3], and [4] does the following sentence best belong?

"These are to be used to reproduce your own brochures and marketing flyers."

(A) [1]
(B) [2]
(C) [3]
(D) [4]

Questions 161-164 refer to the following online chat discussion.

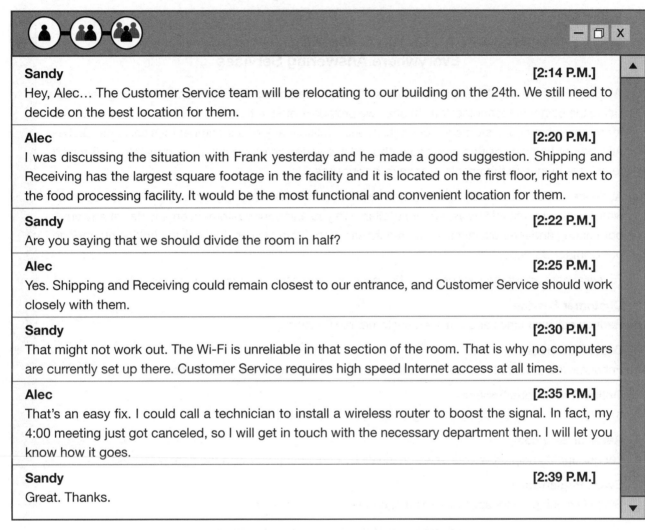

Sandy [2:14 P.M.]

Hey, Alec… The Customer Service team will be relocating to our building on the 24th. We still need to decide on the best location for them.

Alec [2:20 P.M.]

I was discussing the situation with Frank yesterday and he made a good suggestion. Shipping and Receiving has the largest square footage in the facility and it is located on the first floor, right next to the food processing facility. It would be the most functional and convenient location for them.

Sandy [2:22 P.M.]

Are you saying that we should divide the room in half?

Alec [2:25 P.M.]

Yes. Shipping and Receiving could remain closest to our entrance, and Customer Service should work closely with them.

Sandy [2:30 P.M.]

That might not work out. The Wi-Fi is unreliable in that section of the room. That is why no computers are currently set up there. Customer Service requires high speed Internet access at all times.

Alec [2:35 P.M.]

That's an easy fix. I could call a technician to install a wireless router to boost the signal. In fact, my 4:00 meeting just got canceled, so I will get in touch with the necessary department then. I will let you know how it goes.

Sandy [2:39 P.M.]

Great. Thanks.

161. What is indicated about the company?

(A) It is seeking new employees.
(B) It is moving a department.
(C) It is switching Internet providers.
(D) It is purchasing new computers.

162. What did Frank say about the Customer Service team members?

(A) They have complained about the Internet connection.
(B) They will replace the Shipping and Receiving staff.
(C) They will arrive on the 24th.
(D) They should be situated on the first floor.

163. At 2:30 P.M., what does Sandy mean when she writes, "That might not work out"?

(A) She believes the Customer Service staff are unproductive.
(B) She thinks a room is unsuitable for Customer Service.
(C) She recommends changing the date of a project.
(D) She would prefer to work in Shipping and Receiving.

164. Which department will Alec most likely contact at 4 P.M.?

(A) Shipping and Receiving
(B) Customer Service
(C) Food Processing
(D) Information Technology

GO ON TO THE NEXT PAGE

Globe-All
Everywhere Answering Services

We are one of the world's leading providers of outsourced contact centers and answering services. Using the best that technology has to offer, we provide robust, efficient, and cost-effective solutions for our partners and customers around the world. Unlike many of our competitor's services, Globe-All's proven package of incoming and outbound answering solutions can be completely customized to suit the unique requirements of today's businesses.

At Globe-All, we continually look for new and improved methods to help our customers connect with people in profitable ways. We are available to you and your customers on any day at any time, both during and after business hours, regardless of the time of year. Just call the hotline number on our Contact Us page.

To learn more about the services we offer, click on one of the business categories below.

Customer Service
Reduce call wait times and maintain customer relationships.

Order Placement
Enhance your ads for the Web, TV, radio and print by linking to our sales force.

Online Receptions Services
Keep your costs in check by utilizing our virtual receptionist.

Referral Services
Let our agents help grow your sales channels by connecting you with the right matches.

Event Registration
Simplify signing up for special seminars, conferences or classes.

Globe-All. We have answers for everything.

---

165. According to the Web page, what is special about Globe-All?

(A) It helps businesses grow internationally.
(B) It only accepts inbound calls from customers.
(C) It develops services to meet customers' needs.
(D) Its services cost much less than those of its rivals.

166. What service is NOT offered by Globe-All?

(A) 24-hour customer service
(B) Advertisement production
(C) Sales networking
(D) Conference registration

167. According to the Web page, how can Globe-All representatives be contacted?

(A) By sending an e-mail
(B) By using a chat program
(C) By calling a number
(D) By completing an online form

Questions 168-171 refer to the following page from a brochure.

Glacier Bay Tours and Cruises

Have you always dreamed of experiencing the beauty of Glacier Bay aboard a ship?

Glacier Bay Tours and Cruises offers you a choice of four unforgettable boat cruises. — [1] —. Ask at our information booth about receiving a discount when you book two or more cruises for two or more adults. To view the complete schedule, visit our website: glacierbaytoursandcruises.com.

Historic Cruise $85 per person
Join Captain John aboard our tall ship and enjoy a 3-hour, guided tour of Glacier Bay. An experienced local guide will point out cultural landmarks, teaching you about the history of this beautiful bay. — [2] —.

Wilderness Cruise $250 per person
An experienced guide will lead a small group of 10 on an eight-hour wilderness adventure. Depending on the time of year, the group will engage in two of the three following activities: fishing, whale watching, or bear watching. After a delicious lunch at a local restaurant (cost of food included in cruise fee), the group will hike the gorgeous Arbor Trail and delight in sites such as Charles Falls and Silver Cliff.

Stargazer Cruise $125 per person
Enjoy a two-hour guided tour of the bay and then feast in our on-board dining room (cost of food included in cruise fee). Our cruise cuisine has been awarded the Traveler's Choice Award five years in a row! — [3] —. During your four-course dinner, you will be entertained with the sweet sounds of local jazz piano legend Arturo Bernal. Finish the evening off with an informative astronomy lesson on deck. — [4] —.

Culture Cruise $105 per person
After a two-hour guided tour of the bay, the group will disembark in Seaward Bay and hike to a nearby village. There, tourists will learn about the culture of the local people and enjoy a cultural presentation put on by local musicians, singers, actors, and artists.

168. According to the brochure, why should someone visit the information booth?

(A) To save money on bookings for multiple cruises
(B) To request that additional activities be added to an itinerary
(C) To inquire about the likelihood of seeing whales
(D) To learn about fitness levels required for hiking

169. Which cruise's schedule is dependent upon the season?

(A) Historic Cruise
(B) Wilderness Cruise
(C) Stargazer Cruise
(D) Culture Cruise

170. What is true about the Stargazer and Culture Cruise packages?

(A) They appeal to animal lovers.
(B) They include music.
(C) They are the cheapest options.
(D) They have both received awards.

171. In which of the positions marked [1], [2], [3], and [4] does the following sentence best belong?

"Each offers its own unique way to experience one of our area's most precious natural wonders."

(A) [1]
(B) [2]
(C) [3]
(D) [4]

GO ON TO THE NEXT PAGE

Optimized for the Outdoors

Recent research has concluded that human beings are more suited to working and living outside than we realize. Some interesting facts are coming to light.

We all know that tribal peoples lived mostly outside, as did the earliest farmers and workers. Until the advent of electricity, people's lives were ruled largely by cycles of daylight and dark, and no one worked far from a window. It appears that we have evolved to do our best when we maintain some link to the great outdoors. Several studies have recently been conducted that show this.

One study examined the effect of crowded city streets on the brain. Subjects were asked to walk for an hour along a busy street while others were instructed to walk in a large park for an hour. When their brains were mapped immediately afterward, it was shown that those who had walked in the park had less activity in the areas of the brain that show anxiety.

Another study showed that in inner-city slum areas, just the presence of a few trees will lower the rates of violent crime in the area. In particular, the rates for reported family violence decrease.

It seems that we need green, growing things in our environment in order for our minds and brains to function well. Employers and business owners would do well to remember this.

172. The word "maintain" in paragraph 2, line 6, is closest in meaning to

(A) repair
(B) keep
(C) believe
(D) claim

173. What is mentioned about the time before electricity was invented?

(A) Workers were given more breaks.
(B) People were evolving faster.
(C) Windows were more important.
(D) Workplaces were less comfortable.

174. In what section of a newspaper would the article most likely be found?

(A) Gardening
(B) Business
(C) Real estate
(D) Travel

175. What does the article suggest happens when people are around trees?

(A) They find it easier to sleep.
(B) Their brain function speeds up.
(C) They produce a higher quality of work.
(D) They become less aggressive

GO ON TO THE NEXT PAGE

Questions 176-180 refer to the following e-mails.

From:	John Kroft <jkroft@topendmeats.com>
To:	New Zealand Venison Direct Sales <sales@newzealandvenison.com>
Subject:	Product Inquiry

To Whom It May Concern,

We are the largest importer of high quality foreign meats in the New Forest area and would like to make some inquiries regarding your venison, which I recently noticed was advertised on www. kiwimeat.net.

Can you please let us know which cuts of venison you currently offer and the price range of each type? We are interested in venison steak, sausages, and stock and require some samples of each before we place an order. Additionally, we would like to know how long it takes for your products to reach England and if there are any discounts available for bulk orders.

Finally, do you have any testimonials for your products from other buyers that we could view? Also, can you explain why your prices are lower than your competitors? Thank you.

Yours faithfully,

Jon Kroft
Top End Meats

E-Mail Message

From:	Dave Williams <dwilliams@newzealandvenison.com>
To:	John Kroft <jkroft@topendmeats.com>
Subject:	RE: Product Inquiry
Attachment:	📎 price_list_and_order_form.doc

Dear Mr. Kroft,

Thank you for your inquiry on September 20 in which you asked about our venison products.

Our venison is well known throughout the world as it is GE free and generally regarded as the best quality available. We have many testimonials from buyers that we can e-mail to you on request. Our prices are lower than our competitors' because we buy our products directly from local farmers. Since our prices are already so competitive, we only offer discounts on large bulk orders over 600 kilograms. We do, however, offer complimentary samples of all our products.

We have sent, separately, samples of all of our venison products for you to try. As the busy Christmas season is approaching, we would advise you to place an order as soon as possible. Please be aware that once products are shipped, refunds are not possible.

Thank you once again for your interest in our products.

Yours sincerely,

Dave Williams
Managing Director, New Zealand Venison Direct

176. How did Mr. Kroft most likely find out about New Zealand Venison Direct?

(A) He found its ads on a Web site.
(B) He heard about it from other meat importers.
(C) He attended an industry convention.
(D) He visited New Zealand.

177. What does Mr. Kroft want to do before he places an order?

(A) Talk to his co-workers
(B) Try some samples
(C) Contact a rival company
(D) Visit a production plant

178. Why is New Zealand Venison Direct cheaper than other companies?

(A) It runs its own farms.
(B) Its shipping times are longer than average.
(C) It always buys meat in bulk.
(D) It buys directly from producers.

179. What did Mr. Williams attach to his e-mail?

(A) A catalog
(B) A business contract
(C) A contact list
(D) An order form

180. What issue mentioned by Mr. Kroft did Mr. Williams NOT address?

(A) A request for customer testimonials
(B) An explanation of low pricing
(C) The shipping time to England
(D) Information regarding bulk orders

GO ON TO THE NEXT PAGE

Give us a new look and be entered to win!!

Live Landscape Design wants a new look and we need your help. Design a new logo for our company and be entered to win a makeover for your garden and a $10,000 trip to visit famous gardens in Italy, France and Spain.

You need to design a bold logo which reflects our company image. We are committed to preserving nature and helping people achieve their landscape design goals. The logo should be submitted on an A4-sized page and you will also need to include a 500-word submission which explains the meaning of the logo. We require both a color and black and white version of the logo.

Be aware that if you win the competition, you must agree to a photograph of yourself being published. You need to be over 18 years of age to enter.

You may enter anytime between November 21 and December 30. The winner will be notified on January 15.

Please submit your entries by e-mail to Lily Penny at l.penny@livelandscape.com.

From:	Hunter Jones <hjones@hunterdesign.co.uk>
To:	Lily Penny <l.penny@livelandscapes.com>
Date:	November 23
Subject:	Competition questions

Dear Ms. Penny,

I am writing regarding your recently advertised logo design competition. I have a few questions that I hope you can answer for me.

Is the competition only open to amateur designers, or can professional designers also submit entries? I work as a designer at a landscape company, so that is why I am asking this question. Also, is the competition only open to US residents, or can residents of other countries enter the competition? Are late entries accepted?

I hope you will be able to answer my questions and that I will be able to enter the competition. I'd love to win the trip overseas, as I always enjoy visiting those countries.

Yours sincerely,

Hunter Jones

181. What is a requirement to enter the competition?

(A) You must be an American citizen.
(B) You must be an experienced gardener.
(C) You must be at least 19.
(D) You must be a professional designer.

182. What needs to be included with the entry?

(A) A color photograph
(B) A letter of recommendation
(C) A detailed résumé
(D) A written description

183. When will participants find out if they have won?

(A) November 21
(B) November 23
(C) December 30
(D) January 15

184. What information is NOT requested by Mr. Jones?

(A) Whether he can send his entry after the closing date
(B) Whether non-US residents may enter the competition
(C) Whether the prize can be exchanged for cash
(D) Whether professionals are eligible to participate

185. What is suggested about Mr. Jones?

(A) He is an employee of Live Landscape Design.
(B) He does not currently have a garden.
(C) He has traveled to France in the past.
(D) He will assist in judging competition submissions.

GO ON TO THE NEXT PAGE

Questions 186-190 refer to the following notice, e-mail, and feedback form.

Fiesta Tropico Resort - August Guest Activities

All activities are free of charge for guests unless otherwise stated.

When?	What?	Who?
Every Monday/Wednesday	**Scuba Diving Lesson:** Explore the beautiful underwater world beneath the waves surrounding El Nido.	Led by Olly Galvez
Every Tuesday/Friday	**Fire Dancing on the Beach:** Your instructor will teach you the graceful art of traditional fire dancing.	Led by Isla Agustin
Every Wednesday/Saturday	**Island Hopping Tour:** Experience numerous small islands around El Nido and have lunch on your boat.	Led by Ricky Reyes
Every Thursday/Sunday	**Filipino Cooking:** Learn to cook local Filipino dishes. (Total cost of ingredients added to guests' bill.)	Led by Martin Alonzo

Please visit the Guest Activities Office to obtain detailed timetables and to register.

E-Mail Message

From: Jenny Kim <jennykim@fiestatropico.com>
To: Activities Team Members <activitiesteam@fiestatropico.com>
Subject: Important developments
Date: August 1

Hi everyone,

I'd like to draw your attention to this month's activities program. I've just found out that Isla Agustin and Martin Alonzo will be attending an advanced training workshop from August 7 to August 13, so they'll be unavailable to lead their respective activities during that time. Therefore, I will lead Isla's activities and Jenny Gonzales will lead Martin's. Once Isla and Martin come back to work on August 14, everything will continue as normal.

Regards,

Jenny Kim
Activities Team Manager
Fiesta Tropico Resort

Fiesta Tropico Resort

Name: Cathy Beringer

Date: August 15

Number of guests: 4

Date of stay: August 8 – August 12

Feedback:

I'd like to thank you for the excellent service you provide at your resort. I recently stayed there with my family, and we all had so much fun taking part in the activities on offer. I was unable to join the excursion with Mr. Reyes, but my traveling companions seemed to have a great time. My husband and I thought the fire dancing class was a lot of fun, and he is planning to utilize some of the skills he learned in Ms. Gonzales's class in our kitchen at home. Also, my mom and dad had a great time with Mr. Galvez. They will use all of his tips and techniques during their trip to Bali in October.

SUBMIT

186. When does an activity that includes an extra charge take place?
(A) Every Wednesday
(B) Every Friday
(C) Every Saturday
(D) Every Sunday

187. What is the purpose of the e-mail?
(A) To recommend two new staff members
(B) To outline some schedule changes
(C) To encourage staff to attend a workshop
(D) To introduce new activities for guests

188. In the e-mail, the phrase "found out" in paragraph 1, line 1, is closest in meaning to
(A) searched for
(B) located
(C) looked at
(D) learned

189. Who taught Ms. Beringer how to perform a fire dance?
(A) Mr. Galvez
(B) Ms. Kim
(C) Mr. Reyes
(D) Mr. Alonzo

190. What are Ms. Beringer's parents most likely intending to do in Bali?
(A) Take a tour of some islands
(B) Learn local dances
(C) Enjoy some scuba diving
(D) Make traditional food

GO ON TO THE NEXT PAGE

Questions 191-195 refer to the following flyer, customers review, and online response.

Madras Magic – Authentic Indian Cuisine

If you're looking for authentic Indian food cooked using traditional family recipes, Madras Magic is the place for you!

We have several branches throughout Los Angeles, and our award-winning food has been recommended in several leading local food guides.

Check out our newly-opened branch at 547 Wilbur Road! It boasts wonderful food, a courteous wait staff, and amazing decorations.

Regular Menu: Seven days a week
Buffet Style Menu available: Saturday and Sunday

---

http://www.losangelesguide.com/restaurants/indian/madrasmagic/review089   ▼   — ▢ X

Rating : 8.5/10

This restaurant is really worth checking out. I eat out fairly often, and Indian cuisine is one of my favorites, and the new branch of Madras Magic on Wilbur Road is one of the best places I've tried. It has a very extensive menu, and the interior design is very welcoming. Although some dishes on the standard menu are a little expensive, I'm sure they are worth it. Since we had the buffet, we were able to try a wide variety of dishes. The only complaint I have about the place is the lack of vegetarian dishes. My wife struggled to find anything that she could eat. In spite of this, I was generally very impressed with the service and the food.

Posted
by *Christopher Earle*
February 11

Response from Anjit Anwar (Proprietor, Madras Magic)

We were very pleased to read that you had a pleasurable experience at the new Wilbur Road branch of Madras Magic. Please allow me to address the issue you raised in your review. I'm sorry that one aspect of the meal failed to meet your expectations. Our Reed Avenue branch might be a better choice for you the next time you are dining with your wife. The branch on Reed Avenue offers the same excellent dining experience as the one on Wilbur Road, but it has some extra offerings that your wife would enjoy. However, this branch is on the outskirts of town, so it may not be convenient to visit. You can check the location and menu at www.madrasmagic.com/branches/reedavenue.

Posted
February 13

191. What is NOT mentioned in the flyer about the Wilbur Road branch of Madras Magic?

(A) The quality of the food
(B) The attractiveness of the interior
(C) The affordability of meals
(D) The politeness of servers

192. What is indicated in the customer review?

(A) The Wilbur Road branch of Madras Magic is difficult to locate.
(B) Mr. Earle was pleased with his meal at Madras Magic.
(C) Madras Magic's prices are very low compared to its rivals.
(D) Diners should book a table at Madras Magic in advance.

193. What is suggested about Mr. Earle?

(A) He dined at Madras Magic on a weekend.
(B) He has allergies to specific ingredients.
(C) He rarely goes out to eat Indian food.
(D) He has visited several branches of Madras Magic.

194. Why does Mr. Anwar recommend the Reed Avenue branch to Mr. Earle?

(A) It has a larger selection of desserts.
(B) It is more conveniently located.
(C) It is more reasonably priced.
(D) It has more vegetarian options.

195. In the online response, the word "raised" in paragraph 1, line 2, is closest in meaning to

(A) increased
(B) brought up
(C) looked after
(D) inquired

TEST 6

Chester Film Appreciation Society (CFAS)

The CFAS is proud to announce a special event to honor one of our local celebrities. For almost 25 years, director Julius Beauly has not only been an accomplished documentary maker, but also a keen supporter of arts and culture in our local community. We will host a film retrospective to honor Mr. Beauly on September 12 at 2 P.M. in the main auditorium of Edison Movie Theater. A talk by renowned film critic Harvey Miller will follow the triple showing of films.

Julius Beauly's works will be of interest to anyone interested in the birth of cinema. His first documentary, *Stage to Screen*, shows how preferences in the 1900's gradually shifted from theatrical plays to motion pictures, as the film industry became well-established in the US. *Life Through The Lens*, his next documentary, involves interviews with several cameramen who discuss the evolution of their equipment in the early days of cinema. His third documentary, *Stars of Yesteryear* (featuring a musical score composed by Frank Dunwoody), traces the careers of several of the world's first movie stars.

To book seats for the event, please visit www.edisonmovietheater.co.uk. Edison Movie Theater will offer a special rate on some seats for the event. Visit http://www.edisonmovietheater.co.uk/events/cfas for more details.

---

http://www.edisonmovietheater.co.uk/events/cfas ▼ — ☐ X

Special Event: Chester Film Appreciation Society's Julius Beauly Retrospective

Reserve your seat now for the film retrospective on September 12. Attendees are invited to book seats at a special rate available from August 15 to September 4. This price includes free beverages at the snack bar plus a speech by a prominent film critic. For details about this offer and seat availability, call 555-1878.

When making your reservation, use an Osiris credit card and receive 100 reward points if you are part of the Edison Movie Theater Membership Program. We are currently offering a variety of discounts and promotions in conjunction with Osiris. This particular offer is good until the end of September.

Edison Movie Theater

Receipt Date: September 7
Guest: Allan Barrymore
Film: "Julius Beauly Retrospective" (3 films)
Film Showing Date: September 12
Film Showing Time: 2 P.M. to 8:30 P.M.
Seat Number: 3C
Membership Card No.: 938330
Membership Points Awarded: 100
Seat Price: (Chester Film Appreciation Society)
Credit Card Number: XXXX-XXXX-XXX-1987

We hope you enjoy the movie showings!

196. What is featured in all of Mr. Beauly's listed works?

(A) A story about a famous stage actor
(B) A music soundtrack by Frank Dunwoody
(C) A focus on the origins of filmmaking
(D) An emphasis on the role of film crews

197. In the notice, the word "traces" in paragraph 2, line 8, is closest in meaning to

(A) draws
(B) follows
(C) detects
(D) returns

198. What event will be covered by the cost of a seat?

(A) A book signing event
(B) A talk by a celebrity
(C) An on-site filmmaking workshop
(D) A reception with a popular actor

199. What is indicated about the special offer?

(A) It is available on a first come, first served basis.
(B) It covers refreshments and complimentary meals.
(C) It can only be obtained by visiting the theater in person.
(D) It can be applied together with other special offers.

200. What is suggested about Mr. Barrymore?

(A) He visited Edison Movie Theater on September 7.
(B) He helped to organize the film retrospective.
(C) He would prefer not to join the theater's membership program.
(D) He booked seats with an Osiris credit card.

Stop! This is the end of the test. If you finish before time is called, you may go back to Parts 5, 6, and 7 and check your work.

정답 p.470 / 점수 환산표 p.476

실전모의고사
TEST 7

TEST 7 해설

바로 보기

- 시작 시간 _____시 _____분
- 종료 시간 _____시 _____분

▶ 중간에 멈추지 말고 처음부터 끝까지 풀어보세요. 문제를 풀 때는 실전처럼 답안지에 마킹하세요.

READING TEST

In the Reading test, you will read a variety of texts and answer several different types of reading comprehension questions. The entire Reading test will last 75 minutes. There are three parts, and directions are given for each part. You are encouraged to answer as many questions as possible within the time allowed. You must mark your answers on the separate answer sheet. Do not write your answers in your test book.

PART 5

Directions: A word or phrase is missing in each of the sentences below. Four answer choices are given below each sentence. Select the best answer to complete the sentence. Then mark the letter (A), (B), (C), or (D) on your answer sheet.

101. When a recent survey revealed that customer satisfaction rates were low, the CEO of Green Travel completed a report by ------- on how to fix the problem.

(A) him
(B) his
(C) himself
(D) he

102. The brochure for our new product ------- designed to appeal to young adults between the ages of 18 and 24.

(A) has
(B) was
(C) be
(D) are

103. To effectively ------- employees, supervisors must understand their job duties and be willing to listen to their concerns.

(A) compare
(B) relate
(C) manage
(D) locate

104. Prior to providing a cost estimate for your service, please make sure that you understand exactly ------- the client wants.

(A) that
(B) though
(C) what
(D) if

105. Mr. Tanaka wanted to show a short interview filmed with the focus group at the end of his presentation, but there was no DVD player -------.

(A) available
(B) used
(C) occupied
(D) aware

106. Next Monday's sales seminar is intended primarily for full-time employees, but part-time staff are ------- welcome to attend.

(A) also
(B) therefore
(C) beside
(D) yet

107. Olsen Outdoor Sports' annual profits have grown ------- more than fifty percent this year, and we expect similar increases next year.

(A) over
(B) in
(C) by
(D) of

108. Mr. Alvarez, the head of the International Relations Office, is responsible for ------- all client communication written in English.

(A) translate
(B) translated
(C) translating
(D) translation

109. It is vital to keep all manufacturing equipment in good working order since there are no ------- machines.

(A) redundant
(B) inoperable
(C) spare
(D) vacant

110. Experts predict that, with this unstable economy, consumers and bankers alike will become more ------- managing their money on a daily basis.

(A) caution
(B) cautiously
(C) cautious
(D) cautions

111. Pacific Utilities Inc. will charge a late fee of 10 dollars the following month if customers fail ------- make a payment for services.

(A) of
(B) that
(C) to
(D) and

112. Tomorrow's staff meeting will move to Thursday at 9 A.M. in order to ------- the attendance of Mr. Glenn, the sales director.

(A) use up
(B) believe in
(C) make into
(D) allow for

113. We regret to inform you that, due to a recent policy change, new employees will receive ------- after a three-month trial period.

(A) benefited
(B) benefits
(C) benefiting
(D) beneficiaries

114. According to a recent news report, Robertson Telecoms, the largest telephone service provider in the region, improperly managed the personal information of ------- two million customers.

(A) around
(B) within
(C) above
(D) beyond

115. Unfortunately, a second customer called in to report his magazine arrived in the mail with ------- cover torn off.

(A) his
(B) its
(C) her
(D) their

116. Before you accept the position, we recommend you take a few days to review your contract and even seek the ------- of a contract lawyer.

(A) notice
(B) counsel
(C) application
(D) deliberation

117. The board is set to discuss a new strategic plan the day after the company workshop, ------- they will announce the company's new motto, too.

(A) which
(B) then
(C) when
(D) what

118. Ms. Kim was reluctant to purchase the new model before ------- with a mechanic, so the agent gave her a referral to an authorized auto shop.

(A) consults
(B) consulted
(C) consult
(D) consulting

119. Business analysts argue that an increase in the number of large discount stores will ------- lead to the closure of many small, locally-owned retailers.

(A) reservedly
(B) consecutively
(C) thoroughly
(D) ultimately

GO ON TO THE NEXT PAGE

120. Mr. Kelly's leadership strategy includes positive reinforcement, which contributes to a -------, cooperative work environment.

(A) comfort
(B) comforts
(C) comfortable
(D) comfortably

121. The frequent substitution of materials that occurs in the production process is ------- to cause defective products to appear on the market in greater volumes.

(A) essentially
(B) roughly
(C) likely
(D) overly

122. The grand opening event at Marty's Department Store was ----- due to a need for further remodeling work.

(A) postpone
(B) postponement
(C) postpones
(D) postponed

123. Please be advised that our clients are expecting not only ample graphics in our -------, but video content as well.

(A) presented
(B) presenter
(C) presentation
(D) presents

124. After three consecutive months of record-breaking sales, Aviana Inc. was selected as one of the most ------- start-up businesses of the year by Business Beat magazine.

(A) successful
(B) successfully
(C) success
(D) succeed

125. The negative response to our new logo indicates that our customers are strongly loyal to the original one, ------- over 25 years ago.

(A) design
(B) designing
(C) designs
(D) designed

126. To attract young professionals, Jamieson and Sons will pay $5,000 ------- new employees' student loans, provided that they sign a three-year contract with the company.

(A) toward
(B) above
(C) by
(D) on

127. The KMI Knoxville store will be closing at noon on Friday to give the contractors time to ------- for the renovation that will take place over the weekend.

(A) call back
(B) set up
(C) hold on
(D) sign up

128. We need to seriously consider the fact ------- the public perceives us to be an environmentally-friendly company, as our packaging is recyclable.

(A) which
(B) whereas
(C) that
(D) what

129. Mr. Wayne assured management that the installation of the new computer system would ------- the number of errors in financial records.

(A) reduction
(B) reduced
(C) reduces
(D) reduce

130. You can be assured that once today's computer workshop is over, you will be ------- in creating advanced customer databases.

(A) sufficient
(B) proficient
(C) practical
(D) limited

PART 6

Directions: Read the texts that follow. A word, phrase, or sentence is missing in parts of each text. Four answer choices for each question are given below the text. Select the best answer to complete the text. Then mark the letter (A), (B), (C) or (D) on your answer sheet.

Questions 131-134 refer to the following letter.

Dear Ms. Golding,

I am writing in reply to the complaint you sent to our company last Tuesday. After receiving your letter, I ------- the manager in charge of your office building repair work.
131.

After discussing the matter of the substandard roofing repairs with him, I referred the matter to the head of the regional office, ------- requested a full report from the manager.
132.

The complete report concluded that the repairs were not up to standard, as you claim. Accordingly, we will either refund you the amount paid for the work or send another contractor to fix the roof.

-------. I have to inform the regional director of your decision by the end of this month.
133.

I apologize for the problems you ------- , and will do everything I can to resolve this matter as soon
134.
as possible.

Yours sincerely,

Jane Worthington

131. (A) contact
     (B) contacted
     (C) will contact
     (D) should contact

132. (A) who
     (B) what
     (C) he
     (D) which

133. (A) Please confirm which option you would prefer.
     (B) I personally believe that this will be an excellent choice.
     (C) The regional director should contact you about this shortly.
     (D) I promise the report will be completed much sooner next time.

134. (A) to experience
     (B) experience
     (C) experiencing
     (D) have experienced

Questions 135 -138 refer to the following notice.

When you join Huntington Dry Cleaners' customer service database, your details will be retained by our company. We ------- to keep all information up-to-date so that we can contact our customers
135.
with various special offers and discounts. With this in mind, we ask you to ------- permission for us
136.
to retain your information on file for two years.

Your details will only be used by our company. -------. However, on occasion, we may e-mail you to
137.
ask ------- you would like to receive offers from our partner companies.
138.

---

135. (A) strive
(B) assume
(C) contend
(D) state

136. (A) decline
(B) grant
(C) submit
(D) determine

137. (A) We truly apologize for this careless
distribution of secure data.
(B) Your information should be entered by
you using our online form.
(C) They will not be given to other businesses
without your permission.
(D) We assume that's why you choose
Huntington Dry Cleaners.

138. (A) although
(B) either
(C) whether
(D) unless

Questions 139-142 refer to the following e-mail.

From:	Robyn Duncan <r.duncan@hotmedia.com>
To:	Rhys Jones <r.jones@coffeeworks.com>
Date:	September 1
Subject:	Advertising schedule

Dear Mr. Jones,

I am writing regarding your advertising schedule for the month. A few changes ------ recently at
139.
our newspaper while we have been reverting our publication back to a weekly format. ------ the
140.
completion of this transition, your advertising package will need to be rearranged. ------ .
141.

I have put together a new package for you and a complete catalog that outlines available slots and

prices. Could you please arrange a suitable time for us to ------ this matter?
142.

We appreciate your continued business and will do our best to make this transition as smooth and

seamless as possible. I look forward to hearing back from you soon.

Kind regards,

Robyn Duncan

---

139. (A) have made
(B) are made
(C) have been made
(D) had been made

140. (A) Owing to
(B) Prior to
(C) Without
(D) Provided that

141. (A) We have listened carefully to our
customers' suggestions.
(B) However, I am still interested in
purchasing the advertising space.
(C) We hope you continue to enjoy reading
our articles.
(D) For instance, we can no longer offer the
daily advertising you are currently using.

142. (A) reject
(B) discuss
(C) refer
(D) argue

GO ON TO THE NEXT PAGE

Questions 143-146 refer to the following article.

New York, 15 October – Freeville Film Studios Ltd. reported a record profit for the third quarter with a rise of 35 percent. The ------- in revenue can be attributed to the company's recent purchase of rival
143.
movie studio, Skynet Pictures Ltd. Since the merger deal, Freeville Film Studios ------- the largest
144.
film studio in North America. -------, the outlook for the industry as a whole is not so bright. Despite
145.
the upswing in profits, the slow economy has led to a decrease in movie theater attendance. -------.
146.

143. (A) downturn
(B) increase
(C) leveling
(D) development

144. (A) became
(B) will become
(C) had become
(D) has become

145. (A) Nonetheless
(B) Likewise
(C) For example
(D) As a result

146. (A) As a result, the company has recently decided to postpone its expansion plan until next year.
(B) The new film is expected to be released in time for the beginning of the holiday season.
(C) Freeville Film Studios just can't seem to make a wrong decision.
(D) It remains to be seen if Skynet Pictures will continue to be competitive.

PART 7

Directions: In this part you will read a selection of texts, such as magazine and newspaper articles, e-mails, and instant messages. Each text or set of texts is followed by several questions. Select the best answer for each question and mark the letter (A), (B), (C), or (D) on your answer sheet.

Questions 147-148 refer to the following advertisement.

Transform your business events with Starlight!

Are you tired of paying far too much for meals and refreshments for your corporate guests? Then we at Starlight may have the perfect solution for you. We offer a range of luxurious hot and cold dishes delivered and served to your visitors that are sure to leave a lasting impression. Furthermore, our affordable prices mean that we are sure to have a package suitable for any business. And with premises in the cities of Middleton, Haverbrook and Ogden, you are guaranteed to be able to use our services — no matter where you are in the state!

---

147. What kind of business is Starlight?

(A) A transportation company
(B) An accounting firm
(C) A catering company
(D) A real estate agency

148. What is indicated about Starlight?

(A) Services offered are non-refundable.
(B) It has facilities at multiple locations.
(C) Its package prices are negotiable.
(D) It was founded last year.

GO ON TO THE NEXT PAGE

Questions 149-150 refer to the following text-message chain.

Mario [5:08 P.M.]
Daphne, quick question… So, this time next month, we will be working in sunny California with our new team, right?

Daphne [5:13 P.M.]
That's right. Has Ryan given you all the paperwork for relocation assistance? I am just starting to sort through it.

Mario [5:19 P.M.]
Yes. He said he would explain all the details to us next week at our Tuesday meeting.

Daphne [5:25 P.M.]
Oh, he did? What a relief. I was so overwhelmed by it all, to be honest. There is so much to fill out on the forms.

Mario [5:30 P.M.]
Yes, there sure is. Would you like to read through them together before the meeting? We could talk about it tomorrow during our lunch break.

Daphne [5:37 P.M.]
Good idea.

149. What will the writers most likely do next month?

(A) Meet with Ryan
(B) Relocate for work
(C) Begin a new project
(D) Give a presentation

150. At 5:25 P.M., what does Daphne mean when she says, "I was so overwhelmed by it all"?

(A) Some paperwork is difficult to understand.
(B) The daily expenses are higher than expected.
(C) The weekly meetings are inconvenient to attend.
(D) Ryan's explanations are confusing.

BYRON'S HOME FURNISHINGS

SALE

After fifteen years of serving the Bracetown community, we regret to inform you that we have been forced to file for bankruptcy. This is due to the skyrocketing costs of rent within the city. As such, we are holding a sales event while stocks last. Customers will be able to purchase items for their kitchens, bedrooms and lounges at an 80% discount. Products for bathrooms will continue to be sold at full price. We appreciate your support and hope to see you next week.

151. What can be inferred about Byron's Home Furnishings?

(A) It is celebrating its founding.
(B) It is opening a new branch.
(C) It is going out of business.
(D) Many of its items are out of stock.

152. What items are likely NOT to be included in the sale?

(A) Sofas
(B) Showerheads
(C) Dining tables
(D) Beds

Questions 153-154 refer to the following letter.

February 8

Donnamarie Tucker
Accounts Manager

Bank of the Islands
985 Front Street
Honolulu, Hawaii 83233

Dear Ms. Tucker,

I have done business with your bank for over eight years, and until now, I have always been pleased with your services. However, I believe a mistake has been made, and I would like you to correct it.

Please find enclosed copies of my last two bank statements. As you can see, I was charged $15 each month in bank fees on my checking account. Until now, I did not pay any monthly fees because I had a no-charge account. If I kept a balance of at least $1,000 in my account, I was not charged fees. I have kept my balance over $1,000 for many years now.

I called the bank to discuss this error and I was told that the limit for a no-charge account has now been raised to $1,500. I was not informed of this. I now have over $1,500 in my account, so I will not be charged for the current month. Because your bank did not inform me when it changed its terms, I believe that you should refund my checking fees for the last two months.

Thank you for your prompt attention to this. I look forward to continuing to do business with you.

Yours sincerely,

Nicholas Belvedere

153. Why did Mr. Belvedere write the letter?

(A) To request a bank statement
(B) To change his bank account details
(C) To inquire about a new banking service
(D) To complain about an error

154. What does Mr. Belvedere expect the bank to do?

(A) Refund some money
(B) Reduce a monthly fee
(C) Increase his account's minimum limit
(D) Provide a higher interest rate

Memo

To: Ayako Shibata, Human Resources Manager
From: Alexandra Watt, Senior Advisor
Date: Tuesday, May 6
Subject: Cancelation of Friday's meeting

I would like to begin by stating that I think our regular Friday meetings have been very helpful. It is important for me to be aware of morale levels and any policies that might influence them. Whenever I implement a new policy, or judge the effectiveness of a current policy, feedback from the people affected by it is essential.

I regret, however, that I will be unable to attend our meeting this Friday, as I will be attending a conference. The topic of the conference is "Responding to Grievances," which is quite relevant to our Friday discussions. I expect we will be able to resume our Friday meetings on the following week, and I look forward to reporting back to you and discussing the topics covered at the conference.

If you have any specific questions or concerns that you would like me to address at the conference, please feel free to send me an email and I will certainly take them into consideration. I regret that I cannot invite you to the conference, but space is, unfortunately, limited.

---

155. What is discussed at the Friday meetings?

(A) The willingness of staff to attend conferences
(B) The attitude of the staff towards policies
(C) The ability of the staff to improve sales
(D) The effectiveness of staff training sessions

156. When will Mr. Shibata and Ms. Watt likely meet next?

(A) This Monday
(B) Next Monday
(C) This Friday
(D) Next Friday

157. What most likely will be the topic of the next meeting?

(A) How to attract new customers
(B) How to deal with complaints
(C) How to delegate tasks
(D) How to organize events

GO ON TO THE NEXT PAGE

Questions 158-160 refer to the following e-mail.

To:	Maria Coates <mcoates@syprex.com>
From:	John Paul Little <jplittle@syprex.com>
Date:	October 15
Subject:	Online training materials

Hi Maria,

The statistics from our Computer Services Department arrived today and they highlighted a problem we need to take care of. It seems that there is something wrong in the corporate software that we use to train our sales team. The number of employee complaints about the software has risen dramatically since we had the upgrade a month ago. They are reporting screens "getting stuck", selections taking them to the wrong page, and other unusual issues.

It seems that most of the complaints are coming from employees in your Vaccine Sales Department. The Drug Sales section seems to be working just fine. I don't know whether there is something else going wrong, but we do need to take steps to quickly resolve the issue as it is wasting a lot of valuable employee time.

Please conduct a survey of your sales associates in Vaccine Sales, and pin down exactly what is happening, how often, etc. Then get back to me with a detailed report that I can pass along to the Computer Services Department so they can fix it.

Thanks,

John Paul Little

Internal Operations Manager

158. What problem is being discussed?

(A) Vaccine sales are dropping.
(B) Computers need to be replaced.
(C) Software is not working properly.
(D) Employees are wasting time.

159. Which department does Maria work in?

(A) Computer Services
(B) Vaccine Sales
(C) Internal Operations
(D) Drug Sales

160. What is Maria asked to do?

(A) Hire computer programmers
(B) Answer employee complaints
(C) Contact computer services
(D) Survey her employees

Questions 161-164 refer to the following online chat discussion.

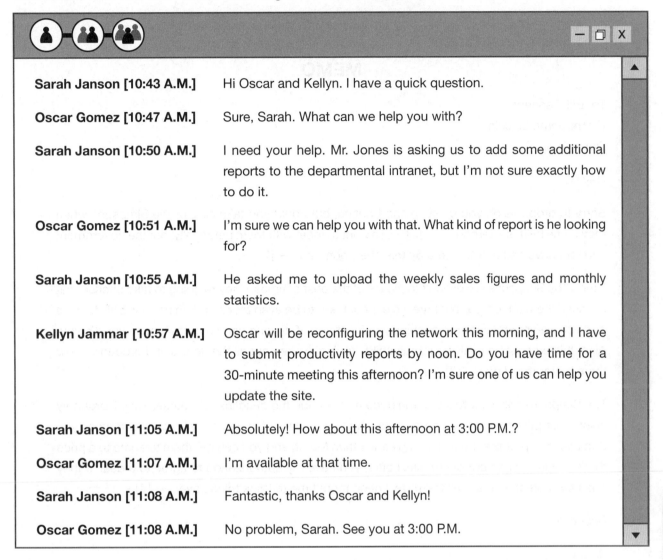

Sarah Janson [10:43 A.M.]	Hi Oscar and Kellyn. I have a quick question.
Oscar Gomez [10:47 A.M.]	Sure, Sarah. What can we help you with?
Sarah Janson [10:50 A.M.]	I need your help. Mr. Jones is asking us to add some additional reports to the departmental intranet, but I'm not sure exactly how to do it.
Oscar Gomez [10:51 A.M.]	I'm sure we can help you with that. What kind of report is he looking for?
Sarah Janson [10:55 A.M.]	He asked me to upload the weekly sales figures and monthly statistics.
Kellyn Jammar [10:57 A.M.]	Oscar will be reconfiguring the network this morning, and I have to submit productivity reports by noon. Do you have time for a 30-minute meeting this afternoon? I'm sure one of us can help you update the site.
Sarah Janson [11:05 A.M.]	Absolutely! How about this afternoon at 3:00 P.M.?
Oscar Gomez [11:07 A.M.]	I'm available at that time.
Sarah Janson [11:08 A.M.]	Fantastic, thanks Oscar and Kellyn!
Oscar Gomez [11:08 A.M.]	No problem, Sarah. See you at 3:00 P.M.

161. In which department does Ms. Janson most likely work?

(A) Art & Design
(B) Marketing
(C) Sales
(D) Human Resources

162. According to the discussion, what does Ms. Janson need help with?

(A) Submitting some documents
(B) Logging in to a website
(C) Understanding a company policy
(D) Increasing sales

163. What does Oscar need to do before he helps Ms. Janson?

(A) Submit productivity reports
(B) Update the network
(C) Upload sales figures
(D) Attend a meeting

164. At 11:05 A.M., what does Ms. Janson mean when she writes, "Absolutely"?

(A) She is available to meet for 30 minutes.
(B) She will create productivity reports for Kellyn.
(C) She will help Oscar with his work assignment.
(D) She knows how to get to a meeting location.

GO ON TO THE NEXT PAGE

Questions 165-167 refer to the following memo.

MEMO

To: Bill Flannery
From: Sarah Lincoln
Date: April 7

Hey Bill,

Sorry to drop this on you on such short notice, but could you take care of the Simpsons when they come by this afternoon? — [1] —. I meant to meet with them personally, but the government auditors have decided to come by this afternoon, too. — [2] —.

I know the Simpsons are difficult to please at the best of times. They're going to take offense that I passed them off to a subordinate, so expect them to be even touchier than normal. Still, they've met you before and seem to genuinely respect you. If anyone can smooth things over, it's you. Also, this proposal is really your brainchild. You've worked out all the details and probably know them better than I do. — [3] —.

The Simpsons will want to lower the price and change the deadline, of course. They'll probably want more performance guarantees, too. Negotiate with them as best you can. As long as you don't have to promise them anything earlier than March and you can get them to agree to a price that's within ten percent of our initial offer, you have my authorization to agree to a deal. If they push for more than that, tell them we'll need more time to think things over. — [4] —.

Best of luck,

Sarah

---

165. What is NOT true of Bill?

(A) He knows the project well.
(B) He outranks Sarah.
(C) He is liked by the client.
(D) He suggested the project.

166. How should Bill proceed if the Simpsons insist on the project being completed before March?

(A) Agree to the earlier deadlines
(B) Insist on lowering the price by ten percent
(C) Tell them that the deadline is unacceptable
(D) Ask for more time to make a decision

167. In which of the positions marked [1], [2], [3], and [4] does the following sentence best belong?

"As a result, I have an unavoidable conflict in my schedule and require your help."

(A) [1]
(B) [2]
(C) [3]
(D) [4]

Questions 168-171 refer to the following notice.

Corporate IT Staff Update

October 15

1. Service Desks: Please note that due to last month's roll-out of the new timesheet software, most sites are experiencing larger numbers of service requests than usual. It is suggested that the requests be prioritized. Some of the less important requests, such as "where do I find such-and-such" can be passed on to the caller's supervisor, who should be able to answer such things. — [1] —.

2. Progress has been made in the replacement of the server infrastructure at corporate HQ here in Dallas. — [2] —. The period of interrupted service should be ending on October 20.

3. We are hiring! Three employees have left the corporate IT Department in the last month. If you would like to be considered for transfer from your current site to the Dallas office, please be sure to apply by October 31. If you have friends who are qualified to work here, we are accepting new résumés after November 1. — [3] —.

4. The duty roster for Christmas holiday coverage is now out. — [4] —. Check the company Web site. We understand you may not want to work then, but we do rotate the names yearly, so please take your turn. You can also find details about our staff Christmas party on our site.

5. This month's brain teaser is a good one! It was contributed by Jenny Rue. See her puzzle on the Web site. Have fun and keep those brains active!

Richard Light

---

168. What is the purpose of this notice?

(A) To outline a job application process
(B) To keep a large department informed
(C) To welcome new employees to the company
(D) To explain new software to employees

169. What is stated about service requests?

(A) They should all be directed to supervisors.
(B) They are gradually decreasing in number.
(C) They should be prioritized by importance.
(D) They will be handled by part-time staff.

170. What is NOT found on the Web site?

(A) A brain puzzle
(B) The holiday schedule
(C) Party information
(D) Department goals

171. In which of the positions marked [1], [2], [3], and [4] does the following sentence best belong?

"Requirements and duties for each position are available upon request."

(A) [1]
(B) [2]
(C) [3]
(D) [4]

GO ON TO THE NEXT PAGE

Questions 172-175 refer to the following e-mail.

To:	Dan Hale <feedback@naturalpulp.com>
From:	Jessica Freeman <jfreeman@saveourforrest.org>
Subject:	Logging Decision
Date:	August 22

Dear Mr. Hale:

I am writing this e-mail to protest your company's decision to start logging in Redwood Forest. There are plenty of other forests you can log in this state. Indeed, many of them are second or third growth forests due to previous logging carried out by your firm or those like it. There's no need to destroy yet another piece of pristine wilderness rich in old growth trees and biodiversity just to get some lumber.

I realize, of course, that the wood from old growth trees commands a higher price on the market than the wood from newer trees. Indeed, I assume that the extra profit is your main reason for applying for a logging permit in that area. I won't waste words here trying to convince you that unspoiled wilderness has an inherent value that cannot be measured in dollars. Nor will I argue that we have a duty to preserve such wilderness areas for future generations, though that is also true.

I will, however, point out that any extra money you hope to make off of the trees you cut down will be more than balanced out in lost profits due to negative publicity and environmental boycotts. Today, consumers are very environmentally conscious, and protestors can get their message out via social networking in a blink of an eye. Look at what happened to Logging Industries, Inc, out in Ohio when they moved into old growth areas. They lost so much money due to the boycotts that they now no longer operate in that state at all.

In closing, I hope you reconsider your rash and ill-advised attempt to log areas best left free from the harm caused by modern industry.

Sincerely,

Jessica Freeman
Director, Save Our Forrest Association

172. Who most likely is Dan Hale?

(A) An environmentalist
(B) A scientist
(C) A business owner
(D) A journalist

173. What argument does Ms. Freedman think will be most convincing to Mr. Hale?

(A) That old growth wilderness areas are important to scientific research
(B) That Redwood Forest is a popular location for community events
(C) That the area he hopes to log is too remote to be profitable
(D) That logging the forest might cost him more than he will make

174. How does Ms. Freeman expect consumers to react to the company's decision?

(A) By sending protest letters
(B) By creating advertising campaigns
(C) By boycotting the company
(D) By launching online petitions

175. The word "measured" in paragraph 2, line 4 is closest in meaning to

(A) lengthened
(B) evaluated
(C) checked
(D) limited

GO ON TO THE NEXT PAGE

August 30

Mr. Charles Penchant
Mainland Media Ltd
110 Granger Avenue, 56089, Manchester, England

Dear Mr. Penchant,

I am writing in reply to your advertisement for freelance writers, which I saw at www.journalismcareers. net. I have over three years of journalism and editing experience. I have been working at a small community paper here in London since I graduated from journalism school.

On October 1, I will be returning to my hometown of Manchester. I will be seeking part-time work while I complete further studies at a local college. One of my former colleagues works at your newspaper and speaks highly of it.

Is the position still available, and how many hours work does it involve per week? I would also like to know if I can work from home or if I need to work at the office. Do you pay an hourly rate or a salary? I have included copies of recent articles I wrote for *The London Sun* and also reference letters from my editor.

Thank you.

Yours faithfully,

James Jones

September 1

James Jones
110 Smith Street, 56089, London, England

Dear Mr. Jones,

Thank you for your inquiry on August 30 regarding freelance writing positions. I have reviewed your résumé, articles, and reference letters and I was very impressed by the range of articles you have written.

Unfortunately, all of our freelance positions have been filled, but we do have a part-time position coming up in November that you may be interested in. That would involve working four mornings per week in our central city office. If this schedule fits in with your studies, then it could work out well for you.

I would like to meet with you in person. Please let me know when we can set up a suitable time to meet shortly after you arrive in Manchester. Also, the position may involve some court reporting, which I see you have done in London. I would appreciate it if you could e-mail me any court articles you have written.

Thank you for your interest in working for our company.

Yours sincerely,

Charles Penchant
Editor

176. How did Mr. Jones find out about the job vacancy at Mainland Media Ltd.?

(A) He saw it listed online.
(B) His co-worker recommended it.
(C) He attended a career fair.
(D) He knows the company's editor.

177. What does Mr. Jones want to know?

(A) If his portfolio can be returned
(B) If the job is still available
(C) If the job is full-time
(D) If his articles are acceptable

178. What does Mr. Penchant suggest to Mr. Jones?

(A) He should stay in London longer.
(B) He needs to obtain a qualification.
(C) He should start work immediately.
(D) He should apply for a position.

179. When will Mr. Penchant and Mr. Jones most likely meet?

(A) In August
(B) In September
(C) In October
(D) In November

180. What information is Mr. Jones asked to provide?

(A) A letter of recommendation
(B) A copy of his résumé
(C) Previous articles
(D) Business proposals

GO ON TO THE NEXT PAGE

Helpers wanted for charity show

The City Mission is looking for passionate actors to be involved in our Christmas Charity Play. The roles are voluntary, with all proceeds going towards helping needy children.

The family show has a fun Christmas theme. Actors need to be willing to attend all rehearsals, which will take place from 7 P.M. to 10 P.M. on Tuesdays and Thursdays from November 10 to 30. The play will be staged from December 1 to 10 with shows nightly at 6 P.M. except for Sundays when the show starts at 4 P.M.

Along with actors, we also need set designers, painters, make-up artists, and ushers. The hours will vary with each position. Apart from the set designers and make-up artists, the other positions do not require any special skills - anyone can apply!

Although the positions are voluntary, each person involved in the production will receive a reference letter and a movie voucher donated by the City Council Youth Services Center.

If you are interested, please come on Saturday, November 2, at 10 A.M. to an open audition. Those interested in the non-acting positions are asked to come along at 11 a.m. to register their details.

For further information please contact Susan Bell at 555-0121 or by e-mail at susan.bell@hotwire.com

---

E-Mail Message

From:	Jeffrey Jackson <jackson@wemail.net>
To:	Susan Bell <susan.bell@hotwire.com>
Date:	October 3
Subject:	Helpers wanted

Dear Susan,

I am writing regarding your notice requesting helpers for an upcoming charity show. I have a few questions that I hope you can answer for me.

Are you only looking for amateur actors, or can professional actors also get involved in the show? I teach acting classes at a local university and would love to act in the show, if possible. I also occasionally design sets, so I would be happy to help out in this area too.

Unfortunately, I am out of town on the audition day, so I was hoping to come in the day before that and meet you in person.

Thank you in advance. I will look forward to your reply.

Yours sincerely,

Jeffrey Jackson

181. What is required to participate in the show?

(A) A donation to charity
(B) A valid photo ID
(C) Attendance at practices
(D) Previous acting experience

182. When will the show start on weekdays?

(A) At 10 P.M.
(B) At 7 P.M.
(C) At 4 P.M.
(D) At 6 P.M.

183. What is recommended for those interested in a non-acting position?

(A) Proving their qualifications
(B) Making a call to Susan Bell
(C) Submitting personal information
(D) Attending an audition

184. What is indicated about Mr. Jackson?

(A) He works for a charity.
(B) He has directed several plays.
(C) He is an acting teacher.
(D) He wants to purchase a ticket for a show.

185. When does Mr. Jackson want to meet with Ms. Bell?

(A) On November 1
(B) On November 2
(C) On November 9
(D) On November 10

GO ON TO THE NEXT PAGE

TEST 7

http://www.mccallbusinessschool.com/upcomingevents/21 ▼

MCCALL BUSINESS SCHOOL OF TEXAS
Professional Development Seminar

For all individuals embarking on a new career path or hoping to enhance their current career, don't miss the professional development seminar organized by the McCall Business School of Texas. The event will be held in the school's newly constructed Roberta James Auditorium on Wednesday, 24 October, from 9:15 A.M. to 5:00 P.M.

The seminar has steadily grown in size, with more and more attendees every year, so if you are interested in attending, call us straight away at 555-3987 or CLICK HERE to purchase a ticket.

As always, we will bring you talks from various successful business experts. This year, the following four talks will take place during the event:

1. Preparing for Job Interviews (9:15 A.M. – 10:00 A.M.)
2. Writing Research Proposals (10:15 A.M. – 11:30 A.M.)
3. Utilizing Consumer Feedback (1:00 P.M. – 3:15 P.M.)
4. Overcoming Financial Obstacles (3:30 P.M. – 4:45 P.M.)

E-Mail Message

To:	Patricia Warburton <pwarburton@bestlogistics.com>
From:	Arnold Haim <ahaim@bestlogistics.com>
Date:	15 October
Subject:	Need a favor

Hi Patricia,

As you know, I've been asked to give a talk at McCall Business School of Texas next week. I've been busy, so I need your assistance with reserving an airline ticket. I'd like you to just book a one-way flight for me, as I'm not completely sure how long I'll stay in town. Ideally, I'd like to arrive in Dallas between 10 and 11 A.M. as I plan to meet an old friend for lunch before my talk at 1 P.M. Please make sure you choose a flight that offers seat selection, as I'd like you to get an emergency exit row seat so that I have some extra leg room. Also, the accounting manager has strictly told me to take a flight that's no more than $300, as I've already spent a lot on accommodation.

Please let me know the itinerary once you've made the booking for me. Thanks.

Arnold Haim

https://www.airtravelplus.com/tickets/search02879 ▼ — ☐ X

Available Flights	Seat Selection	Menu Options	Baggage Policy	Payment & Confirmation

Passenger: One Adult

Date: Wednesday, 24 October

Route: Minneapolis/St. Paul (MSP) to Dallas Fort Worth International (DFW)

Departure Time	Arrival Time	Seat Selection	Price	Airline
07:05 A.M.	09:25 A.M.	YES	$280	Pegasus Air
07:35 A.M.	10:00 P.M.	YES	$290	Air Sprint
08:15 A.M.	10:30 P.M.	NO	$295	Southern Air
08:40 A.M.	10:55 P.M.	YES	$325	Air Rapido

186. On the first Web page, the word "embarking" in paragraph 1, line 1, is closest in meaning to

(A) commencing
(B) boarding
(C) considering
(D) applying

187. What is NOT indicated about the seminar?

(A) It is held on an annual basis.
(B) It will take place in a new venue.
(C) It is increasing in popularity.
(D) It will last for two days.

188. Who most likely is Ms. Warburton?

(A) A seminar organizer
(B) A Web site designer
(C) A personal assistant
(D) A business school lecturer

189. What topic will Mr. Haim discuss at the seminar?

(A) Preparing for Job Interviews
(B) Writing Research Proposals
(C) Utilizing Consumer Feedback
(D) Overcoming Financial Obstacles

190. What airline will Mr. Haim probably use to travel to Dallas?

(A) Pegasus Air
(B) Air Sprint
(C) Southern Air
(D) Air Rapido

TEST 7

GO ON TO THE NEXT PAGE

Here is one more excellent reason to choose Gravity Resort, Bali!

To celebrate our being in business for ten years, Gravity Resort is running a special offer. In collaboration with Jade Coral Scuba Diving, guests who stay with us for three consecutive nights will receive a complimentary half-day diving trip. Only guests who stay at Gravity Resort between 1 July and 31 October may sign up for this special offer. An individual taking advantage of the offer can choose between two world-renowned dive sites: Padang Bay and Crystal Cove. You will receive a two-hour diving tutorial beforehand in the resort pool, and all equipment rental is included. To sign up for a dive excursion, or to hear more about the trip itineraries, check the dive company's Web site at www.jadecoraldives.com. Guests must e-mail Jade Coral Scuba Diving one month before the date on which they would like to go diving. Dive participants must be over 15 years old and display a competent level of swimming ability, in accordance with safety regulations.

E-Mail Message

From: Ricki Antonius <ricki@jadecoral.com>
To: Stefani Indriani <sindriani@gravityresort.com>
Date: 30 September
Subject: Gravity Resort Scuba Diving Excursions
Attachment: 📎 Jade Coral Scuba Diving Invoice

Dear Ms. Indriani,

Please find my invoice for the September dive excursions attached to this e-mail. You may be confused about the additional charge listed on the document. Perhaps you'll remember that I ended up chartering a boat in order to visit a more remote dive site at Gili Selang on September 15. This was a special request made by three employees of Cheng Systems who had heard about the location from their CEO.

As you can see, it was a disappointingly slow month for the complimentary dive excursions, with only 14 people taking advantage of the offer. I'm afraid you failed to reach the 50 individuals per month target you had set, and by some margin. I feel that I should point out that almost all of them chose Padang Bay over Crystal Cove for their dive experience. I'd recommend replacing the cove with another spot if you ever run the offer again in the future, as it has a relatively poor reputation compared to other options.

Regards,

Ricki

Jade Coral Scuba Diving Invoice

Date: 30 September

Bill to: Gravity Resort

Service Details	Number of Individuals	Standard Rate (Rupiah)	Subtotal (Rupiah)
Pool Training Session	14	450,000	6,300,000
Half-Day Scuba Dive	14	750,000	10,500,000
Equipment Rental	14	350,000	4,900,000
Extra Charge	1	300,000	300,000

Total 22,000,000 Rupiah

---

191. According to the advertisement, what is NOT true about the resort's special offer?

(A) Guests must stay for at least three nights to qualify.
(B) The offer will end in October.
(C) Only large groups are eligible to participate.
(D) Participants must be over a certain age.

192. What is suggested about the employees from Cheng Systems?

(A) They were visiting Gravity Resort for a business meeting.
(B) They sent an e-mail to Jade Coral Scuba Diving in August.
(C) They had a diving tutorial at Padang Bay.
(D) They changed the original date of their diving trip.

193. In the e-mail, the word "reach" in paragraph 2, line 2, is closest in the meaning to

(A) arrive
(B) communicate
(C) stretch
(D) achieve

194. What does Mr. Antonius suggest?

(A) Raising some prices
(B) Changing an advertising strategy
(C) Selecting an alternative dive site
(D) Contacting a former customer

195. Why was Gravity Resort charged 300,000 rupiah by Jade Coral Scuba Diving?

(A) Mr. Antonius was required to take a boat to Gili Selang.
(B) Mr. Antonius provided additional pieces of diving equipment.
(C) The Cheng Systems CEO joined his employees for diving.
(D) The Cheng Systems employees visited several diving locations.

GO ON TO THE NEXT PAGE

TEST 7

Hawthorne Ballroom to Host
Battle of the Bands Final

Hawthorne Ballroom has been closed for refurbishment for a few weeks, but it will be ready to host the final concert of this year's Deacon County Battle of the Bands contest, which will take place throughout September. Although the modification work was supposed to take place two months from now, the project start date was brought forward so that the venue would be ready to host the final of our county's popular annual music contest. As in previous years, various unsigned bands from across the county will compete to win a lucrative recording contract with Down Home Records.

Although Hawthorne Ballroom is one of the county's most historical and prestigious entertainment venues, it is the only venue in the county that has never hosted a Battle of the Bands concert, so the ballroom's owners are delighted to have an opportunity to participate this year. The ballroom will officially reopen on the day that the final concert takes place. The concert is certain to draw thousands of music fans, and a capacity crowd of 5,000 people is quite likely. While Hawthorne Ballroom's main door used to be on Hawkins Road, attendees should now enter through the new door around the corner on Billings Street.

Deacon County Battle of the Bands

First Round Concerts			
The Great Apes Vs. Head Candy 8 September, 7 P.M. Burton Concert Hall Burton	Sky Bandits Vs. Rolling Thunder 9 September, 7 P.M. Halley Music Hall Shelbyville	The New Noise Vs. Over the Top 10 September, 7 P.M. Wesley Theater Harrisburg	Northern Lights Vs. White Fire 11 September, 7 P.M. Clyde Amphitheater Meadowside

Second Round Concerts	
Winners of 8 September and 9 September concerts 14 September, 6 P.M. Halley Music Hall, Shelbyville	Winners of 10 September and 11 September concerts 15 September, 6 P.M. Clyde Amphitheater, Meadowside

Final Concert

Winners of 14 September and 15 September concerts
17 September, 6 P.M.
Hawthorne Ballroom, Harrisburg

Make sure you only purchase tickets from verified ticket sellers to avoid paying increased fees. Tickets can be purchased directly from each venue and from selected record stores in each town or city.

News Update
KPRX RADIO 98.5 FM

....

Entertainment – Live Music, 8 September

Today marks the beginning of this year's Deacon County Battle of the Bands! At 7:00 P.M., the first of the first-round concert battles will take place between The Great Apes and Head Candy, both of whom were originally formed in Meadowside. Our entertainment correspondent, Dale Cooper, will be covering the event live on our station.

And don't forget to tune in for more live coverage tomorrow night, when our guest reporter, Maria Shandy, will be checking out the music at Halley Music Hall in Shelbyville.

---

196. In the article, the word "draw" in paragraph 2, line 5, is closest in meaning to

(A) outline
(B) attract
(C) direct
(D) fill in

197. According to the article, what will be changed at Hawthorne Ballroom?

(A) Its ticket prices
(B) Its seating capacity
(C) Its entrance location
(D) Its name

198. When will the first concert be held at a new host venue?

(A) On September 8
(B) On September 10
(C) On September 14
(D) On September 17

199. In the schedule, what are people advised to do?

(A) Purchase tickets in advance to receive a discount
(B) Arrive at concert venues early to get a good seat
(C) Avoid buying tickets from unofficial vendors
(D) Contact venues to inquire about special offers

200. Where will Mr. Cooper be reporting from?

(A) Burton
(B) Shelbyville
(C) Harrisburg
(D) Meadowside

TEST 7

Stop! This is the end of the test. If you finish before time is called, you may go back to Parts 5, 6, and 7 and check your work.
정답 p.471 / 점수 환산표 p.476

실전모의고사
TEST 8

TEST 8 해설

바로 보기

시작 시간 _____시 _____분

종료 시간 _____시 _____분

READING TEST

In the Reading test, you will read a variety of texts and answer several different types of reading comprehension questions. The entire Reading test will last 75 minutes. There are three parts, and directions are given for each part. You are encouraged to answer as many questions as possible within the time allowed. You must mark your answers on the separate answer sheet. Do not write your answers in your test book.

PART 5

Directions: A word or phrase is missing in each of the sentences below. Four answer choices are given below each sentence. Select the best answer to complete the sentence. Then mark the letter (A), (B), (C), or (D) on your answer sheet.

101. The reimbursement request for your trip last month to Chicago has ------- to be processed because there is a missing receipt for the car rental.

(A) yet
(B) already
(C) after
(D) too

102. The Clothing Recyclers purchases ------- clothing in good condition and refurbishes it for sale on their Web site at a low price.

(A) used
(B) using
(C) to use
(D) uses

103. ------- a power failure in the assembly line area, a backup power generator will start automatically to prevent interruption of production.

(A) For example
(B) In the meantime
(C) In particular
(D) In the event of

104. The construction of the sports stadium is likely ------- at least 800 employment opportunities in the Langhorne Creek region.

(A) to create
(B) creation
(C) creative
(D) creates

105. Please ------- that Ms. Tower is going to announce changes to employee sick leave policies at this afternoon's meeting.

(A) remind
(B) refer
(C) notify
(D) note

106. With the cost of transportation becoming ------- high, we have had to raise our prices by 5 percent in order to compensate for losses.

(A) increasingly
(B) increasing
(C) increased
(D) increase

107. The retirement dinner for the vice president was a success, as ------- 90 percent of the company's workers attended the event.

(A) normally
(B) generously
(C) approximately
(D) evenly

108. The entire Human Resources Department must participate in the upcoming training ------- designed to promote interpersonal communication.

(A) session
(B) movement
(C) center
(D) force

109. Refunds will be given on electronics purchases only if they are returned within 30 days and -------.

(A) unopened
(B) unoriginal
(C) inapplicable
(D) intended

110. We regret to say that the delivery of your order has been delayed by 10 days ------- a shipping problem.

(A) except for
(B) because of
(C) however
(D) although

111. While developing a new operating manual for the customer service representatives, Mr. Harley was ------- able to take a day off.

(A) surely
(B) hardly
(C) thoroughly
(D) completely

112. We are happy to report that sales of our new cell phone model have ------- exceeded investors' expectations.

(A) closely
(B) more
(C) but
(D) far

113. Through the introduction of more quality control -------, JS Electronics hopes to reduce defective products reaching store shelves.

(A) measures
(B) accomplishments
(C) observances
(D) assurances

114. After reviewing this month's sales figures, the CEO decided to ------- a more aggressive marketing strategy.

(A) accompany
(B) implement
(C) inform
(D) reduce

115. An employee satisfaction survey conducted ------- full-time staff identified managers' openness as one positive aspect of our working environment.

(A) into
(B) toward
(C) over
(D) among

116. Morgan Inc.'s acquisition of a foreign firm will bring about a variety of drastic changes to the way the company -------.

(A) operated
(B) operation
(C) to operate
(D) operates

117. The hotel spa offers a variety of packages that can be mixed and matched according to your tastes to provide you with a fully ------- experience.

(A) personally
(B) personality
(C) personalize
(D) personalized

118. Mr. Gardner drew up a document outlining the details of the agreement ------- both parties could finish reviewing the contract well before the planned signing date.

(A) in order to
(B) so that
(C) such as
(D) even so

119. Before making any major career decisions, it is best to seek appropriate advice from a more expert ------- in your field.

(A) profession
(B) profess
(C) professionally
(D) professional

GO ON TO THE NEXT PAGE

TEST 8

120. ------- the company's continuous effort to adapt to the slow economy, management is cautiously considering a corporate restructuring.

(A) Despite
(B) Now that
(C) Nonetheless
(D) Yet

121. Please be aware that the staff parking lot will be inaccessible ------- starting next Tuesday, and will remain closed until further notice.

(A) temporary
(B) temporarily
(C) temporality
(D) temporalities

122. I'd like to extend my ------- to all full- and part-time staff for our being voted Company of the Year for the third consecutive year.

(A) sympathy
(B) qualification
(C) exposure
(D) gratitude

123. A government commission has recently been created to make dramatic ------- to the current tax system.

(A) modifying
(B) to modify
(C) modifications
(D) modify

124. Since our factory ------- technical difficulties several months ago, its output has been continuously dropping to new lows.

(A) excused
(B) experienced
(C) exhausted
(D) experimented

125. While plant managers ------- agree that immediate action must be taken to improve productivity, few of them support the schedule most recently proposed by Mr. Hill.

(A) concurrently
(B) feasibly
(C) extremely
(D) unanimously

126. Ms. Stone is in charge of the buyout negotiations with the company's direct -------, which would substantially increase its market share.

(A) competing
(B) competitive
(C) compete
(D) competitor

127. The desserts ------- in the company cafeteria are not only incredibly delicious, but healthy and beautifully presented, too.

(A) offering
(B) offers
(C) to offer
(D) offered

128. Although it was not mandatory, Mr. Wang signed up for the IT training session, showing a strong interest in ------- new things.

(A) will learn
(B) learning
(C) learned
(D) to learn

129. After interviewing Mr. Lyle and reviewing his work history, we conclude that he is the most ------- candidate for the job.

(A) qualification
(B) qualifies
(C) qualify
(D) qualified

130. All the team members have a lot of ------- respect for Ms. Smith because she is a competent manager who has always led the team to success.

(A) deepen
(B) deep
(C) deeply
(D) depth

PART 6

Directions: Read the texts that follow. A word, phrase, or sentence is missing in parts of each text. Four answer choices for each question are given below the text. Select the best answer to complete the text. Then mark the letter (A), (B), (C) or (D) on your answer sheet.

Questions 131-134 refer to the following advertisement.

The Client Pro+ Software Suit
Build Solid Relationships With Your Customers With Minimal Effort!

In today's extremely competitive market, providing a quality product or service just isn't enough. You need to connect with your customers to build loyalty and encourage them to ------- rely on your **131.** business to meet their needs.

Want to make things easier and faster? Then you need the Client Pro+ Software Suite. This powerful program will allow you to:

- Identify your most profitable customers so you can focus your marketing efforts and ------- revenue. **132.**
- Send out regular e-mails offering customers discounts on specific products, free gifts, or other specials that will encourage ------- to buy. **133.**
- Keep track of customer contact information so you can stay in touch.

For a limited time, we are offering the Client Pro+ Software Suite for $499.99. -------. Call us **134.** at 1- 800-803-7777 to place your order now. This incredible deal won't last long!

131. (A) consist
(B) consisted
(C) consistent
(D) consistently

132. (A) complete
(B) employ
(C) maximize
(D) restrict

133. (A) they
(B) them
(C) their
(D) themselves

134. (A) Our customer support team will be happy to process your refund.
(B) This price includes unlimited technical support for two years.
(C) With the Client Pro+ Software Suite, you can also save time.
(D) Make sure you let your customers know about this amazing discount.

GO ON TO THE NEXT PAGE

Questions 135-138 refer to the following e-mail.

To: Harry Henderson
From: Moretz Picture Frames
Subject: Your Order

Dear Mr. Henderson,

I am pleased to ------- that your order placed on March 3 is now ready for early shipping.
　　　　　　　　135.

When submitting your order, you emphasized the importance of prompt delivery, and I am glad to say
that by ------- a special effort, I will be able to send them a few days earlier than agreed upon. The
　　　　136.
items will arrive no later than April 1, so you will have plenty of time to frame your paintings before
your exhibition in Geneva.

You mentioned earlier that you would prefer to receive your order at your workshop in Zurich. So, I
now await your shipping instructions. ------- receiving them, I will send you an invoice. Detailed terms
　　　　　　　　　　　　　　　　　137.
are available upon request. ------- .
　　　　　　　　　138.

---

135. (A) comply
(B) confirm
(C) remind
(D) apply

136. (A) made
(B) make
(C) makes
(D) making

137. (A) Plus
(B) Even
(C) Upon
(D) While

138. (A) Thank you for agreeing to attend our
exhibition.
(B) Your items have been sent out via express
shipping.
(C) I am very pleased with the quality of your
service.
(D) I always appreciate your continued
business.

Questions 139-142 refer to the following e-mail.

From: akio@mercorp.com
To: chiyo@mercorp.com
Subject: Contract Negotiations
Date: April 11

Dear Chiyo:

As requested, I am providing an update on the status of our contract negotiations with New Directions Perfume. I met with three of the company's representatives today, including the CEO. I am extremely pleased to say that we made a lot of progress.

The individuals I met with were ------- with our advertisement samples. They were also excited when
                                    139.
I told them about some of our past campaigns for well-known fragrances. We were all in agreement that developing online marketing strategies is crucial.

Currently, the main ------- to our finalizing the contract is money. The cost of a basic package is
                      140.
within the company's budget. However, they also want a 30-second radio spot. ------- .
                                                                              141.

Please let me know what you think as soon as possible. I told them that I would get back to them

------- tomorrow.
142.

Sincerely,

Akio

---

139. (A) impression
(B) impresses
(C) impressed
(D) impressing

140. (A) obstacle
(B) prospect
(C) route
(D) breach

141. (A) They added that the famous announcer will not be available for a while.
(B) So, it remains to be seen whether the fragrances will be ready before the launch.
(C) Due to recent changes, our basic package is not currently available.
(D) Obviously, this will substantially increase the final price.

142. (A) until
(B) by
(C) during
(D) near

Questions 143-146 refer to the following notice.

Staff Notice: Changes to Procedures For Handling Client Complaints

Over the past six months, we have failed to respond to 11 client complaints. To prevent similar incidents in the future, we are introducing several changes. -------.
143.

1. Respond to the client -------. Verify that the complaint was received as soon as you read it, and
144.
   assure the customer that it will be resolved as quickly as possible.

2. Access the shared "Client Complaint" page on our internal server. Record the time and date the
   call or e-mail was received. Provide a detailed description of the problem.

3. Check the page within seven business days to make sure the complaint is marked as "solved." *(If
   it is not, flag it as "urgent.")*

4. ------- the client is still unhappy, forward the details directly to Sherri in Customer Relations. She
   145.
   will handle the matter from there.

We believe these small procedural changes will help us satisfy all of our clients and rebuild our -------
146.
for providing exemplary service.

Sincerely,

Management

---

143. (A) If this happens again, we will be forced to
take the following measures.
(B) We assure you that your complaints are
taken seriously by our customer support
team.
(C) From now on, please complete the
following steps whenever you receive a
complaint.
(D) We sincerely apologize for keeping you
waiting while your request was being
processed.

144. (A) mutually
(B) regularly
(C) continually
(D) immediately

145. (A) Unless
(B) If
(C) While
(D) So

146. (A) reputation
(B) acquaintance
(C) confirmation
(D) recognition

PART 7

Directions: In this part you will read a selection of texts, such as magazine and newspaper articles, e-mails, and instant messages. Each text or set of texts is followed by several questions. Select the best answer for each question and mark the letter (A), (B), (C), or (D) on your answer sheet.

Questions 147-148 refer to the following announcement.

Latin Tastes Closing Event - Final Week!

As owners Robert and Michelle Sanchez announce their retirement, we would like to invite you to a week of discounted tasting events at their restaurant:

Latin Tastes

85 Meaning Street

Downtown Area, Appleton

April 15-21

Food as always will be prepared by chef Roland Tarquez. A long-time friend of the restaurant owners, Rachel Tarley, will also bring along her guitar to perform some tracks from her latest album. Tickets for each evening will be sold on a first-come, first-served basis.

147. What will most likely happen on April 22?

(A) A new chef will be hired.
(B) A business will be closed.
(C) A new tasting menu will be announced.
(D) Some fresh ingredients will be delivered.

148. What is indicated about Rachel Tarley?

(A) She has cooking experience.
(B) She owns a business.
(C) She will be selling tickets.
(D) She is a musician.

GO ON TO THE NEXT PAGE

Questions 149-150 refer to the following text-message chain.

Ryan [6:09 P.M.]
Hey, Brianna… It's that time of year again. Performance reviews are next week.

Brianna [6:13 P.M.]
Yes, it is. I really don't enjoy this time of year. Setting goals and targets is stressful, especially when the outcome affects my salary for next year.

Ryan [6:17 P.M.]
It is a good opportunity for individual growth, though. Since you have to do it, it would be beneficial to make sure that the targets you are setting with Nathan are in line with your career goals.

Brianna [6:20 P.M.]
That's true. I am aiming to become a manager one day, so I will definitely make sure that I make the most of it. Thanks for the reminder.

Ryan [6:25 P.M.]
No problem. Would you like to work together to help set targets during our lunch break tomorrow?

Brianna [6:27 P.M.]
That would be great.

149. What does Ryan say about performance reviews?

(A) They are personally useful.
(B) They are not required for all staff.
(C) They don't usually match company goals.
(D) They are performed once a month.

150. At 6:27 P.M., what does Brianna mean when she says, "That would be great"?

(A) She is impressed by Ryan's work targets.
(B) She will reschedule her meeting with Nathan.
(C) She wants to collaborate with Ryan on a task.
(D) She is grateful to receive a lunch break extension.

Questions 151-152 refer to the following information.

Oakware
Furniture Rental

Unit 2, Main Street

Tel: 553-555-0116

www.oakwarefurniture.com

"Quality with a personal touch!"

Visit our warehouse :

Monday - Wednesday   9:00 A.M. – 4:00 P.M.

Thursdays and Fridays   10:00 A.M. – 5:00 P.M

Weekends & Holidays   11:00 A.M. – 2:00 P.M.

Our sales lines are open:

Monday – Wednesday   2:00 P.M. – 8:00 P.M.

Thursdays & Fridays   9:00 A.M. – 4:00 P.M.

Weekends & Holidays   12:00 P.M. – 4:00 P.M.

Enter your details online to receive a free catalog.

Next-day delivery guaranteed.

151. When can customers call a sales advisor?

(A) On Monday at 11:00 A.M.
(B) On Thursday at 5:00 P.M.
(C) On Saturday at 3:00 P.M.
(D) On Sunday at 7:00 P.M.

152. How can customers receive a catalog?

(A) By calling a sales line
(B) By visiting a Web site
(C) By going to a warehouse
(D) By ordering some furniture

GO ON TO THE NEXT PAGE

Questions 153-154 refer to the following e-mail.

From:	orders@wildriveronline.ca
To:	joliver@mymail.ca
Subject:	Wildriver Camping Supplies Order
Date:	June 4

Dear Mr. Oliver,

Wildriver Camping Supplies has received the order you placed on June 3 via our online store.

Your order for the following item(s) is now being processed:

Catalog No.	Description	Quantity	Cost per unit
FV-375	Fovex 2-person tent	1	$349.99
LS-83	Lista down sleeping bag	2	$95.00
			Sales Tax $22.25
			TOTAL $562.24

We expect to be able to fill your order within five business days. Since your order exceeds $100 before tax, shipping charges will be waived. Payment will be billed to your credit card when the order is shipped. You will receive another e-mail at that time.

If you have any questions about your order, please call 555-0128.
Thank you for shopping at Wildriver Camping Supplies.

153. What is the purpose of the e-mail?
(A) To announce that an order has been shipped
(B) To confirm receipt of an order
(C) To inform a customer that an item is out of stock
(D) To explain a price change

154. What is indicated about Mr. Oliver's order?
(A) Sales taxes have been waived.
(B) He received a $100 discount.
(C) He placed it over the telephone.
(D) There is no delivery charge.

Von Dreyer Medical Supply

3738 W Reno Ave, Oklahoma City, OK 73107

October 19

Mr. Adrian Coyne
Northview Apartments 388
400 Welland Road
Norman, OK 73071

Dear Adrian,

As discussed following your interview on October 15, we are pleased to offer you a one-year contract of employment at Von Dreyer Medical Supply. The position will commence on November 1 and continue until October 31 next year.

The yearly salary for the position is $42,000. In addition to public holidays, you are entitled to two weeks' paid vacation. You will also receive healthcare and dental coverage.

On your first morning at work, before going to your department, please report to Chad Finn in the Personnel Department at 9:00. He will explain the benefits and working conditions in detail and provide you with a copy of your contract. You will also be expected to sign a confidentiality agreement, which will be prepared for you by Chad.

We look forward to having you on the team.

Regards,

Maureen Hughes

Maureen Hughes
Vice President of Operations

155. When will Adrian begin working at Von Dreyer Medical Supply?

(A) October 15
(B) October 19
(C) October 31
(D) November 1

156. What is NOT stated in the letter?

(A) The duration of Adrian's contract
(B) The amount of vacation time Adrian will receive
(C) The department Adrian will work for
(D) The medical benefits Adrian will receive

157. According to the letter, what will Adrian have to do on the first day?

(A) Sign an official document
(B) Submit a personnel report
(C) Undergo a medical check-up
(D) Prepare a presentation

GO ON TO THE NEXT PAGE

Important Notice

You may have noticed recently that your tap water appears somewhat cloudy. We'd like to assure all our tenants that the water is still perfectly safe to drink. The cloudiness is due to higher-than-normal levels of rainfall in the Gulf Mountains area. The heavy precipitation has caused the rivers that supply the city's water to flow faster than usual. As a result, there is a greater amount of sediment being carried into the water supply tanks. This sediment is what causes the water to appear cloudy.

As a precaution, the city has tested the water to check that the drinking quality is acceptable. Health officials have indicated that there is no risk involved in drinking it or using it for other purposes, and there is no need to boil the water before use.

If the government does issue a water safety advisory at some point, we will put notices in your mailboxes immediately.

Regards,

The management

Jersey Heights Apartments

158. Who is the notice intended for?

(A) Government workers
(B) Water plant inspectors
(C) Apartment residents
(D) Health officials

159. What has caused a change in the water?

(A) Pollution
(B) Heavy rainfall
(C) Low water levels
(D) Damaged pipes

160. What is indicated about the water?

(A) It is safe for consumption.
(B) It should be boiled before use.
(C) It will be temporarily unavailable.
(D) It may contain harmful substances.

Questions 161-163 refer to the following advertisement.

Bellingham's
Now also at 454 Torrance Drive (Next to Pastel Art Supplies)
Pittsburgh, PA 15213
555-9237

Business hours:
9 A.M. to 5 P.M., Monday to Friday
9 A.M. to 6 P.M. Saturdays

Free crystal flower vase when you spend over $100
(Kingsway Plaza Store Only)

To celebrate this store's first week in business:
15% off all rugs and carpets
20% off curtains (plain linen only)
25% off all picture frames

The above discounts will be offered from May 2 to May 8

For only $30 per year, you can sign up for the Bellingham's
customer rewards card and receive an additional 5% off all purchases
made at our Torrance Drive location, our flagship store on Bertrand Street,
and on our Web site!

Also, until May 8, order any item of bedding
directly from www.bellinghams.com and get 10% off!

---

161. What type of merchandise does Bellingham's sell?

(A) Building materials
(B) Home furnishings
(C) Art supplies
(D) Flowers

162. What is indicated about Bellingham's?

(A) It has stores in more than one city.
(B) It opens seven days a week.
(C) Its merchandise is second-hand.
(D) It is opening a new location.

163. For which item will the customers get an online-only discount?

(A) A bathroom rug
(B) A decorative vase
(C) A bed cover
(D) A set of curtains

GO ON TO THE NEXT PAGE

Local Company Set to Expand Production

M&G Plastics announced yesterday that it has obtained approval for the addition of a new assembly line to produce a type of plastic sheeting. — [1] —. A new building will be built to house this line, which will be operated by at least fifty new full-time workers when it is up and running.

A spokesman for the company, Mike Jones, said that making plastic sheeting was an obvious choice for expansion since the company already produces most of the raw materials necessary to make it. He added that there is a shortage in the market, which provided an added incentive. — [2] —.

Construction and instrumentation companies interested in bidding for this work should contact M&G immediately, as it hopes to start construction as soon as possible. It is estimated that construction will be finished in March or April, with full production achieved by the start of June. — [3] —.

Shares in M&G Plastics rose by two points after the announcement was made, and there was much excitement among local jobseekers and business owners here in Indianapolis. Two other cities were considered for the new facility. — [4] —. In the end, the decision to build it here in Indianapolis was made partly because of the good economic climate in our city

---

164. What is the purpose of this article?

(A) To announce an expansion
(B) To advertise for new employees
(C) To profile a new company
(D) To encourage investment

165. What is NOT mentioned about M&G Plastics?

(A) Its stock prices recently increased.
(B) It aims to take advantage of a market shortage.
(C) It is relocating its headquarters.
(D) It will have a new building constructed.

166. What is indicated about the workforce of M&G Plastics?

(A) It will increase in size.
(B) Employees will be transferred overseas.
(C) It includes temporary workers.
(D) Staff work on various shifts.

167. In which of the positions marked [1], [2], [3], and [4] does the following sentence best belong?

"However, shareholders raised concerns about the proposed sites in Toledo and Kalamazoo."

(A) [1]
(B) [2]
(C) [3]
(D) [4]

Questions 168-171 refer to the following online chat discussion.

Kelly Esparza [9:05 A.M.]	Hi, Tony, thank you for contacting us. What can I help you with today?
Tony Orleans [9:06 A.M.]	Hi, Kelly, I have a question about your mid-weight spring jackets. Can you tell me how long the warranty lasts and if they are waterproof?
Kelly Esparza [9:07 A.M.]	Sure, I can give you more information. Are you talking about the Merilo Men's Lightweight Jacket?
Tony Orleans [9:08 A.M.]	That's right. I'm thinking of taking it on my tour of Europe in May, but I want to make sure it will be suitable for the weather.
Kelly Esparza [9:09 A.M.]	No problem. That specific jacket is water-resistant, not waterproof. You may want to purchase a waterproofing spray to add additional protection.
Tony Orleans [9:09 A.M.]	Okay, I can do that. Will the spray stain the material?
Kelly Esparza [9:10 A.M.]	We always recommend testing the product on an inconspicuous area of the jacket before spraying the rest. You can tell if it will change the color within an hour.
Tony Orleans [9:11 A.M.]	Thanks, Kelly. What about the warranty?
Kelly Esparza [9:12 A.M.]	All our products come with a 5-year warranty that covers all manufacturer defects. It doesn't cover normal wear and tear, stains, etc.
Tony Orleans [9:13 A.M.]	Okay, that seems reasonable. Thank you very much for your help.
Kelly Esparza [9:14 A.M.]	You're welcome, Tony. Please contact us anytime.

TEST 8

168. Who is Tony most likely speaking to?

(A) A shipping clerk
(B) A tour guide
(C) A fashion designer
(D) A customer service agent

169. What does Kelly recommend?

(A) Choosing a larger size
(B) Buying a protective spray
(C) Avoiding inclement weather
(D) Purchasing a more expensive jacket

170. What type of defect probably will not be covered by the warranty?

(A) A faulty zipper
(B) Missing stitches
(C) Stained material
(D) Broken buttons

171. At 9:13 A.M., what does Tony mean when he says, "Okay, that seems reasonable"?

(A) He is satisfied with the warranty terms.
(B) He thinks the price of a jacket is fair.
(C) He will try the jacket on before buying it.
(D) He does not think the product will last long.

GO ON TO THE NEXT PAGE

Questions 172-175 refer to the following e-mail.

```
╔═══════════════════════════════════════════════════════════════╗
║                        E-Mail Message                          ║
╠═══════════════════════════════════════════════════════════════╣

    To:        Sandra Wilcot <swilcot@bcmart.com>
    From:      Madeline Stark <mstark@bcmart.com>
    Subject:   New business hours
    Date:      June 24

─────────────────────────────────────────────────────────────────

    Hi Sandra,

    I wanted to e-mail you about the meeting we had last week in regard to the proposal to change our
    business hours. — [1] —. Pushing our opening and closing hours back by one hour certainly seems like
    a smart decision. — [2] —. Therefore, in order to evaluate all aspects of the proposal, I gathered the
    opinions of staff at yesterday's training workshop.

    First of all, several of our employees complained that the new schedule would put them in the middle
    of rush hour. This would lengthen everyone's commute by approximately half an hour. — [3] —. Also,
    several of our workers are parents and must drop their children off at school in the morning. The new
    schedule would impede that. — [4] —. And lastly, our deliveries often come at 8:00 a.m. Many of our
    packages must be signed and accounted for, which will be impossible if there's nobody there at that
    time.

    I understand that the proposed change of schedule would allow workers to sleep a bit later. But
    unfortunately, the drawbacks are rather significant, and it is not possible to meet everyone's preferences.

    Best regards,

    Madeline Stark
    Operations Manager
```

172. According to the e-mail, approximately how much extra time would be required for commuting?

(A) 15 minutes
(B) 30 minutes
(C) 60 minutes
(D) 90 minutes

173. What is NOT mentioned as a disadvantage of the new schedule?

(A) Employees will be unable to attend a daily meeting.
(B) Employees will be stuck in rush hour traffic.
(C) Employees will miss morning deliveries.
(D) Employees will have difficulty taking their kids to school.

174. What can be inferred about Ms. Stark?

(A) She would prefer to keep the current schedule.
(B) She will make an announcement to all employees.
(C) She is impressed with Ms. Wilcot's proposal.
(D) She is responsible for receiving deliveries at the company.

175. In which of the positions marked [1], [2], [3], and [4] does the following sentence best belong?

"At the same time, we must consider the potential negative implications of such a move."

(A) [1]
(B) [2]
(C) [3]
(D) [4]

GO ON TO THE NEXT PAGE

Questions 176-180 refer to the following e-mails.

To:	Genevieve Lowe <glowe@goodmail.com>
From:	Marcus Bronson, HR Manager <mbronson@bestfood.com>
Subject:	Employment
Date:	May 19

Hi Genevieve,

I am very happy to tell you that your application for the post of research assistant has been successful. A formal letter will follow, but I thought you would like to know as soon as possible.

You will report to Mr. Angus O'Toole, whom you interviewed with while you were here. He runs the Flavoring and Preservatives Department, which I am sure you will find interesting. You will be designing and testing various new preservatives for our vegetable products.

We were impressed by your thesis, and we would be happy if you continue to publish the results of any research conducted while in our employment. Of course, we would maintain the rights to any patents developed in our own laboratories.

Your start date is set for June 16 and we will expect to see you then. You can report to me for your initial orientation. We are also conducting an open house on June 12, so you are welcome, of course, to come and look round then.

Congratulations, and I wish you every success in your future career.

Marcus Bronson

E-Mail Message

To: Marcus Bronson, HR Manager <mbronson@bestfood.com>
From: Genevieve Lowe <glowe@goodmail.com>
Subject: RE: Employment
Date: May 19

Hello, Mr. Bronson,

I am so glad to hear that I have a job with your company! I am looking forward to it. I liked Mr. O'Toole when I met him and I am glad I will be working with him.

I hate to ask for a favor before I have even started work, but I feel I have to. I have just learned that I have won the Lily Jermison Award for Excellence in Food Science, which as you know is very prestigious. Unfortunately, the presentation is in Alabama on the day I am supposed to start working for you! I would really like to attend the award ceremony, so would it be possible for me to start working a day or two later? I do hope this will not cause any problem.

Thank you for letting me know the good news so soon. I appreciate the heads up, and I know I will enjoy working for you!

Best wishes,
Genevieve Lowe

176. What is the purpose of the first e-mail?

(A) To offer a research grant
(B) To arrange an interview
(C) To introduce a new employee
(D) To notify a successful applicant

177. Who most likely is in charge of food preservatives research?

(A) Marcus Bronson
(B) Genevieve Lowe
(C) Angus O'Toole
(D) Lily Jermison

178. What will Genevieve's job duties involve?

(A) Editing research papers
(B) Developing new food additives
(C) Training new employees
(D) Planning company events

179. When will Genevieve receive her award?

(A) On May 19
(B) On June 12
(C) On June 16
(D) On June 19

180. What request does Genevieve make?

(A) To postpone her first day of work
(B) To be transferred to the Alabama office
(C) To work for Mr. O'Toole
(D) To attend the open house

GO ON TO THE NEXT PAGE

TEST 8

Questions 181-185 refer to the following notice and letter.

Theater Closure

The Grand Theater, the most historic theatre in Oak Town will be closed from July 1 until September 1 in order to complete renovations. Patrons are aware that the roof of the foyer leaks during heavy rain storms, and it is time to repair it. We are also taking this opportunity to refurbish the bathrooms, cast dressing rooms, box office and front foyer. The main audience seating area was refurbished just two years ago, so it will be left as is at this time.

We hope this does not cause any undue inconvenience to our loyal audience, and we look forward to re-opening in the fall, in greater splendor than ever before.

Thank you,

Melodee Carnahan
Secretary to the Board, The Grand Theater

April 22

Dear Ms. Carnahan,

I am glad to see that the Grand Theater is going to be repaired at last. My wife is a loyal theater-goer, and she has commented on the need for repairs.

I would like to acquaint you with my business, Heritage Homes. We have been in the local area for twenty-two years, and we specialize in remodelling and upgrading older homes. We aim to restore, repair and renew the fittings in these homes in such a way that their historical authenticity is not compromised, while at the same time making them comfortable and practical for the modern family. Unfortunately, I was not able to submit a bid for the work you did on your main audience seating area in the past, as it happened during a year that I took off work for health reasons.

I am now fully healthy again and I would like to submit a bid to renovate your dressing rooms and bathrooms. We could also do the work required in the foyer and box office.

Please let me know who I should contact for the details.

Yours sincerely,

Scott Lyle

Scott Lyle

181. In the notice, the word "opportunity" in paragraph 1, line 3, is closest in meaning to

(A) advantage
(B) chance
(C) vacancy
(D) offer

182. What is suggested about the Grand Theater?

(A) It is the largest theater in town.
(B) It needs a new seating area.
(C) Its bathroom pipes often leak.
(D) Its roof is in poor condition.

183. What is the purpose of the letter?

(A) To ask for an employment application
(B) To offer to perform some work
(C) To announce a business closure
(D) To advertise construction products

184. What is NOT suggested about Heritage Homes?

(A) It has been in business for more than two decades.
(B) It provides an initial consultation free of charge.
(C) It strives to maintain the historical value of buildings.
(D) It converts old properties into contemporary homes.

185. When most likely was Mr. Lyle ill?

(A) Last month
(B) Late last year
(C) Two years ago
(D) Two months ago

GO ON TO THE NEXT PAGE

Basketfuls of Joy

833 Oceanview Avenue, Vancouver, British Columbia V5K 1P4

Phone: (604) 555-6411

Fruit baskets for all occasions!

Basket designer and company owner: Elizabeth Schmelar
We use a variety of locally-grown fruits in our baskets,
as well as exotic fruits from a wide range of tropical countries.
We guarantee the freshest, most flavorful fruits in our baskets.

- Baskets are available in a variety of colors and designs with options available for custom, personalized designs.
- Same-day delivery in Vancouver and the surrounding areas* is available for orders placed before 1:00 P.M. during weekdays and by 12:00 P.M. on the weekends. Our delivery rates are the lowest in the region.
- Orders can be placed at our store, by phone, or online (www.basketfulsofjoy.ca)
- Customers ordering for the first time get free delivery (the promo code MN1337 can be used in the online form for this discount).

* Within 30 kilometers of the borders of Vancouver

BASKETFULS OF JOY – Order Form

Date of order: Thursday, May 1
Delivery priority: Same-day delivery
Ordering customer: Tilda Swanson
Recipient(s): Timothy and Theresa Pilton, Acceleration Business Solutions
Delivery Address: 44 Boardwalk Street, Vancouver, British Columbia V5K 2V1

Basket Number	Details	Quantity	Price
58C	Lucky Basket Personalized message: Best of luck with your new consulting business!	2	$45 CAD each

Promo Code: MN1337	Delivery fee	$0
Credit Card Number: 1234-5585-6676-****		$90 CAD

http://www.localbusinessratings.com/vancouver/92080

Basketfuls of Joy (833 Oceanview Avenue, Vancouver, British Columbia V5K 1P4)

Overall rating: 3.5/5.0
Reviewed by: Tilda Swanson
Date of review: May 4

I recently ordered some baskets of fruit from this company for some friends of mine and I was mostly satisfied with the products and service. When I visited my friends at their workplace, I had a chance to see the baskets, and I was very impressed with the quality of fruits and the presentation of the baskets themselves. The only problem is that they arrived two days later than expected, so I was slightly disappointed about that. However, my friends were still delighted to receive the gift, even if it was a little late, so I guess everything worked out well in the end.

186. What is indicated about Basketfuls of Joy?

(A) It has several stores in the Vancouver area.
(B) It specializes in locally-grown flowers.
(C) It provides fruits that were grown overseas.
(D) It is currently hiring new delivery drivers.

187. What is suggested in the advertisement about delivery?

(A) Overnight deliveries are only available during weekdays.
(B) It is free of charge at any time on weekends.
(C) It is currently unavailable for online orders.
(D) It is cheaper compared to any other similar services.

188. What can be inferred about Mr. and Ms. Pilton?

(A) They recently started a business.
(B) They are related to Ms. Swanson.
(C) They sent multiple orders for baskets.
(D) They are seeking consultation services.

189. What is indicated about Ms. Swanson?

(A) She wants to express her condolence.
(B) She placed her order in the evening hours.
(C) She is a first-time customer of Basketfuls of Joy.
(D) She works close to Basketfuls of Joy.

190. When did the baskets arrive at 44 Boardwalk Street?

(A) On May 1
(B) On May 2
(C) On May 3
(D) On May 4

TEST 8

GO ON TO THE NEXT PAGE

E-Mail Message

To: Annabeth Farley <afarley123@maximail.com>
From: Brian Earnshaw <bearnshaw@eveinteriors.com>
Date: June 13
Subject: Decorating at 311 Grant Avenue

Dear Ms. Farley,

It was a pleasure talking with you earlier this week about the interior design plan for the property you recently purchased. Now that I have visited the house and calculated the dimensions of your rooms, I have a better idea of what sizes of curtains are required for the windows, and I have a suggestion regarding the large window in your living room. Because you and your family will spend a lot of time in this room, I'd recommend hanging Zola curtains. They include a thermal lining that helps to prevent heat-loss, so it will keep your living room nice and warm. Please visit www.zolacurtains.com/premium and let me know which type you prefer.

Regarding your bedroom, because the southeast-facing window is more exposed than the others, the sun will shine directly through it for much of the day, especially in the morning. Therefore, I'll send you some samples of our special 'blackout' curtains that would help keep that room dark while you are sleeping. These should arrive by courier tomorrow afternoon. Once you've had a chance to consider your options for both rooms, please get back to me.

Regards,

Robert Earnshaw
Eve Interiors Inc.

---

http://www.zolacurtains.com/premium

ZOLA CURTAINS

At Zola Curtains, we are especially proud of our premium range of curtains. Our premium curtains are available in four different types, all of which boast attractive and tasteful designs or patterns. Available colors include: Dark Grey, Dark Blue, Dark Green, Light Brown, and Dark Red.

Curtain type	Width/Length	Description
Osbourne	W: 330 cm L: 240 cm	Eyelet or pencil pleat style, 100% polyester
Bonham	W: 320 cm L: 210 cm	Pencil pleat or rod pocket style, 100% polyester
Shannon	W: 330 cm L: 240 cm	Double pinch pleat or pencil pleat style, 50% polyester / 50% cotton
Lescott	W: 340 cm L: 230 cm	Rod pocket or double pinch pleat style, 50% polyester / 50% cotton

To:	Brian Earnshaw <bearnshaw@eveinteriors.com>
From:	Annabeth Farley <afarley123@maximail.com>
Date:	June 14
Subject:	RE: Decorating at 311 Grant Avenue

Dear Mr. Earnshaw,

I just checked out the Web site link you sent to me yesterday, and I would prefer the curtains that have the greatest length so that they will definitely reach the floor. But, I would rather not have the ones that are composed entirely of polyester. If possible, can you try to get me a pencil pleat set in Dark Green? Also, the courier just arrived. Thank you so much! I'll wait until my husband gets home and we can discuss the plans for the bedroom together.

Regards,

Annabeth Farley

191. What can be inferred about Mr. Earnshaw?

(A) He measured the windows at 311 Grant Avenue.
(B) He worked with Ms. Farley on a previous project.
(C) He recommended a property to Ms. Farley.
(D) He has recently purchased a new house.

192. What does Mr. Earnshaw mention about Zola curtains?

(A) They are currently being discounted.
(B) They help to conserve heat.
(C) They are a best-selling brand.
(D) They are available in several colors.

193. What is indicated about Ms. Farley's bedroom?

(A) It only has one window.
(B) It will be painted next week.
(C) It does not currently have a carpet.
(D) It receives a lot of natural light.

194. What type of curtains does Ms. Farley choose for her living room?

(A) Osbourne
(B) Bonham
(C) Shannon
(D) Lescott

195. Why most likely does Ms. Farley thank Mr. Earnshaw?

(A) For sending a business contract
(B) For performing some repairs
(C) For recommending Zola Curtains
(D) For providing some sample

GO ON TO THE NEXT PAGE

Questions 196-200 refer to the following agenda and e-mails.

Tentative Agenda Created on March 5

Interns Video Game Seminar Schedule
OCP Software Company
March 12 - Computer Suite A

9:30 A.M. – 10:30 A.M.	Coffee and introductory talk by company founder
10:30 A.M. – 12:00 P.M.	Seminar 1: Modern trends in the industry
12:00 P.M. – 1:30 P.M.	Seminar 2: Devising novel game concepts
1:30 P.M. – 2:15 P.M.	Break (Lunch provided in staff cafeteria)
2:15 P.M. – 4:00 P.M.	Seminar 3: Utilizing programming languages
4:00 P.M. – 4:30 P.M.	Refreshments and socializing
4:30 P.M. – 6:00 P.M.	Seminar 4: 3D graphics development

E-Mail Message

To: Shona Glover <sglover@ocpsoft.com>
From: Sven Kallstrom <skallstrom@ocpsoft.com>
Date: March 9
Subject: Seminar series update

Hi Shona,

We will need to make a change to the series of seminars we are running for those who recently joined our internship program. I just heard that Mr. Hoffman has an appointment and won't be coming in to the office until 10:30 that day. That means he won't be able to give the welcome talk while the attendees are all having morning coffee.

None of the other executives are free to give a talk that day, so I think we should give a presentation about our past, current, and future video game projects instead. Lead software developer Dan Bushell has offered to help out with that.

I'm sorry that I can't help out on the day of the seminar series, but I'm sure you'll do an excellent job of organizing the event. Please remember to revise the agenda to reflect the change I mentioned, and then send me a finalized version.

Have a good day,

Sven

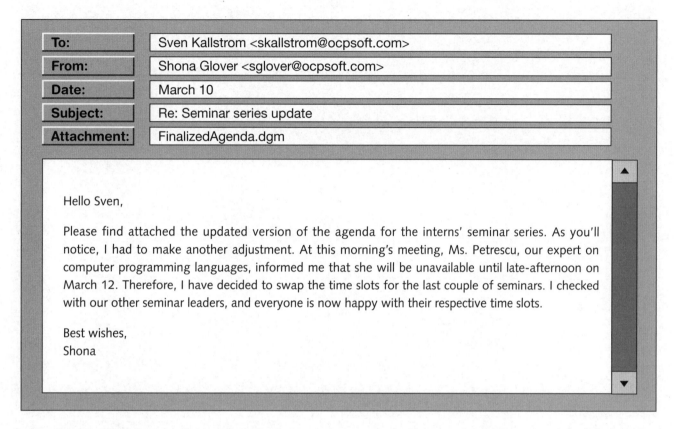

To:	Sven Kallstrom <skallstrom@ocpsoft.com>
From:	Shona Glover <sglover@ocpsoft.com>
Date:	March 10
Subject:	Re: Seminar series update
Attachment:	FinalizedAgenda.dgm

Hello Sven,

Please find attached the updated version of the agenda for the interns' seminar series. As you'll notice, I had to make another adjustment. At this morning's meeting, Ms. Petrescu, our expert on computer programming languages, informed me that she will be unavailable until late-afternoon on March 12. Therefore, I have decided to swap the time slots for the last couple of seminars. I checked with our other seminar leaders, and everyone is now happy with their respective time slots.

Best wishes,
Shona

196. What will the interns do from 12:00 P.M. to 1:30 P.M.?

(A) Meet for lunch in the staff cafeteria
(B) Watch a presentation about the company's projects
(C) Learn how to come up with innovative ideas
(D) Discuss recent trends in the software industry

197. Who is the founder of OCP Software Company?

(A) Mr. Hoffman
(B) Mr. Bushell
(C) Ms. Glover
(D) Ms. Petrescu

198. In the first e-mail, the word "free" in paragraph 2, line 1, is closest in meaning to?

(A) empty
(B) available
(C) complimentary
(D) occupied

199. What does Mr. Kallstrom ask Ms. Glover to do?

(A) Deliver a talk on programming languages
(B) Help to lead one of the seminars
(C) Make an update to a schedule
(D) Attend a meeting with colleagues

200. When will the interns most likely learn about creating 3D graphics?

(A) From 9:30 A.M. to 10:30 A.M.
(B) From 10:30 A.M. to 12:00 P.M.
(C) From 2:15 P.M. to 4:00 P.M.
(D) From 4:30 P.M. to 6:00 P.M.

TEST 8

Stop! This is the end of the test. If you finish before time is called, you may go back to Parts 5, 6, and 7 and check your work.

정답 p.471 / 점수 환산표 p.476

실전모의고사
TEST 9

TEST 9 해설

바로 보기

- 시작 시간 _____시 _____분
- 종료 시간 _____시 _____분

▶ 중간에 멈추지 말고 처음부터 끝까지 풀어보세요. 문제를 풀 때는 실전처럼 답안지에 마킹하세요.

READING TEST

In the Reading test, you will read a variety of texts and answer several different types of reading comprehension questions. The entire Reading test will last 75 minutes. There are three parts, and directions are given for each part. You are encouraged to answer as many questions as possible within the time allowed. You must mark your answers on the separate answer sheet. Do not write your answers in your test book.

PART 5

Directions: A word or phrase is missing in each of the sentences below. Four answer choices are given below each sentence. Select the best answer to complete the sentence. Then mark the letter (A), (B), (C), or (D) on your answer sheet.

101. Mr. Turner has someone in mind for the new position, but the ------- decision will not be made for a week or so.

(A) finalize
(B) final
(C) finals
(D) finally

102. Despite his popularity with many employees, Tim O'Brian has ------- hope of becoming personnel manager at BA Financial Corporation.

(A) little
(B) a number of
(C) a few
(D) several

103. The west wing of the Gerald Building will be closed from December 26 to 31 for -------, but will reopen with a more spacious employee lounge.

(A) renovates
(B) renovate
(C) renovator
(D) renovations

104. Last week, MCA Manufacturing, Inc.'s sales associates convened to ------- concerns that the lack of new contracts in recent months would result in a sharp decrease in sales.

(A) address
(B) remark
(C) improve
(D) comment

105. After months of negotiations, Mr. Kenneth has reached an agreement with JM Logistics Co., ------- support is crucial for his business's economic recovery.

(A) which
(B) whose
(C) that
(D) what

106. Last week, a power failure caused all computer systems to stop functioning, ------- interrupting the presentation to our important clients.

(A) usefully
(B) readily
(C) precisely
(D) briefly

107. To motivate employees in the sales division, anyone selling over 100 units of merchandise this month will receive additional ------- on their paychecks.

(A) compensates
(B) compensated
(C) compensatory
(D) compensation

108. All of the food served at the company's 10th anniversary dinner ------- by Hartford Catering Services.

(A) provide
(B) was provided
(C) provided
(D) providing

109. Mr. Hambleton will assume responsibility ------- employee travel reimbursement while the accounting manager is on vacation.

(A) on behalf of
(B) as well
(C) for
(D) by

110. We are concerned that the ------- figures from the last quarter will lower our advertising budget for the rest of the year.

(A) disappointing
(B) disappoint
(C) disappointment
(D) disappointed

111. The color scheme of our new office building was ------- selected by an award-winning local interior designer.

(A) skilled
(B) skillfully
(C) skill
(D) skillful

112. ------- mentioned during the staff meeting last week, beginning May 1, lunch time will be extended by 30 minutes to give employees the chance to participate in fitness activities.

(A) As
(B) If
(C) After
(D) For

113. Some of the major hotels in Hokkaido have reduced room rates as a way of ------- travelers during the off season.

(A) attracts
(B) attraction
(C) attracting
(D) attracted

114. If you would like to ------- from our group life insurance policy, please contact our Special Sales Team at 324-555-3528 before the end of the month.

(A) benefit
(B) serve
(C) assist
(D) help

115. Under the leadership of the new CEO, KPL Corporation's customer service has improved significantly in terms of ------- wait times and quality of service.

(A) also
(B) between
(C) both
(D) additionally

116. It became ------- that the client was not satisfied with the consulting team led by Ms. Cruz and requested its replacement.

(A) apparent
(B) negligible
(C) contingent
(D) prerequisite

117. The editor advised her assistant to proofread all documents more ------- before submitting them to avoid any minor errors in the future.

(A) considerately
(B) generously
(C) willingly
(D) carefully

118. Carl came ------- recommended by his former employer, a well-known accountant who once worked with us in the past.

(A) high
(B) higher
(C) highest
(D) highly

119. You will be required to send a proposal ------- your project to the executive board before any funding is granted.

(A) describing
(B) telling
(C) promising
(D) informing

120. Once the corporation is in the ------- stage of moving its manufacturing facilities, it will offer workers substantial incentives to relocate.

(A) initial
(B) ahead
(C) forward
(D) present

GO ON TO THE NEXT PAGE

121. Any new advertisers seeking to purchase space in our magazine are asked to consult our ------- for submission, available on our Web site.

(A) issues
(B) references
(C) guidelines
(D) resources

122. ------- we have the budget to buy new computers, we regret that our outdated photocopier cannot be replaced until later this year.

(A) But
(B) While
(C) Before
(D) However

123. Since Mr. Brownloe requested a second round of corrections, the project deadline has been extended to accommodate ------- revisions.

(A) his
(B) he
(C) him
(D) himself

124. We will reopen after two months of renovations with a grand sale ------- on the 29th.

(A) start
(B) started
(C) starting
(D) starter

125. BTC's Tokyo office manager Sylvie Wu has accepted a new position at the head office and will ------- at the end of the month.

(A) update
(B) retire
(C) relocate
(D) demote

126. To avoid serious accidents, all refinery workers should follow standard safety ------- at work.

(A) procedures
(B) developments
(C) categories
(D) qualifications

127. Because many clients have requested longer store hours, we will now stay open until 10 P.M. during the week, but will continue ------- at 9 P.M. on Saturdays and Sundays.

(A) closing
(B) closed
(C) close
(D) have closed

128. With so many clients not sending in their financial records in time, we will set deadlines ------- submission and charge a processing fee of $15 for each late document.

(A) about
(B) for
(C) of
(D) to

129. Johnson Elevators is planning to expand the size of its ------ team by hiring eight more engineers.

(A) maintain
(B) maintained
(C) maintenance
(D) maintainable

130. The real estate agent urged Mr. Kwan to purchase the larger house immediately, but he was reluctant due to his ------- budget.

(A) potential
(B) distinct
(C) limited
(D) assorted

PART 6

Directions: Read the texts that follow. A word, phrase, or sentence is missing in parts of each text. Four answer choices for each question are given below the text. Select the best answer to complete the text. Then mark the letter (A), (B), (C) or (D) on your answer sheet.

Questions 131-134 refer to the following letter.

Thank you for becoming a First Bank credit card customer. ------- is your new credit card.
131.

Before using your card, please ------- read the accompanying documents describing your rights and
132.
responsibilities as a First Bank credit card user. If you have any further questions, call 255-HELP. To

activate your card, call 255-CARD to confirm that you have received your card. Your card will not be

valid for use ------- you call this number.
133.

In an unlikely event of loss or theft, please call 255-LOST immediately. -------.
134.

Thanks.

131. (A) Enclosed
(B) Enclosure
(C) Enclosing
(D) Enclose

132. (A) unanimously
(B) eagerly
(C) thoroughly
(D) conveniently

133. (A) earlier
(B) rather
(C) whether
(D) unless

134. (A) If you are interested, please contact us.
(B) Thank you for informing us about the missing card.
(C) We look forward to serving you in the future.
(D) There are several First Bank account types available.

GO ON TO THE NEXT PAGE

Questions 135 -138 refer to the following notice.

Welcome to Trinity Advertising's third annual staff conference. -------. With such a large number of
135.
employees attending, we will be keeping to a ------- timetable during the event to ensure that we
136.
complete all of our activities on time.

Keeping this in mind, we ask you to ------- from missing any scheduled events. You should all already
137.
know how vital it is to attend each one.

Tonight, we will gather in the ballroom for a formal dinner followed by our annual awards ceremony.
Tomorrow there will be a series of speakers and workshops. We apologize that no lunch will be
provided in between the workshops. ------- , sandwiches and beverages may be purchased from the
138.
vending machines in the lobby.

---

135. (A) We hope your stay with us has been an
enjoyable one.
(B) Please give a warm welcome to our
guests and make them feel at home.
(C) Allow me to describe some of the topics
that will be discussed during the event.
(D) We are set to break previous records with
over 500 staff attending this year.

136. (A) rigorous
(B) various
(C) numerous
(D) hazardous

137. (A) obtain
(B) refrain
(C) prevent
(D) mind

138. (A) For instance
(B) In addition
(C) However
(D) Otherwise

Questions 139 -142 refer to the following e-mail.

From: Rebecca Vercoe <r.vercoe@tgarchitectural.com>

To: All Staff

Date: December 1

Subject: Company relocation schedule

I am writing regarding our recently confirmed office relocation to the Gasson Street business park, which is ------- to take place on January 5 next year.
139.

Before moving into the new office, we asked that all staff pack up their personal belongings by putting them in boxes, which will be distributed ------- the next two weeks. ------- . Considering this,
140. **141.**
we will require you to have your boxes ready for moving by December 20. ------- , we have decided
142.
to allow you to finish work early on December 19 to allow sufficient time for everyone to organize their belongings.

Thank you for your cooperation in this matter.

Regards,

Rebecca

---

139. (A) considered
(B) measured
(C) scheduled
(D) presented

140. (A) under
(B) among
(C) between
(D) within

141. (A) The new furniture will match the office interior nicely.
(B) We anticipate having many items to move to our new premises.
(C) Many of the boxes have already been stacked near the main entrance.
(D) Some belongings will be arriving late.

142. (A) Therefore
(B) Still
(C) Although
(D) Prior to

GO ON TO THE NEXT PAGE

Questions 143-146 refer to the following article.

Los Angeles, 23 April – Local station JSV Television has lost millions so far this year with a record second quarter loss of $22 million and could even face bankruptcy by the end of the year. The downturn in revenue can be ------- to the global decline of media companies and a difficult economic
143.
environment.

-------. This move into print media is worrying some shareholders who voiced their opposition to the
144.
purchase at a recent meeting.

JSV Television is the largest privately-owned television station in the state of California and has become one of the ------- companies in the industry ever since its ------- by Harry Smithson in 1964.
145. **146.**
The company currently employs 6,800 staff.

---

143. (A) attributed
(B) contributed
(C) committed
(D) applied

144. (A) Industry analysts predict that the sluggish economy will soon recover.
(B) Despite the drop in earnings, JSV Television recently acquired a daily newspaper.
(C) Media companies need to find ways to adapt to how people consume media.
(D) It saw many customers drop their service in favor of cheaper plans.

145. (A) leading
(B) accustomed
(C) originated
(D) moving

146. (A) founding
(B) found
(C) founder
(D) founded

PART 7

Directions: In this part you will read a selection of texts, such as magazine and newspaper articles, e-mails, and instant messages. Each text or set of texts is followed by several questions. Select the best answer for each question and mark the letter (A), (B), (C), or (D) on your answer sheet.

Questions 147-148 refer to the following invoice.

Fresh Scent Flower Delivery

98 Houston Highway, Mainstown, Arkansas 92049

Delivery Invoice

Date: Feb 27
Invoice No: 49302
Purchased by: Bob Bradley
Delivery Address: The Cottage, Jupiter Drive, Brekonsville, Arkansas

Mixed Roses Economy Bundle	$49.95
Deluxe Greeting Card	$4.95
Helium Greeting Balloon	$19.95
Gift Chocolates: 12 pc. set	$ 9.95
Subtotal	$84.80
Returning Customer Discount	- $10.00
Tax	$8.35
Shipping*	$4.00
Total	$87.15
Adjusted Total	$83.15

* Shipping fees are waived during the month of February.

We at Fresh Scent appreciate your business.

---

147. What is suggested about Mr. Bradley?

(A) He is employed by Fresh Scent.
(B) He is unsatisfied with the quality of a product.
(C) He requested a refund from Fresh Scent.
(D) He has shopped at Fresh Scent before.

148. What is the total amount that Mr. Bradley must pay?

(A) $83.15
(B) $49.95
(C) $84.80
(D) $87.15

GO ON TO THE NEXT PAGE

Questions **149-150** refer to the following article.

The Hatfield Gazette

Travel Eye

February 21

The CEO of local travel firm Golden Dreams today announced plans to expand its business. The firm, well known for offering holiday packages exclusively to people over 65, is reported to have experienced a dramatic increase in sales over the last year. Cruises to various Central American destinations have proven to be particularly popular over this time.

Golden Dreams was originally founded in Mayville before moving its offices to Redberry, where it has been ever since. Customers have come from all over the state following a successful advertising campaign in the Dustlane area. CEO Michael Phillips today announced plans to open a new office in Edmonton later this year.

149. What is suggested about Golden Dreams?
(A) It provides its services only to senior citizens.
(B) Its profits have been steadily decreasing.
(C) It is being sold to its rival company.
(D) It offers holiday packages to Africa.

150. Where are Golden Dreams' offices currently located?
(A) Edmonton
(B) Mayville
(C) Dustlane
(D) Redberry

Questions 151-152 refer to the following text-message chain.

Ben [7:30 P.M.]

We have been doing the bookkeeping and preparing all the financial reports without any help. I've put in over 25 extra hours so far this month. This is getting really difficult.

Julia [7:42 P.M.]

I know. The extra pay from overtime is great. However, I am seriously close to burning out. When are they going to hire someone? Should we schedule a meeting with Charles?

Ben [7:45 P.M.]

I actually spoke with him yesterday. He hired a couple of new assistants, but they can't start for another two weeks.

Julia [7:50 P.M.]

I see. I wonder if someone from Customer Support would be able to come help us out temporarily.

Ben [7:52 P.M.]

Actually, Peter just returned early from his cruise. I bet he could help.

151. At 7:42 P.M., what does Julia mean when she says, "However, I am seriously close to burning out"?

(A) She will take a bookkeeping course.
(B) She will hire an assistant by herself.
(C) She is struggling with her workload.
(D) She would like a higher overtime rate.

152. What will happen in two weeks?

(A) Peter will transfer to the Billing Department.
(B) Ben and Julia will meet with Charles.
(C) Charles will interview job applicants.
(D) New employees will start working.

Questions 153-154 refer to the following letter.

Personnel Director
Metatron Software
Route de Moncor 14 - PO Box 49
Zurich, Switzerland

Dear Sir or Madam,

I am writing to express my interest in the position of senior programmer posted on Metatron's Web site. As I indicate on my enclosed résumé, I previously worked for over 10 years as a programmer at O.G.Soft, where I was involved in the development of many of its applications. Among other projects, I was the primary designer on its best-selling spreadsheet software CalQLate. In addition to overseeing a team of software programmers, my duties at O.G.Soft included programming new applications, maintaining and updating existing software, and managing quality control processes.

I look forward to discussing this employment opportunity with you in person. Thank you for your time and consideration.

Sincerely,

Cecil Vyse

Cecil Vyse

153. What is indicated about CalQLate?

(A) It took 10 years to develop.
(B) It is no longer available for purchase.
(C) It was commercially successful.
(D) It was produced by Metatron.

154. According to the letter, in which area does the writer NOT have experience?

(A) Marketing software
(B) Managing employees
(C) Conducting product tests
(D) Creating software

Questions 155-157 refer to the following e-mail.

To:	bhinton@worldnet.com
From:	inge@barnaby.com
Subject:	Upcoming Work
Attachment:	Projects.doc

Hi Brandon,

I hope this e-mail finds you well. My name is Inge Samuelsson. As you probably know, Sheila Campbell left Barnaby Communications last month, and I have taken over her position. According to Sheila's notes, you are the primary translator for outsourced projects, so I assume we will be working together a lot.

We have a number of translation projects under development, and I'd like to give you the first chance at claiming them. Please consult the attached file which shows the projected due dates and estimated word counts of each assignment. Needless to say, the deadlines are likely to change, but hopefully not by too much. The English drafts of the first project will be assigned to translators next week. If you are interested in any of the projects or if you have any questions, please reply by e-mail by the end of the day tomorrow.

Best regards,

Inge Samuelsson
Editor
Barnaby Communications

155. Who most likely is Brandon?

(A) A prospective client
(B) A freelance writer
(C) A job applicant
(D) A project manager

156. What is included with the e-mail?

(A) A cost estimate for a project
(B) A document to be translated
(C) A tentative work timeline
(D) A renewed contract to be signed

157. What will most likely happen next week?

(A) Brandon will apply for one of the projects.
(B) Some documents will be distributed.
(C) Ms. Samuelsson will meet with Brandon.
(D) A finished work will be submitted.

Questions 158-160 refer to the following article.

Smokers are less likely to show up for work than their non-smoking counterparts. That's the conclusion of a new Danish study published in the medical journal *Side Effects*, which reports that smokers average seven more days of sick leave per year than non-smokers.

Over 12,000 people in seven countries took part in the 10-year survey, which compared smokers and non-smokers on a number of issues, including work absences, hospitalization times, diet, and personal finances. Overall, people in the survey took an average of 12 days of sick leave each year. The average was 16 days for smokers and 9 for non-smokers. Among countries surveyed, the number of working days lost each year due to sickness was highest in Denmark (18) and lowest in the United States (10).

The study also found that smokers are more likely to be obese and have chronic health problems. Jens Gronkjaer, the author of the study, says: "On one level, the data shows what we already know – smoking is bad for individual health. But it also shows there are secondary effects that we usually don't consider, like a negative impact on the work quality and productivity of staff."

158. What was the purpose of the survey?

(A) To measure the impact of smoking on workers
(B) To express support for anti-smoking campaigns
(C) To compare the effectiveness of different diet programs
(D) To study popular methods for quitting smoking

159. What issue was NOT addressed by the study?

(A) Eating habits
(B) Time spent in hospitals
(C) Employee performance
(D) Fitness activities

160. What does Jens Gronkjaer imply about the findings?

(A) Smoking is just an individual habit.
(B) Smoking is more than a health problem.
(C) They contradict the results of previous studies.
(D) Many people don't think smoking is dangerous.

Questions 161-164 refer to the following online chat discussion.

Hiroto Nara [11:33 A.M.]	Hi Mari, Jungeun and I have a few questions about the new-hire training that will start next week.
Mari Busov [11:40 A.M.]	Hi, Hiroto and Jungeun. Sorry for taking so long, I was in a meeting. I'm happy to answer any questions you might have.
Jungeun Lee [11:41 A.M.]	Can you confirm the exact number of trainees that we will have on Monday?
Mari Busov [11:41 A.M.]	Sure. Right now, we are expecting 17. I still need to follow-up with a few candidates, so that number might increase to 20. I will let you know by the end of the day.
Hiroto Nara [11:42 A.M.]	Okay, that's great. We have prepared 30 training manuals, but I wanted to make sure we didn't need more. Will the trainees need only the software, shipping, and customer service modules?
Mari Busov [11:42 A.M.]	These new trainees will be assigned to a special project that will involve the key skills taught in the data entry and quality control modules, so you should definitely include those modules. I'm not sure why you've included the customer service module, as they won't come face-to-face with any customers.
Jungeun Lee [11:43 A.M.]	Oh, okay. That's different from what Jen told us last week.
Mari Busov [11:45 A.M.]	Sorry about that. Perhaps she got a little confused about it.
Hiroto Nara [11:46 A.M.]	Oh, no worries. This actually makes our job easier. Thanks for your help, Mari!

161. What department do Jungeun and Hiroto most likely work in?

(A) Training
(B) Customer Service
(C) Accounting
(D) Delivery

162. What is indicated about the manuals?

(A) They need to be photocopied.
(B) They will be distributed by e-mail.
(C) There are enough of them prepared.
(D) Some employees haven't received them.

163. According to the discussion, what skill is essential for the special project?

(A) Quality control
(B) Maintaining equipment
(C) Customer service
(D) Sales

164. At 11:43 A.M., what does Ms. Lee imply when she says, "That's different from what Jen told us last week"?

(A) She heard that the customer training session took place last week.
(B) She believed that the new trainees would deal with customers.
(C) She hopes that the new associates are qualified to work with them.
(D) She disagrees with Jen's suggestion about the training modules.

GO ON TO THE NEXT PAGE

Questions 165-167 refer to the following advertisement.

Portable music players allow you to enjoy your favorite tunes while walking on the street, sitting in an airplane, or working at your desk. But while it's easy to bring your music with you, it's not so easy to avoid background noise. That's why Resonance Audio Inc. has developed our exclusive NB (Noise-Block) headphones.

Our products provide you with the ultimate listening experience. Our revolutionary noise-blocking technology cuts background noise by 70%, which is at least 20% more than any other brand on the market. Resonance Audio Inc. is a leader in sound quality, and these new headphones live up to our high standards.

NB headphones have been designed with your comfort and convenience in mind. They have a compact shape, making them easy to carry or put in your bag. The soft padding around the earpieces allows you to wear them for hours without discomfort. Besides, they weigh only 16g: one of the lightest headphones on the market.

Visit www.rai.com to learn more. Order now and you can try NB headphones risk-free for 30 days. If you are not completely satisfied, we will give you a full refund.

165. What kind of product is being advertised?

(A) Online music service
(B) Audio accessories
(C) Car stereo systems
(D) Audio editing software

166. What is mentioned as an advantage of the product over other brands?

(A) Its sound quality
(B) Its attractive design
(C) Its reasonable cost
(D) Its compact size

167. What is NOT a feature of the product?

(A) Comfortable padding
(B) Lightweight
(C) A carrying case
(D) A money-back guarantee

Questions 168-171 refer to the following notice.

Professionally Yours - The HR Manager's Resource

Start the new year off right. Professionally Yours is offering a set of workshops tailored to the challenges facing today's Human Resources managers. Reserve your place now for an in-depth look at the latest in HR management. Come for one day or for the whole week.

When: January 10-13
Where: Myra Schultz Convention Center, 23 The Plaza, Dallas, Texas
Registration: 423-555-0123 or workshopinfo@professionallyyours.com
Early registration earns a 10% discount.

Be a Legal Eagle – Monday 10

Learn about recent changes in federal and state laws and policies. — [1] —. Includes information on income tax, persons with disabilities, environmental requirements, equal opportunities and more. Presented by local law firm Brown, Lyons & Richie.

Fostering Corporate Culture – Tuesday 11

— [2] —. Award-winning author and psychologist Peter Leland discusses what determines corporate culture and how it affects the bottom line. See how small changes in the workplace and procedures can dramatically affect productivity and output. You'll come away with some great tools for making your company more competitive.

Restructuring – Wednesday 12

— [3] —. See the latest research on corporate downsizing and outsourcing – and learn the benefits and drawbacks. Afternoon seminar on dealing with accompanying issues.

HR Software Update – Thursday 13

A comprehensive survey of all the major vendor software available for managing employee time-sheets, expense account, vacation time, etc. — [4] —. See which package will best fit your particular needs. Presented by our own expert, Roger Halley.

Visit our Web site at www.professionallyyours.com for more information.

---

168. What is the purpose of the notice?

(A) To announce a company meeting
(B) To seek volunteers for a survey
(C) To publicize a four-day event
(D) To advertise a university class

169. According to the notice, who has written a book?

(A) Myra Schulz
(B) Brown, Lyons & Richie
(C) Peter Leland
(D) Roger Halley

170. When will computer programs be discussed?

(A) On January 10
(B) On January 11
(C) On January 12
(D) On January 13

171. In which of the positions marked [1], [2], [3], and [4] does the following sentence best belong?

"Learn strategies for deciding where to focus in times of economic difficulties."

(A) [1]
(B) [2]
(C) [3]
(D) [4]

GO ON TO THE NEXT PAGE

Office Interiors Inc.

Make your workspace work for you!

Are you moving to a new office location? Expanding your floor space? Reorganizing your workflow? — [1] —. Office Interiors Inc.'s team members have many years of experience in designing and implementing workspaces that work for you. We pay attention to your office's every need, from choosing colors that promote productivity in your particular industry, to computer-aided designs for furniture placement in high traffic areas. We do it all.

— [2] —. We maintain a large inventory of office furnishings and design elements, as well as a qualified staff of interior designers and architects. Ask us for a referral list of satisfied customers.

— [3] —. We will observe your workflow and talk to your employees as well as making a comprehensive study of your needs and wants. You will be given a choice of plans/materials/designs with price ranges included, but you will make the final decisions yourself.

— [4] —. Choose Office Interiors and improve productivity and comfort at your office!

172. What is the purpose of the advertisement?

(A) To describe brand-new products
(B) To announce a company's relocation
(C) To promote a company's services
(D) To outline an upcoming project

173. What is mentioned about Office Interiors Inc.?

(A) It specializes in designing workspaces.
(B) It charges less than its competitors.
(C) It has offices all around the world.
(D) It provides free estimation service.

174. According to the advertisement, what will Office Interiors Inc. NOT do?

(A) Have discussions with employees
(B) Provide customer referrals
(C) Examine how a potential client works
(D) Make a final design selection

175. In which of the positions marked [1], [2], [3], and [4] does the following sentence best belong?

"One of the most important steps of our service is the information gathering process."

(A) [1]
(B) [2]
(C) [3]
(D) [4]

GO ON TO THE NEXT PAGE

Questions 176-180 refer to the following invitation and letter.

You are invited to join
James Leem, personal investor and
Chief Executive Officer at JL Financial,
for a Black Tie event on July 29
at the Pink Horizon Inn and Spa
on the banks of the Pacific Ocean.
Guests will enjoy an internationally-acclaimed three-course meal,
after which they will be treated to
a sunset cruise on Cardinal Bay.

For those who would like to stay the night,
one night's accommodation for two
has been reserved for each guest.
Each couple will also receive a voucher for the spa,
all courtesy of Mr. Leem.

This evening is for preferred clients only.
Thank you for referring over 10 new clients to Mr. Leem this year.

Kindly RSVP by June 21
to Mr. Leem's secretary.

Ms. Jasmine Park
JL Financial
532 Humboldt Street
Santa Rosa, California 95404

Dear Ms. Park,

Thank you for the invitation to Mr. Leem's Black Tie event. I must say I was quite surprised to receive it. It is the first time I have been recognized in this way by an investment banker. It will certainly encourage me to remain a "preferred client." Smart business move!

Unfortunately, I am unable to attend the event due to a prior business engagement. Because I am the sole proprietor of my business, I am kept quite busy, and I will be overseas the night of the event. My wife is also sorry she will miss out on the evening and the chance to meet with Mrs. Leem.

I wonder if we will be invited next year to make up for our absence this year. I would be honored to attend another time, if this is the sort of thing Mr. Leem does regularly. In the future, I need at least two months' notice instead of three weeks in order to make a commitment to an event such as this one.

Thank you again for the invitation. I am pleased with my decision to invest with Mr. Leem and look forward to meeting you in the future.

Regards,

Daniel Sujek

Daniel Sujek
President, Sujek Consulting

176. What is the purpose of the event?

(A) To mark a company's founding day
(B) To attract potential investors to a project
(C) To celebrate a CEO's retirement
(D) To thank clients for their referrals

177. What does Mr. Sujek suggest about the event?

(A) It is a unique way to grow business.
(B) It includes only business owners.
(C) It is being poorly organized.
(D) It should be held on a weekend.

178. Who is Jasmine Park?

(A) James Leem's secretary
(B) Daniel Sujek's wife
(C) An investor at JL Financial
(D) The receptionist at Pink Horizon

179. In the letter, the word "move" in paragraph 1, line 3, is closest in meaning to

(A) location
(B) advice
(C) progress
(D) strategy

180. Why is Mr. Sujek unable to attend the event?

(A) He has a business meeting.
(B) His wife has a prior appointment.
(C) He will be traveling abroad.
(D) He will be attending a convention.

GO ON TO THE NEXT PAGE

Questions 181-185 refer to the following notice and e-mail.

Notice to All Residents of Skyline Condominium
April 24

Recently there was an increasing number of complaints from our tenants about noise, theft and the lack of parking spaces. To address those issues, we had a resident meeting last week. As a result of a vote that included all tenants, three new rules have been added to our Condominium Agreement. You can find a description of the rules that have been approved below:

1. Any guest visiting the building who requires a parking space for over one week must pay a fee of $5 per day.

2. Any renovation requiring electrical or plumbing changes must be approved by the newly-appointed Condominium inspector prior to the commencement of the renovations.

3. All windows must be closed and locked if your suite is vacant for a period of 48 hours or more.

Each resident is asked to sign the attached form and return it to the President of the Resident Council in Suite #313 before the end of April.

The changes will be considered in effect starting May 1. Any resident who does not follow these rules will be fined $150 per offense.

Sincerely,

Stacey Partel
President, Resident Council
Skyline Condominium

E-Mail Message

To: Stacey Partel <spartel@skyline.com>
From: Hans Schoenberg <hans@schoenbergmedia.com>
Subject: Window Fine
Date: May 3

Dear Ms. Partel,

I would like to request that the fine I received today be waived.

I was away on business when the notice regarding our Condominium Agreement was posted, so I just found out about the changes today.

Prior to my trip, I had arranged for a friend to come into my suite and open the windows over the weekend to let in some fresh air. I made these arrangements before the changes to the Agreement took effect. Therefore, I ask that you reconsider the fine and treat it as a notice for future offenses. I assure you I will have no difficulty obeying the rules.

Thank you for your understanding.

Sincerely,

Hans Schoenberg

Suite #405

181. What most likely caused the agreement to be changed?

    (A) Ms. Partel wanted to increase security.
    (B) Many residents reported issues to the council.
    (C) The condominium hired a new manager.
    (D) Some tenants failed to pay fines.

182. What is each resident asked to do?

    (A) E-mail the condominium inspector
    (B) Pay a $150 fee to Ms. Partel
    (C) Acknowledge receipt of the changes
    (D) Request a personal parking space

183. Who most likely is Hans Schoenberg?

    (A) The maintenance manager
    (B) A colleague of Ms. Partel's
    (C) An association founder
    (D) A current resident

184. Why did Mr. Schoenberg write to Ms. Partel?

    (A) To request that she withdraw a fine
    (B) To ask for a copy of the Condominium Agreement
    (C) To give her notice that he will be out of town
    (D) To arrange for an inspector to check his suite

185. What is indicated about Mr. Schoenberg?

    (A) He will travel for business this month.
    (B) He was not at home on April 24.
    (C) He shares a condominium with a friend.
    (D) He believes the new rules are unfair.

GO ON TO THE NEXT PAGE

Blue Blocker Glasses

Did you know that many electronic devices produce a type of blue light that can be extremely harmful? Many doctors recommend wearing Blue Blocker glasses whenever you are looking at a phone, tablet, e-reader, or computer screen. If you have trouble sleeping, it is beneficial to wear these glasses for at least an hour before you fall asleep at night. We have thousands of testimonials from loyal buyers, including many celebrities, who say that this amazing product has made a world of difference to their quality of life.

Wearing Blue Blocker glasses can help you:
• sleep better
• improve your focus
• prevent headaches
• reduce eye problems
• look fashionable

Many office managers have expressed interest in our product, so we are pleased to offer a generous corporate discount. If you buy between five and ten pairs of glasses, you'll receive a discount of ten percent. Any orders of more than ten pairs will be reduced in price by twenty percent.

BLUE BLOCKER INC.

Order #32876

Order submitted: July 15
Order shipped: July 22
Expected delivery date: July 30

Description	Quantity	Total
Blue Blocker Glasses	15	$360.00 USD**

** Corporate Discount Applied

Customer's shipping information

Bill@LuxuryFlooring.com
Bill Brown, CEO
Luxury Flooring
1000 4th Street
New York City, NY 10108

Customer Satisfaction guaranteed!

If you are not happy with our product in the first 30 days, we will give you your money back.

Blue Blocker Inc.

Product Review

Customer's Name: Bill Brown
Date Posted: August 15

I love these Blue Blocker glasses and I have been wearing them for the past two years. I run my own business, and I am in front of the computer for several hours during the day, scheduling work projects and ordering materials such as tiles, hardwood, etc. Not surprisingly, my screen time began to negatively affect my vision and sleep habits. Since coming across these glasses, however, life has changed for both me and my employees! Now, I wear Blue Blocker glasses whenever I am doing work for my business and it makes a great difference to the way I feel. In fact, I think everyone who works in an office should have a pair of these glasses. It will definitely improve your performance at work.

If I have only one complaint, it would be that it can take a while to receive items after placing an order. I ordered several pairs of glasses back on July 15, and I received them almost a full week after the scheduled delivery date. This caused some inconvenience for me and my staff. Despite this issue, I still feel that the glasses are worth the wait.

186. In the advertisement, the word "beneficial" in paragraph 1, line 3, is closest in meaning to

(A) informative
(B) respected
(C) helpful
(D) profitable

187. What is indicated about Blue Blocker glasses?

(A) They protect device screens.
(B) They must be used for outdoors only.
(C) You may use them before sleeping.
(D) They require a doctor's approval.

188. What type of business does Bill Brown most likely run?

(A) A glasses manufacturer
(B) An eye care clinic
(C) A flooring company
(D) A Web design firm

189. What discount was most likely applied to Mr. Brown's order?

(A) 5 percent
(B) 10 percent
(C) 15 percent
(D) 20 percent

190. What does Mr. Brown indicate about Order #32876?

(A) It contained fewer items than ordered.
(B) It was shipped to an incorrect location.
(C) It included some defective items.
(D) It arrived at his workplace in August.

GO ON TO THE NEXT PAGE

Questions 191-195 refer to the following advertisement, e-mail, and review.

The Best Party Planner

Are you having a difficult time planning an amazing celebration? My name is Janet Rivers and I am the owner of The Best Party Planner. My company is eager to arrange a wonderful event for all of your guests to enjoy. We will provide guidance and support throughout the entire party planning process. There will be no pressure on you because we always take care of any issues that could occur before or during your party.

I can arrange a party in one of the four following locations, all of which provide a wide range of delicious food.

- Golden Sands (Mexican Food)
- The Circle Landmark (Classic American Burgers)
- Seven (French Cuisine)
- Marchetti's Pizzeria (Pizza and Pasta)

Please call me immediately to schedule a free consultation where we will discuss your specific needs and vision for your event. The Best Party Planner can't wait to help you plan the most beautiful affair that you will remember for the rest of your life.

E-Mail Message

To:	Nigel Givens, Kathryn Benson
From:	Rhonda Lees
Subject:	Jerry Sawyer's Retirement Party
Date:	May 3

Dear Colleagues,

As you know, Jerry will be retiring at the end of this year. To honor all his years of hard work and dedication here at APL Real Estate, we will be throwing him a surprise retirement party. After all, throughout his time working for APL, he made the most home sales our company has ever seen!

We have hired Janet Rivers from The Best Party Planner to take care of organizing the event. She has suggested four locations, and I'm going to discuss these with her and choose the best one.

Kathryn, I'd like you to inform the rest of our employees about the plan. Also, Janet will make sure that whichever restaurant we choose will have vegetarian options for you. And, Nigel, I'd like you to put you in charge of making sure Jerry attends the event. Just tell him you'd like to treat him to dinner, but remember that the party is supposed to be a surprise!

Please mark your calendars for May 14 at 6:00 P.M. I will send more details about the location and menu soon.

Thanks,
Rhonda Lees

"The WORST Party Planner"

Date: May 19

I attended a work event last week that "The Best Party Planner" had planned. It was very disappointing. First of all, Janet Rivers, the owner of the company, never communicated to the restaurant that a vegetarian would be attending the party. With no apology, she brought us a platter of Mexican tacos and burritos, all of which contained either steak or chicken, which I am obviously unable to eat. In addition, all the decorations that were hung up throughout the room had my colleague's name spelled incorrectly. After all his years of incredible hard work with our real estate company, this easily avoidable oversight was insulting.

— Anonymous

191. What is indicated about the The Best Party Planner?

(A) It is a privately-owned company.
(B) It specializes in providing musical entertainment.
(C) It offers discounts to returning clients.
(D) It provides catering for office parties.

192. What does Ms. Lees say about Mr. Sawyer?

(A) He has selected a restaurant for an event.
(B) He has experience in arranging parties.
(C) He has accepted a new position.
(D) He is a successful salesperson.

193. Where did Mr. Sawyer's party most likely take place?

(A) Golden Sands
(B) The Circle Landmark
(C) Seven
(D) Marchetti's Pizzeria

194. Who most likely posted the review?

(A) Jerry Sawyer
(B) Nigel Givens
(C) Kathryn Benson
(D) Rhonda Lees

195. What is suggested about Janet Rivers?

(A) She is a detail-oriented worker who cares about clients.
(B) She does not always follow through with her promises.
(C) She offers a full refund to dissatisfied clients.
(D) She manages the kitchens of many restaurants.

GO ON TO THE NEXT PAGE

Questions 196-200 refer to the following job advertisement and e-mails.

CLS TOYS INCORPORATED

Job Vacancy: Promotional Events Team Leader

Our famous toy company, CLS Toys, is seeking an enthusiastic and personable team leader to work during the Christmas shopping season from November 2 to January 5. Applicants must be able to organize and supervise promotional events according to our specific company guidelines. It is required to have a polite and courteous manner when dealing with our customers. Professionalism is key! Occasionally workers may be asked to visit our corporate headquarters in Kansas City for work purposes, so please let us know during your interview if you are willing to travel.

We are eager to hire individuals who can work independently as well as be part of a team. Our monthly wages are competitive and we offer employee discounts. You must have at least two years of experience in events promotion to be considered for this position.

Interested individuals should submit a cover letter and a résumé to the Human Resources Department at hrmanager@clstoys.com. Applications will be accepted until 5 P.M. on September 30.

E-Mail Message

To:	Human Resources <hrmanager@clstoys.com>
From:	Jane Ryan <janeryan@worldnet.com>
Date:	Team Leader Job Opportunity
Subject:	September 28
Attachment:	📎 Resume.doc

Dear Sir or Madam,

My name is Jane Ryan and I am applying for the promotional events team leader position at CLS Toys, as advertised in this week's newspaper. I am a reliable, determined, and passionate worker with diverse work experience that has prepared me to be successful as a team leader.

For the past three years, I have been working a variety of freelance jobs, and I particularly enjoy picking up work and helping out with promotional events during this time of year. Last year, I sold candy at a local candy shop. The year before, I enjoyed playing the part of Santa's elf in Rivers County Mall in my hometown of Des Moines. My CV provides more details about my variety of experiences in this field.

Thank you in advance for your consideration.

Sincerely,

Jane Ryan

To:	Jane Ryan <janeryan@worldnet.com>
From:	Robert Klepner <rklepner@clstoys.com>
Subject:	Welcome to the team
Date:	October 26
Attachment:	LocationDetails.jpg

Dear Ms. Ryan,

I am pleased to hear that you have accepted our job offer. We are thrilled to welcome you to the team. Leslie Raxenberg, our Human Resources manager, put your application at the top of the pile because she knew that I used to be Santa Claus in the mall when I was a college student. I look forward to exchanging stories.

I would like to invite you to join our team for an optional training session on October 29 from 9:00-5:30 at our training facility located in your hometown. I have attached a map and directions to this e-mail. In addition to providing you with your standard hourly pay, our payroll manager, Ben Davies, will cover your transportation costs and all meals. Your new colleague, Shai Greene, has just confirmed her attendance. Please let me know if you would like to join us.

Regards,

Robert Klepner, CEO

196. According to the advertisement, what is true about the job?

(A) Regular commuting is required.
(B) The position is seasonal.
(C) All meals are complimentary.
(D) It is an hourly paid position.

197. What is indicated about Jane Ryan?

(A) She managed a candy shop.
(B) She has experience as a team leader.
(C) She has had several jobs.
(D) She is seeking a full-time position.

198. In the first e-mail, the word "part" in paragraph 2, line 3, is closest in meaning to

(A) section
(B) share
(C) piece
(D) role

199. Who most likely posted the job advertisement?

(A) Robert Klepner
(B) Leslie Raxenberg
(C) Shai Greene
(D) Ben Davies

200. What is indicated about the training session?

(A) It will be held at CLS Toys' headquarters.
(B) It will be led by Shai Greene.
(C) It is mandatory for new hires.
(D) It will take place in Des Moines.

Stop! This is the end of the test. If you finish before time is called, you may go back to Parts 5, 6, and 7 and check your work.

정답 p.472 / 점수 환산표 p.476

실전모의고사
TEST 10

TEST 10 해설

바로 보기

시작 시간 _____시 _____분

종료 시간 _____시 _____분

▶ 중간에 멈추지 말고 처음부터 끝까지 풀어보세요. 문제를 풀 때는 실전처럼 답안지에 마킹하세요.

READING TEST

In the Reading test, you will read a variety of texts and answer several different types of reading comprehension questions. The entire Reading test will last 75 minutes. There are three parts, and directions are given for each part. You are encouraged to answer as many questions as possible within the time allowed. You must mark your answers on the separate answer sheet. Do not write your answers in your test book.

PART 5

Directions: A word or phrase is missing in each of the sentences below. Four answer choices are given below each sentence. Select the best answer to complete the sentence. Then mark the letter (A), (B), (C), or (D) on your answer sheet.

101. Greenhouse Plus Inc.'s Web site regularly offers ------- deals on its newly-released lines of gardening products.

(A) excel
(B) excellence
(C) excellent
(D) excellently

102. Ms. Oh was chosen as an event coordinator because of her extensive experience in ------- a variety of public festivals around the city.

(A) organizing
(B) summarizing
(C) retailing
(D) applying

103. To recognize those ------ have been staying late to finish the Stevenson case earlier, management will be holding a dinner party.

(A) what
(B) which
(C) who
(D) whom

104. Ms. Saito will provide you with an estimate if she has received the ------- for the renovations.

(A) specific
(B) specifics
(C) specifically
(D) specified

105. It is common sense that with new management come new ------- for motivating employees.

(A) strategic
(B) strategize
(C) strategies
(D) strategically

106. The majority of the keynote speakers will be talking about social networking developments ------- the upcoming technology conference.

(A) at
(B) as
(C) though
(D) of

107. Our new anti-virus software will ------- your computer against viruses as well as remove unnecessary files from the machine.

(A) deliver
(B) pretend
(C) ensure
(D) protect

108. Rudy and Isobel were unable to stay at ------- preferred accommodations in Toronto because the company's travel budget was too small.

(A) them
(B) themselves
(C) their
(D) theirs

109. I am writing this letter ------- behalf of
Chester City Utility Authority to remind you
that your account is two months overdue.

(A) on
(B) over
(C) to
(D) for

110. Salaries are ------- decided by Ace Tech's
personnel manager, but the CFO might
recommend some minor adjustments.

(A) typically
(B) scarcely
(C) recently
(D) relatively

111. Between 8 and 9 A.M., Highlands bus
passengers can use neither concession cards
------- free tickets on any city services.

(A) nor
(B) with
(C) and
(D) or

112. After ------- herself, Ms. Chang described her
personality and previous work experience in
great detail.

(A) introduce
(B) introduced
(C) introduces
(D) introducing

113. Although your order has been received, it
may be a week ------- we can ship it because
the item is out of stock.

(A) while
(B) before
(C) if
(D) but

114. We will issue you a full ------- as long as
the item has the sales tag attached and is
returned within two weeks of purchase.

(A) purchase
(B) deposit
(C) receipt
(D) refund

115. The Negotiating Team manager informed the
board members that we could expect to earn
------- $25 million from the sale of our Home
Appliances Division.

(A) approximate
(B) approximating
(C) approximation
(D) approximately

116. Unfortunately, I won't be able to ------- your
offer for the marketing director position as I
am looking for a finance-related job.

(A) accept
(B) assert
(C) admit
(D) appear

117. Please be aware that your e-mail address will
only be used for our promotional purposes
and will never be disclosed to third parties
------- written permission from you.

(A) without
(B) within
(C) except
(D) unless

118. The new tourist information center is currently
seeking ------- staff that can help visitors with
any questions they may have.

(A) qualified
(B) qualifier
(C) qualify
(D) qualification

119. All flight attendants are required to -------
in a professional manner when dealing with
complaints from passengers.

(A) invite
(B) respond
(C) attach
(D) advise

GO ON TO THE NEXT PAGE

120. We were disappointed to discover that the antique vase had been broken in transit due to the lack of ------- handling.

(A) hospitable
(B) appropriate
(C) subsequent
(D) separate

121. Throughout the month of July, United Travel Agency will ------- all travelers with a free cabin bag and luggage tags to use on their holiday.

(A) offer
(B) provide
(C) notify
(D) contribute

122. Officials said that an ------- investigation is underway to identify individuals involved in Nutripharm's fraudulent business dealings.

(A) activate
(B) actively
(C) activity
(D) active

123. Rushden Inc. plans to build a new facility in Scargill Park, ------- popular with young residents due to its drive-in movie theater.

(A) past
(B) once
(C) as
(D) former

124. The half-price voucher is valid for a ------- time and can only be used one time during the summer.

(A) partial
(B) deficient
(C) controlled
(D) limited

125. In such a ------- growing business environment, it is most important to determine the changing needs of potential customers.

(A) patiently
(B) deeply
(C) greatly
(D) rapidly

126. The multinational coffee company found that their sales were quite strong ------- countries where they offer the widest range of flavors.

(A) by
(B) in
(C) on
(D) at

127. We were able to increase sales of our organic cereal by an impressive 25 percent last year ------- by changing the packaging.

(A) simple
(B) simpler
(C) simply
(D) simplify

128. As a result of the recent railway strike, Ms. Hawthorne had to ------- her monthly visit to her family in France.

(A) emerge
(B) postpone
(C) decorate
(D) reflect

129. Some staff still fail to arrive at work on time ------- the fact that we introduced a strong penalty for being late.

(A) while
(B) despite
(C) indeed
(D) although

130. Please note that all reservations must be ------- by phone at least 24 hours ahead of your scheduled departure date.

(A) confirmed
(B) written
(C) composed
(D) formed

PART 6

Directions: Read the texts that follow. A word, phrase, or sentence is missing in parts of each text. Four answer choices for each question are given below the text. Select the best answer to complete the text. Then mark the letter (A), (B), (C) or (D) on your answer sheet.

Questions 131-134 refer to the following letter.

Mr. Frank Hollman

25 Madison Avenue

San Francisco, CA 98203

Dear Mr. Hollman,

Thank you for visiting our office last week at such ------- notice. We were impressed with your range
131.

of staff training programs. We have now finished reviewing documents from all the employee training

providers who applied for the role.

At a meeting held yesterday afternoon, we selected a number of staff training programs which we

believe are ------- for our company and your program is near the top of our list.
132.

We would like to invite you back for a final interview on September 22 at 10 A.M. ------- . So, please
133.

prepare some materials and we will provide ------- special equipment you need.
134.

Please contact me at 555-5693 and let me know if you can attend the interview.

Yours sincerely,

Daisy Jenkins

131. (A) heavy
(B) short
(C) regular
(D) perfect

132. (A) suitable
(B) suits
(C) suitability
(D) suit

133. (A) Applications should be submitted along
with a résumé.
(B) We wish you the best of luck in your future
endeavors.
(C) You will be asked to present a trial training
program.
(D) Positions are hard to come by during this
slow economy.

134. (A) several
(B) almost
(C) every
(D) any

GO ON TO THE NEXT PAGE

Questions 135-138 refer to the following notice.

Cafeteria to Be Closed Temporarily

All staff, please note that the cafeteria will be closed for the rest of the week ------- renovations, as we
                                                                                           135.
are expanding the room in order to provide staff with much more space to enjoy their lunch breaks.

With this in mind, we ask you to please remove any personal items which could be ------- during the
                                                                                     136.
building work that will begin tomorrow morning.

------- you will be unable to access the cafeteria, we have decided to give each staff member a $50
137.
café voucher to use at Quick Bite Café, which is just around the corner from our office. -------.
                                                                                          138.

Thank you for your understanding and cooperation.

---

135. (A) for
(B) beyond
(C) as such
(D) apart from

136. (A) damage
(B) damaged
(C) damaging
(D) damages

137. (A) So that
(B) Additionally
(C) Now that
(D) Until

138. (A) We are confident that you will all be
satisfied with the new equipment.
(B) I hope there is enough space to
accommodate all our employees at the
event.
(C) Please make sure that these vouchers are
distributed to all of our customers.
(D) We apologize for any inconvenience you
may experience during the renovation.

Questions 139-142 refer to the following notice.

Notice

It has come to our attention that we have had thefts of personal items that were left unattended in the gym. ------- members are reminded that you bring valuable personal belongings to the gym at
                    139.
your own risk.

This problem has become so common these days ------- we are considering installing a CCTV
                                        140.
system in the building. If you want to bring valuables to our facilities, please be sure to keep them with you at all times or lock them away in the lockers ------- in the changing rooms.
                                                    141.

We are unable to reimburse any gym member for their missing or stolen items. ------- .
                                                                        142.

---

139. (A) Every
(B) Much
(C) Any
(D) All

140. (A) because
(B) for
(C) that
(D) since

141. (A) provided
(B) providing
(C) provide
(D) provides

142. (A) Speak with an instructor for reimbursement details.
(B) Always take care when using the exercise machines.
(C) This change will go into effect immediately.
(D) Therefore, think carefully before bringing your valuables with you.

GO ON TO THE NEXT PAGE

Questions 143-146 refer to the following article.

Oxford, England, October 23 – A proposal for a 500-hectare housing development near Oxford has angered local residents who want to ------- the unique historical character of the city.
143.

Residents have presented a petition ------- by 5,900 people to officials at the town hall.
144.

It calls for an immediate halt to the new development while community meetings are held to

explain the nature of the housing development to local residents.

-------. A town hall spokesperson said that city officials, ------- the housing developers, would be
145.   **146.**
present at the meeting, which takes place at 7 P.M. on Wednesday, November 17.

143. (A) approach
(B) preserve
(C) select
(D) educate

144. (A) handled
(B) entitled
(C) restored
(D) signed

145. (A) Residents are concerned about the environmental impact on the city.
(B) Several council members were instrumental in stopping the project.
(C) The final meeting will be organized at the town hall to address the issue.
(D) Some residents met with council members in person.

146. (A) nearby
(B) across
(C) out of
(D) along with

PART 7

Directions: In this part you will read a selection of texts, such as magazine and newspaper articles, e-mails, and instant messages. Each text or set of texts is followed by several questions. Select the best answer for each question and mark the letter (A), (B), (C), or (D) on your answer sheet.

Questions 147-148 refer to the following advertisement.

Dream Living
14 Main Street, Boise, Idaho

Whether you envision yourselves living in a trendy downtown apartment or a spacious townhouse in a leafy suburb, Dream Living has everything you need! Our experienced staff will strive to help you find the perfect place to suit your tastes and needs. Furthermore, for the rest of this month, we are offering a 50% discount on all fees. In addition to this, we will pick you up from your location to save you the hassle of driving. To find out more, just visit us online at our recently re-designed Web site, www.dreamliving.org.

---

147. What type of business is Dream Living?

(A) A real estate agency
(B) A dining facility
(C) A Web design company
(D) A financial consulting firm

148. What is NOT indicated about Dream Living?

(A) It plans to relocate its head office.
(B) It offers a transportation service.
(C) It is running a special promotion.
(D) It has recently modified its Web site.

GO ON TO THE NEXT PAGE

Questions 149-150 refer to the following text-message chain.

Louis [6:08 P.M.]
Good evening, Hiro and Roberta. Tomorrow we are going to have a meeting at 11:00 in my office. It's about your career objectives.

Roberta [6:22 P.M.]
Could you please explain further?

Louis [6:30 P.M.]
We need to make a final decision on what your goals are for this year so that we can submit the forms to the CEO by next Friday.

Roberta [6:32 P.M.]
Oh, okay. Is there anything we should do to prepare?

Louis [6:36 P.M.]
Actually, I just sent you some documents by e-mail. Why don't you have a look? They contain guidelines on how to set objectives for your career goals. It would be great if you could check them out before we get together tomorrow.

Hiro [6:42 P.M.]
Will do. Thanks, Louis.

149. What must Hiro and Roberta do by next Friday?

(A) Submit some information
(B) Attend a training workshop
(C) Update their résumés
(D) Prepare for interviews

150. At 6:42 P.M., what does Hiro mean when he says, "Will do"?

(A) He will contact the CEO directly.
(B) He will explain the agenda in further detail.
(C) He will submit his career goals by e-mail.
(D) He will read some documents before the meeting.

Easyride Car Rental

$100 GIFT VOUCHER

We at Easyride have decided to launch a loyalty scheme to thank our repeat customers for continuing to choose us as their vehicle rental service. The voucher holder may redeem this special discount when paying their next bill.

** This voucher may only be redeemed by the named recipient. It may only be used to reduce the total cost of your bill and is not exchangeable for cash. Please note that this voucher may not be used in conjunction with any other offer. Vouchers presented after the expiration date will not be honored. **

Voucher Recipient: Jamie Neville

Expiration Date: December 31

---

151. Why was the gift voucher most likely given to Mr. Neville?

(A) He is a first-time customer.
(B) He recommended the company to friends.
(C) He spent a specific amount of money.
(D) He has used Easyride previously.

152. What is true about the gift voucher?

(A) It cannot be used with another promotion.
(B) The expiration date may be extended.
(C) It may be exchanged for $100 in cash.
(D) It can be transferred to another person.

The Himelton Times
Zooatron CEO Richard Player Celebrates

The founder of sportswear company Zooatron was in high spirits today as he attended the ribbon cutting of his new downtown store. The clothing brand has grown rapidly over the last year, and Richard Player thanked the large crowd for their continued support of the business. Speaking to reporters afterwards, Mr. Player stated that the expansion will help in maximizing profits and increasing the company's stock value.

Zooatron is well known for its ethical business values, particularly making headlines for its work in helping The Himelton Orphanage, which was badly damaged during the recent flooding. While many volunteers in the town have donated their time to hosting fundraising events for the orphanage, Zooatron has gone a step further by directly giving 10% of its profits to the cause. With the new branch, Mr. Player hopes numerous other charitable organizations will also benefit from Zooatron's increased earnings.

153. What is the article mainly about?
   (A) A store opening
   (B) A new product line
   (C) An employment opportunity
   (D) A corporate merger

154. According to the article, how has Mr. Player helped the Himelton Orphanage?
   (A) By organizing fundraising events
   (B) By contributing financial help
   (C) By offering discounted products
   (D) By raising media awareness

Questions 155-157 refer to the following memo.

From: Sue Ragnall, Sales Manager
To: Sales associates
Date: January 4
Re: Cosmetics lines

As you all know, we recently conducted a survey of customer preferences in the Cosmetics Department of the store. Cosmetics are a low-cost, high-volume product and we need to keep up with changes in customer preference.

The data collected has now been analyzed and the results show that we need to make some changes. Here is a brief summary of the most important conclusions:

- The most popular eco-friendly lines were Healthy Face and Feeling Free.
- Customers disliked the Feeling Free cleansing products, but liked the makeup choices.
- The Excellence brand was preferred overall, probably because it has the lowest prices.
- Very few Jancé products were bought, but those customers who did buy it always asked for it by name.

As a result of these findings, we have decided that we will no longer carry the Jancé or Feeling Free lines. Jancé is far too costly to keep in stock if it is rarely sold, and Feeling Free has some questionable products.

NOTE:

If customers ask for a Feeling Free product, please recommend a Healthy Face one instead. Please also take note of what they requested. If we have many requests for Feeling Free makeup, we may re-institute that part of the brand.

155. What is the main topic of the memo?
   (A) Coming changes to products offered
   (B) A proposal to merge with another company
   (C) Recommendations to improve the performance of sales staff
   (D) A comparison of rival companies' products

156. According to the memo, which brand do some customers specifically request?
   (A) Excellence
   (B) Feeling Free
   (C) Healthy Face
   (D) Jancé

157. What is NOT mentioned about Feeling Free products?
   (A) They are environmentally friendly.
   (B) They include cleansers.
   (C) They are inexpensive.
   (D) They will no longer be stocked.

GO ON TO THE NEXT PAGE

Hannah's Weekly Book Review:
From Rags to Riches (by Julian Dempster)

By Hannah Fitts

From Rags to Riches was chosen as this months' book review subject because the author, Mr. Julian Dempster, has recently moved to Longview, just twenty miles away at the other end of our little valley.

This book appears to be just another "rags to riches" story about someone who was very poor before suddenly finding the key to creating a successful business and becoming wealthy. However, after a thorough read, it shows itself to be far more than that.

It is true that Mr. Dempster did at one time find himself homeless, and he did frequent soup kitchens. Furthermore, he now has a comfortable mansion, a family and a happier life. What is different about his story is that it is full of the things he learned along the way.

His journey was not so much about developing his business insight as it was about developing himself. He has chapters on such topics as "Don't follow the rules" and "Learning to be still" as well as "Ask!" He details both personal crises and heart-warming joys with the same utter frankness.

And for those not interested in self-help, Mr. Dempster's engaging writing style makes this a good read.

---

158. What most likely is Hannah Fitts' profession?

(A) Author
(B) Journalist
(C) Teacher
(D) Therapist

159. What is indicated about Mr. Dempster?

(A) He has written several books.
(B) He has collaborated with Ms. Fitts.
(C) He founded a company.
(D) He donates money to the homeless.

160. What is indicated as the reason that Hannah Fitts chose to write about *From Rags to Riches*?

(A) The author lives nearby.
(B) The book has received an award.
(C) The author plans to visit her town soon.
(D) The book helped her to improve her life.

Questions 161-164 refer to the following online chat discussion.

Sivan [3:12 P.M.]

Hello. This is Sivan, your customer service representative for Lose Weight, Feel Great. How may I help you today?

Joshua [3:15 P.M.]

Hi Sivan. I have lost four pounds this week. I am pleased with my results so far. I wanted to know if I could eat white rice with my dinner tonight.

Sivan [3:18 P.M.]

Brown rice is permitted on this diet, but white rice is not. Broccoli rice is also allowed.

Joshua [3:20 P.M.]

Broccoli rice? I have never tried that before.

Sivan [3:24 P.M.]

You should. It is healthy and delicious! Do you have access to the dietary guidebook? Complex carbohydrates are explained in the paperwork that you should have received in your welcome package.

Joshua [3:26 P.M.]

I've actually misplaced those.

Sivan [3:29 P.M.]

Not a problem. Please let me know your e-mail address and I will send them to you. You can also access them online at our Web site.

161. What does Joshua imply about the program?

(A) It is effective.
(B) It is affordable.
(C) It is widely popular.
(D) It is time-consuming.

162. At 3:26 P.M., what does Joshua mean when he says, "I've actually misplaced those"?

(A) He didn't receive the package of broccoli rice.
(B) He cannot find his receipt.
(C) The welcome e-mail didn't arrive.
(D) A handbook is missing.

163. What does Sivan suggest that Joshua do?

(A) Attend a dieting class
(B) Try a new food
(C) Purchase a book
(D) Send an e-mail

164. What will most likely happen next?

(A) Sivan will check the product's Web site.
(B) Joshua will prepare some white rice.
(C) Sivan will cook something for Joshua.
(D) Sivan will e-mail Joshua.

GO ON TO THE NEXT PAGE

Questions 165-168 refer to the following notice.

Due to recent changes in regulations, which will come into effect next month, many airlines have restricted liquid items in carry-on luggage. — [1] —. Please pay attention to the following rules and contact your airline for more specific information:

The maximum amount of liquid that can be packed in carry-on luggage is 100ml per container. The maximum number of containers is 10. — [2] —. The containers must be placed inside a sealed clear plastic bag, which must be presented to airport officials when you are asked to do so. — [3] —. The bag must be removed from the carry-on luggage and scanned separately at the airport.

In addition, any items purchased at duty-free stores must also be contained in a sealed plastic bag. Please be aware that various countries have different duty-free limits and rules regarding liquid items. If you will visit another country before reaching your destination, please be aware that the rules of that country apply to any liquid items you may have purchased. — [4] —.

165. For whom is the information most likely intended?

(A) Airline security staff
(B) Duty-free retailers
(C) Luggage store employees
(D) Airline passengers

166. Who should be contacted for further information?

(A) Airline companies
(B) An airport help desk
(C) A flight attendant
(D) A product manufacturer

167. According to the notice, what might people be asked to do?

(A) Buy fewer duty-free items
(B) Throw away liquid items
(C) Show items to staff
(D) Repack their bags

168. In which of the positions marked [1], [2], [3], and [4] does the following sentence best belong?

"These must be made of clear plastic so that the contents can be easily seen."

(A) [1]
(B) [2]
(C) [3]
(D) [4]

Questions 169-171 refer to the following advertisement.

Leila's Bar and Grill

366 Sherling Street, Portland, OR 97211

(503) 555-8787

www.leilasbarportland.com

Have your next big gathering at Leila's Bar and Grill. Our restaurant provides ample space for birthday parties, office get-togethers, anniversary celebrations and more. We offer many kinds of entertainment, including billiards, ping pong tables, and arcade games.

And don't forget our delicious buffet options!

Two-Meter Sub Sandwich (14–20 servings) A giant submarine sandwich made with the freshest vegetables and your choice of meat and cheese. **$33.00**

Giant Party Pizza (20-25 servings) Our gigantic party pizza has a 100-centimeter diameter and can be divided into 4 sections of different toppings. **$45.00**

Taco Bar (18–23 servings) Includes both hard-shell and soft-shell tacos, which can be filled with a variety of meats, cheese, vegetables, beans, and sauces, as well as beverage options. **$59.00**

Steak Buffet (16–20 servings) For those who don't want to disappoint their party guests. Includes all varieties of Leila's delicious steaks cooked to order. **$129.00**

Other menu options and costs can be found on our Web site. Parties can be scheduled online, although reservations are on a first-come, first-served basis. Returning customers can receive a 20% discount on their order. Gatherings must be scheduled at least three days in advance.

---

169. What is the purpose of the advertisement?

(A) To advertise the grand opening of a tavern
(B) To explain a restaurant's party options
(C) To promote a new recreation area
(D) To detail a restaurant's new menu

170. What option includes beverages?

(A) Two-Meter Sub Sandwich
(B) Giant Party Pizza
(C) Taco Bar
(D) Steak Buffet

171. How can customers receive a discount at Leila's Bar and Grill?

(A) By responding to an online survey
(B) By scheduling an event in advance
(C) By visiting the place more than once
(D) By selecting two or more options

GO ON TO THE NEXT PAGE

Questions 172-175 refer to the following article.

Zoom Motors Leading the Car Industry in Greener Cars

Zoom Motors is a relatively new car manufacturer whose stated goal is to "make the greenest car yet." Not only are they developing cars that do not run on gasoline, but they are trying to make them affordable, too. — [1] —.

"It's no use making a great car that reduces carbon emissions if only a few people can afford it. Here at Zoom Motors, we envision a world where electric vehicles are the industry standard and less pollution is released into the air. The only way to do that is by making an electric car with the lowest cost possible." Zoom Motors chairman, Jacob Holmes stated.

The latest model to roll off the Zoom Motors assembly line is the Zoom Electro. — [2] —. It is an electric car, so there are zero emissions. The power plant that ultimately provides the energy, of course, may release pollution into the air. But the Zoom Electro has no exhaust and is considered the greenest car on the market. — [3] —. But, what distinguishes it from other electric cars?

For one thing, it is made using recycled materials. Secondly, the factory that manufactures the Zoom Electro runs primarily on wind energy. And finally, Zoom Motors has developed technology that reduces costs in manufacturing to make the car affordable. Its price is comparable to many gasoline-powered cars on the market today. — [4] —.

The Zoom Electro battery can go for 300 kilometers before it needs to be recharged, and it is the most environmentally-friendly car on the road today. For a reliable, affordable, eco-friendly ride, Zoom Electro should be your first choice! We expect to see more great things from Zoom Motors in the years to come.

172. What is implied about green cars?

(A) They are not as fast as conventional cars.
(B) They are usually expensive for consumers.
(C) They have more powerful batteries.
(D) They are not very comfortable.

173. What is NOT mentioned as something that motivates Jacob Holmes?

(A) Consuming less fuel
(B) Reducing pollution
(C) Lowering car prices
(D) Minimizing production costs

174. According to the article, what is different about the Zoom Electro?

(A) It can be recycled into useful materials.
(B) It runs on wind energy.
(C) Its price is as low as conventional cars.
(D) It can be recharged while it is running.

175. In which of the positions marked [1], [2], [3], and [4] does the following sentence best belong?

"They are committed to improving green technology while reducing costs."

(A) [1]
(B) [2]
(C) [3]
(D) [4]

GO ON TO THE NEXT PAGE

Questions 176-180 refer to the following e-mails.

E-Mail Message

To: Lisa Berger <lberger@htcinternational.com>
From: Susan Reynolds <sreynolds@htcinternational.com>
Subject: Staffing changes
Date: December 2

Hi Lisa,

I just heard from James Wells that he had to have emergency surgery, so he will not be back at work for at least six weeks. With Julia Markham's baby coming a month before it was expected, that leaves us really short-handed, right at the busiest time of year. Fortunately, both of them will return to work eventually, but that doesn't help us right now.

Do you have any workers whose time is not fully used? If you could lend us one person until mid-January, that would be a big help. I am going to move Julia's assistant, Margaret King, up to do Julia's job while she is gone, so the person you send us does not have to have a great amount of experience. He or she will just need to assist Margaret with her daily tasks. We are trying to see if we can split up James's work between everyone else, so no one is overworked.

Let me know if you can help us out.

Thanks,

Susan

To:	Susan Reynolds <sreynolds@htcinternational.comSSS>
From:	Lisa Berger <lberger@htcinternational.com>
Subject:	Re: Staffing changes
Date:	December 3

Hi, Susan,

What bad timing for this to happen to both of them at the same time! I hope the baby is ok, arriving early.

I do have someone I can send you, but he is not very experienced. We hired a student intern who will start next week and be here for five weeks. We anticipated that we would need him because of the extra work involved in the rollout of the new corporate bookkeeping and accounting software that was supposed to happen this month. They are now telling us they won't be ready to do that until the 15th of next month, and we have already agreed to hire this person.

His name is Jose Alvarez, and he seemed bright and cooperative in the interview. He behaved very professionally and seemed eager to learn. I'll send him along to your department when he gets here.

Good luck with all the extra work!

Lisa

176. What problem does Ms. Reynolds discuss in her e-mail?

(A) There are not enough workers.
(B) There have been too many orders.
(C) Some equipment is unavailable.
(D) A work deadline is too tight.

177. Why is Julia not at work?

(A) She is very ill.
(B) She is on vacation.
(C) She needed surgery.
(D) She had a baby.

178. Who will be assisting Margaret King?

(A) James Wells
(B) Julia Markham
(C) Jose Alvarez
(D) Lisa Berger

179. What is NOT mentioned about the new worker?

(A) He has not started work yet.
(B) He has lots of experience.
(C) He acts professionally.
(D) He is willing to help out.

180. When will the software most likely be installed?

(A) In fifteen days
(B) in December
(C) In mid-January
(D) At the end of this week

GO ON TO THE NEXT PAGE

New Plastics Introduced for Use in Surgery
by Zoe Callahan

Philadelphia, PA – The University of Pennsylvania, in conjunction with Arlex Inc., has developed a line of plastics that promise to revolutionize the implant surgery world.

One of the most challenging aspects of using plastics inside the body is the tendency of body fluids to wear down plastic. In the past, this has meant that devices such as artificial joints and heart valves did not last very long. Patients often need repeat surgeries when their plastic parts wear out. Until now, most plastics that could last inside the body have been found to be more toxic. During a joint project, university and Arlex Inc. chemists developed a new set of polymers, or plastics, which last for an unusually long time. They are also entirely non-toxic to the body.

The new materials have been extensively tested on animals and are now ready for human trials. The University Hospital of Pennsylvania will be the first location to test them. Testing will begin with younger patients, who will benefit the most from longer-life replacement parts. Athletes needing artificial joints and children with faulty heart valves will be considered for the first surgeries.

Arlex produces most of the new plastics and polymers at its manufacturing plants in New Jersey. It is projected that these new materials will be available for universal use within two years.

Arlex Inc.

September 13

Zoe Callahan, Staff Writer
Philadelphia Express
2311 Pilgrim Way
Philadelphia, PA 11239

Dear Ms. Callahan,

Thank you for writing about the new plastics we have developed in conjunction with the University of Pennsylvania. We appreciate the publicity you have given us.

I would like, however, to point out that the undertaking to develop these materials also included collaboration with the Organic Chemistry Department of the University of Toronto in Canada. They provided considerable expertise. In fact, the whole project has been a three-way venture. While not many Canadians may read the Philadelphia Express, I do believe we should give them credit for all their input.

I would also like to add that the materials will actually be manufactured in our plant outside Toronto. Only the final assembly of the artificial devices will be done locally at the facility you mentioned.

Sincerely,
Mark Brennan, Public Relations, Arlex Inc.

181. What is the main subject of the article?

(A) New materials for operations
(B) The environmental impact of plastics
(C) Complications of surgeries
(D) Medical testing on animals

182. What is NOT mentioned as a problem with currently-used plastics?

(A) They wear out too fast.
(B) Some of them are toxic.
(C) Patients require more surgeries.
(D) They are expensive to make.

183. Why will testing be done on younger patients first?

(A) There are many more of them.
(B) Their bodies will adapt better.
(C) They will heal much better.
(D) They will live longer.

184. What takes place at the Arlex site in New Jersey?

(A) Experimental surgery
(B) Plastics manufacturing
(C) Device assembly
(D) Testing procedures

185. What request does Mark Brennan make?

(A) The results of testing should not be revealed.
(B) A third contributor should be acknowledged.
(C) The plant location should be kept secret.
(D) A summary of benefits should be published.

GO ON TO THE NEXT PAGE

Questions 186-190 refer to the following list, program schedule, and e-mail.

Documentary Films Directed by Martin Herzog

The Great Fire
A city in flames. Herzog looks at the impact of the Great Fire of London, which destroyed over 13,000 homes over four days in 1666. The fire resulted in major social and economic problems in the British capital.

Discovering the New World
Herzog charts the course of Italian explorer Christopher Columbus' first voyages across the Atlantic Ocean and learns about his first interactions with the indigenous populations he encountered.

Pyramids from Nowhere
A thought-provoking look at the theories behind one of the greatest engineering mysteries of all time. Herzog follows a team of archaeologists as they attempt to unearth the secrets behind the construction of the Great Pyramid of Giza in Egypt.

Sugar & Spice
Herzog travels from Iran to China, describing the establishment of the Silk Road and the influence that this trade route had on the development of civilizations on the Asian continent.

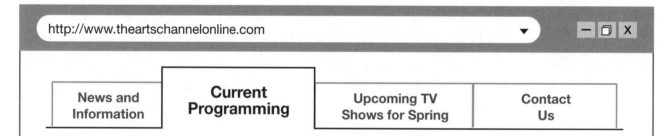

http://www.theartschannelonline.com

| News and Information | **Current Programming** | Upcoming TV Shows for Spring | Contact Us |

The Arts Channel
Night Schedule, January 6

7:30 – Life on Canvas (Hosted by: Charles Maxwell)
Host Charles Maxwell talks about the changing trends in the world of art, from concept and design to material selection and technique.

8:30 – Up Close & Personal (Hosted by: Annette Fielding)
Explorer and filmmaker Martin Herzog is interviewed about what inspired him to make his latest documentary about one of the most iconic and recognizable structures in the world. He shares his own theories on its construction and purpose.

10:00 – Classical Notes (Hosted by: Lily Montague)
Lily Montague takes a look at some contemporary musicians and composers who are making waves in the world of classical music. The show includes several captivating performances and in-depth interviews.

E-Mail Message

From: Carissa Yentob <cyentob@apmmail.net>
To: feedback@theartschannel.com
Date: January 7
Subject: Martin Herzog Feature

I have been a regular viewer of the The Arts Channel ever since it was first introduced five years ago, and I'd like to commend you on the quality of the shows you air. I especially wanted to express how much I enjoyed the newest addition to your programming schedule. The show has featured some interesting individuals over the past few weeks, but the guest on last night's show was of particular interest to me. I remember Martin from one of his filming expeditions. I was a member of the team he followed and filmed during his time in Egypt, and I was impressed by the passion he clearly has for his work. It's pleasing to see that his documentary is generating some interest in the media, and I look forward to seeing it upon its release.

Kindest regards,

Carissa Yentob

---

186. What do Mr. Herzog's documentaries all have in common with one another?

(A) They celebrate famous structures.
(B) They describe the lives of explorers.
(C) They take place in Europe.
(D) They focus on historical events.

187. What film did Mr. Herzog most likely speak about on The Arts Channel?

(A) The Great Fire
(B) Discovering the New World
(C) Pyramids from Nowhere
(D) Sugar & Spice

188. What is indicated about Up Close & Personal?

(A) It airs at 8:30 every evening.
(B) It is a relatively new show.
(C) It is hosted by Charles Maxwell.
(D) It was changed to a different time slot.

189. In the e-mail, the word "introduced" in paragraph 1, line 1, is closest in meaning to

(A) recommended
(B) advanced
(C) released
(D) acquainted

190. What is most likely true about Ms. Yentob?

(A) She interviewed a documentary maker.
(B) She was featured on Classical Notes.
(C) She hosts a very popular television program.
(D) She has worked in an academic field.

GO ON TO THE NEXT PAGE

OFFICIAL NOTICE
OLRD Community Gathering

— The Oxley Leisure & Recreation Department (OLRD) will hold a meeting to decide whether to begin publishing a monthly newsletter for the recreation center, starting from next month. All members must be in complete agreement in order for the proposal to be approved. Voting will be conducted anonymously.

— THE OLRD will convene at City Hall on Monday, February 13, at 9:00 A.M. to review the proposal and cast votes. The gathering is also open to local residents who wish to learn more about the subject and raise any issues they may have regarding the running of the center.

— More information may be obtained from our secretary, Olivia Weller, at 555-0138 or oweller@olrd.com.

Issue No. 1

Date of publication: March 2

Visit Oxley Recreation Center!

Oxley Recreation Center has become a popular meeting place for all residents of Oxley and the surrounding towns. Constructed nearly 25 years ago, it was originally under the administration of the Oxley Community Welfare Committee (OCWC), which ran the facility effectively for almost two decades. The city council dissolved the OCWC and renamed the division as the Oxley Leisure & Recreation Department a few years ago. Since then, the center has become even more popular. Today, the center boasts an abundance of amenities and offers numerous classes and recreational activities.

The center will allow anyone to come along to take part in these specific activities at no cost in the following months:

April – Yoga and Pilates demonstrations in the fitness room
May – Foot and hand massages in the spa/sauna area
June – Water aerobics and diving lessons in the swimming pool
July – Tennis instruction at the outdoor courts

To find out more about our free activities, please visit www.oxleyrecreationcenter.co.ca.

http://www.oxleyrecreationcenter.co.ca

| Recent News | Amenities | Our Staff | Parking Facilities |

NEW CENTER ACTIVITY! Construction of our state-of-the-art indoor climbing wall is finally complete! Whether you are an expert or a beginner, come along and enjoy our wall. Classes are available for all levels, and interested individuals can sign up by clicking

(HERE)

IMPORTANT ANNOUNCEMENT! The center's swimming pool will be unavailable from May 22 to July 5 due to urgent repairs and renovation work. With regret, all scheduled activities during this month will no longer be going ahead. We apologize for this inconvenience.

191. What information is NOT included on the notice?

(A) Details about membership
(B) Contact information for the OLRD
(C) The location of a gathering
(D) The purpose of a public meeting

192. In the excerpt from a newsletter, the word "boasts" in paragraph 1, line 6, is closest in meaning to

(A) advertises
(B) organizes
(C) possesses
(D) exaggerates

193. What is suggested about the OLRD?

(A) It was established twenty years ago.
(B) It does not allow residents to attend meetings.
(C) It works closely with the OCWC.
(D) It recently held a unanimous vote.

194. Which activity will not be offered temporarily at Oxley Recreation Center?

(A) Yoga demonstrations
(B) Massages
(C) Aerobic classes
(D) Tennis lessons

195. What is indicated about the center's climbing classes?

(A) They will take place outside.
(B) They are only for beginners.
(C) They are popular with local residents.
(D) They can be signed up for online.

GO ON TO THE NEXT PAGE

Questions 196-200 refer to the following list, Web page, and e-mail.

Complete Discography of Marissa Lyon

Promise Me Twilight

Rarely is a debut album as captivating and moving as Marissa Lyon's *Promise Me Twilight*. Featuring guest vocals from her friend and collaborator Judith Gehrman, this album still stands up well against her later releases. What makes this all the more remarkable is that the album was recorded on a tiny budget in Marissa's New Orleans apartment.

Best Laid Plans

Marissa Lyon's sophomore release builds on the success of her debut album, exploring richer musical arrangements and more personal lyrical themes. She is assisted on this album by renowned saxophonist Guy LeBlanc, who adds a distinctive jazzy vibe to the record. Recorded at New Orleans' famous Millhouse Studios.

Nights in Manhattan

This is Marissa Lyon's best-selling album, having gone platinum multiple times in numerous countries. Once again recording in Millhouse Studios, Marissa utilized the talents of a wide variety of well-known musicians, including Jerry Singer, lead guitarist of the band High Tension.

Bridging the Gap

Recorded with the help of a full orchestra, The Royal Ealing Philharmonic, in London, England, *Bridging the Gap* is Marissa's most grandiose recording yet. While it has failed to match the record sales of her previous recording, it has been praised by both fans and critics alike.

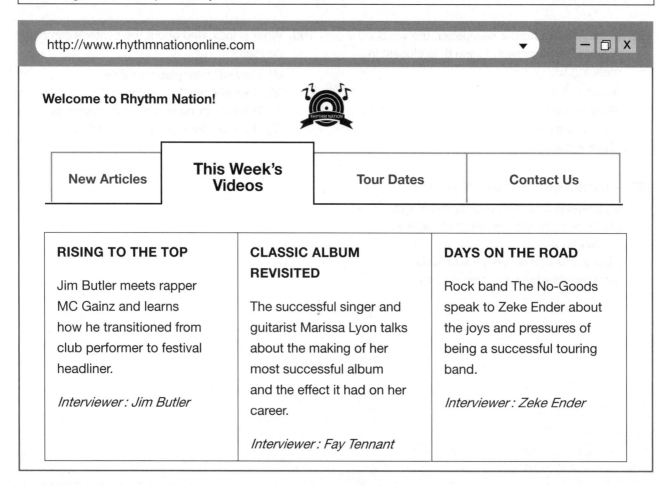

http://www.rhythmnationonline.com

Welcome to Rhythm Nation!

| New Articles | **This Week's Videos** | Tour Dates | Contact Us |

RISING TO THE TOP

Jim Butler meets rapper MC Gainz and learns how he transitioned from club performer to festival headliner.

Interviewer : Jim Butler

CLASSIC ALBUM REVISITED

The successful singer and guitarist Marissa Lyon talks about the making of her most successful album and the effect it had on her career.

Interviewer : Fay Tennant

DAYS ON THE ROAD

Rock band The No-Goods speak to Zeke Ender about the joys and pressures of being a successful touring band.

Interviewer : Zeke Ender

From:	Luke Forsythe <lforsythe@omegamail.net>
To:	Rhythm Nation Online <feedback@rno.com>
Date:	July 2
Subject:	Marissa Lyon Interview

I've been a big fan of Rhythm Nation ever since the site was launched almost ten years ago, and I always really look forward to checking out your new articles and videos. I'm particularly impressed with your newest interviewer, who conducted a really insightful and enjoyable interview recently with Marissa Lyon. I had the distinct honor of working with Ms. Lyon when she recorded in London earlier this year, and I still enjoy being able to hear my own contribution when I listen to that record. Your featured video brought back many fond memories for me. I'd just like to thank you all at Rhythm Nation for providing content as excellent as the Marissa Lyon interview.

Best wishes,

Luke Forsythe

196. What do Ms. Lyon's albums all have in common with one another?

(A) They were recorded in New Orleans.
(B) They each have achieved platinum sales.
(C) They were recorded on a small budget.
(D) They all feature guest musicians.

197. What album did Ms. Lyon most likely discuss on Rhythm Nation Online?

(A) Promise Me Twilight
(B) Best Laid Plans
(C) Nights in Manhattan
(D) Bridging the Gap

198. What is indicated about Fay Tennant?

(A) She is a member of a musical group.
(B) She interviews musicians every day.
(C) She was recently hired by Rhythm Nation.
(D) She runs a popular music Web site.

199. In the e-mail, the word "conducted" in paragraph 1, line 3, is closest in meaning to

(A) watched
(B) acted
(C) led
(D) played

200. What is most likely true about Mr. Forsythe?

(A) He previously resided in New Orleans.
(B) He is seeking a position on Rhythm Nation.
(C) He interviewed Ms. Lyon this year.
(D) He is a member of an orchestra.

Stop! This is the end of the test. If you finish before time is called, you may go back to Parts 5, 6, and 7 and check your work.
정답 p.472 / 점수 환산표 p.476

GO ON TO THE NEXT PAGE

실전모의고사
TEST 11

TEST 11 해설

바로 보기

시작 시간 _____시 _____분

종료 시간 _____시 _____분

▶ 중간에 멈추지 말고 처음부터 끝까지 풀어보세요. 문제를 풀 때는 실전처럼 답안지에 마킹하세요.

READING TEST

In the Reading test, you will read a variety of texts and answer several different types of reading comprehension questions. The entire Reading test will last 75 minutes. There are three parts, and directions are given for each part. You are encouraged to answer as many questions as possible within the time allowed. You must mark your answers on the separate answer sheet. Do not write your answers in your test book.

PART 5

Directions: A word or phrase is missing in each of the sentences below. Four answer choices are given below each sentence. Select the best answer to complete the sentence. Then mark the letter (A), (B), (C), or (D) on your answer sheet.

---

101. After 15 years of service at BCL Apparels as chief designer, Mr. Jason Dash will retire next month after disappointing ------- in the past few seasons.

(A) performed
(B) performing
(C) perform
(D) performances

102. When his company expanded quickly, Mr. Buser found that he couldn't manage the accounts all by -------.

(A) him
(B) himself
(C) his
(D) he

103. The initial response to our new advertising campaign was very positive, which ------- the added expense of hiring a writer and a graphic designer to work on it.

(A) corrected
(B) explained
(C) decided
(D) promoted

104. Please report any damage to corporate property, ------- accidental or not, to the Maintenance Department immediately.

(A) whether
(B) rather
(C) what
(D) although

105. We cannot begin processing your visa application until three different forms of ------- are received at the office.

(A) selection
(B) identification
(C) perception
(D) recognition

106. All employees should be prepared to provide an update on the status of their current projects ------- in Wednesday's business meeting.

(A) yet
(B) whereas
(C) while
(D) over

107. The dream of ------- limitless profits has attracted numerous ambitious people to the online industry over the past decade.

(A) highly
(B) eventually
(C) potentially
(D) unfortunately

108. INO policy requires that every team leader ------- in the communication skills workshop because we believe effective leadership will lead to higher productivity.

(A) enrolling
(B) to enroll
(C) enrolls
(D) enroll

109. The amount of money raised at the year-end fundraiser was ------- to support a full scholarship, so a second event will be held in a few months.

(A) incapable
(B) persuasive
(C) operational
(D) insufficient

110. The Institute of Applied Science provides its attendees with ------- knowledge and skills in the fields of engineering and science.

(A) valuably
(B) valuable
(C) valuing
(D) value

111. Dr. McKenzie received an honorary citizenship for his outstanding ------- to the city's health center for poor residents.

(A) treatment
(B) promotion
(C) analysis
(D) service

112. Factors to consider when planning an office layout include the total space available and the location of ------- office equipment.

(A) share
(B) shares
(C) shared
(D) sharing

113. Please arrive for your flight ------- two hours ahead of schedule to allow adequate time to check your luggage and locate your gate.

(A) rather than
(B) too much
(C) at least
(D) even more

114. To cut costs, WGY Inc. will merge its operations and sales departments ------- it moves to its new headquarters.

(A) as soon as
(B) as though
(C) in order that
(D) as such

115. The 20 percent discount the Shanghai Department Store has been offering only ------- to items in the bathroom and kitchen section.

(A) concedes
(B) applies
(C) includes
(D) lowers

116. The customer service representatives ------- handle sensitive financial information, so it is crucial for them to maintain confidentiality.

(A) frequent
(B) frequents
(C) frequented
(D) frequently

117. Please ------- the form with your credit card information and send it to us in the enclosed prepaid envelope.

(A) complete
(B) cancel
(C) terminate
(D) supervise

118. The ------- of Main Street will be changed dramatically if the city council decides to demolish the town hall and movie theater.

(A) appearance
(B) behavior
(C) operation
(D) system

119. The board of directors is prepared to offer the managerial position to ------- Connor Patrick or Sarah O'Connor.

(A) either
(B) both
(C) neither
(D) still

GO ON TO THE NEXT PAGE

120. We've received several complaints from customers who think our new ------- of advertisements have incorrect information.

(A) process
(B) series
(C) course
(D) operation

121. Goldstone Financial Consulting is currently finalizing a ------- proposal to be presented to one of its largest clients.

(A) detail
(B) details
(C) detailed
(D) detailing

122. The initial step in developing a new product is ------- brainstorming, where all R&D staff will be asked to suggest as many ideas as possible.

(A) typically
(B) necessarily
(C) tensely
(D) obediently

123. This year's street festival in Coburg will be held on a date that ------- the founding of the city.

(A) results in
(B) places on
(C) coincides with
(D) participates in

124. Informal attire ------- jeans, T-shirts, and torn clothing is considered inappropriate at the workplace.

(A) so that
(B) in case
(C) likewise
(D) such as

125. Once you fill out your monthly expense report, e-mail it to Ted Turner in Accounting for review and final -------.

(A) approve
(B) approvingly
(C) approves
(D) approval

126. Please be advised that ------- is able to enter through the West Lobby entrance while the area is being renovated.

(A) whoever
(B) someone
(C) one another
(D) no one

127. Committed to ------- a high level of communication, the Marketing and Graphic Design departments meet every Monday at 9 A.M to share project development updates.

(A) maintain
(B) maintained
(C) have maintained
(D) maintaining

128. Created by the researchers of Ohio's leading pharmaceutical company, our weight loss program is committed to being not only effective ------- safe.

(A) for
(B) but
(C) only
(D) and

129. Industry analysts are concerned that recent increases in corporate tax rates will ------- affect business profits for several years to come.

(A) adversely
(B) fortunately
(C) deliberately
(D) smoothly

130. After receiving positive feedback from several product testing sessions, the ABS Sound Lab decided to ------- the launch of its new stereo system.

(A) recognize
(B) generate
(C) expedite
(D) attract

PART 6

Directions: Read the texts that follow. A word, phrase, or sentence is missing in parts of each text. Four answer choices for each question are given below the text. Select the best answer to complete the text. Then mark the letter (A), (B), (C) or (D) on your answer sheet.

Questions 131-134 refer to the following e-mail.

To: Jenny Pines <jpines@mailmail.com>

From: Mark Teller <humanresources@priceunlimited.com>

Date: February 10

Subject: Welcome to the team!

Dear Jenny,

Congratulations on completing the comprehensive sales training course. I am extremely pleased to have hired a valuable ------- to our company.
131.

I hope that you found the training program to be enlightening and useful in preparing you for this dynamic work environment. To assist you in ------- the content of the course, I have attached our
132.

employee handbook. Please refer to this guide if you feel unsure about any of our departmental procedures.

I have scheduled a meeting for you with our office manager, Jeffrey Kent, today at 10:30 A.M. in regards to getting to know your individual client list. ------- , please familiarize yourself with your workspace and
133.

computer system. ------- .
134.

Sincerely,

Mark Teller

---

131. (A) expertise
(B) particular
(C) service
(D) addition

132. (A) retain
(B) retains
(C) retaining
(D) retained

133. (A) Until now
(B) In the meantime
(C) Since then
(D) In the end

134. (A) Don't hesitate to contact me directly if you encounter any problems.
(B) Should we need you to lead another course in the future, we will contact you immediately.
(C) The feedback we received from your clients was overwhelmingly positive.
(D) I would like to wish you the very best of luck with your upcoming interview.

GO ON TO THE NEXT PAGE

Questions 135-138 refer to the following article.

Vancouver, December 5 — Preston Manufacturing announced this week that it will initiate a three-phase shutdown of the local SBF Automotive factories currently operating in the Vancouver area.

------- .
135.

Preston Manufacturing has been the subject of wide public criticism ------- its purchase of locally-
136.
owned SBF Automotive last year, which caused two of the region's largest plants to be subsequently closed. The remaining three factories will begin the closing process early next year.

While Preston Manufacturing cites financial troubles as the leading reason for the closures, local

residents are uncertain as to ------- the industry will continue to support the region and its workers.
137.

Apart from being a source of tax revenue in the area, each SBF Automotive factory employs

around five hundred individuals.

Preston Manufacturing officials indicate that its plant operations ------- by late May of next year.
138.

---

135. (A) Company officials offered sincere apologies in a press conference yesterday.
(B) Many other companies also have industrial facilities operating in the area.
(C) Despite this, Preston Manufacturing has still remained profitable.
(D) Since the announcement, most employees have been offered renewed contracts.

136. (A) while
(B) as well
(C) instead
(D) following

137. (A) how
(B) what
(C) that
(D) which

138. (A) has been concluded
(B) concluding
(C) were concluded
(D) will have been concluded

Questions 139-142 refer to the following letter.

Dear Mr. Wells,

I am writing in response to your ------- for insurance coverage on the warehouse building located at
139.
174 Falls Street. As per our agreement, the building has been routinely inspected for safety hazards
as is required for approval.

------- receiving the results from the city inspector, I had no choice but to deny your request.
140.

As the warehouse has not been used for several years, it requires numerous repairs in order to receive
coverage. ------- updating the building's heating and ventilation systems, several of the emergency
141.
exits need modifications to be in accordance with current safety standards.

I have sent the inspector's full report to your office. -------.
142.

I wish you the best of luck with your future business.

Sincerely,

Tom Walsh

Policy Manager

Brooks Insurance

---

139. (A) application
(B) apply
(C) applies
(D) applicant

140. (A) Except for
(B) Upon
(C) Later
(D) Unless

141. (A) In addition to
(B) Rather than
(C) Assuming that
(D) Based on

142. (A) Provided all the necessary adjustments
are made, you may apply again at a later
date.
(B) Should you decide to perform a follow-
up inspection, please inform the factory
manager in advance.
(C) Also, I have enclosed several insurance
coverage plans that you may be
interested in.
(D) In short, it will not be safe for your staff to
continue to work under these conditions.

GO ON TO THE NEXT PAGE

Questions 143-146 refer to the following e-mail.

To: Colin Chaplin <cchaplin@tmail.com>

From: Customer Service <customerservice@typhoon.com>

Date: May 7

Subject: Repair Request

Dear Mr. Chaplin,

I am sorry to hear that your Typhoon 670 dishwasher has malfunctioned. I am writing to inform you that we are ------- to repair your appliance until May 14 at the earliest. We apologize for this delay,
143.
but we are severely short-staffed at this time.

-------. I see that you purchased the three-year warranty plan, which means you are eligible for a free
144.
repair service, including replacement parts. Please respond to this e-mail to inform me of a suitable time for our technician to visit you on May 14.

-------, please make sure that your appliance is turned off and do not attempt to perform any repairs
145.
yourself. I have enjoyed ------- you. Thank you for contacting Typhoon Appliances.
146.

Tyrone Carter

Customer Service Department

Typhoon Appliances

---

143. (A) ready
(B) unable
(C) delighted
(D) tentative

144. (A) We have received the faulty appliance.
(B) It was a pleasure serving you at our store.
(C) Please provide a copy of your proof of purchase.
(D) I checked the model number you provided.

145. (A) Additionally
(B) As such
(C) Indeed
(D) Likewise

146. (A) assist
(B) have assisted
(C) assists
(D) assisting

PART 7

Directions: In this part you will read a selection of texts, such as magazine and newspaper articles, e-mails, and instant messages. Each text or set of texts is followed by several questions. Select the best answer for each question and mark the letter (A), (B), (C), or (D) on your answer sheet.

Questions 147-148 refer to the following letter.

March 25
Ms. Laura Michaels
Suite 16, 560 Main Street
Denver, Colorado 80209

Dear Ms. Michaels,

This is in response to your letter dated March 19. You wrote asking whether the cotton in our garments is grown in this country or not.

After consulting with our Procurement Department, I have learned that some of our items are produced in the southern United States, and some come from other countries, most notably in Asia. Our organic cotton children's clothes are all made by a local company in South Carolina. This is what makes them exclusive. Our adult garments may be sourced from several countries, so we must know the production date and location printed on the label in order to tell which country the materials of your particular shirt came from.

Thank you for your inquiry, and we hope that you will continue to buy our products. We do continue to offer the highest quality items at the most reasonable prices.

Yours sincerely,

Linda Esteban

Linda Esteban,
Manager, Cool Comfort Inc.

147. What is the purpose of the letter?

(A) To answer an inquiry
(B) To promote a new product
(C) To apologize for an error
(D) To request product information

148. What type of product does Cool Comfort Inc. most likely sell?

(A) Home appliances
(B) Clothing
(C) Snack foods
(D) Fabrics

GO ON TO THE NEXT PAGE

Questions 149-150 refer to the following text-message chain.

Adam	[4:30 P.M.]

Jennifer, I just came across a course that looks really interesting…

Jennifer	[4:49 P.M.]

Oh, yeah? Tell me about it.

Adam	[4:52 P.M.]

Well, it's called "Relating and Understanding."
I want to see if we can hire this company to give weekly presentations to our workers. The course will improve the way they interact with each other and communicate their ideas and opinions during team meetings. It runs for 12 weeks.

Jennifer	[4:58 P.M.]

A friend of mine said that her company has been running a similar course. She thinks it's made a huge difference in her work environment. I think it would fit into our budget.

Adam	[5:04 P.M.]

If you think so, I'll consider it. But I'm not completely sure, and I still need to gather all the facts and then get Tom's approval, of course.

Jennifer	[5:10 P.M.]

Okay. Please e-mail me any links you find. I will do some research tonight, as well. I really like the idea.

Adam	[5:12 P.M.]

Glad you like it. We will touch base about it tomorrow.

149. What most likely is the topic of the course the writers are discussing?

(A) Settling customer complaints
(B) Improving customer satisfaction
(C) Business management
(D) Employee communication skills

150. At 4:58 P.M., what does Jennifer mean when she says, "She thinks it's made a huge difference in her work environment"?

(A) Her friend recently launched a big hit program.
(B) Her friend believes a course is effective.
(C) Her friend is having difficulties at work.
(D) Her friend is available to lead a course.

Questions 151-152 refer to the following memo.

To: All Sawtooth Inc. Staff
From: Brandon Kim, CEO
Subject: Seminar
Date: January 29

Dear All,

Please be informed that your participation will be required at the Privacy & Security seminar to take place on February 22 from 1:00 P.M. to 4:30 P.M. in the conference room. As of March this year, all regional offices must follow the rules and regulations in accordance with the policies determined by our global office in the US. All staff members must also sign a declaration form upon completion of the seminar.

If you cannot attend the scheduled time above, please speak to your designated manager to arrange attendance at one of the seminars to be held off-site no later than April 15.

In advance of the seminar, please take time to review the pamphlet that has been circulated to all department heads.

I look forward to seeing you at the seminar.

Brandon Kim
CFO

---

151. What are employees required to do after the seminar?

(A) Sign a document
(B) Review a pamphlet
(C) Make an arrangement
(D) Submit event feedback

152. What should employees do if they cannot join the session on February 22?

(A) Speak with Brandon Kim
(B) Sign up for an earlier seminar
(C) Give a written explanation
(D) Contact a specific supervisor

GO ON TO THE NEXT PAGE

Questions 153-154 refer to the following e-mail.

E-Mail Message

To: Belle Choi <bellechoi@epharm.com>
From: Kevin Womack <kwomack@epharm.com>
Date: February 22
Subject: March Trip

On behalf of the board of directors here at Eldridge Pharmaceuticals, I'd like to thank you for your continued efforts in selling our pharmaceutical products in Korea. It will be nice to talk with you and your team about our sales figures when I see you all in Busan next month at our new factory. I will be landing in Seoul in the late afternoon on March 14, and will then take a train down to Busan and check-in to my hotel. I'll be leaving early on March 17.

By the way, I would like to inquire whether you would mind pushing back our dinner reservation by one day. I'm sorry to ask you for this favor, but something urgent has come up that I will need to attend to on March 15, so I won't be available that evening. I have had to hastily schedule a meeting with Erin Suzuki while we are both in Busan. She will be going back to Osaka the next day. Please let me know if you would be happy to change our plans.

Regards,

Kevin Womack
Director of Asian Sales
Eldridge Pharmaceuticals Inc.

---

153. According to the e-mail, what is Mr. Womack planning to do?

(A) Change the venue of a meeting
(B) Postpone a meal with Ms. Suzuki
(C) Organize flights to Osaka
(D) Visit a manufacturing facility in Busan

154. When had Ms. Choi originally planned to have dinner with Mr. Womack?

(A) On March 14
(B) On March 15
(C) On March 16
(D) On March 17

Questions 155-157 refer to the following e-mail.

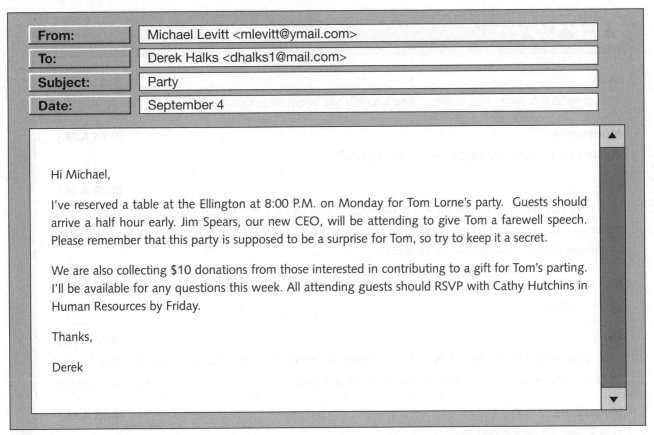

From:	Michael Levitt <mlevitt@ymail.com>
To:	Derek Halks <dhalks1@mail.com>
Subject:	Party
Date:	September 4

Hi Michael,

I've reserved a table at the Ellington at 8:00 P.M. on Monday for Tom Lorne's party. Guests should arrive a half hour early. Jim Spears, our new CEO, will be attending to give Tom a farewell speech. Please remember that this party is supposed to be a surprise for Tom, so try to keep it a secret.

We are also collecting $10 donations from those interested in contributing to a gift for Tom's parting. I'll be available for any questions this week. All attending guests should RSVP with Cathy Hutchins in Human Resources by Friday.

Thanks,

Derek

155. Who is the event being planned for?

(A) Jim Spears
(B) Michael Levitt
(C) Tom Lorne
(D) Cathy Hutchins

156. When should the guests arrive?

(A) At 7:00 P.M.
(B) At 7:30 P.M.
(C) At 8:00 P.M.
(D) At 8:30 P.M.

157. What is the reason for the party?

(A) A new CEO is being introduced.
(B) A coworker is leaving.
(C) The company is celebrating a successful year.
(D) The company wants to reward staff.

GO ON TO THE NEXT PAGE

Questions 158-161 refer to the following online chat discussion.

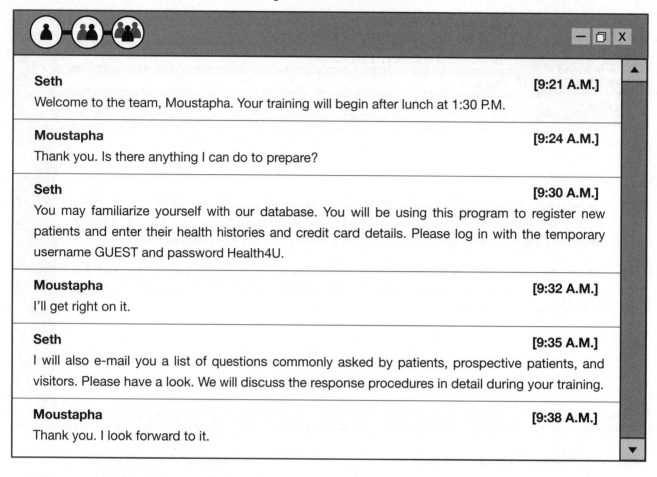

Seth [9:21 A.M.]

Welcome to the team, Moustapha. Your training will begin after lunch at 1:30 P.M.

Moustapha [9:24 A.M.]

Thank you. Is there anything I can do to prepare?

Seth [9:30 A.M.]

You may familiarize yourself with our database. You will be using this program to register new patients and enter their health histories and credit card details. Please log in with the temporary username GUEST and password Health4U.

Moustapha [9:32 A.M.]

I'll get right on it.

Seth [9:35 A.M.]

I will also e-mail you a list of questions commonly asked by patients, prospective patients, and visitors. Please have a look. We will discuss the response procedures in detail during your training.

Moustapha [9:38 A.M.]

Thank you. I look forward to it.

158. Where most likely does Moustapha work?

(A) In a train station
(B) In a visitor's center
(C) In a public library
(D) In a medical office

159. What does Seth say about the database?

(A) It is easy to use.
(B) It stores financial information.
(C) It requires a personalized password.
(D) It is updated once per day.

160. At 9:32 P.M., what does Moustapha mean when he writes, "I'll get right on it"?

(A) He will contact some clients.
(B) He will practice using a program.
(C) He will submit some information.
(D) He will create new user information.

161. What will Seth most likely do next?

(A) He will make a list of participants.
(B) He will create Moustapha's e-mail account.
(C) He will update the payroll database.
(D) He will send a FAQ sheet to Moustapha.

Questions 162-164 refer to the following notice.

Date posted: March 19

To all exam takers:

In preparation for our annual language proficiency test, we will be hosting a workshop for all employees who have registered for the test.

The workshop will be held at the Camak Auditorium from April 9 to 15. All employees who have registered for the proficiency test can participate in the workshop. Those who are taking the language test for the first time must attend. There is no cost for the workshop. However, there will be an optional supplementary course the following week. Employees who enroll in the supplementary course will take a practice exam every night. The cost will be $100.

If you are interested in the supplementary course, please submit your payment before the beginning of next month. It is scheduled to start on April 18 at 6:00 P.M.

---

162. Who may attend the workshop?

(A) All company staff
(B) Employees who recently joined the company
(C) Staff who have signed up for a test
(D) Employees who failed a previous test

163. What is the last day that individuals may pay for the supplementary course?

(A) March 31
(B) April 1
(C) April 18
(D) April 30

164. What is indicated about employees who are taking the test for the first time?

(A) They must register online.
(B) They must attend a workshop.
(C) They must pay $100 to register.
(D) They must take the supplementary course.

GO ON TO THE NEXT PAGE

Questions 165-168 refer to the following form.

Employee Review Form

Name: _Conrad Jacobs_	Date of Evaluation: _July 14_
Job Title: _Job Placement Officer_	Evaluator: _Mindy Smith_
Months in this position: _22_	Review Period: _January-June_

Mr. Jacobs clearly finds great joy in matching employees with employers and has had a high success rate. He has shown initiative in creating a computer program that searches for jobseekers and their skills in order to match them with job advertisers. He then assists jobseekers in applying for the jobs to which they are well-suited and communicates with employers to set up interviews.

Mr. Jacobs' commitment to his clients can be demonstrated in the monthly workshops he hosts. During these workshops, he gives helpful advice on writing cover letters and résumés. — [1] —. He also conducts practice interviews to prepare jobseekers for the next step in the process.

Furthermore, Mr. Jacobs speaks regularly with the hiring staff that will be reviewing applications and conducting interviews. This helps him better prepare his clients, and it helps him to better match jobseekers with jobs. — [2] —.

One suggestion I would make to Mr. Jacobs is to follow up on successful matches. — [3] —. Learning which matches have been successful and which have failed will guide him in future job placement endeavors.

Overall, I am very happy with Mr. Jacobs' performance. — [4] —. Therefore, I would like to recommend he be granted a pay raise.

Mindy Smith

---

165. What does Mr. Jacobs do?

(A) Manage hiring processes
(B) Maintain the computer system
(C) Help jobseekers
(D) Create job advertisements

166. What can be inferred about Mr. Jacobs?

(A) He finds his position rewarding.
(B) He recently started a new job.
(C) He mentors new hires.
(D) He is Ms. Smith's direct supervisor.

167. What will Mr. Jacobs most likely do in the future?

(A) He will receive more responsibility.
(B) He will check on past clients.
(C) He will train for a more suitable job.
(D) He will attend an interview with Ms. Smith.

168. In which of the positions marked [1], [2], [3], and [4] does the following sentence best belong?

"In fact, I feel he is deserving of improved compensation for all his efforts."

(A) [1]
(B) [2]
(C) [3]
(D) [4]

Harbor Village Café is a recently renovated restaurant on St. Maarten Avenue. What was an old warehouse is now a trendy hotspot on the waterfront. Owner Miles Bukowski purchased the building in September. Just two months later, renovations were completed and the café was open for business.

"I felt like the old warehouse was an eyesore on our waterfront. Now it is a piece of history that everyone can enjoy," said Mr. Bukowski.

The warehouse dates back to 1867 when it was built to store supplies for a shipping company. In 1926 it was sold and used as storage for commercial fishing boats. When commercial fishing was restricted to several small zones in 1971 in order to restore abundance, the fishing industry began to decline rapidly and the warehouse was left unoccupied. It remained empty until Mr. Bukowski purchased it.

So the next time you find yourself on St. Maarten Avenue and want a quick bite to eat, stop by the Harbor Village Café. The new renovations and spectacular waterfront view will surely amaze you.

169. In what month did the café most likely open?

(A) February
(B) June
(C) September
(D) November

170. Why was the warehouse abandoned in the 1970s?

(A) Because a shipping company went out of business
(B) Because local residents demanded its closure
(C) Because its condition had become unsafe
(D) Because fishing was prohibited

171. The word "decline" in paragraph 3, line 4, is closest in meaning to

(A) decrease
(B) reject
(C) weaken
(D) deteriorate

GO ON TO THE NEXT PAGE

Questions 172–175 refer to the following e-mail.

E-Mail Message

To: Lacey Tregembo <laceyt@bitoeng.com>
From: James Dimon <jdimon@wellsdimon.com>
Date: August 5
Subject: Upcoming visit

Dear Ms. Tregembo,

I have been notified that you will visit our company next week. We are happy to have you meet with us and learn more about our engineering practice. — [1] —.

I wanted to give you an itinerary to prepare you for your arrival. On Monday morning, you will meet with our Senior Engineer, Mark Trabajo. He will give you a safety briefing and then introduce you to the team that you will be observing. Each morning afterward, you will meet with them to learn about our data collection process. — [2] —.

You are invited to join us for lunch each day. I have several different project managers that would be happy to meet with you. Each of them is considered to be among the top engineers in our field.

In the afternoon, you will meet with Yui Lee in our experimental laboratory. — [3] —. You will also learn how our experimentation process works. Hopefully, this data can be useful in your own engineering field.

On your last day, we will have a seminar with guest speakers from our research facility in Germany. — [4] —. During that event, we ask that you share a few words about your experience at Wells-Dimon.

We will have a car pick you up at your hotel on Monday morning at 8:00 A.M. Thanks for your interest in our program. We look forward to meeting you soon.

Sincerely,

James Dimon
CEO, Wells-Dimon

172. What will Mr. Trabajo do?

(A) Introduce Ms. Tregembo to a team
(B) Give a lecture on data collection
(C) Send Ms. Tregembo a trip itinerary
(D) Perform laboratory experiments

173. What is Ms. Tregembo encouraged to do on a daily basis?

(A) Submit a report to Mr. Dimon
(B) Check some safety equipment
(C) Join her colleagues for a meal
(D) Attend a professional seminar

174. What will Ms. Tregembo most likely do on the last day of her visit?

(A) Tour a research facility
(B) Meet with Yui Lee
(C) Make some remarks
(D) Return to Germany

175. In which of the positions marked [1], [2], [3], and [4] does the following sentence best belong?

"This is where you will observe our cutting-edge experiments."

(A) [1]
(B) [2]
(C) [3]
(D) [4]

GO ON TO THE NEXT PAGE

Questions 176-180 refer to the following e-mails.

To:	Steven Spurrier <sspurrier@himail.com>
From:	Danny Ford <hrjobs@deloitte.com>
Subject:	Network Administrator Vacancy

Dear Mr. Spurrier,

I am contacting you because I noticed that you applied to our company as a network systems engineer. I'm afraid that position was already filled, but I'd like to inform you that there is also an opening for a network administrator in our Loans Division you may be interested in. Having reviewed your résumé, we would like to know more about you and your qualifications. Although the position is different from the one you had been seeking, we believe there is considerable overlap in both scope and in requirements.

We are hoping that you can come in for an interview on Monday, December 2. However, we also have dates available on December 3, 5, and 9. We will hold our interviews at 11:00 A.M. Please choose whichever is most convenient for you. As you know, this position requires a proficiency in programming languages and large-scale computer networking. So please arrive prepared to take an exam to test your skills. When you come to the interview, please remember to bring a copy of your engineering license.

Thank you,

Danny Ford

E-Mail Message

To:	Danny Ford <hrjobs@deloitte.com>
From:	Steven Spurrier <sspurrier@himail.com>
Subject:	Re: Network Administrator Vacancy

Dear Mr. Ford,

Thank you for your e-mail. I am very excited to hear from Deloitte and I am interested to learn more about the opportunity. I would be happy to come in on the second interview date you mentioned. However, I am hoping it will be possible to rearrange the time. I am working with another company part-time, so rescheduling for some time in the afternoon will work for me. Also, I am waiting for a copy of my engineering license to be approved. I can bring a letter of certification as a temporary substitute if that is acceptable. Please let me know when we can reschedule. I will also need to know the address and location of the interview.

Regards,

Steven Spurrier

176. Why did Mr. Ford contact Mr. Spurrier?

(A) To inform him about a job vacancy
(B) To request that he submit an application
(C) To reschedule a job interview
(D) To inquire about a position

177. What is implied about Mr. Spurrier in the first e-mail?

(A) He was not selected for the position he wanted.
(B) He was previously working for Mr. Ford.
(C) He is overqualified for the network administrator role.
(D) He doesn't have to take an exam that is usually required.

178. What does Mr. Ford ask Mr. Spurrier to bring with him?

(A) His résumé
(B) A portfolio of past work
(C) A letter of certification
(D) His engineering license

179. When does Mr. Spurrier want to visit Mr. Ford's workplace?

(A) December 2
(B) December 3
(C) December 5
(D) December 9

180. What problem does Mr. Spurrier mention?

(A) One of his documents is not available.
(B) He is not available in the afternoons.
(C) His home is located far from Deloitte's offices.
(D) He is unable to submit an application before a deadline.

GO ON TO THE NEXT PAGE

Questions 181-185 refer to the following e-mails.

To:	Anita Gray, Manager
From:	Lynette Quade, Sales Representative
Subject:	Staff morale

Dear Anita,

I was intrigued by our discussion about improving morale. I have observed over the past few months that, while our efforts to improve productivity have been effective, they may be having a negative effect on morale. For example, our decision to monitor computers for social network usage has significantly reduced the number of worker hours wasted online, but it has also created an atmosphere in which employees feel like they are not trusted.

My proposal is not to reverse our monitoring procedures, but rather to try to add some morale-boosting initiatives. One idea is to create incentives for employees to be more productive. Perhaps instead of having quotas that must be met, we could reward certain levels of achievement. Another is staff appreciation dinners on Friday evenings. This might reduce the impulse people feel to engage in social networking sites as they will have the opportunity to network face to face with their colleagues in a non-competitive environment with no expectations for performance.

I am interested to hear what you think about my suggestions. Perhaps we could arrange a meeting for next Monday.

Regards,

Lynette

E-Mail Message

To:	Lynette Quade, Sales Representative
From:	Anita Gray, Manager
Subject:	RE: Staff morale

Dear Lynette,

Thank you for your suggestion regarding morale-boosting initiatives. I am interested in your ideas and would like to meet to discuss them further. Please contact my secretary to arrange a time to meet.

In particular, I would be interested to hear about other companies that have used these kinds of initiatives. Have they been effective in the long run? Will increased productivity result in increased profits sufficient to cover the costs? I would like to see some figures addressing these concerns if you have any.

Regarding the social gatherings you proposed, I think that staff appreciation lunches on Fridays would be preferable.

I look forward to meeting you next Monday and discussing these ideas. I think we can come up with a good plan of action.

Best wishes,

Anita

181. What is the main purpose of the first e-mail?

(A) To complain about a policy change
(B) To express gratitude to a colleague
(C) To propose some ideas
(D) To discuss an employee

182. What will Ms. Quade likely do to prepare for the next meeting?

(A) Research the effectiveness of some incentives programs
(B) Calculate appropriate production quotas for the coming month
(C) Invite staff representatives in order to get their input
(D) Propose a system for evaluating employee performance

183. What can be inferred about online social networking?

(A) It doesn't help improve work efficiency.
(B) It is an important part of Ms. Quade's job.
(C) It has a negative effect on customer relations.
(D) It creates opportunities to relax while at work.

184. On what matter did Ms. Quade and Ms. Gray disagree?

(A) When to hold staff parties
(B) How to measure work efficiency
(C) How much to pay as incentives
(D) When to meet each other

185. What was NOT suggested as a way to improve the mood around the company?

(A) More time dedicated for online social networking
(B) Opportunities to encourage direct relationship
(C) The end of the quota system in favor of an incentives program
(D) Regular events to show employee appreciation

GO ON TO THE NEXT PAGE

E-Mail Message

To:	Victor Manfred <vmanfred@futuracorp.com>
From:	Jerome Dash <jeromedash@futuracorp.com>
Date:	June 23
Subject:	Limousine
Attachment:	📎 brochure.doc

Dear Mr. Manfred,

I have attached some information about a vehicle that I think we should consider adding to our fleet of company cars. I believe that this vehicle would impress our clients when we shuttle them between the airport, their hotel, and our headquarters.

One of our primary goals here at Futura Corporation is to promote environmental awareness and maintain our reputation for eco-friendly business practices. The new Skylark Senator is an electric limousine that would show this dedication to our clients. It runs on a 24-KWh battery, which is enough power for journeys of up to 60 kilometers on a single charge – more than adequate for driving our clients from place to place. Its new Level 3 charging port allows it to be recharged in approximately one and a half hours. Upon release, it will retail for $59,995, but advance orders placed before July 1 will knock the price down to $54,995.

Any company purchases have to go through you first, so I'd like you to think this over and then let me know if I can go ahead with it or not.

Best regards,

Jerome Dash

Skylark Auto – Promotional Brochure

Introducing the brand-new Skylark Senator, a revolution in electric vehicle design!

When it is officially launched on July 15, the Skylark Senator will be the most advanced electric limousine model on the market. With its impressive 24-kWh battery, the Senator can travel up to 75 kilometers before it needs to be recharged, and charging only takes around 90 minutes thanks to the revolutionary Level 3 charging port.

The Senator's creator, Dean Salinger, has worked in the motor industry for more than 30 years. He began his career as an engineer at Ezio Motors, but swiftly rose up the ranks and finally left that company to focus on design and development in Skylark Auto's electric vehicle division.

The official launch of the Skylark Senator will take place at the KMS Auto Show in Los Angeles, and the car will be available for $59,995. However, early purchases (made before July 1) can take advantage of the lower price of $54,995.

To find out more about the Skylark Senator, visit our Web site at www.skylarkauto.com. For further information about the KMS Auto Show and our launch event, go to www.kmsautoshow.com/info.

To:	Jerome Dash <jeromedash@futuracorp.com>
From:	Victor Manfred <vmanfred@futuracorp.com>
Date:	June 24
Subject:	Re: Limousine

Hi Jerome,

Thanks for contacting me regarding the Skylark Senator. I'm definitely interested in purchasing one, but I don't want to be too hasty. We have plenty of money left in our purchasing budget, so I'd rather wait until the new model is released and reviewed by auto experts before I make a final decision. Also, I'm allocating an allowance for you to attend the vehicle's official launch event in July. I want you to find out more about the vehicle and report back to me with your thoughts.

Regards,

Victor Manfred
Chief Financial Officer
Futura Corporation

186. What is the purpose of the first e-mail?

(A) To seek approval for a purchase
(B) To advertise a new vehicle
(C) To discuss an upcoming client visit
(D) To suggest repairing company cars

187. In the first e-mail, the word "primary" in paragraph 2, line 1, is closest in meaning to

(A) prior
(B) main
(C) initial
(D) potential

188. What has Mr. Dash misunderstood about the vehicle?

(A) Its retail price
(B) Its battery power
(C) Its driving range
(D) Its recharge time

189. What is suggested about Mr. Salinger?

(A) He currently works at Ezio Motors.
(B) He works closely with Futura Corp.
(C) He organizes the KMS Auto Show.
(D) He designs electric vehicles.

190. What can be inferred about Mr. Manfred?

(A) He would prefer to buy a vehicle at a reduced price.
(B) He plans to attend an upcoming auto show himself.
(C) He would like Mr. Dash to travel to Los Angeles.
(D) He will compare the performance of two vehicles.

GO ON TO THE NEXT PAGE

A REMINDER FOR EVERYONE

– Visitors on Friday –

Games World Magazine is sending a journalist and film crew to conduct interviews with us on Friday, August 24, at 1:00 P.M., so make sure that you look presentable and are prepared to discuss our upcoming software release. This especially applies to all lead developers.

We want all of you to be present during their visit, so you should be at your workstations by 1:00 P.M. that day. We think the interviews and filming will take no more than ninety minutes. I know most of you are not keen on speaking to the media, but this type of thing is important as part of the marketing for the games we will launch soon. Please make a good impression.

To:	Anthony North <anorth@logistasoft.com>
From:	Miranda Fantano <mfantano@gamesworldmag.com>
Date:	Tuesday, August 21
Subject:	Friday's arrangements

Dear Mr. North,

I would just like to confirm that we will be arriving at your headquarters in Silicon Valley at one o'clock this Friday. As I mentioned previously, we would like to interview the lead developers of your upcoming video game, Fantasy Legends. The weather should be perfect, so the best place to do this will be next to your swimming pool. The filmed interviews will be posted to the online version of our publication. You mentioned that your employees usually return from lunch at 1:30 P.M. Thanks for making an adjustment in order to accommodate our schedule.

Best regards,

Miranda Fantano
Games World Magazine

Logista Software: Changing Video Gaming from the Inside

By Clinton Kelsey

Walking into Logista Software's impressive headquarters, I was surprised to see employees lounging around reading graphic novels or indulging in a game of table tennis. "We encourage our staff to relax and stimulate their minds, and this helps them to stay creative," says Anthony North, the software company's founder and CEO.

Logista was established only four years ago and has rapidly risen to prominence in the video game industry. Its headquarters is comprised of contemporary workspaces designed by Annalise Peel. She stated, "I tried to give the work environment a fresh, invigorating appearance, as well as a feeling of openness and freedom."

In a recent interview, Kyle Channing, founder of renowned electronics firm Muvo Technologies, shared his thoughts on Logista's approach. "I think they've succeeded in fostering a work atmosphere that prioritizes innovation," he said. "This is apparent in the work it produces, and this is especially true in the case of its upcoming release."

Logista Software's headquarters is located in Silicon Valley, and the building itself reflects the creativity of the team busily working within. The interior is brightly painted, with several areas containing comfortable bean bags, books, and games. A rooftop patio runs alongside a beautiful pool where staff can cool down during their break periods.

Click the video link below for our full piece on Logista Software and our interviews with the senior developers of the firm's upcoming game, Fantasy Legends.

191. Who most likely posted the notice?

(A) Ms. Fantano
(B) Mr. North
(C) Ms. Peel
(D) Mr. Kelsey

192. What are employees instructed to do on August 24?

(A) Attend a product development meeting
(B) Suggest locations for a media event
(C) Contribute an article to a magazine
(D) Take a shorter lunch break than usual

193. What is indicated about the lead developers?

(A) They should visit Games World Magazine's head office.
(B) They will be interviewed on a rooftop patio.
(C) They will give a demonstration of a new video game.
(D) They have been featured in Games World Magazine before.

194. What is suggested about Logista Software?

(A) It posts videos on its Web site.
(B) It recently merged with Muvo Technologies.
(C) It has gained a good reputation in its field.
(D) It has relocated its headquarters.

195. What does Mr. Channing imply about Fantasy Legends?

(A) Its release date has been changed.
(B) It is likely to sell out quickly.
(C) It is an innovative piece of work.
(D) It will be launched in August.

GO ON TO THE NEXT PAGE

Questions 196-200 refer to the following e-mails and invoice.

E-Mail Message

To:	Mary Findlay <mfindlay@truemail.net>
From:	Henry Poole <hpoole@innerwellness.com>
Subject:	Inner Wellness
Date:	February 10

Dear Ms. Findlay,

Thank you for your interest in Inner Wellness, the leading supplier of health foods, vitamins, and supplements in Kelsey County. As you noted, our store is indeed located in downtown Overton, but we also provide shipping for online shoppers who reside in surrounding counties. Shipping rates are as follows:

- Cooper County: $5.00
- Bennett County: $7.00
- Netting County: $8.00
- Beaufort County: $10.00

Furthermore, if you wish to join the Inner Wellness Store Membership program, you will receive a ten percent discount on any order exceeding $150. To sign up, you can simply visit our Web site at www. innerwellness.com/membership or respond to this e-mail. I would be happy to assist you with the registration process.

Best wishes,

Henry Poole
Owner & Proprietor
Inner Wellness

Inner Wellness

Order #: 59379

Customer: Mary Findlay

Date of Purchase: February 12

Delivery Address: 548 Olsen Avenue, Bridgeton

Date of Delivery: February 14

Item	Quantity	Unit Price	Net Amount
Vitamin C 1000 mg (250 tablets)	1	$36.99	$36.99
ABC Daily Multivitamin (240 tablets)	2	$39.99	$79.98
Children's Multivitamin (200 tablets)	1	$32.99	$32.99
Chunky Peanut Protein Bar 60g	12	$2.50	$30.00
If you are dissatisfied with your order, you must contact us within three days of the delivery receipt date in order to obtain a refund or request an exchange.	Shipping		$10.00
	Sub-total		$184.96
	10% Discount		-$18.99
	Total		$161.97

To:	Henry Poole <hpoole@innerwellness.com>
From:	Mary Findlay <mfindlay@truemail.net>
Subject:	Recent Order
Date:	February 20

Dear Mr. Poole,

I am writing with regard to my recent order from Inner Wellness, which arrived promptly on February 14. Before I discuss the main issues, let me begin by saying that I am extremely satisfied with the Vitamin C tablets, the adult multivitamins, and the protein bars. Unfortunately, I ordered the wrong multivitamins for my young son and daughter; I had intended to purchase the chewable tablets. Would it be possible to exchange the product for the chewable version?

Also, based on my invoice, it seems as though I was overcharged by three dollars for shipping. It's not necessary to arrange a refund for such a small sum, but I would hope that this does not happen again in the future.

I look forward to hearing from you.

Regards,

Mary Findlay

196. What is the purpose of the first e-mail?

(A) To promote new health products
(B) To announce a store sale
(C) To respond to an inquiry
(D) To apologize to a customer

197. What can be inferred about Ms. Findlay?

(A) She is a returning customer of Inner Wellness.
(B) She visited the Inner Wellness store in person.
(C) She works in the health food industry.
(D) She applied for a store membership.

198. What item did Ms. Findlay order by mistake?

(A) Vitamin C 1000 mg
(B) ABC Daily Multivitamin
(C) Children's Multivitamin
(D) Chunky Peanut Protein Bar

199. Why will Ms. Findlay's request most likely be denied?

(A) She used a discount coupon to purchase items.
(B) She did not spend enough money on products.
(C) She was too late in contacting the company.
(D) She failed to attach a copy of her invoice.

200. Where most likely does Ms. Findlay live?

(A) In Cooper County
(B) In Bennett County
(C) In Netting County
(D) In Beaufort County

Stop! This is the end of the test. If you finish before time is called, you may go back to Parts 5, 6, and 7 and check your work.

정답 p.473 / 점수 환산표 p.476

실전모의고사
TEST 12

TEST 12 해설

바로 보기

시작 시간 _____시 _____분

종료 시간 _____시 _____분

▶ 중간에 멈추지 말고 처음부터 끝까지 풀어보세요. 문제를 풀 때는 실전처럼 답안지에 마킹하세요.

READING TEST

In the Reading test, you will read a variety of texts and answer several different types of reading comprehension questions. The entire Reading test will last 75 minutes. There are three parts, and directions are given for each part. You are encouraged to answer as many questions as possible within the time allowed. You must mark your answers on the separate answer sheet. Do not write your answers in your test book.

PART 5

Directions: A word or phrase is missing in each of the sentences below. Four answer choices are given below each sentence. Select the best answer to complete the sentence. Then mark the letter (A), (B), (C), or (D) on your answer sheet.

101. Sales figures and teamwork are important, but the number one thing we expect from employees is that they make a significant ------- to our organization.

(A) contribute
(B) contributing
(C) contributor
(D) contribution

102. A monthly update will be sent out to all investors to keep ------- informed of new projects and challenges.

(A) them
(B) they
(C) their
(D) themselves

103. Any form of written ------- sent by our company must include our logo and our contact information.

(A) communicate
(B) communicated
(C) communicates
(D) communication

104. The board's decision was ------- by data included in the presentation given by the financial consultant.

(A) influenced
(B) negotiated
(C) engaged
(D) involved

105. It is difficult to find qualified temporary workers during the winter ------- employee absenteeism rates are highest.

(A) where
(B) what
(C) when
(D) which

106. Mr. Talbot's duties include collecting feedback from our customers and ------- orders.

(A) verifies
(B) verifying
(C) verified
(D) verifications

107. Before making a home purchase, ------- buyers should consider property taxes and ongoing maintenance costs.

(A) delicate
(B) continuous
(C) potential
(D) suspect

108. After February 20, subway passengers can use either cash ------- credit cards to pay for monthly travel passes.

(A) but
(B) with
(C) and
(D) or

109. The west wing of the company building is a ------- area, where all personnel must enter a code to gain entry.

(A) predicted
(B) situated
(C) restricted
(D) confirmed

110. The value of our stock continues to ------- despite efforts to improve the image of our sportswear brand.

(A) cease
(B) decline
(C) delay
(D) maintain

111. Successful candidates for the sales consultant position should have a minimum ------- five years of relevant experience.

(A) of
(B) at
(C) to
(D) in

112. To ensure that all contact with our clients is professional, ------- with our guidelines regarding e-mail and phone communication is crucial.

(A) disclosure
(B) compliance
(C) enthusiasm
(D) connection

113. Regrettably, your application was unsuccessful ------- the high number of qualified candidates for the position of maintenance manager.

(A) due to
(B) except for
(C) regarding
(D) in spite of

114. With house prices ------- record lows, there has never been a better time to purchase a new property.

(A) obtaining
(B) announcing
(C) reaching
(D) renovating

115. You must fill out the ------- form and bring it with you to your hospital appointment next week.

(A) attached
(B) invented
(C) exceeded
(D) directed

116. Please retain your ------- as proof of purchase and make sure you bring it into the store if you find any defects in the product.

(A) notice
(B) procedure
(C) receipt
(D) option

117. Members of our staff seem to get tired during the afternoon hours, ------- we opened a company gym to give them more energy.

(A) unless
(B) so
(C) if
(D) otherwise

118. After a brief introduction, the new senior manager will outline his plans for ------- the entire company.

(A) streamline
(B) streamlined
(C) to streamline
(D) streamlining

119. The Westwood Bank will not give out any personal details to a third party ------- written permission from the customer.

(A) without
(B) notwithstanding
(C) providing
(D) given

GO ON TO THE NEXT PAGE

120. Renovations ------- in the Administration Office this month, so please make sure to pack up your desk and move all your personal belongings to the third floor.

(A) to begin
(B) will begin
(C) beginning
(D) begins

121. We have a ------- pack of materials for all new interns, which covers every aspect of our legal firm and will help familiarize you with our company.

(A) tidy
(B) brief
(C) frequent
(D) complete

122. Jamison International Inc. is ------- seeking a competent financial specialist to join the firm as its current financial director is retiring at the end of the year.

(A) typically
(B) actively
(C) extremely
(D) unusually

123. Although we have experienced a slight downturn in revenue this quarter, our sales figures are still ------- high.

(A) enough
(B) closely
(C) quite
(D) even

124. During the upcoming workshop, Dr. Jones will discuss ------- methods for dealing with issues involving patients and their families.

(A) durable
(B) effective
(C) constant
(D) stressed

125. New hires are advised to take ------- care with your work to ensure that you don't make the same mistake twice.

(A) little
(B) many
(C) lots
(D) great

126. For your -------, I have included a detailed description of all services that will be provided in the package.

(A) reference
(B) conclusion
(C) expectation
(D) occurrence

127. Next year, a team of medical experts will investigate ------ sunlight patterns influence human behavior and skin conditions.

(A) about
(B) that
(C) whether
(D) whose

128. Resignation letters are ------- submitted a month prior to the termination of employment, but in exceptional cases a shorter notice may be granted.

(A) generally
(B) finally
(C) nearly
(D) approximately

129. Any ------- electronic devices that are still under warranty may be returned by mail to the product manufacturers for repairs.

(A) accurate
(B) qualified
(C) defective
(D) expired

130. According to Professor Patel, the demand for low-income housing is expected to ------- despite the current economic slowdown.

(A) reserve
(B) surpass
(C) expand
(D) assemble

PART 6

Directions: Read the texts that follow. A word, phrase, or sentence is missing in parts of each text. Four answer choices for each question are given below the text. Select the best answer to complete the text. Then mark the letter (A), (B), (C) or (D) on your answer sheet.

Questions 131-134 refer to the following notice.

Infinity Productions will reimburse employees for travel expenses incurred when performing the various functions of their jobs. Travel expenses include the ------- of transportation, accommodation,
131.
and meals consumed over the duration of the business trip.

Employees seeking reimbursement for expenses must file an expense report no later than the

first day of each month. ------- item should be entered separately and include the date, the amount,
132.
the reason for the expense, and a scanned copy of the receipt. Reimbursements will be deposited

------- into employees' bank accounts on the fifteenth day of each month, along with regular pay.
133.

------- .
134.

Thank you for your continued commitment to Infinity Productions.

131. (A) length
(B) cost
(C) share
(D) content

132. (A) All
(B) Which
(C) Such
(D) Each

133. (A) direct
(B) directs
(C) direction
(D) directly

134. (A) Please ensure that you send a copy of your trip itinerary this week.
(B) Don't forget that products may only be returned with a valid receipt.
(C) Thank you for helping us to reduce our monthly business expenses.
(D) You will be notified if payments are likely to be later than the 15th.

GO ON TO THE NEXT PAGE

Questions 135-138 refer to the following e-mail.

To: Management <managerlist@kpt.com>

From: HR Department <humanresources@kpt.com>

Subject: Leadership Retreat

Date: April 2

The company president would like to extend an invitation to all of our management staff here at KPT Industries to a company retreat. This retreat will take place on the third weekend in May. ------- . For example, you will have the opportunity to attend workshops led by some of the industry's
    135.

most ------- managers. Each attendee will work with a mentor who will guide you in becoming an
        136.

effective leader. ------- , you will work with one another to complete a set of objectives and techniques
            137.

to be implemented back at the office.

The retreat aims to reward our hard-working managers with quality dining, fun recreational activities, and time for socializing. And after what we expect will be productive mornings, you will be free to enjoy the retreat. The golf course, horse stables, and exercise rooms are free for all to enjoy.

If you wish ------- the retreat, please reply to this e-mail, and you will be provided with details on
          138.

shuttle services.

---

135. (A) Inclement weather is expected, so bring appropriate clothing.
(B) Speakers should prepare their presentation files in advance.
(C) Attendance is voluntary, but we will certainly make it worth your while.
(D) This does not allow us much time to prepare properly.

136. (A) successful
(B) available
(C) promotional
(D) possible

137. (A) However
(B) Instead
(C) Also
(D) In fact

138. (A) attending
(B) attend
(C) to attend
(D) attended

To: Reggie Clide

From: Dennis Kang

Subject: Parking changes

Date: March 10

Dear Mr. Clide,

-------. It will be no longer possible to allow your customers to park their cars in front of the lot.
139.
-------, the land has been acquired by the local government ------- a compulsory purchase order.
140.   **141.**

It is my best assumption that a city park is scheduled to be built there, and a new school will be right next to it. I am sorry that I am not giving you much notice, but this has all happened rather suddenly over the past few days.

I hope that you will not have ------- difficulty making other parking arrangements.
142.

Sincerely,

Dennis Kang

---

139. (A) I received your request for a parking permit.
(B) Thanks for your interest in using our services.
(C) Our parking lot is scheduled to be closed for renovations.
(D) I am contacting you with some regrettable news.

140. (A) Surprisingly
(B) Initially
(C) Alternatively
(D) Unfortunately

141. (A) by
(B) under
(C) upon
(D) with

142. (A) any
(B) many
(C) every
(D) such

GO ON TO THE NEXT PAGE

TEST 12

Questions 143-146 refer to the following letter.

Dear Ms. Lockhart,

------- . I understand that we will meet in the dining hall of the Canton Hotel at one o'clock. In
143.
attendance will be our Marketing team, which includes Monty Warren and Martha Solomon. Mandy
Eason and Clarice Bernard of our Sales team will be attending, too. Regrettably Michelle Goldberg
will be unable to join us due to a scheduling ------- .
144.

We hope to discuss techniques for improving sales in the upcoming months, and are eager to hear
your ideas. I know that you have a wealth of experience and I feel that our team can benefit hugely
------- your expertise. I would also like to thank you in advance for agreeing to meet with us. I am
145.
confident that together we will be able to identify the strengths and weaknesses of our current
strategy and create a plan that will help ------- our market share.
146.

I look forward to our meeting and future correspondence.

Sincerely,

Samantha Kasten

---

143. (A) I would like to thank you for arranging my
accommodation during my stay.
(B) Please proceed with the booking of a
room for our upcoming meeting.
(C) We have many items to add to our sales
meeting agenda.
(D) I am writing to confirm the details of our
meeting scheduled for this Friday.

144. (A) conflict
(B) conflicts
(C) conflicting
(D) conflicted

145. (A) over
(B) from
(C) out of
(D) as

146. (A) grant
(B) suggest
(C) improve
(D) register

PART 7

Directions: In this part you will read a selection of texts, such as magazine and newspaper articles, e-mails, and instant messages. Each text or set of texts is followed by several questions. Select the best answer for each question and mark the letter (A), (B), (C), or (D) on your answer sheet.

Questions 147-148 refer to the following article.

Book Review:
Creative Structure: The Path to Change in Business

Timothy Chouinard's book *Creative Structure: The Path to Change in Business* offers a new approach to integrating successful strategic change in big business. Instead of encouraging companies to revise their mission and vision statements, which is the traditional method to implement strategic change, Chouinard emphasizes the creation of company culture as the most important step. "Without knowing who your company is from the bottom up," writes Chouinard, "you cannot begin to find a strategy that will serve both staff and clients." The author conducted case studies of numerous large corporations and, based on his findings, argues that company culture not only dictates the best direction for the company but also guides the company through effective strategic change.

147. According to the article, what is needed for strategic change?

(A) Well-trained staff members
(B) A clear corporate culture
(C) Comprehensive market research
(D) A loyal customer base

148. What is suggested about Timothy Chouinard?

(A) He founded his own corporation.
(B) He has researched a number of businesses.
(C) He has expertise in public relations.
(D) He regularly lectures on business-related topics.

GO ON TO THE NEXT PAGE

Questions 149-150 refer to the following text-message chain.

Edward   **[4:02 P.M.]**

What did you think about Mr. Harrison, our most recent candidate?

Donna   **[4:12 P.M.]**

I believe he has the required base skills in addition to his masters' degree, but he has only worked for one year as a technology coordinator. Before that, he worked in customer support. Is he sufficiently qualified for this role?

Christina   **[4:18 P.M.]**

I don't think it's enough. However, he came with a strong recommendation from Mr. Tuchman. Apparently, he is a very fast learner and eager to train.

Donna   **[4:20 P.M.]**

He also graduated with high distinction in his computer science program. I suppose he is a hard worker.

Edward   **[4:24 P.M.]**

I actually think that his prior experiences working with people make him stand out as a candidate in our field. He must be able to work well in a team, keep organized, and give clear explanations to our callers.

---

149. At 4:18 P.M., what does Christina mean when she says, "I don't think it's enough"?

(A) The candidate does not have a suitable degree.

(B) The candidate lacks relevant work experience.

(C) The candidate's base skill is not satisfactory.

(D) The candidate has never worked in customer support before.

150. What does Edward say about Mr. Harrison?

(A) He will be offered a management role.

(B) He has several key job skills but is not cooperative.

(C) He should explain some information more clearly.

(D) His experiences give him an advantage.

Need help planning your next conference?

Look no further! Executive Conference Services can handle all aspects of planning your next conference. Your own administrative staff will no longer be stretched too thin, trying to manage the details. As professional planners, the staff at ECS know all the tricks of the trade to save you money at every turn. On the spot disasters can be turned over to us for safe and efficient handling. We work in cities nationwide.

You can choose a planning package that suits your company and your conference style. Your contract may include any or all of the following items:

- Event booking – major and minor venues
- Scheduling within the conference (e.g. workshops and breakout sessions)
- Catering coordination
- Printing and publishing requirements
- Local hotel recommendations
- Audio-visual equipment (basic and specialty)
- Host services, secretarial and janitorial services during the conference
- Special needs – ask us if you need additional services
- Conference advertising

For more information call 914-555-0112 or e-mail info@executiveconference.com

151. What is being advertised?

(A) A new conference center
(B) A city planning company
(C) An executive hotel package
(D) A conference planning service

152. Which service is among those being offered?

(A) Providing projectors
(B) Booking hotel rooms
(C) Handling special diets
(D) Leasing vehicles

GO ON TO THE NEXT PAGE

Questions 153-154 refer to the following notice.

Earthquake Preparedness for Homeowners
Central Insurance

Did you know that most homeowners' and renters' insurance policies do not include coverage for damage from earthquakes? Because of recent events, the Regional Preparedness Authority (RPA) is recommending that everyone in the Bay Area check their policy to see if they are covered. Central Insurance is one of just a few licensed insurers that can sell an RPA approved policy. If you are not sure what your policy covers, consult an authorized provider, such as Central Insurance, to find out.

Whether or not you are covered, there are a few additional things you can do to better prepare yourself and your family for when the next big one strikes.

1. Brace the hot water tank in your home to reduce the risk of water damage or fire.

2. Secure cupboard doors to prevent them from swinging open.

3. Make sure gas appliances have shut-off valves that can be used.

4. Inspect the foundations of your wood home to ensure they're sturdy and secure.

5. Attach open shelves to the wall to avoid spillage of their contents during shaking.

153. What is true about the notice?

(A) Central Insurance is the only licensed company in the region.
(B) The Regional Preparedness Authority offers insurance.
(C) Many policies do not include earthquake damage.
(D) Many homeowners do not have house insurance.

154. What tip is NOT provided in the notice?

(A) Ensure gas devices can be turned off
(B) Fix shelving units to a wall to prevent spills
(C) Remove unnecessary items from cupboards
(D) Check the foundation of one's property

Questions 155–157 refer to the following memorandum.

From: Johnathan Brewer, Warehouse Manager
To: Brenda Davenport, Human Resources
Date: August 11
Subject: Parking problems

Ms. Davenport,

This is Jonathan Brewer, head of our Warehouse and Shipping Department. As I'm sure you know, last week's storm caused significant damage to the roof of our warehouse. Because of this, we will have to empty portions of our warehouse while construction crews make repairs. The construction crew will arrive on Friday, September 4, and they will work through Tuesday, September 8.

Employees should be aware of the following change in procedure. Because we have to empty the warehouse to make room for construction crews, shipments cannot be processed until after completion. If your clients need anything, it should be shipped before or after the construction.

Also, the construction crews will bring in lots of heavy equipment, so employees will not be able to park in our parking lot until the day after the work is finished. Instead, they may park along Ashcott Avenue or at the Brice Hotel. As such, employees may need to leave for work earlier than they usually do.

Thank you for your time. Please forward this to all employees as soon as possible.

Regards,
Johnathan Brewer

155. What needs to be repaired as a result of the storm?

(A) The assembly line machinery
(B) The warehouse roof
(C) The shipping area
(D) The parking lot

156. What are employees encouraged to do during the repairs?

(A) Clean their own workstations
(B) Reschedule shipping dates
(C) Volunteer for a construction project
(D) Find an alternative parking space

157. What day can employees return to their normal morning routines?

(A) Monday
(B) Tuesday
(C) Wednesday
(D) Friday

GO ON TO THE NEXT PAGE

Questions 158–160 refer to the following e-mail.

```
┌─────────────────────────────────────────────────────────────┐
│                     E-Mail Message                          │
├─────────────────────────────────────────────────────────────┤
│                                                               │
│  From:        Greg Clayton <gclayton1@mail.com>              │
│  To:          Maurice Wright <mwright@swiftcars.com>         │
│  Subject:     Employee Mike Stratton                          │
│                                                               │
├─────────────────────────────────────────────────────────────┤
```

Dear Mr. Wright,

This e-mail is in regard to one of your employees, Mike Stratton. On Saturday, March 25, my wife and I were traveling to San Francisco. On the way, our SwiftCars rental car broke down. We were stuck in a countryside area and it was getting very late. We were very worried. My wife called your emergency roadside hotline to get some help.

We were informed that it would take three hours before a tow truck could come and get us. So, your employee, Mike Stratton, drove to pick us up himself. While we waited for our new rental car, Mr. Stratton bought us dinner and gave us the new car for free. Because we were running late, he also contacted the hotel on our behalf.

We could have been stuck on the side of the road for hours. But Mr. Stratton went out of his way to help us. His generous attitude made us forget our bad luck. Our trip was wonderful, and if it weren't for him, it could have been ruined. I hope you know what a wonderful employee you have.

Thanks,

Greg Clayton

---

158. What is the purpose of the e-mail?

(A) To explain a traffic problem
(B) To offer a dinner invitation
(C) To praise a company worker
(D) To complain about a service

159. Who is Greg Clayton?

(A) A service center repairman
(B) The owner of a rental agency
(C) A customer of SwiftCars
(D) A hotel manager

160. What did Mr. Stratton do?

(A) Arranged for a taxi to pick up the customers
(B) Made dinner for his customers
(C) Booked a trip to San Francisco
(D) Reserved a hotel for Greg Clayton

Questions 161–163 refer to the following memo.

To: Anonville Staff
From: Rob Schrab, Manager
Date: Friday, Oct. 3

Dear staff,

It has come to my attention that a few of you have been neglecting your duties when it comes to cleaning up the store before shutting it down for the day. The cleanup process is important for both sanitation and security reasons. I already have the names of those who have not been following protocol, but I would prefer not to take any sort of disciplinary action.

Instead, why don't we try splitting up the work? Everyone can take turns moving displays to the back room, vacuuming the main room, taking out the garbage, etc. Janice and I will work on a schedule that will coincide with everyone's work schedules for the next few weeks, and we can start this on Monday. After that, we'll see how it's working out and go from there.

161. What is the purpose of the memo?

(A) To remind staff to perform their duties
(B) To apologize for the unclean condition of a store
(C) To announce a deal with a cleaning company
(D) To solicit ideas from employees

162. What task is NOT mentioned by Mr. Schrab?

(A) Removing the garbage
(B) Cleaning the carpets
(C) Mopping the floors
(D) Shifting items to another room

163. When will the new cleaning schedule begin?

(A) October 3
(B) October 4
(C) October 5
(D) October 6

GO ON TO THE NEXT PAGE

A New Dawn for Kitchen Knives?

June 10 – With the rise of celebrity chefs and cooking shows on television, high-quality kitchen knives are in higher demand than ever before. — [1] —. Typically, kitchen knives have always been widely produced all over the world, for both professional and personal use. And, with new knife-manufacturing methods that utilize computers and new technology, manufacturers are now succeeding in making knives that are not only sharper than ever before, but also aesthetically appealing and easy to handle.

— [2] —. There is, however, one aspect of kitchen knives that some manufacturers seem to have forgotten about: their longevity. British chef Leah McKellan believes that some of the advanced knives being produced today are much more likely to break compared with older types. "I remember when knives were much sturdier and could last for a much longer length of time," she says.

Ms. McKellan noted that knives have grown slightly less durable over the years, so chefs and individuals who cook frequently at home often find themselves needing to replace broken blades. This did not use to be such a concern in the past, but as time has gone on, emphasis seems to have shifted more towards style rather than prolonged use.

— [3] —. She aims to develop a range of extremely robust knives without losing any of the performance and appearance we expect from modern-day knives. — [4] —.
"I think it's possible with today's technology to produce high-quality knives that stay sharp for several years without any breakage," she says. Ms. McKellan hopes to release her signature range early next year.

---

164. What characteristic of the knives does the article focus on?

(A) Their sharpness
(B) Their weight
(C) Their length
(D) Their durability

165. How has the manufacture of knives changed?

(A) Knives are now made using computers.
(B) Knives are now produced worldwide.
(C) Knives are now created for commercial use.
(D) Knives are now manufactured using different metals.

166. What is indicated about Ms. McKellan?

(A) She is the author of several books.
(B) She is involved with the food industry.
(C) She has worked in several countries.
(D) She is the owner of a manufacturing plant.

167. In which of the positions marked [1], [2], [3], and [4] does the following sentence best belong?

"It is true that the knives we use today function incredibly well and look stylish."

(A) [1]
(B) [2]
(C) [3]
(D) [4]

Questions 168-171 refer to the following online chat discussion.

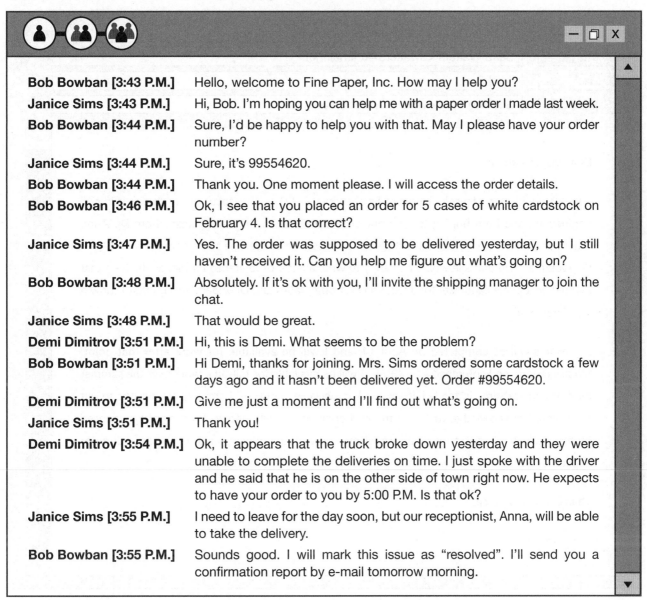

Bob Bowban [3:43 P.M.]	Hello, welcome to Fine Paper, Inc. How may I help you?
Janice Sims [3:43 P.M.]	Hi, Bob. I'm hoping you can help me with a paper order I made last week.
Bob Bowban [3:44 P.M.]	Sure, I'd be happy to help you with that. May I please have your order number?
Janice Sims [3:44 P.M.]	Sure, it's 99554620.
Bob Bowban [3:44 P.M.]	Thank you. One moment please. I will access the order details.
Bob Bowban [3:46 P.M.]	Ok, I see that you placed an order for 5 cases of white cardstock on February 4. Is that correct?
Janice Sims [3:47 P.M.]	Yes. The order was supposed to be delivered yesterday, but I still haven't received it. Can you help me figure out what's going on?
Bob Bowban [3:48 P.M.]	Absolutely. If it's ok with you, I'll invite the shipping manager to join the chat.
Janice Sims [3:48 P.M.]	That would be great.
Demi Dimitrov [3:51 P.M.]	Hi, this is Demi. What seems to be the problem?
Bob Bowban [3:51 P.M.]	Hi Demi, thanks for joining. Mrs. Sims ordered some cardstock a few days ago and it hasn't been delivered yet. Order #99554620.
Demi Dimitrov [3:51 P.M.]	Give me just a moment and I'll find out what's going on.
Janice Sims [3:51 P.M.]	Thank you!
Demi Dimitrov [3:54 P.M.]	Ok, it appears that the truck broke down yesterday and they were unable to complete the deliveries on time. I just spoke with the driver and he said that he is on the other side of town right now. He expects to have your order to you by 5:00 P.M. Is that ok?
Janice Sims [3:55 P.M.]	I need to leave for the day soon, but our receptionist, Anna, will be able to take the delivery.
Bob Bowban [3:55 P.M.]	Sounds good. I will mark this issue as "resolved". I'll send you a confirmation report by e-mail tomorrow morning.

168. Why does Ms. Sims contact Fine Paper Inc.?

(A) To ask for a discount on paper
(B) To learn more about paper products
(C) To find out about a missing order
(D) To purchase paper products

169. At 3:48 P.M., what does Mr. Bowban mean when he says, "Absolutely"?

(A) He will consider Ms. Sims' suggestion.
(B) He can guarantee fast shipping.
(C) He is confirming the location of a package.
(D) He is willing to assist Ms. Sims.

170. When does the delivery driver expect to arrive at Ms. Sims' workplace?

(A) In 5 minutes
(B) In about one hour
(C) In the morning
(D) Tomorrow afternoon

171. What does Ms. Sims say about the suggested delivery arrangement?

(A) Her office will be closed by 5:00 P.M.
(B) A staff member will receive the package.
(C) She wants the driver to arrive sooner.
(D) She will meet the driver in another area.

GO ON TO THE NEXT PAGE

Questions 172-175 refer to the following e-mail.

To:	Joanne Blenkhorn <jblenkhorn@lincolncity.gov>
From:	Sean Walters <swalters@unimail.net>
Date:	April 2
Subject:	Seeking Employment Opportunities

Dear Ms. Blenkhorn,

I am a student at the Lincoln School of Engineering. — [1] —. The focus of my studies is in civil engineering and I am hoping to gain practical experience in the field. I heard from Dr. Anna Alderman that the city council hires students for various roles over the summer months. — [2] —. Dr. Alderman said that she would be happy to write a letter of reference for me, as she feels that I would be a prime candidate for a job. I have strong grades and Dr. Alderman says that I show a lot of potential.

My exams will be completed on April 14, and I will be available for work after that point. Studies resume on September 4. — [3] —. I will be available for full-time work over the summer months and part-time in the fall, if any work is available. — [4] —. I am very enthusiastic to put my theoretical knowledge to use in the civil engineering field and to learn from experienced professionals in a hands-on way. Please let me know of any openings and of the procedure for application.

Thank you in advance,

Sean Walters

172. What is the purpose of the e-mail?

(A) To apply for a scholarship
(B) To inquire about jobs
(C) To request a transfer
(D) To recommend a course

173. Where does Ms. Blenkhorn likely work?

(A) At a university
(B) At an advertising firm
(C) At a government office
(D) At an architectural firm

174. When can Sean Walters begin work?

(A) After he graduates
(B) After he finishes his exams
(C) After his summer vacation
(D) After his classes begin

175. In which of the positions marked [1], [2], [3], and [4] does the following sentence best belong?

"I would be very interested in learning about these opportunities."

(A) [1]
(B) [2]
(C) [3]
(D) [4]

GO ON TO THE NEXT PAGE

Technologically Speaking: Shiftless
by Sarah Henry, Torend Tribune

(March 5) - The latest addition to Shift's new and innovative product line comes out next week, and a lot of people are excited. Others, however, aren't too keen on the release, saying that they weren't impressed by the company's demonstration.

When the company released the first edition of their tablet, Shiftless, it was instantly crowned the most innovative tablet on the market.

Unfortunately, the tablet doesn't seem to be rousing the same amount of admiration this time around. There have been a few improvements, but they aren't as innovative as customers initially hoped.

The latest version has a memory boost and is able to store up to three times as much data as the first edition. The screen is the latest in touch screen technology, which is great, but not innovative. The camera has also been updated with a great increase in quality, but again, where's the innovation?

When the new version of the Shiftless is launched on March 13, will it be a success? Probably, but it seems as though most of that will be due to the brand more than the product itself.

Shift.com

FEEDBACK

Device purchased: ___Shiftless___
User: ___Tina Shield___
Posted: ___March 20___
User Rating: ___3/5___

I got my tablet just a couple of days after the official launch day, but I didn't want to review it until I'd had enough time to use every feature extensively. Overall, the product is good, but it seems like there haven't been many improvements since the last version of the Shiftless came out.

The application store is a good addition, but there are too many pointless apps that clutter up the store and make the useful ones too hard to find. I also noticed that the touch screen is overly sensitive on the factory settings. It can be adjusted in the options menu, but I'm having a hard time finding a level that works well for me. I definitely don't regret my purchase, but I do hope that they will address these issues in the next update.

176. What is the purpose of the article?

(A) To announce a new camera
(B) To share user tips
(C) To review a new electronic device
(D) To report on market trends

177. In the article, what is NOT mentioned about the tablet?

(A) The memory
(B) The camera
(C) The screen
(D) The price

178. When did Ms. Shield probably purchase her tablet?

(A) On March 5
(B) On March 12
(C) On March 15
(D) On March 20

179. What is indicated about the application store?

(A) It is filled with useless apps.
(B) It requires special registration to use.
(C) It will open in the near future.
(D) It suffers from frequent crashes.

180. What can be inferred about Ms. Shield's experience using the device?

(A) She believes many issues are resolved with this release.
(B) She thinks she wasted her money.
(C) The device was difficult to learn how to use.
(D) The touch screen did not meet her expectations.

TEST 12

GO ON TO THE NEXT PAGE

Questions 181-185 refer to the following e-mails.

To:	service@wells.com
From:	bgrimm@alc.com
Date:	August 2
Subject:	Request for customer service

To Whom It May Concern:

My name is Benjamin Grimm, and I currently have a loan request being processed at the Boston branch of Wells Bank. I'm in London at the moment, but I don't have time to visit the branch and speak with a teller. I'll be here until the 10th, but I'm hoping that the issue can be resolved before I return to Boston.

The reason I am contacting you is because there is a recent change in the amount of money being invested in my start-up business. Because of this, I would like to adjust the arrangement that the bank and I currently have. If it's impossible to alter the arrangement through e-mail, please at least halt the process until I return.

Thank you,

Benjamin Grimm

E-Mail Message

To:	bgrimm@alc.com
From:	mfrink@wells.com
Date:	August 2
Subject:	Your e-mail message

Dear Mr. Grimm,

I am Melissa Frink, a representative from Wells Bank. I'm writing to you in response to your earlier e-mail about the loan. Unfortunately, for security reasons, we are unable to alter anything related to your account over e-mail. However, we have halted the loan process as you have requested, and it will be frozen until you reactivate it. You'll be able to reactivate it over the phone, but I recommend that you visit your home branch to speak with a loan officer before making any changes.

Beforehand, you should consider several issues concerning the loan. Be sure that the loan is for the proper amount of money so that you aren't borrowing more than you need and that the interest on the account is at a level that you'll be able to afford in the future. There are several different loan options, too; ensure you are choosing the one that best suits your financial situation.

Once you're back in your hometown, gather your account information and discuss your plans with a loan officer at the branch. Thank you for choosing Wells Bank.

Sincerely,

Melissa Frink

181. What is the purpose of the first e-mail?

(A) To apply for a job at a bank
(B) To cancel an account at the bank
(C) To change an arrangement with a bank
(D) To solicit investment in a business

182. What is most likely true of Mr. Grimm?

(A) He has founded a new company.
(B) He wants to relocate to the London area.
(C) His investors are withdrawing.
(D) He requires a large loan from the bank.

183. What does Mrs. Frink recommend that Mr. Grimm do?

(A) Take out several long-term loans
(B) Choose a different bank for the loan
(C) E-mail the loan officer that he worked with
(D) Speak with a bank employee directly in Boston

184. What is NOT mentioned as a factor that Mr. Grimm should consider when deciding on a type of financing?

(A) The type of loan that he should take out
(B) The amount of money that is required
(C) The length of repayment time he would need
(D) The amount of interest that he can afford

185. In the second e-mail, the word "concerning" in paragraph 2, line 1, is closest in meaning to

(A) worrying
(B) regarding
(C) including
(D) addressing

GO ON TO THE NEXT PAGE

TEST 12

PLATINUM OFFICE SUPPLIES
Your Best Source for All Your Office Needs!

Please join us in celebrating our 30th year in business!

To mark the founding of our company on January 1, we will be offering a variety of special deals to our customers at our main branch on 11th Street in downtown Pittsburgh. Throughout January, customers who make a one-time purchase of $500 or more during specific time periods will receive one of the following special items**:

January 1 – January 8: Veritron 1TB Portable Hard Drive
January 9 – January 16: Digisonic 20″ LED Monitor
January 17 – January 24: Streamjet 200 Mini Printer
January 25 – February 1: Basscom Portable Wireless Speaker

(** Available while stocks last)

We hope to see you at our 11th Street branch in January!

INVOICE

Platinum Office Supplies

11th Street, Pittsburgh, PA 15222

Orders Received On: January 21   **Customer:** Carruth Publishing
To Be Delivered On: January 27   **Order Number:** #67198

Product code	Quantity	Price Per Unit	Total Price
#56700	125	$3.49	$436.25
#46007	150	$8.99	$1,348.50
#24505	15	$15.49	$232.35
#34590	100	$12.99	$1299.00
Balance Due:			**$3,316.10**

Your payment is due in full within 15 days of the outgoing delivery date.

We appreciate your patronage.

E-Mail Message

To:	Jesse Hull <jhull@platinum.com>
From:	Andrea Lacey <alacey@carruthpub.com>
Date:	February 3
Subject:	Order #67198

Dear Mr. Hull,

Our stationery order (#67198) just arrived this morning and I'm currently reviewing the invoice that came with it. Platinum Office Supplies came highly recommended to us, but there must have been an error made when you took our recent order. According to the invoice, we have been billed for 150 black inkjet printer cartridges, but we only put in an order for 15 printer cartridges. We received only the amount we originally requested. Furthermore, we placed an order for 100 colored file folders (#56788). Not only were these missing from the order we received, but they are not even shown on the invoice. When I originally e-mailed you in January, you assured me that you had everything we need in your warehouse ready to be sent out.

These colored file folders are very important as we need them for our new magazine division that is set to open and begin publishing next week. Since I will be going on vacation from tomorrow, I have notified my assistant, Jeff Krause, and instructed him to call you in the morning to ensure that the colored file folders will be sent out. As soon as we receive these missing products and an amended invoice, we will make the payment in full. We are willing to excuse these inconveniences on this occasion, but I hope this does not happen again in future.

Sincerely,

Andrea Lacey

Business Operations Manager

Carruth Publishing

---

186. What is the main purpose of the advertisement?

(A) To announce the opening of a store
(B) To introduce a new range of products
(C) To describe a limited-time offer
(D) To give details of a closing down sale

187. What was most likely included with Carruth Publishing's order?

(A) A hard drive
(B) A monitor
(C) A printer
(D) A speaker

188. For what product was Carruth Publishing billed incorrectly?

(A) #56700
(B) #46007
(C) #24505
(D) #34590

189. What does Ms. Lacey mention about the products she ordered?

(A) She contacted Mr. Hull last month to inquire about availability.
(B) She made an error when estimating the number of units required.
(C) She would prefer to substitute product #56788 with a different item.
(D) She wants Platinum Office Supplies to allow a further discount for its mistake.

190. In the e-mail, the word "excuse" in paragraph 2, line 5, is closest in meaning to

(A) apologize
(B) substitute
(C) remove
(D) overlook

GO ON TO THE NEXT PAGE

Questions 191-195 refer to the following e-mails and invoice.

E-Mail Message

To:	Janette Lim <janettelim@bestmail.com>
From:	Paul Jacoby <sales@eternitygowns.com>
Date:	Saturday, October 4
Subject:	SPECTACULAR DRESSES

Don't miss out! We are currently offering a wide array of beautiful Eternity wedding gowns in our yearly end-of-season sale. These dresses are all unique and handmade, so make sure you take advantage of this opportunity to get your ideal dress at an affordable price. You can view our full range of gowns and accessories on our Web site, but we recommend that you visit our High Street location in person. That's the best way to ensure that you find the dress that is right for you. If you visit our store before October 31, we'll offer you an initial dress fitting free of charge, and if you purchase a wedding gown that costs more than $7,500, we will provide a matching pair of shoes at no extra cost. So, if you're planning your wedding, come and check out what we have available!

Paul Jacoby
Sales Manager
Eternity Wedding Gowns

** This e-mail was sent to you automatically because you have inquired about our products in the past.

INVOICE

CUSTOMER: JANETTE LIM

PAYMENT PROCESSED ON: October 27

Thank you for choosing Eternity Wedding Gowns. The following items have now been reserved and can be picked up at your convenience. Please note that alterations can be made at our competitive, low rates.

Item#	Item Description	Quantity	Price Per Unit	Total
E5894	Eternity Luna Silk Wedding Gown	1	$6,500	$6,500
E4738	Eternity Luna Silk Wedding Veil	1	$600	$600
E0177	Eternity Regal Silk Wedding Gloves	1	$150	$150
JF471	Jean Fournier White Shoes	1	$300	$300
Initial Fitting Cost				$0.00
Total				$7,550

To:	Paul Jacoby <sales@eternitygowns.com>
From:	Janette Lim <janettelim@bestmail.com>
Date:	November 8
Subject:	Bridal Garments

Dear Mr. Jacoby,

You may remember me from my dress fitting at your store last month. Well, I finally had time to pick up all of the garments yesterday, and I couldn't resist trying them on once I got home. My first impression was that the gown is even more beautiful than I remembered! I certainly made the right choice. The gloves are extremely tight, however; I guess the wrong size may have been included in my order. Thankfully, there are no such problems with the shoes or veil. Can you tell me a suitable time for me to bring in the ill-fitting item and have it exchanged? I think it might be better if I deal directly with you, just to avoid any similar mistakes.

Best wishes,

Janette Lim

191. According to the first e-mail, why should customers visit the store instead of shopping online?

(A) To obtain a complimentary item
(B) To browse a larger range of merchandise
(C) To avoid paying an extra charge
(D) To find the most suitable products

192. What is suggested about Ms. Lim?

(A) She is a designer of custom wedding dresses.
(B) She works as a wedding planner.
(C) She has contacted Eternity in the past.
(D) She recently purchased several gowns.

193. What is indicated about the items ordered?

(A) They will be worn at an event in October.
(B) They must be returned to Eternity after use.
(C) They can be modified relatively cheaply.
(D) They will be delivered to Ms. Lim's home.

194. How could Ms. Lim have benefited from an additional special offer?

(A) By purchasing a more expensive gown
(B) By writing a review on the Web site
(C) By ordering through the Web site
(D) By ordering a greater number of items

195. Which item would Ms. Lim like to exchange?

(A) E5894
(B) E4738
(C) E0177
(D) JF471

GO ON TO THE NEXT PAGE

Questions 196-200 refer to the following e-mails and flyer.

E-Mail Message

To:	Leanne Trumbo <ltrumbo@swiftmail.net>
From:	Max Hedberg <mhedberg@wessexgallery.com>
Subject:	Upcoming Workshop
Date:	August 22
Attachment:	🔗 flyer.doc

Dear Ms. Trumbo,

Thank you for your interest in the upcoming Arts & Crafts Workshop at Wessex Art Gallery. It would be my pleasure to tell you some more details about the event. First, you are completely correct regarding registration. There is no specific deadline, although I would encourage you to sign up in advance as we expect classes to fill up by the end of this week.

Regarding the class teachers, I can assure you that they are all highly skilled artists and craftspeople. Enid Bliss and Ingrid Karlsson have displayed their paintings all over the world, while our life drawing expert was recently profiled in the July issue of *Art World Monthly*.

I have taken the liberty of attaching a copy of our event flyer for your reference. This includes all the information you'll need to know regarding location, class times, registration, and payment methods. Please note that Graeme Moon has been called overseas due to a family matter, so we are currently seeking a suitable replacement to instruct the 8:30 A.M. class.

I hope I have answered all of your questions sufficiently, and I look forward to seeing you on August 28.

Sincerely,

Max Hedberg

Annual Arts & Crafts Workshop
Wessex Art Gallery, 376 Bloor Street South, Edenville
8:30 A.M. to 6:30 P.M., Sunday, August 28

Class Time	Class Topic	Teacher
8:30-10:00 A.M.	Introduction to Pottery	Mr. Graeme Moon
10:15-11:45 A.M.	Watercolor Techniques	Ms. Enid Bliss
1:00-2:30 P.M.	Stone Carving & Sculpture	Mr. Harold Tibbs
2:45-4:30 P.M.	Oil Painting Basics	Ms. Ingrid Karlsson
4:45-6:30 P.M.	Life Drawing	Mr. Hugh Hewitt

Registration fees:
Single Session: Attend a single class for $35
Morning Session: Attend the two morning classes for $50
Afternoon Session: Attend the three afternoon classes for $75
Full-day Session: Attend all of the classes for the low price of $100

Registration may be performed either in person, over the phone (555-0129), or by visiting our Web site at www.wessexartgallery.ca.

To:	Max Hedberg <mhedberg@wessexgallery.com>
From:	Leanne Trumbo <ltrumbo@swiftmail.net>
Date:	August 30
Subject:	Gallery Workshop

Dear Mr. Hedberg,

I just wanted to contact you to thank you for organizing such an enjoyable and educational event. All three of the classes I attended at the recent workshop were well run and the teachers were clearly experts in their respective fields. It was certainly money well spent, in my opinion. Next year, I'll pay the full $100 so that I don't miss out on any of the sessions. Please add me to your mailing list so that I can be kept informed about all future workshops and exhibitions.

Best regards,

Leanne Trumbo

196. Why did Mr. Hedberg write to Ms. Trumbo?

(A) To inform her about payment options
(B) To remind her about a registration deadline
(C) To suggest that she change classes
(D) To respond to her previous inquiry

197. According to Mr. Hedberg, which teacher was featured in a magazine?

(A) Ms. Bliss
(B) Mr. Hewitt
(C) Ms. Karlsson
(D) Mr. Tibbs

198. What is indicated about Graeme Moon?

(A) He will teach more than one class at the workshop.
(B) He has offered to substitute for another teacher.
(C) He will be unable to participate in the event.
(D) His class will begin later than scheduled.

199. What is NOT indicated about the Wessex Arts & Crafts Workshop?

(A) Discounts are offered to groups.
(B) Online registration is available.
(C) It takes place every year.
(D) There will be a break for lunch.

200. What type of registration did Ms. Trumbo most likely pay for?

(A) Single Session
(B) Morning Session
(C) Afternoon Session
(D) Full-day Session

Stop! This is the end of the test. If you finish before time is called, you may go back to Parts 5, 6, and 7 and check your work.

정답 p.473 / 점수 환산표 p.476

실전모의고사
TEST 13

TEST 13 해설

바로 보기

시작 시간 _____시 _____분

종료 시간 _____시 _____분

READING TEST

In the Reading test, you will read a variety of texts and answer several different types of reading comprehension questions. The entire Reading test will last 75 minutes. There are three parts, and directions are given for each part. You are encouraged to answer as many questions as possible within the time allowed. You must mark your answers on the separate answer sheet. Do not write your answers in your test book.

PART 5

Directions: A word or phrase is missing in each of the sentences below. Four answer choices are given below each sentence. Select the best answer to complete the sentence. Then mark the letter (A), (B), (C), or (D) on your answer sheet.

101. I would like to ------- you that your city design plan has been selected as a finalist in our national design competition.

(A) say
(B) recommend
(C) inform
(D) announce

102. It is widely known that the lawyer was a ------- professional who had won nearly all of her recent court cases.

(A) talent
(B) talented
(C) talentless
(D) talents

103. *The Sun Times* has identified its strongest readership market as those aged ------- 15 and 30 years old.

(A) along
(B) between
(C) through
(D) among

104. The merger of the two major semiconductor manufacturers was expected to be worth about 50 million dollars with all figures ------- into account.

(A) takes
(B) taken
(C) taking
(D) take

105. Please ------- from smoking during the flight, and ensure you stay seated while the seatbelt sign is on.

(A) avoid
(B) stop
(C) prohibit
(D) refrain

106. Our newly-hired designer's job involves ------- Web sites for businesses in the San Francisco area.

(A) creating
(B) create
(C) creator
(D) creation

107. One of the ovens we recently ordered had to be returned to the store as the timer was ------- when the appliances arrived at the facility.

(A) delayed
(B) faulty
(C) unnecessary
(D) packaged

108. It was regrettable that rain and hail ------- the start of the annual football match between the two rival high schools.

(A) to delaying
(B) delaying
(C) delays
(D) delayed

109. ------- you have picked up your tickets, please proceed to your designated gate and prepare for departure.

(A) Before
(B) Once
(C) Should
(D) Owing to

110. Please make sure to call the computer help desk if you need ------- with updating your virus software.

(A) assistance
(B) assistant
(C) assist
(D) assisted

111. All guests of the Grey Lily Hotel receive ------- access to the Grey Lily Spa across the street from the hotel.

(A) reasonable
(B) complimentary
(C) approximate
(D) exemplary

112. The head of the maintenance team advised the technicians only to use ------- tools to ensure safety and effectiveness.

(A) certificate
(B) certified
(C) certifying
(D) certification

113. The company has expanded its catalog to include several innovative new products, many of ------- will be in demand on the international market.

(A) theirs
(B) them
(C) where
(D) which

114. The sales manager is pleased that the recent surge in sales after the release of the new marketing campaign has been ------- incredible.

(A) by far
(B) absolutely
(C) much
(D) a lot

115. Effective immediately, all hotel guests are ------- to return their room keys to the front desk upon check-out.

(A) asked
(B) talked
(C) followed
(D) revised

116. ------- strong sales in the European market, our office supplies line is overall going down and will be discontinued as of next April.

(A) Although
(B) Despite
(C) Furthermore
(D) Yet

117. It is a potentially beneficial idea which ------- to be fully explored and developed in the future.

(A) deserve
(B) deserving
(C) deserves
(D) is deserved

118. We have to find ways to create a strong brand by continuing to innovate while ------- a loyal customer base.

(A) motivating
(B) selling
(C) retaining
(D) working

119. Even though operating expenses have been falling recently, management is concerned that labor costs have been rising -------.

(A) steady
(B) steadier
(C) steadiest
(D) steadily

GO ON TO THE NEXT PAGE

120. Our luxury airline's executive class section lets you fly in comfort, allowing you ------- for the duration of your flight.

(A) relaxation
(B) relaxing
(C) to relax
(D) relax

121. Please be aware that, due to unforeseen circumstances, there will be a slight ------- to the conference program.

(A) modification
(B) explanation
(C) organization
(D) illustration

122. AJ Electronics Inc. has decided to change its company logo in the hope that it can broaden the range of customers it -------.

(A) is attracted
(B) attracts
(C) attracting
(D) attract

123. The more responsibility an employee is given, the more ------- they will complete their work tasks.

(A) effects
(B) effect
(C) effectively
(D) effective

124. Sharko's board members seem unsure ------- to continue with their current strategy or to take the company in a new direction.

(A) whether
(B) so as
(C) either
(D) although

125. According to the employment contract, Ms. Ma's job description includes ------- of the communications and marketing team.

(A) supervise
(B) supervising
(C) supervisor
(D) supervision

126. All staff are reminded to attend Mr. Almar's retirement celebration tonight and to thank him for his life-long dedication ------- the company.

(A) to
(B) at
(C) of
(D) in

127. Cheeka Athletics has launched a new advertising campaign that ------- combines animated images and colorful photography.

(A) skilled
(B) skillful
(C) skillfully
(D) skills

128. When ------- the printer toner cartridge, insert the new cartridge with the colored arrows facing up, as shown in the diagram.

(A) replaced
(B) replace
(C) to replace
(D) replacing

129. As soon as the fire alarm sounds, please evacuate the building ------- and stay at the designated meeting point until further notice.

(A) currently
(B) previously
(C) forcefully
(D) promptly

130. The training sessions will be held over three ------- days from next Tuesday at the company headquarters in Tokyo.

(A) consecutive
(B) following
(C) weekly
(D) simultaneous

PART 6

Directions: Read the texts that follow. A word, phrase, or sentence is missing in parts of each text. Four answer choices for each question are given below the text. Select the best answer to complete the text. Then mark the letter (A), (B), (C) or (D) on your answer sheet.

Questions 131–134 refer to the following e-mail.

From: Peter Tobin <ptobin@bluemountainair.com>

To: Graham Vaughn <gvaughn@wizmail.com>

Subject: Your complaint

Dear Ms. Vaughn

I am writing in reply to the feedback form you filled out on your flight from Rome to New York last week. I want to assure you that I ------- the matter fully and I have given your complaint serious consideration.
                                           131.

After receiving the flight report, I forwarded the information ------- the regional director, who requested
                                                                  132.
a full internal investigation into the flight. The investigation found that the flight path could have been altered to lessen the impact of the turbulence.

We would like to offer you either a 50 percent refund of your flight ticket price or a 25 percent ticket price refund and a voucher for an upgrade to business class on your next flight with us. ------- . -------
                                                                                              133.   **134.**
Transatlantic Airways, I wish to apologize for the problems you experienced onboard our aircraft.

Yours sincerely,

Peter Tobin
Customer Service Manager
Blue Mountain Air

---

131. (A) investigate
   (B) have investigated
   (C) will investigate
   (D) have been investigated

132. (A) with
   (B) over
   (C) among
   (D) to

133. (A) You will be assured that our flights offer premium comfort and convenience.
   (B) I would like to know which option you would prefer.
   (C) I promise that the change in the route will be effective immediately.
   (D) Please be sure to bring your passport when you check in.

134. (A) On behalf of
   (B) In case of
   (C) As a result
   (D) As if

GO ON TO THE NEXT PAGE →

Questions 135-138 refer to the following announcement.

Job Fair for Bright Start Industries

Bright Start Industries is one of the nation's leading producers of lamps and other lighting fixtures. We will ------- a job fair on September 30 in the Community Arena. Individuals interested in working
135.
in our main store in Carson City or in one of our other 12 locations across the country are encouraged to attend. We currently have openings for all positions, but are particularly interested in candidates who have interior design knowledge. -------. They would help our customers decide ------- to best
136.   137.
incorporate our products into the design of a home or office space.

To be considered for any position, individuals must have a grade 12 education and previous experience in retail and hospitality. Please bring a current résumé and contact information for three references. Bright Start Industries offers a ------- salary, medical benefits, and opportunities for
138.
training and advancement.

We are excited to speak with all attendees on September 30.

135. (A) held
(B) have held
(C) be held
(D) be holding

136. (A) They have performed well in this capacity without training.
(B) Please send your résumé to the hiring manager at your convenience.
(C) Unfortunately, we could not fill all of these positions.
(D) These individuals could potentially be hired as consultants.

137. (A) what
(B) how
(C) which
(D) that

138. (A) reflective
(B) competitive
(C) collaborative
(D) portable

Questions 139-142 refer to the following e-mail.

To: Shinsuke Ito <s.Ito@bestapparel.com>

From: Grant Wood <gwood@mbtextiles.com>

Subject: Samples

Dear Mr. Ito,

We welcome the inquiry you made on June 20 and thank you for your interest in our products. Our catalog and some working samples are being sent to you today ------- express mail. Unfortunately,
    139.
we cannot send you a full range of samples at the present time, but the working samples are of the same high quality as the finished products.

-------. Mr. Kim, our overseas director, will be in Japan early next month and will be pleased to call
140.
on you. He will have with him a wide range of our products, and when you see them, we believe you will agree that the quality of the material and the high standard of craftsmanship will appeal to even the most ------- buyer.
            141.

We very much look forward to ------- an order from you.
                142.

Regards,

Grant Wood

---

139. (A) with
(B) by
(C) for
(D) in

140. (A) We would like for you to come to our head office.
(B) Our products will be sent out to you tomorrow.
(C) Thank you for sending your feedback on our products.
(D) I have an idea for how you can see our merchandise.

141. (A) preferable
(B) curious
(C) selective
(D) prominent

142. (A) receive
(B) received
(C) be received
(D) receiving

GO ON TO THE NEXT PAGE

Questions 143-146 refer to the following letter.

November 24

Dear Mr. Sanchez,

Thank you for your letter regarding your recent visit to our newly-opened Mexican restaurant.

First, let me offer my sincere apologies that the appetizer was not to your liking. Most people who visit our establishment enjoy spicy food, but we understand that ------- do not. For that reason, we
                                                                                              143.
offer all menu selections in mild, medium, and hot versions. This is something your server should have told you when you placed your order.

I also understand that you are disappointed we do not offer free refills on soft drinks. This was a hard decision. However, we felt it was the right one, as it will allow us to keep prices reasonable and minimize waste. -------, we offer filtered ice water at no cost.
                      144.

We would like another chance to make you one of our many satisfied customers. So, I ------- a gift
                                                                                        145.
certificate for two free meals with drinks and dessert at any of our locations. -------.
                                                                                  146.

Sincerely,

Penelope Lopez
Customer Relations Specialist

143. (A) any
     (B) some
     (C) all
     (D) one

144. (A) Likewise
     (B) Otherwise
     (C) For example
     (D) Instead

145. (A) had been enclosing
     (B) have enclosed
     (C) enclosing
     (D) was enclosed

146. (A) I hope you and a guest will join us for dinner in the near future.
     (B) I look forward to hearing about your recommendations for other restaurants.
     (C) Thank you for staying with us during these difficult times.
     (D) We would be pleased to do business with your company again.

Directions: In this part you will read a selection of texts, such as magazine and newspaper articles, e-mails, and instant messages. Each text or set of texts is followed by several questions. Select the best answer for each question and mark the letter (A), (B), (C), or (D) on your answer sheet.

Questions 147-148 refer to the following advertisement.

Do you have a great business idea but don't quite have the money to get it started?

We want to hear from you!

Our business, Capital Factory, is a business incubator that provides support to start-up businesses for ten weeks. Over the course of those 10 weeks, we will provide free office space while our team of 20 business veterans gives free legal advice and guides you towards success. In addition to this, each of our 20 entrepreneurs invests $5,000 into each company that we select.

Visit us online to apply today. Every year, we choose 5 promising start-ups to invest in and help promote. Last year alone, we had over 300 applicants, so submit your application for consideration soon.

147. Who is this service intended for?

(A) Business graduates seeking internships
(B) People planning to start a business
(C) People who have recently retired
(D) Established businesses with financial problems

148. What is NOT mentioned as a benefit available to applicants?

(A) Financial support
(B) A free workspace
(C) Management training
(D) Legal advice

GO ON TO THE NEXT PAGE

Questions 149-150 refer to the following text-message chain.

Sheila [7:08 P.M.]
Did you hear about Richard's new work-from-home policy?

Tony [7:08 P.M.]
Yes, I did. I have never heard of a policy where employees are required to share a picture of their home office space. It seems odd.

Sheila [7:10 P.M.]
Actually, this type of policy is becoming more common in the corporate world. It's a way of building trust and making sure that employees have a positive environment to work in. It's perfectly legitimate.

Tony [7:11 P.M.]
I see. Well, having the flexibility to work from home is certainly a privilege. So, I won't complain. When are the photos due?

Sheila [7:12 P.M.]
They must be e-mailed to Richard by next Friday so he can forward them to the CEO.

149. What is implied about the new type of policy?

(A) It has been beneficial for other businesses.
(B) Sheila is unfamiliar with it.
(C) It will lead to an increase in profits.
(D) It is required by law.

150. At 7:11 P.M., what does Tony mean when he says, "So, I won't complain"?

(A) He will share a photo of his home office.
(B) He does not like to voice his opinion.
(C) He would prefer to work in the office.
(D) He thinks managers should be more flexible.

One of the small but annoying problems that crops up in many small offices is the mess that accumulates in the lunch room, and especially in the shared refrigerator. Use these tips to clean up your shared food spaces.

- Tell your staff that everything should be labeled with the person's name and date. Keep pens and labels nearby. Remove unlabeled items daily and workers will soon remember to do it.

- At the end of the work week, simply clear out the fridge. Long-term items that don't spoil (like preserves or ketchup) may be color-coded with labels, and everything else disposed of. Do it at the same time each week, so workers know it will happen.

- In a very small office, consider providing inexpensive but non-perishable snack items to reduce refrigerator usage from the start.

151. Who is the article most likely intended for?

(A) Corporate CEOs
(B) Office managers
(C) Part-time employees
(D) Restaurant owners

152. What is NOT suggested as a way of encouraging employee participation?

(A) Being consistent with the disposal times
(B) Designating a person for each daily task
(C) Providing cheap snacks to employees
(D) Throwing out unlabeled food

Big City Mall is pleased to announce that its new wing will be open for business as of March 8. Over a dozen new stores, including Giant Electronics, Brand Name Clothing, and Various Miscellany, are holding grand openings. Bring your appetites, too! The new wing includes a second food court with seven new restaurants catering to all tastes. And finally, now you have a reason to leave your car at home! The wing connects the mall directly to the subway station, making it even easier for shoppers to visit us. Celebrate the opening by checking out the mall-wide sale, with all stores offering a 10% savings on all merchandise on top of the annual March Madness promotional offers. Come see all that we have to offer, new and old, at Big City Mall on March 8!

153. What is primarily being advertised?

(A) An addition to a shopping center

(B) A new restaurant franchise

(C) An expanded subway line

(D) A year-end seasonal sale

154. How will the business mark the event?

(A) With free giveaways

(B) With extended hours

(C) With free parking

(D) With a discount on goods

Questions 155-157 refer to the following memo.

From: Adele Renard, Office Manager

To: All employees

Date: December 28

Re: New Year's Day Celebrations

The city police have informed us that due to the New Year's Day celebrations in Washington Square, they are closing several blocks of Broad Street (including the block where our office is) during the morning parade and the evening fireworks display. This means employees will not be able to access the company parking lot from 7:00 A.M. until noon, and again from 4:00 P.M. until 9:00 P.M. on January 1.

This does not affect many employees since it is a statutory holiday, but as you know we do have some service departments that run around the clock. It is suggested that these employees park in the Central Parking public lot, which is located four blocks south of the office on Broad Street. If you submit your parking tickets, you will be reimbursed for the extra cost. Anyone needing to unload a vehicle or anyone with mobility problems should make prior arrangements so that problems can be avoided.

Thank you, and Happy New Year to you all.

155. Why will the company parking lot be unavailable to staff at certain times?

(A) There will be a delivery truck arriving.
(B) It will be used only by customers.
(C) It will be closed for repairs.
(D) Some roads will be closed.

156. When will the parking lot be open on January 1?

(A) 9:00 A.M.
(B) 1:00 P.M.
(C) 5:00 P.M.
(D) 8:00 P.M.

157. What are employees NOT encouraged to do?

(A) Work from their own home
(B) Park in a local parking lot
(C) Keep their parking receipts
(D) Plan in advance for special circumstances

GO ON TO THE NEXT PAGE

Questions 158-161 refer to the following online chat discussion.

Anna Paxton [2:33 P.M.]	Hi everyone. I wanted to talk about the company picnic tomorrow and make sure everything is in order.
Sam Kim [2:34 P.M.]	Hi Anna, I can fill you in on details about catering. Allison can tell you about the venue and Nancy knows about attendance.
Anna Paxton [2:34 P.M.]	And what about the gifts?
Allison McGuire [2:34 P.M.]	I can tell you about that as well.
Anna Paxton [2:35 P.M.]	Great. Sam, why don't you start? Is everything set with the catering company?
Sam Kim [2:36 P.M.]	Yes, I spoke with them earlier today. They will arrive at the picnic site at 11:30 A.M. and everything will be set up and ready to serve at 12:00 P.M. We have ordered a total of 275 servings, including chicken, beef, and vegetarian options. This means we will have an extra 10 servings in case more people show up.
Anna Paxton [2:38 P.M.]	Good, and are they supplying all of the table settings?
Sam Kim [2:40 P.M.]	They are only supplying plates and cutlery. I ordered napkins separately and will bring them with me tomorrow.
Anna Paxton [2:40 P.M.]	Fantastic. Nancy, you're up. How many people are we expecting?
Nancy Clemens [2:42 P.M.]	About 265. They have all received their entry tickets.
Anna Paxton [2:43 P.M.]	Perfect. Allison, is everything OK with the venue and gifts?
Allison McGuire [2:44 P.M.]	The venue had assigned us a much smaller picnic location. I told them it was unsuitable, so they moved us to the adjacent site, which will be big enough. The gifts arrived yesterday and are in the back of my car. We are all set at my end.
Anna Paxton [2:45 P.M.]	Great, thank you all for all your hard work. I'm sure everyone will enjoy the picnic tomorrow.

158. What part of the company picnic is Nancy responsible for?

(A) Activities
(B) Attendance
(C) Catering
(D) Gifts

159. What is indicated about the menu?

(A) Visitors should bring their own meat to cook at the picnic.
(B) It has not been finalized yet.
(C) Attendees will have two options for dessert.
(D) Some dishes without meat will be served.

160. What does Sam mention regarding the food?

(A) He contacted an experienced catering company.
(B) He has ordered more than they need.
(C) He does not have enough table settings for the staff.
(D) He plans to submit the food orders soon.

161. At 2:44 P.M., what does Allison imply when she says, "We are all set at my end"?

(A) She doesn't have time to help out with other tasks.
(B) The gifts will be ordered soon.
(C) The tables in her section have been set.
(D) She has her assignments under control.

Theater Group Raises Money to Save Building

By Phil Sakiyama

The Players Theater Group raised over $30,000 at its latest theatrical fundraiser to save the historic Dominion Bank building. They are hoping to purchase the building and convert it into a theater.

In early April, the building's current owner, Simon Bradley, announced his intention to sell the building to an apartment developer. When the theater group members heard the news, they set out to raise enough money to buy it. Bradley, a prestigious mutual fund investor, has given the group until August 1 to come up with $80,000 in cash to put toward the sale of the building. If the group cannot raise the capital, the building will be sold, as planned, to the developer in September.

To show his support, Bradley, a long-time fan of the theater group and its stage productions, personally attended the fundraiser and made a generous donation. The group currently has $65,000 in cash and intends to hold more fund-raising performances throughout June and July to raise the rest of the money.

162. Why is the Players Theater Group raising money?

(A) To expand the theater company
(B) To produce a national show
(C) To save a historic building
(D) To support local arts community

163. Who is Simon Bradley?

(A) A best-selling writer
(B) A property developer
(C) A financial professional
(D) An architect

164. What can be inferred about Mr. Bradley?

(A) He owns several historic buildings.
(B) He enjoys watching plays.
(C) He invests in housing developments.
(D) He lives near the theater.

GO ON TO THE NEXT PAGE

Questions 165-168 refer to the following contract.

This document outlines an agreement between Brandon Skelly and Eric Wright, independent contractor, made on June 11.

Eric Wright will complete the task of renovating the home of Brandon Skelly. Details of this project will be outlined below. The task is to be completed by August 30 at a cost that shall not exceed $10,000.00.

Project details:

The kitchen will have new flooring and a new countertop installed. — [1] —. The door will also be replaced. The living room will be painted and new carpets will be installed.

An addition to the house will be constructed adjoining the living room. It will include four windows and two doors. One door provides entry to the living room. — [2] —. The plans for the addition are attached to the contract.

Both bathrooms will be painted and new tile flooring installed. — [3] —.

Conditions:

- All materials will be purchased at Hal's Hardware, where an account has been set up. Eric Wright will be able to obtain all necessary materials, and the cost of said materials will be added to the bill after being approved by Brandon Skelly. — [4] —

- Eric Wright will provide Brandon Skelly with weekly invoices showing hours worked. The rate of pay is set at $40.00 per hour and will be paid weekly.

- Any disputes that cannot be resolved between Eric Wright and Brandon Skelly shall be decided by an independent mediator.

- As Eric Wright is an independent contractor, he is not entitled to benefits and no deductions shall be made from his pay.

---

165. What is indicated about Eric Wright in the contract?

(A) He will submit a daily progress report.
(B) He will begin work on August 30.
(C) He will subcontract some work to another company.
(D) He will charge $10,000.00 or less.

166. What is mentioned about building materials?

(A) They will come from a single supplier.
(B) They will be created from recycled materials.
(C) They will be delivered to the work site by Mr. Skelly.
(D) They should be approved by Eric Wright to be paid later.

167. What is indicated about Mr. Skelly's house?

(A) It has two bathrooms.
(B) A basement will be added.
(C) New flooring will be installed in its living room.
(D) It currently has no kitchen appliances.

168. In which of the positions marked [1], [2], [3], and [4] does the following sentence best belong?
"The other one exits to the backyard."

(A) [1]
(B) [2]
(C) [3]
(D) [4]

Questions 169-171 refer to the following notice.

Dear valued customer,

Tyson Bank appreciates and values your loyalty. For over thirty years, we have served the greater Cincinnati area. We started out as a small bank, and now we have over two hundred branches across the Midwest.

We would like to remind you that our branch at 442 East Main Street will be closed on Monday, June 9. It will reopen on Monday, June 16. We apologize for any inconvenience. However, we are renovating our lobby and expanding our parking facility to better serve you in the future.

Although customers can visit our Harbor View location, which is only a few blocks away, we strongly recommend that you make transactions, transfer money, and check your balance from our Web site.

Thank you for thirty years of business. We hope to continue to serve you for many more.

Regards,

Michelle Constanza
CEO

169. Who is Michelle Constanza?

(A) A Tyson Bank executive
(B) A Tyson Bank customer
(C) The CEO of a renovation company
(D) The mayor of Cincinnati

170. What is NOT mentioned about the bank?

(A) It is located in Cincinnati.
(B) It is the largest bank in the Midwest.
(C) It will be temporarily closed.
(D) It is increasing the size of its parking lot.

171. What does Ms. Constanza advise customers to do during the renovations?

(A) Contact the bank manager directly
(B) Access the building through the rear entrance
(C) Use the bank's Web site
(D) Visit the Harbor View branch

GO ON TO THE NEXT PAGE

To: All staff
From: Personnel Office
Re: Fire safety
Date: Monday, July 3

Due to a number of recent fires in our region, the city council requires all businesses to have stricter fire safety plans in place by July. — [1] —. So, we must start preparing for these changes now. We have decided to implement a series of fire safety measures to ensure the safety of all staff working in our company.

We will have a number of fire safety events over the next two months. The first event will be this Wednesday when the fire department comes to inspect our building. There will be a mandatory fire safety seminar next week. Employees should also be prepared for three fire drills which will be carried out at random. — [2] —.

As part of this process, I would like to ask all staff to report any potential fire hazards they come across in the building to Lucy Jenkins using the form that has been e-mailed to you. You should print the form and fill it in before giving it to Ms. Jenkins.

— [3] —. As many of the recent fires occurred outside normal working hours, we will restrict after-hours access to the building. If you need to stay late, please e-mail your supervisor, who will submit a list of those people who will remain in the building after 5:30 P.M. to Mr. Jones. Friends and family members should not visit the premises after-hours without permission from Mr. Jones.

Before Wednesday's building inspection, please clean the area around your desk and remove any items which may be blocking the stairwell. We will carry out a building check tomorrow at 5 P.M. to ensure that everything is neat and organized.

The fire safety seminar will take place on Thursday, so you are asked to fill in the form at reception to confirm your attendance. You may choose to take the seminar at 10 A.M., 2 P.M. or 4 P.M. — [4] —.

172. Why are the fire safety measures being introduced?

(A) Many staff don't know what to do in case of a fire.
(B) There are many risk factors in the office.
(C) The company failed a recent safety inspection.
(D) There have been several fires in the area.

173. How should hazards be reported?

(A) By contacting the fire department
(B) By submitting a form
(C) By calling a supervisor
(D) By sending an e-mail

174. When will the fire department inspect the building?

(A) On Monday
(B) On Tuesday
(C) On Wednesday
(D) Next week

175. In which of the positions marked [1], [2], [3], and [4] does the following sentence best belong?

"However, attendance at one of these is compulsory for all staff."

(A) [1]
(B) [2]
(C) [3]
(D) [4]

GO ON TO THE NEXT PAGE

R&L Office Supply
334 Main Street, Portland, Oregon

Billing Address: Luland Box Company, P. O. Box 147, Eugene, Oregon
Shipping Address: 1297 West Technology Ave., Eugene, Oregon

Purchase order number: 10062033
Purchase order date: November 30
Payment due: January 31
Terms: Net 60 days
Shipped: December 6

Shipped	Quantity	Price	Net Amount
19-inch monitor	6	$250.00	$1,500.00
SensoMax keyboard	6	$25.00	$150.00
Extra laptop cable	12	$12.50	$150.00
External hard drive	1	$50.00	$50.00
		Subtotal	$1,850.00
		Shipping	$25.00
		Total	$1,875.00

* Shipping will be paid by the store if the order is over $1,500.

* Please report errors or damage to Jonathan Black at jonathanblack@rlsupply.com within five business days.

E-Mail Message

To:	Jonathan Black <jonathanblack@rlsupply.com>
From:	Heather Vangelis <heatherv@lulandco.com>
Re:	Order Number 10062033
Date:	December 10

Dear Mr. Black,

Thank you for our order for computer peripherals, which arrived promptly the day after you shipped it. Everything we ordered has arrived. It has taken us a few days to distribute the items and start using them. We have found in the last two days that three of the extra laptop cables and one of the keyboards do not work. We have tried them with different computers, and in different offices, and they just do not work at all. They act as if they are not plugged in.

As a result, we are returning the defective items with a request for replacement. Their original packaging was not damaged, so we assume that the parts were defective after being manufactured, and not damaged in transit. We will be withholding full payment until working replacements have been received. We do understand that you do not manufacture these items yourselves, and so you are not responsible for the defects. However, you might consider testing them more carefully in the future, before sending them out to your customers.

Lastly, it seems that I have been overcharged by $25. I was eligible for a shipping waiver by ordering more than $1,500. I would like you to take care of this too.

Thank you,

Heather Vangelis

176. In the invoice, what is suggested about the order?

(A) It took over a week to be delivered.
(B) The items can be returned within 5 days.
(C) The customer has been overcharged.
(D) The order consists of kitchen appliances.

177. How long does a customer have to report a problem with an order?

(A) 5 days
(B) 6 days
(C) 31 days
(D) 60 days

178. In the e-mail, the word "found" in paragraph 1, line 3, is closest in meaning to

(A) determined
(B) located
(C) recovered
(D) acquired

179. When did the order arrive at Luland Box Company?

(A) November 30
(B) December 6
(C) December 7
(D) January 31

180. What does Ms. Vangelis say about R&L Office Supply?

(A) It should send out a repair technician.
(B) It needs to send out orders more promptly.
(C) Its manufacturing standards are too low.
(D) It should check if items work before shipping them.

GO ON TO THE NEXT PAGE

Questions 181-185 refer to the following e-mails.

To:	Frank Cruise <fcruise@primeedu.com>
From:	Sally Bullard <sbullard@primeedu.com>
Subject:	Meeting of the board of executives
Date:	March 20

Dear Frank,

As the newest member of the board of executives, your attendance is requested at our next meeting. It will be held on Wednesday, March 27, at 1:00 in the board room on the seventh floor.

I know that your particular area of expertise is trends in sales, so I would like to request that you come prepared with a presentation covering the past twelve months and expectations for the next twelve months. We are hoping to improve our market share in the coming year, and I would like for us to brainstorm ideas for doing just that at this meeting.

Other items on the agenda include staff morale, career development, and training. If you have any thoughts on these topics, we welcome any and all suggestions. A few specific questions for you to consider are as follows:

1. How would you assess morale currently, and what can be done to make improvements?
2. What can we do to be more competitive?
3. We would like to train our current staff to move up in our organization rather than hiring from outside. How can we provide such training without hindering productivity?

Please respond to confirm your attendance.

E-Mail Message

To:	Sally Bullard <sbullard@primeedu.com>
From:	Frank Cruise <fcruise@primeedu.com>
Subject:	Re: Meeting of the board of executives
Date:	March 20

Dear Sally,

I am writing to confirm my attendance at the March 27 meeting of the executive board. I have done a great deal of research and will share my findings with you all on the topic of improving our market share. I have some figures to share that illustrate some problem areas we are experiencing, and I feel confident that we can address these problems together. I will also take the other questions into consideration, and I am especially looking forward to sharing my ideas with you regarding the third question you mentioned in your e-mail. I think that this is going to be a very productive meeting.

I also wanted to thank you for your confidence in me and for nominating me to the board of executives. This is a tremendous opportunity for me and I will not let you down!

181. What is the purpose of the first e-mail sent to Mr. Cruise?

(A) To request a work report
(B) To inform him of a job opportunity
(C) To nominate him to the board
(D) To invite him to a meeting

182. In the first e-mail, the word "items" in paragraph 3, line 1, is closest in meaning to

(A) issues
(B) products
(C) traits
(D) notices

183. What topic is Mr. Cruise most looking forward to discussing at the meeting?

(A) Ways to improve morale
(B) Ways to train existing staff
(C) Ways to be more competitive
(D) Ways to boost factory production

184. What can be inferred about Mr. Cruise?

(A) He has shown interest in an upcoming promotion opportunity.
(B) He will meet with Ms. Bullard prior to the meeting on March 27.
(C) He recently joined the company from one of its competitors.
(D) This will be his first meeting with the board of executives.

185. Why does Mr. Cruise thank Ms. Bullard?

(A) For helping him research sales trends
(B) For providing advice on presentation techniques
(C) For recommending him to the board
(D) For putting him in charge of a project

GO ON TO THE NEXT PAGE

White Orchid Hotel Renovations Completed

April 7 (Montreal) – After two months of extensive remodeling work, White Orchid Hotel was pleased to mark the re-opening of its largest function room by holding a banquet in the elegantly decorated event space. Among the new features of the room are a very large performance stage and newly-installed floor-to-ceiling windows that run along the west and south sides of the room. Guests at the reopening event remarked on the beautiful decorations in the room as well as the stunning view across downtown Montreal.

White Orchid Hotel & Function Rooms

458 Montblanc Avenue, Montreal, Quebec H2Z 1R1

The Matthews Room ·· $435 per evening

This 65-square-meter room can accommodate up to 60 people seated. It is suitable only for meetings and seminars. Elegantly decorated in a contemporary fashion, and features a small stage. Located on the second floor.

The Tipton Room ·· $550 per evening

This 72-square-meter room can accommodate up to 75 people seated. Suitable for banquets, meetings, and seminars. A medium-sized stage is set up in the corner, and audio/visual equipment is provided. Located on the second floor.

The Akerman Room ·· $610 per evening

This 84-square-meter room can accommodate up to 80 people seated. It is suitable for banquets, meetings, and seminars. A stage is in place for live music, and the room is fully equipped with presentation equipment. Located on the first floor.

The Underwood Room ·· $875 per evening

This 90-square-meter room can accommodate up to 95 people. It is suitable for meetings, banquets, and seminars. Fully equipped with A/V equipment, with a spacious stage along the northern wall. Tall windows along the west and south sides. Located on the second floor.

For booking inquiries, please contact Alice Livingstone at alivingstone@whiteorchid.com.

To:	Alice Livingstone <alivingstone@whiteorchid.com>
From:	Brianna Hooper <bhooper@tyrus.com>
Date:	April 21
Subject:	Function Room Hire

Dear Ms. Livingstone,

I have been handed the responsibility of organizing my firm's year-end banquet, which we would like to hold on December 28 or December 29. Your cousin, Matthew Bright, is my personal assistant, and he recommended that I contact you. We are looking for a function room that will hold up to 75 employees and clients who have been invited to attend. Also, we will need a stage and audio/visual equipment, as we will be presenting awards to those employees at our law firm who have performed exceptionally over the year. I checked your list of rooms, and it seems that the Tipton Room would be the best choice.

I would like to make the payment for the room as soon as possible to ensure that the space is reserved. Please let me know how I should proceed. Thanks in advance.

Regards,

Brianna Hooper

TEST 13

186. According to the article, which function room was recently renovated?

(A) The Matthews Room
(B) The Tipton Room
(C) The Akerman Room
(D) The Underwood Room

187. What do the four function rooms have in common with one another?

(A) They are located on the same floor.
(B) They are all suitable for banquets.
(C) They each contain a stage.
(D) They can accommodate at least 70 guests.

188. What is indicated about Ms. Livingstone?

(A) She is related to one of Ms. Hooper's staff.
(B) She has been nominated for a company award.
(C) She will be giving a presentation to employees.
(D) She has previously provided services to Ms. Hooper.

189. What information does Ms. Hooper NOT provide in the e-mail?

(A) The approximate number of expected guests
(B) The time she would like the event to begin
(C) The reason she would like to reserve a space
(D) The type of company she works for

190. How much will Ms. Hooper most likely pay to hire the function room?

(A) $435
(B) $550
(C) $610
(D) $875

GO ON TO THE NEXT PAGE

Questions 191–195 refer to the following advertisement, e-mail, and reference letter.

The United Bedfordshire Hospitals Group

- Internal Vacancies -

The following positions within our hospitals and clinics are being advertised internally in an effort to find the most suitable and qualified candidates among our current UBHG members. E-mail Jerry Sandoval at jsandoval@ubhg.co.uk for further details or to put yourself forward for a position. Please include your résumé.

Physiotherapist (Luton) - A space has opened up for a permanent Band 5 physiotherapist to join the team within the Physiotherapy Department at Luton Health Center. This role will also involve 'on call' cover for the evenings as well as occasional weekend work.

Health Care Support Worker (Bedford) – This is an exciting opportunity to join a large multi-disciplinary team on the Clinical Decision Unit at Bedford Royal Hospital. This role requires an enthusiastic individual who can remain calm under pressure and can prioritize workload.

Urology Staff Nurse (Dunstable) - Join our existing team of urology nurse specialists and practitioners at Dunstable Health Clinic. This position is being advertised in order to cover maternity leave. It is expected that the duration will be approximately 10 to 12 months.

Endoscopy Staff Nurse (Luton) - The Endoscopy Unit in Luton City Hospital performs a variety of endoscopic procedures. Candidates should have a professional nursing qualification, excellent interpersonal skills, and a willingness to work on weekends.

E-Mail Message

To:	Jerry Sandoval <jsandoval@ubhg.co.uk>
From:	Edith Kapranos <ekapranos@bedfordhosp.org>
Subject:	UBHG Vacancies
Date:	October 11

Dear Mr. Sandoval,

As a long-time member, I normally check the United Bedfordshire Hospitals Group Web site every Tuesday once you have added all the latest available positions. After the recent update, I noticed a new vacancy that would suit me well. Therefore, I have included my résumé and ask that I be considered for the position of endoscopy staff nurse.

For the past 4 years I have served as a staff nurse in the Ear, Nose & Throat Department at Bedford Royal Hospital, and I spent two years at Dunstable Health Clinic prior to that. I hold a degree from Mellor Nursing College, and I have learned a great deal over the past few years in my current position. However, I feel that it is time to move on and gain further experience in a fresh, challenging environment. My supervisors have always noted my communication skills, both when speaking with patients and with my superiors. On occasion, I have even been asked to supervise a small team of junior nurses and delegate tasks accordingly. Weekend work has never been a problem for me, and I am used to working on a flexible schedule.

Please consider me for the vacancy, and I will look forward to receiving your reply.

Edith Kapranos

Dear Mr. Sandoval,

I am writing to you in reference to Ms. Edith Kapranos, who is in the process of applying for a new position within United Bedfordshire Hospitals Group.

I have had the pleasure of working closely alongside Edith for the past few years, during which time I have served as her department manager. Edith has always excelled in her role, both in terms of showing individual dedication and a willingness to contribute to the team as a whole.

I can safely say that I have never had any problems with Edith when it comes to her attitude, effort, punctuality, and performance. Therefore, I can recommend her to you without any hesitation, and I have no doubt that she would prove to be a valuable asset to your team. If you would like to discuss Edith's specific job duties or skills in more detail, please contact me at 555-0125.

Sincerely,

Trevor Ogilvie

191. For whom is the advertisement most likely intended?

(A) Board members at Luton Health Center
(B) Recruiters from local medical institutions
(C) Individuals interested in training workshops
(D) Members of a professional association

192. What position is being offered on a temporary basis?

(A) Physiotherapist
(B) Health Care Support Worker
(C) Urology Staff Nurse
(D) Endoscopy Staff Nurse

193. What is indicated about the United Bedfordshire Hospitals Group?

(A) It updates online job listings every week.
(B) It offers advice about health on its Web site.
(C) It has organized job fairs in local towns.
(D) It advertises job vacancies in several publications.

194. What does Ms. Kapranos mention that is NOT relevant to the position for which she is applying?

(A) Her availability on weekends
(B) Her degree from nursing school
(C) Her experience managing others
(D) Her ability to communicate well

195. Where does Mr. Ogilvie most likely work?

(A) Luton City Hospital
(B) Bedford Royal Hospital
(C) Mellor Nursing College
(D) Dunstable Health Clinic

GO ON TO THE NEXT PAGE

Questions 196-200 refer to the following flyer, online form, and e-mail.

Beresford Wild Salmon Market

The Freshest Wild Salmon - From Natural Freshwater Sources Straight to Your Kitchen

Beresford Wild Salmon Market, located in Anchorage, Alaska, invites you to join its innovative and convenient membership program. Members enjoy fresh wild salmon during our fishing season from May to October.

Sign up for market membership and receive the following perks:
- Discounted pink and red salmon, collected from surrounding streams and packaged on ice
- Complimentary small shellfish caught by Roper & Co. occasionally included with salmon orders
- Access to the members page of our Web site, which includes exclusive weekly offers and promotions
- Reduced admission fees for our annual seafood festival. Tickets typically cost $30, but members can enter for only $20.

Members receive one shipment per month. A full shipment consists of 20 whole salmon and costs $300, while a half shipment consists of 10 whole salmon and costs $170.

For over ten years, our wild salmon has been sourced only from the streams and rivers surrounding Anchorage, so you can be assured of its freshness. To sign up for a membership, please visit our Web site at www.beresfordsalmon.com.

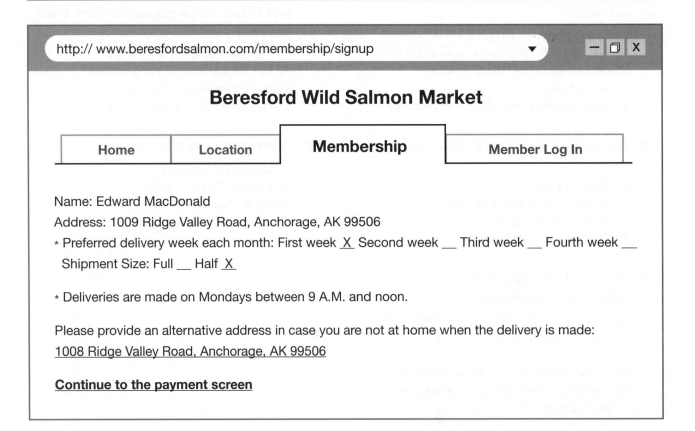

http:// www.beresfordsalmon.com/membership/signup   ▼   — ⟳ X

Beresford Wild Salmon Market

| Home | Location | **Membership** | Member Log In |

Name: Edward MacDonald
Address: 1009 Ridge Valley Road, Anchorage, AK 99506
* Preferred delivery week each month: First week <u>X</u> Second week __ Third week __ Fourth week __
  Shipment Size: Full __ Half <u>X</u>

* Deliveries are made on Mondays between 9 A.M. and noon.

Please provide an alternative address in case you are not at home when the delivery is made:
<u>1008 Ridge Valley Road, Anchorage, AK 99506</u>

Continue to the payment screen

To:	Customer Service <inquiries@beresfordsalmon.com>
From:	Edward MacDonald <emacdonald@seafoodheaven.com>
Subject:	General Inquiry
Date:	June 10

Hello,

I'd like to start by extending my gratitude to you for providing such a high-quality, efficient service. The salmon that you've been delivering to my restaurant has been absolutely delicious, and my diners have remarked on its taste and freshness several times. In addition, the $20 tickets for this year's seafood festival will be a welcome bonus. The one thing I'm confused about is that I haven't had anything from Roper & Co. thus far. I'm hoping that will change in the coming weeks. However, please let me know if you've decided to change this policy.

Thanks,

Edward MacDonald

TEST 13

196. What is the purpose of the flyer?

(A) To invite local residents to an event
(B) To promote a new fish market
(C) To announce the start of a fishing season
(D) To advertise a special membership

197. What is suggested about the workers at Beresford Wild Salmon Market?

(A) They package salmon from May to October.
(B) They update the market's Web site once a month.
(C) They import specific items from overseas.
(D) They distribute products to several retailers.

198. What is NOT indicated about Beresford Wild Salmon Market?

(A) It keeps its salmon chilled.
(B) It only sells locally-caught salmon.
(C) It hosts an event every year.
(D) It serves meals on-site.

199. How much will Mr. MacDonald pay per month for his membership?

(A) $20
(B) $30
(C) $170
(D) $300

200. What problem does Mr. MacDonald most likely refer to in the e-mail?

(A) He was charged full price for festival tickets.
(B) His recent order of salmon was smaller than expected.
(C) He has not received any free shellfish.
(D) He is waiting for confirmation of a payment.

Stop! This is the end of the test. If you finish before time is called, you may go back to Parts 5, 6, and 7 and check your work.

정답 p.474 / 점수 환산표 p.476

실전모의고사
TEST 14

TEST 14 해설

바로 보기

시작 시간 _____ 시 _____ 분

종료 시간 _____ 시 _____ 분

▶ 중간에 멈추지 말고 처음부터 끝까지 풀어보세요. 문제를 풀 때는 실전처럼 답안지에 마킹하세요.

READING TEST

In the Reading test, you will read a variety of texts and answer several different types of reading comprehension questions. The entire Reading test will last 75 minutes. There are three parts, and directions are given for each part. You are encouraged to answer as many questions as possible within the time allowed. You must mark your answers on the separate answer sheet. Do not write your answers in your test book.

PART 5

Directions: A word or phrase is missing in each of the sentences below. Four answer choices are given below each sentence. Select the best answer to complete the sentence. Then mark the letter (A), (B), (C), or (D) on your answer sheet.

101. Dr. Taylor and Dr. Holmes are high-achieving, distinguished scientists and perform research effectively on -------.

(A) their
(B) their own
(C) theirs
(D) them

102. As part of our plan ------- outstanding loan payments, we will be recruiting additional staff in our finance department.

(A) recovering
(B) for recovery
(C) to recover
(D) recovered

103. All departments should be aware of the new policies ------- procurement contracts and make sure to update their internal documentation.

(A) that
(B) whereas
(C) besides
(D) concerning

104. To maintain our reputation as a leading communications company, we must ------- current trends in the marketplace extremely closely.

(A) monitor
(B) focus
(C) adhere
(D) achieve

105. According to our employee handbook, the machinery should be repaired ------- after the Mechanical Department has been consulted.

(A) because
(B) during
(C) still
(D) only

106. As you can see, we have ------- the photocopier in a central location, so all employees can access it more easily.

(A) engaged
(B) situated
(C) consigned
(D) prompted

107. The team's ability to perform ------- well in adverse circumstances has really impressed the president.

(A) exceptional
(B) exception
(C) except
(D) exceptionally

108. There simply is no ------- in this year's budget to replace outdated equipment in the laboratory.

(A) occupation
(B) volume
(C) room
(D) structure

109. The purpose of the upcoming workshop is to train the staff in the most ------- techniques for contract negotiations.

(A) innovate
(B) innovation
(C) innovatively
(D) innovative

110. According to its press release, the research paper focuses on the ------- of patients with various types of bone disease.

(A) precaution
(B) situation
(C) manufacture
(D) treatment

111. Quarx Electronics has begun to follow the trend ------ larger screens on its latest line of smartphones.

(A) toward
(B) beside
(C) into
(D) among

112. Having ------ to offer multilingual customer service, the Northbridge Cardiac Hospital hopes to attract international patients.

(A) decisive
(B) decided
(C) deciding
(D) decision

113. ------ the relocation of the Marketing Department to Taipei, internal communications have been carried out using our new videoconferencing software.

(A) Therefore
(B) However
(C) Because
(D) Since

114. Although it is a newcomer in the domain of e-learning, Goldwave Education has been highly ------- by many experts in that field.

(A) regardless
(B) regards
(C) regarding
(D) regarded

115. Your reservation is not ------- until you make the final payment, so please contact our office to organize your payment schedule by the end of the day.

(A) confirmed
(B) expected
(C) arrived
(D) exchanged

116. This year, we are ------- to welcome Brandford Inc.'s European regional management team to our annual general meeting.

(A) please
(B) pleased
(C) pleasing
(D) pleasure

117. As business is robust in the fall and all staff members are needed in the office, Ms. Stevens recommended only one employee ------- the industry trade show this year.

(A) attend
(B) attends
(C) will attend
(D) has attended

118. The managers' use of company vehicles is an issue ------- the CFO has been meaning to discuss with Mr. Carey.

(A) which
(B) what
(C) whom
(D) where

119. The CEO of Sashagiri Enterprises has led the ------- with great integrity, invaluable knowledge, and life-long dedication.

(A) organizing
(B) organize
(C) organized
(D) organization

GO ON TO THE NEXT PAGE

120. Mr. Mansour shows creativity and sound management skills, and he has not ------- had a project go over budget.

(A) yet
(B) also
(C) still
(D) already

121. Each new employee must submit a personal profile form and up-to-date tax information ------- their first day of work.

(A) prior to
(B) as long as
(C) until
(D) afterward

122. This small gift is a token of our appreciation for all the hard work you have done over the ------- 25 years in our town.

(A) past
(B) next
(C) long
(D) recent

123. ------- meticulous planning and cost control, the construction project went over budget by approximately $17 million.

(A) Thanks to
(B) In view of
(C) Despite
(D) In case of

124. By the time he retires next year, Bill Malayam ------- for Phillips Telecom for almost two decades.

(A) will have worked
(B) has worked
(C) will be working
(D) had worked

125. At first, we were delighted to visit the new Gala restaurant, but we were disappointed to find out that the service was ------- slow.

(A) noticeably
(B) diligently
(C) critically
(D) successively

126. Unfortunately, the company's 10th anniversary celebration was postponed due to ------- weather conditions.

(A) severe
(B) appropriate
(C) extensive
(D) responsive

127. If Mr. Song had known he was being considered for a promotion, he ------- the project on time.

(A) has finished
(B) would have finished
(C) was finished
(D) will finish

128. The community festival had a ------ better turn-out compared to the one last year, where it rained every single day.

(A) too
(B) much
(C) so
(D) very

129. Every year, the Stroweman Foundation charity ------- over $100,000 to Stevenson University scholarship funds.

(A) donates
(B) publishes
(C) observes
(D) seeks

130. ------- we complete one of our projects before the deadline, we get to leave the office an hour early.

(A) Soon
(B) Whenever
(C) That
(D) Sometimes

PART 6

Directions: Read the texts that follow. A word, phrase, or sentence is missing in parts of each text. Four answer choices for each question are given below the text. Select the best answer to complete the text. Then mark the letter (A), (B), (C) or (D) on your answer sheet.

Questions 131–134 refer to the following e-mail.

From: Russell Egerton <regerton@fastfashion.com>

To: Kevin Livingstone <klivingstone@xyzmail.com>

Date: March 28

Subject: Job application

Dear Mr. Livingstone,

I am writing regarding your recent application for the store manager job. I am sorry for the delay in replying to you, but we received ------- 500 applications for the position.
131.

-------, you were not selected for the position, but we have another one which would be suitable for
132.
you. This position is for an assistant store manager in our city's busy central location, which is always packed with shoppers. I wanted to offer you a chance to apply for this position before we advertise it. ------- .
133.

If you are ------- in the position, could you please e-mail or call me as soon as possible so that we
134.
can arrange a suitable time for an interview? It would be best if you could contact me between 12 P.M. and 5 P.M. as I will be out of the office in the morning.

---

131. (A) more
(B) rough
(C) over
(D) many

132. (A) In fact
(B) In addition
(C) Moreover
(D) In case

133. (A) We think your skills and qualifications are an excellent match for this job.
(B) We encourage you to seriously reconsider our offer and contact us again.
(C) I look forward to reviewing your résumé and recommendation letters.
(D) However, this position was filled and the posting has been removed.

134. (A) interested
(B) interesting
(C) interestingly
(D) interest

GO ON TO THE NEXT PAGE

Questions 135-138 refer to the following notice.

From now until January 25, whenever you make a purchase at www.sureshopping.com, you will be entered into our Sure Shopper Contest, in which two lucky winners will be awarded a year of free shipping and a $250 gift -------. To qualify for this, simply check the contest box on your purchase
135.
form and your name and e-mail address will automatically be registered for the draw.

Customers can be ------- that their details will not be shared with any outside sources. We consider
136.
our customers' contact information to be ------- confidential. The contest closes on January 25.
137.
-------. The winners will be notified by e-mail on January 28.
138.

135. (A) certify
(B) certificate
(C) certified
(D) certification

136. (A) inspired
(B) applied
(C) assured
(D) committed

137. (A) strictly
(B) customarily
(C) heavily
(D) narrowly

138. (A) Please ensure that our customers follow these rules accordingly.
(B) Your entry has been received and you will be notified when the contest closes.
(C) Customers are advised not to share their personal information with anyone.
(D) Until then, customers are free to enter anytime they make a purchase.

Questions 139-142 refer to the following article.

Lee's Tires and Rims Recognized for Innovation

By Cho Eun-Seong

Mr. Lee Tae-Hyun of Lee's Tires and Rims received the esteemed "Innovator of the Year" award at last night's ceremony celebrating creative business successes in Seoul. The reward recognized a new ------- in winter tires which experts say is far safer than that of standard winter tires.
139.

Lee's patented tire has been shown to improve traction, thereby ------- the likelihood that a driver will
140.
lose control of their vehicle in slippery conditions. Furthermore, these tires are more durable and less susceptible to wear and tear. This means that the tires stay safer for longer periods of time.

"I want our roads to be safe for everyone, and there is something I want to make very clear—these tires do not make you absolutely safe. -------. But if you must drive, these tires are significantly better
141.
than anything else on the market," Lee said in an interview ------- the award ceremony. Lee vows to
142.
continue his work in improving tires and making the roads a safer place to travel.

---

139. (A) franchise
(B) scheme
(C) design
(D) resignation

140. (A) reducing
(B) ensuring
(C) releasing
(D) resuming

141. (A) Accidents have decreased significantly this year.
(B) As a result, the cost of insurance continues to increase.
(C) If the roads are slippery, stay home if you can.
(D) Drivers have praised the deep tread of the tires.

142. (A) except
(B) following
(C) along
(D) provided

GO ON TO THE NEXT PAGE

Questions 143-146 refer to the following e-mail.

To: Ida Fitzgerald <ifiz@daox.net>

From: Jennifer Rushmore <jrushmore@tvnradio.com>

Subject: My gratitude

Dear Ms. Fitzgerald,

About a decade ago, I took a field trip to a radio station. I was fascinated by the voices and music that were being broadcast on air. -------, it has been my greatest wish to become a radio announcer, **143.** all the way through my adolescence. However, I knew it would be an almost impossible dream to achieve.

One day, I built up enough courage to ask you, my homeroom teacher, about it. You offered me a lot of good advice, saying, "Only with a single step does a journey of a thousand miles -------." You **144.** also said that you had a friend at a radio station and gave me his phone number. Had it not been for you, I might never have had ------- an opportunity. Now, I work at the station and am learning how to **145.** become a professional radio announcer. -------. **146.**

Sincerely,

Jennifer Rushmore

---

143. (A) Specifically
(B) Since then
(C) Likewise
(D) Rather

144. (A) began
(B) begun
(C) begin
(D) begins

145. (A) great
(B) such
(C) each
(D) too

146. (A) Your work has truly been an inspiration to me.
(B) I have been dreaming of joining you at your station.
(C) I am truly grateful that you chose to employ me.
(D) Thanks for encouraging me to pursue my dream.

PART 7

Directions: In this part you will read a selection of texts, such as magazine and newspaper articles, e-mails, and instant messages. Each text or set of texts is followed by several questions. Select the best answer for each question and mark the letter (A), (B), (C), or (D) on your answer sheet.

Questions 147-148 refer to the following business card.

Akmed & Sons Ltd.

Terry Bullard

Financial Advisor, West Drayton area

"Helping small businesses get big tax returns for over 15 years"

Hours: Mon – Fri, 9 A.M. – 5 P.M.

Weekend appointments
available on request

34 Drayton Road, West Drayton, 39220

Call: 555-0129

E-mail: tbullard@wirenet.com

http://www.akmednsons.com

---

147. Who most likely is Mr. Bullard?

(A) An accountant
(B) A business investor
(C) An insurance sales agent
(D) A recruitment specialist

148. What is indicated about Mr. Bullard?

(A) He has been recently hired.
(B) He specializes in assisting large businesses.
(C) He has his own personal Web site.
(D) He is available on Saturdays.

GO ON TO THE NEXT PAGE

Questions 149-150 refer to the following text-message chain.

KARL TYSON   [7:20 A.M.]

Hi, Polly. I just got on the bus. I'll probably get to downtown Los Angeles by 9:30 at the latest.

KARL TYSON   [7:21 A.M.]

Have you gotten there already? I hope our company booked us into a nice hotel.

POLLY HOGAN   [7:25 A.M.]

Hey, Karl. I just arrived, and the hotel is pretty reasonable. Remember, our budget for this trip is limited.

KARL TYSON   [7:27 A.M.]

That's true. Well, as long as it's comfortable. I'd like to take a short nap before the meeting with the potential suppliers. Is it far from downtown?

POLLY HOGAN   [7:28 A.M.]

It's a little far out. The good news is there's a free shuttle bus from the bus terminal to our hotel.

KARL TYSON   [7:30 A.M.]

Oh, that's good to know. Is it hard to find the shuttle bus pick-up point?

POLLY HOGAN   [7:31 A.M.]

It couldn't be simpler. Just exit the downtown bus terminal through the main entrance, and you'll see it right outside.

KARL TYSON   [7:32 A.M.]

Great. Okay, I'll let you know once I arrive. See you soon, Polly.

---

149. What can be inferred about Mr. Tyson and Ms. Hogan?

(A) Ms. Hogan is on the way to the hotel.
(B) They will stay in separate hotels.
(C) They do not live in Los Angeles.
(D) Mr. Tyson knows how to get to his destination.

150. At 7:31 A.M., what does Ms. Hogan mean when she writes, "It couldn't be simpler"?

(A) She is sure that a shuttle bus runs frequently.
(B) She agrees to meet Mr. Tyson outside a bus station.
(C) She thinks Mr. Tyson will easily find a hotel.
(D) She had no difficulty in locating a bus stop.

Rocket Automotives Ltd.

Vacancy: General Manager

Hoxbridge Branch

Rocket Automotives is expanding.

We are currently in the process of opening a new distribution facility in Hoxbridge.

We require an experienced manager to supervise employees at this branch.

The successful applicant will have:

• At least five years of industry experience

• A relevant Master's degree

• Strong collaborative skills

The closing date for applications is March 15.

Interviews will take place during the week of March 18.

To apply, please fill in an application form on our Web site at

www.rocketcars.net/opportunities

TEST 14

151. What is mentioned about Rocket Automotives Ltd.?

(A) Some staff will retire soon.
(B) It is launching a new product.
(C) It is opening a new business location.
(D) It runs skill development courses for staff.

152. Which of the following are applicants NOT expected to have?

(A) Advanced education in the field
(B) Excellent customer service skills
(C) Prior experience in the auto industry
(D) The ability to work as part of a team

GO ON TO THE NEXT PAGE

Questions 153-154 refer to the following e-mail.

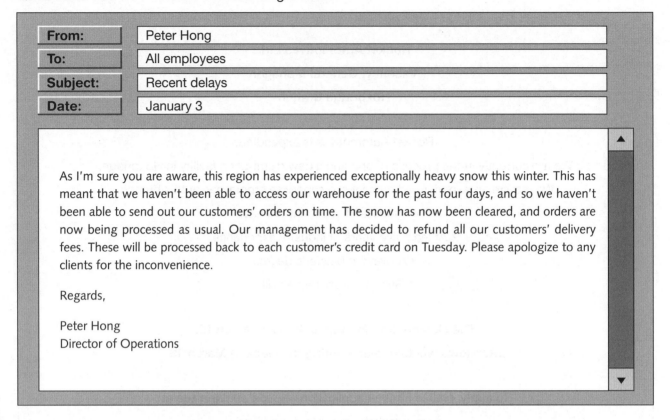

From:	Peter Hong
To:	All employees
Subject:	Recent delays
Date:	January 3

As I'm sure you are aware, this region has experienced exceptionally heavy snow this winter. This has meant that we haven't been able to access our warehouse for the past four days, and so we haven't been able to send out our customers' orders on time. The snow has now been cleared, and orders are now being processed as usual. Our management has decided to refund all our customers' delivery fees. These will be processed back to each customer's credit card on Tuesday. Please apologize to any clients for the inconvenience.

Regards,

Peter Hong
Director of Operations

153. What does the e-mail indicate about the warehouse?

(A) It has recently undergone an expansion.
(B) It was recently inaccessible.
(C) It ran out of stock due to high demand.
(D) It was damaged during a snowstorm.

154. What will happen next Tuesday?

(A) Refunds will be processed.
(B) Orders will be delivered.
(C) A store will reopen after renovation.
(D) A new product will launch.

Local Portland News

Hysteria at Solid Gold Soundz as Music Fans
Line Up Around the Block

Fans of pop star Carla Jean Stetson began turning up at the Mitchell Street location of Solid Gold Soundz at around midnight last night, nine hours before the store opened for business this morning. The reason for such enthusiasm is that fans are excited to get their hands on Ms. Stetson's long-awaited new CD, *Written in the Stars*, which went on sale nationwide from today. Ms. Stetson has amassed a legion of fans after touring continuously over the past 12 months and performing concerts in all major U.S. cities.

Another reason for the pop singer's rapidly increasing fame is the extensive advertising campaign that has been running online and in print media ever since she signed her first record contract with BTM Entertainment Company. The campaign has consisted of various full-page spreads in music magazines and Web site advertisements specifically targeting teenaged music fans. The record label has stated that it poured an unprecedented amount of money into the marketing of Ms. Stetson, as it expects her to become the most profitable of all its artists.

Solid Gold Soundz fully anticipated the large and enthusiastic turnout of music fans and planned accordingly. In response to complaints from music fans who were left disappointed and empty-handed on the release day of Ms. Stetson's previous album, the store made sure to order a sufficient number of CDs this time. Also, until the end of the week, customers can enter a raffle at the store to win an opportunity to meet Ms. Stetson backstage after her concert at Portland Arena on August 8.

155. Why were some people waiting in line for hours?

(A) To meet a famous singer
(B) To buy a new music release
(C) To watch a musical performance
(D) To enter a prize drawing

156. What is indicated about the advertising campaign?

(A) It required a relatively low amount of financing.
(B) It was first developed approximately one year ago.
(C) It was designed to attract customers to Solid Gold Soundz.
(D) It was funded by BTM Entertainment Company.

157. What is suggested about Solid Gold Soundz?

(A) It will sponsor an upcoming concert series.
(B) It will invite Ms. Stetson to sign copies of her CD in-store.
(C) It pays attention to its customers' needs.
(D) It does not stock Ms. Stetson's previous albums.

GO ON TO THE NEXT PAGE

22 Crayford Street
Montgomery, AL 36043
July 2

Dear Mr. Connors

We are very happy to provide our services in helping you set up your new restaurant. I've included some sample interiors including fixtures and designs that are standard for restaurants. Custom decorations, such as logos or paintings, are optional, but will increase the overall cost of the renovations by 20%. We will have an open house with models of many of these interiors at our headquarters on July 13 from 3 P.M. to 7 P.M.

We ask that you let us know your decision on what style of interior you would like for your restaurant by August 12, so that we have one month to finish the construction. Feel free to call me with any questions at 205-555-1388.

Best wishes,
Kyle Langley
Founder, Storefront Interiors

Enclosures.

158. What is the purpose of the letter?

(A) To give directions to an open house
(B) To request payment for restoration services
(C) To ask for a custom design layout
(D) To inform about ordering procedures

159. What is suggested about Storefront Interiors' custom designs?

(A) They must adhere to construction regulations.
(B) They will be shown at a grand opening.
(C) They are more expensive than standard designs.
(D) They are made by well-known designers.

160. When will Mr. Connors' restaurant open?

(A) On July 2
(B) On July 13
(C) On August 12
(D) On September 12

Questions 161-164 refer to the following online chat discussion.

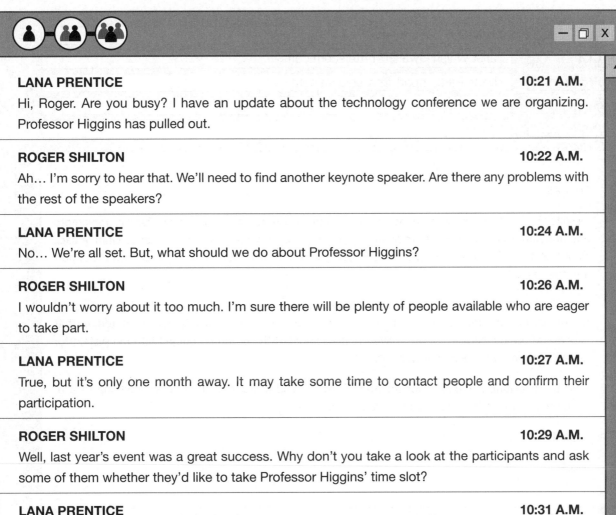

LANA PRENTICE   10:21 A.M.

Hi, Roger. Are you busy? I have an update about the technology conference we are organizing. Professor Higgins has pulled out.

ROGER SHILTON   10:22 A.M.

Ah... I'm sorry to hear that. We'll need to find another keynote speaker. Are there any problems with the rest of the speakers?

LANA PRENTICE   10:24 A.M.

No... We're all set. But, what should we do about Professor Higgins?

ROGER SHILTON   10:26 A.M.

I wouldn't worry about it too much. I'm sure there will be plenty of people available who are eager to take part.

LANA PRENTICE   10:27 A.M.

True, but it's only one month away. It may take some time to contact people and confirm their participation.

ROGER SHILTON   10:29 A.M.

Well, last year's event was a great success. Why don't you take a look at the participants and ask some of them whether they'd like to take Professor Higgins' time slot?

LANA PRENTICE   10:31 A.M.

That's a good idea. I'll get on it right away.

161. Why did Ms. Prentice contact Mr. Shilton?

(A) To discuss potential event venues
(B) To request his assistance at an event
(C) To invite him to talk at a conference
(D) To inform him of a cancelation

162. At 10:24 A.M., what does Ms. Prentice mean when she writes, "We're all set"?

(A) She would like Mr. Shilton to confirm his attendance.
(B) All other speakers have been confirmed.
(C) She is grateful for Mr. Shilton's advice.
(D) It is too late to change the dates of a conference.

163. Why is Ms. Prentice concerned?

(A) There are no suitable venues available.
(B) There is a lack of interest in the event.
(C) There is not much time to find a participant.
(D) There are several speaking positions to be filled.

164. What does Mr. Shilton suggest?

(A) Postponing the event
(B) Meeting with Professor Higgins
(C) Reducing the number of attendees
(D) Contacting previous speakers

GO ON TO THE NEXT PAGE

Questions 165-168 refer to the following e-mail.

To:	Marketing Department
CC:	Janet Walsh <jwalsh@nrttelecom.com>
From:	Nicole Park <npark@nrttelecom.com>
Subject:	Meeting update
Date:	August 3

Dear All,

Despite the threat of bad weather, we are going ahead with the reception dinner for Mr. Yamamoto and his team from JHK Media from Japan. — [1] —. I have pushed our reservation at La Grande back from 6:00 P.M. to 7:00 P.M. in order to give our guests from JHK more time to travel from the airport into the city. — [2] —.

Since Cynthia Yu will be away on business, I have arranged to have Ken Lee from Ace Editorial attend the dinner in order to provide interpretation for the evening. Janet, would you mind adding that expense to the budget? — [3] —. I have already submitted the proposed budget into the system for review, but it has not been approved yet.

I will be circulating the agenda for the evening by the end of the day. If you have anything to add, please send it to me by e-mail before 2:00 P.M. today. — [4] —.

Regards,

Nicole

---

165. What can be inferred about Cynthia Yu?

(A) She speaks Japanese.
(B) She works for Ace Editorial.
(C) She is traveling in Japan.
(D) She is responsible for expenses.

166. Who will provide the translation service?

(A) Janet Walsh
(B) Nicole Park
(C) Ken Lee
(D) Cynthia Yu

167. What will Nicole do later today?

(A) Distribute an updated document
(B) Change the meeting schedule
(C) Add an item to the budget
(D) Contact Janet Walsh

168. In which of the positions marked [1], [2], [3], and [4] does the following sentence best belong?

"His fee is for four hours at the usual rate."

(A) [1]
(B) [2]
(C) [3]
(D) [4]

Questions 169-171 refer to the following e-mail.

E-Mail Message

To:	All Staff
From:	Oliver Carruthers
Subject:	Annual staff party
Date:	October 29

Greetings,

We are all winding down as we approach the end of the fiscal year. I trust that each of you is looking forward to a well-deserved break. As a team, we have had a very productive year and on behalf of the management here at PQR Enterprises, I would like to invite you to our annual staff party for an opportunity to get to know your colleagues better in a relaxed environment. You all deserve it!

The event will be held in the ballroom at Reitman Hotel on November 8 at 6:00 P.M. It will be catered by Stonewall Catering. Entertainment will be provided by the Reitman Hotel Band, as well as the popular comedian, Wayne Rally.

We understand that many of you have children, which makes it difficult to attend evening functions. Because we hope to accommodate as many of you as possible, we have hired childcare staff who will provide free babysitting on the night of the party. Children will be fed a healthy meal which will be followed by a family movie. Qualified babysitters will be there to attend to the children's needs. After the movie, there will be games and arts and crafts to keep the youngsters entertained until their parents are ready to go home.

We sincerely hope to see everyone there!

TEST 14

169. What is the main purpose of the e-mail?

(A) To congratulate the team on a successful fiscal year
(B) To invite staff to a celebratory company party
(C) To inform staff that they will receive an extra bonus
(D) To request childcare services during a staff party

170. What is NOT mentioned as something the children will enjoy?

(A) A movie
(B) Music
(C) Games
(D) Arts and crafts

171. What can be inferred about Mr. Carruthers?

(A) He is planning a monthly meeting.
(B) He is concerned about sales.
(C) He plans to hire new employees.
(D) He represents management.

GO ON TO THE NEXT PAGE

Questions 172-175 refer to the following e-mail.

To:	Sales Department <sales@seaviewresorts.com>
From:	Anna Thompson <athompson@seaviewresorts.com>
Subject:	Results of Survey
Date:	April 4

Dear Sales Team,

I am writing on behalf of the Marketing Department to share the results of the recent survey we conducted.

First, clients rated the friendliness of the reservations staff at 4.3/5. We were pleased with this ranking because many of you attended the workshop on how to achieve customer satisfaction last month. Well done.

Second, clients gave us 4.1/5 on promotions. — [1] —. We recognize that not all of you are authorized to offer upgrades or last-minute deals, so we will be discussing this issue with the appropriate managers. — [2] —. We hope to see some improvement in this area before the next survey in two months.

Last, clients rated us 2.8/5 on honoring discount codes. — [3] —. We will be holding a follow-up meeting with you to determine whether clients are trying to use fake or expired discount codes or if you are not informed of new discount codes being circulated.

Overall, we are happy with your ratings. — [4] —. You can expect a more detailed analysis, including manager comments, in the final results, which will be e-mailed late next week.

If you have any questions, please e-mail me.

Anna

172. What is the purpose of the e-mail?

(A) To ask staff members to complete a survey
(B) To request staff attendance at a meeting
(C) To communicate the results of a survey
(D) To introduce new reservations procedures

173. What is suggested about reservations staff?

(A) They require more experience.
(B) They received customer service training.
(C) They offer too many last-minute upgrades.
(D) They are not authorized to give online discounts.

174. What will staff receive next week?

(A) Clearance to offer discounts
(B) New training to improve survey results
(C) A copy of the survey
(D) Feedback from managers

175. In which of the positions marked [1], [2], [3], and [4] does the following sentence best belong?

" All three generally matched our expectations at the beginning of the survey."

(A) [1]
(B) [2]
(C) [3]
(D) [4]

GO ON TO THE NEXT PAGE

The 10th Annual New Orleans Business Expo
Arrange a booth for your business now!

The country's biggest business exposition will be held next spring from April 9 to 11 at the Show Grounds Exhibition Center. Plan now to promote your business at this prestigious event. Choose one of the packages below.

Rent a Room for Demo or Display
A whole room in the conference center, rented by the half day. Tables and chairs provided. Electronics available on request (extra charge). Rooms are limited, so book early.

Main Exhibition Hall Booth
Standard 5m by 5m booth space with one electricity outlet. 2 tables and 2 chairs provided on request. Corner booths (no extra charge) are in great demand.

Food Vendor Booth
Standard 5m by 5m booth but with additional power outlets and a sink area. All food booths are on the western side of the exhibition hall. Chairs are not provided but are available in a central location for customer use.

Outside Booth
Outdoor booth space in parking lot in front of exhibition hall (on the south side). Tents and chairs will be provided. No electricity power outlets available. No refunds due to weather.

No-Booth Business Pass
Businesses wishing to showcase their products without a booth must purchase a pass. Roaming vendors without passes or booths will not be permitted.

** Booths are issued on a first come, first served basis until they are all gone.

** 50% down payment required for rental. Refundable up until two months before the show.

** Contact the Show Grounds office (office@showgrounds.com) for information or to reserve your space.

E-Mail Message

To:	Show Grounds Office <office@showgrounds.com>
From:	Leroy Hutchison <lhutchison@donutdelites.com>
Date:	September 8
Subject:	10th Annual New Orleans Business Expo

Dear Sir/Madam,

I would like to reserve a booth at the Annual Business Expo in April next year. I would like one food vendor space, please. I plan to serve hot and cold drinks and pastries.

I do have one concern, however. Your notice states that the food vendors will all be located in one area of the hall. I am familiar with the Show Grounds and I understand the exhibition hall is surrounded by parking lots. One of my employees is disabled and uses a wheelchair. He needs a parking space relatively near to the area where we will be setting up our booth. Please let me know if there will be any disabled parking available on the side of the hall where we will be located.

We would also like to request a booth in an easily accessible spot, if possible. Many thanks for your attention to this.

Yours sincerely,

Leroy Hutchison
Donut Delites

176. What is indicated about the business expo?

(A) It will be held in multiple cities.
(B) It will run for three days.
(C) It takes place twice a year.
(D) It includes foreign companies.

177. Where will chairs NOT be provided?

(A) In the food vendor booths
(B) At the outside booths
(C) In the demo rooms
(D) In the main exhibition hall booths

178. What is suggested about corner booths?

(A) They do not have any electric outlets.
(B) They are only available in the main hall.
(C) They get booked up quickly.
(D) They are bigger than regular booths.

179. In the e-mail, the word "spot" in paragraph 3, line 1, is closest in meaning to

(A) position
(B) mark
(C) stain
(D) observation

180. On which side of the exhibition hall would Mr. Hutchison like to have a booth?

(A) North
(B) South
(C) East
(D) West

GO ON TO THE NEXT PAGE

Maplewood Printing to Close Locations

Maplewood Printing will close three of its eight print shops by January 15, says manager Sarah Piu. According to her, more and more customers upload files online instead of coming into the stores, so there is less need for physical locations. She believes they can meet their clients' printing needs while reducing their costs.

Maplewood insists that the company is not struggling financially and that clientele is steadily rising. However, the decision to consolidate was made to better serve customers. "More people upload files online nowadays," explains Piu. "It will be more efficient if we hire more people to work behind the scenes."

Customers are encouraged to upload their work online, and then drop by their chosen location to pick up the completed product. The company also offers a courier service for people who are not comfortable using the online service.

The locations set to close are Copy Cat on Huntington Street, Copy King on Dufferin Avenue, and Carbon Copy on Mannix Street.

Maplewood will be hiring extra print technicians for the stores that remain open. They will also be hiring staff dedicated to processing Web orders. In order to improve the online uploading process, improvements to the Web site are set to occur in the new year.

Ms. Sarah Piu
Manager, Maplewood Printing, Inc.
245 Elderwood St
Berkeley, CA 19405

Dear Ms. Piu,

I saw the article in the *Berkeley Herald* announcing the closure of your Huntington Street location, and I am writing to share with you my dissatisfaction with this news.

I am a regular customer at that location, and your staff members know me well. I come into the store two or three times a week for print orders for my real estate firm, which is located just across the road.

Like many of your clients, I frequently require print materials immediately. Mailing them in would not suit me, nor would sending my order by courier. I require my material quickly and often spontaneously, and cannot afford the time to wait for the mail.

Your other suggestion of uploading the files online doesn't help for two reasons. First, I have difficulty with computer software. I do not know how to convert the templates I use for my work into the required format. Second, even if I could convert the files, I still wouldn't have the time to drive all the way to your Copy World location on Main Street to pick up the material.

I have supported your company for many years, partially because of the good work you produce, but mostly because you are conveniently located for my business. Now I regret to inform you that due to your decision to close the Huntington location, you are losing a valued customer.

Sincerely,

Martin Showers

Martin Showers

181. What does the article imply about most of Maplewood Printing's customers?

(A) They normally visit the Carbon Copy store.
(B) They prefer to use an online service.
(C) They believe the company should lower its prices.
(D) They find the company's Web site difficult to access.

182. What is mentioned as a reason for closing stores?

(A) Other companies offer faster services.
(B) The stores need better locations.
(C) The company needs more printing technicians.
(D) The needs of customers have changed.

183. Why did Mr. Showers write to the company?

(A) To apply for employment
(B) To inquire about a new location
(C) To complain about a store closure
(D) To request a correction to the article

184. In the letter, the word "suit" in paragraph 3, line 1, is closest in meaning to

(A) satisfy
(B) match
(C) adapt
(D) become

185. Which location's closing impacts Mr. Showers?

(A) Copy World
(B) Copy Cat
(C) Copy King
(D) Carbon Copy

GO ON TO THE NEXT PAGE

Questions 186-190 refer to the following advertisement, recipe, and e-mail.

Hello Delicious

Are you tired of spending hours searching for recipes and going food shopping? We have the perfect service for you! Hello Delicious is a popular food delivery service that sends amazing recipes and fresh ingredients straight to your home once per week. With this service, you can easily cook incredible meals without having to deal with the hassle of planning and shopping. You can sign up for our unique service by visiting our Web site at www.hellodelicious.co.uk. Join now and get 40% off your first meal package by entering Coupon Code FOOD4U when registering.

Hello Delicious guarantees your complete satisfaction. If you are unhappy for any reason, simply contact our Customer Service Department at support@hellodelicious.com.

Hello Delicious – This Week's Amazing Recipe!

Dear Ms. Natalie Rodriguez,

Welcome to Hello Delicious! The meal package you have received contains the following ingredients, which you can use to make this week's recipe: CHINESE OMELET!

2 tsp. canola oil / ¼ lb. shitake mushrooms / 2 tsp. soy sauce / 4 spring onions
4 eggs / 2 cups peas / 2 cups bean sprouts / ½ bell pepper

Prepare for cooking by slicing the mushrooms and peppers, chopping the spring onions, and beating the eggs. Then follow these steps:

1. In a large pan, heat the oil until it is hot.

2. For 2-3 minutes, fry the mushrooms until they turn brown.

3. Add the soy sauce and spring onions. Stir for one minute.

4. Reduce the heat to low. Pour in the eggs. Cover and cook until the egg is set. Then, move it to a warm plate.

5. Increase the heat to high. Add a teaspoon of oil and fry the peas, bean sprouts, and peppers until they are hot.

6. Put the vegetables on half of the omelet. Fold the omelet in half over the vegetables.

E-Mail Message

To: Customer Service <support@hellodelicious.com>
From: Natalia Rodriguez <natalia1@boomail.com>
Subject: Complaint
Date: November 14

To Whom It May Concern:

Yesterday, I was excited to receive my first food package from Hello Delicious. As a busy working mother, I was so relieved to have found a service that would make preparing food for my family a bit easier, and we were all excited to try the Chinese omelet recipe you sent. Also, when signing up online, I entered the code mentioned in your advertisement, so I really felt like we were making a good decision.

Unfortunately, I was quite disappointed to find that there was a key ingredient missing from the package. Without the soy sauce, I had to improvise and make do with whatever I could find in my own kitchen. The closest thing I had was Worcestershire sauce, so I used that as a substitute. I'm afraid the end result tasted a little strange!

I would appreciate it if you could check the contents of next week's package, and all subsequent ones, prior to shipping. I'm looking forward to receiving it!

Regards,

Natalia Rodriguez

---

186. What is indicated about Hello Delicious in the advertisement?

(A) It recently expanded its range of services.
(B) It visits customers at home to provide consultations.
(C) Recipes can be downloaded from its Web site.
(D) An incentive is offered to its first-time customers.

187. In the advertisement, the word "straight" in paragraph 1, line 3, is closest in meaning to

(A) directly
(B) successively
(C) evenly
(D) precisely

188. According to the recipe, what should Ms. Rodriguez do after the oil is heated?

(A) Cook the mushrooms
(B) Chop the vegetables
(C) Wait for 2-3 minutes
(D) Take out a large pan

189. What is most likely true about Ms. Rodriguez's food package?

(A) It was delayed during delivery.
(B) A discount was applied to it.
(C) A free welcome gift was included with it.
(D) It contained some spoiled food items.

190. Which step of the recipe did Ms. Rodriguez change?

(A) Step 2
(B) Step 3
(C) Step 4
(D) Step 5

GO ON TO THE NEXT PAGE

Book Club

Are you seeking a group of like-minded individuals who love reading novels and having thought-provoking discussions? Browne's Books, a small independent store owned by former author and book critic Margaret Browne, is hosting its next book club on November 19. The book chosen for this month's chat is the award-winning novel by Jayne Friedman, *The Boy and the Chair*, a tale about a quirky and imaginative young child who creates a world of his own in an attempt to escape the trials and tribulations of modern-day elementary school. Jayne Friedman is also the author of *The Swings at Sunset* and *Blue's Bicycles*. All of her novels are based on the life of her son.

To RSVP, please contact the club president at booklover@diomail.com by Thursday, November 12.

To:	Hannah Stone <booklover@diomail.com>
From:	Dale Levine <dalelevine@allmail.net>
Subject:	The Boy and the Chair
Date:	November 10

Dear Ms. Stone,

I would love to attend the gathering at Browne's Books on the 19th. I recently moved here, so I have been looking for a way to meet people in the area. I always glance at the bulletin board in my apartment building for community events, and I recognized the name of the bookstore because I walk past it every day on my way to work.

I am particularly excited about meeting local people with similar interests. Thanks so much for organizing it. I would be happy to bring some appetizers from my restaurant to the event, if you think people would like that. You can take a look at the menu by visiting my Web site at www.levinesrestaurant.com/menu. Let me know your thoughts.

Regards,

Dale Levine

November 24

Book Review – *The Boy and the Chair*

Review by *Dale Levine*

I first started reading this book for a book club, and I was instantly hooked. *The Boy and the Chair's* imaginative descriptions of Zach's fantasies were palpable; I felt as if I were living life through his eyes and escaping his difficulties in school alongside him. Throughout the story, there were countless moments of humor, kindness, and strength. By the end of the book, I was truly inspired.

I highly recommend this book to anyone who appreciates the creativity and resilience of children. In addition to it being an addictively enjoyable read, the main character's unique way of seeing the world brings to light the importance of understanding and respecting young children with special needs.

191. What does the advertisement suggest about the book club?

(A) It discusses three books at each meeting.
(B) It typically gathers once a month.
(C) It has been held in several different bookstores.
(D) It was established by Jayne Friedman.

192. How did Mr. Levine find out about the book club?

(A) By reading a newspaper
(B) By attending a community event
(C) By visiting a Web site
(D) By checking a notice board

193. What is suggested about Ms. Stone?

(A) She owns a local bookstore.
(B) She is the president of a club.
(C) She has recently moved to the area.
(D) She has published several novels.

194. In the review, the word "appreciates" in paragraph 2, line 1, is closest in meaning to

(A) admits
(B) raises
(C) values
(D) estimates

195. What is indicated about Jayne Friedman?

(A) All of her novels have won awards.
(B) She experienced difficulties in school.
(C) She writes science fiction novels.
(D) Her son has special needs.

TEST 14

GO ON TO THE NEXT PAGE

Questions 196-200 refer to the following internal memo, schedule, and e-mail.

To: All RT Technology Employees
From: Wesley Russo, Personnel Manager
Subject: Information Technology Convention

Dear Team,

On May 5, we will be hosting an IT convention at RT Technology's headquarters. Speakers and vendors from all over the world will be arriving to give lectures and share their expertise. In order to reserve a seat, please let me know the session that interests you the most.

The theme of this year's convention is "Inspire & Evolve." You will be able to see and try out all different kinds of technology. Augmented reality is becoming very popular, so there will be many vendors with virtual reality goggles as well as fun new games for you to play. Artificial intelligence is also extremely popular nowadays. ZX Robotics Corporation will even be presenting robots that can clean your house or be your personal assistant! Please note that this will be your last opportunity to hear that company's current CEO speak publicly, as he is retiring from his position in a few months.

Make sure you take the time to review the schedule of lectures and sign up soon to avoid disappointment.

Regards,

Wesley

Information Technology Convention
Saturday, May 5, at RT Technology Headquarters

Lecture Schedule

2:00 Stanley White - "The Future of Artificial Intelligence"
Stanley is the CEO of ZX Robotics Corporation. His lecture includes a history of artificial intelligence (AI) and thoughts on how AI could change the world in our lifetime. He will also be displaying some of his company's products, including his incredibly life-like personal assistant, Violet.

3:00 Georgina Rogers - "Will Virtual Reality Become the New Reality?"
Georgina graduated last year from Massachusetts Institute of Technology (MIT). She currently works for Virtuoso, a company that develops virtual reality software. Her presentation shows how socializing with other people in the future will take place online more often than in person.

4:00 Fred Bradbury - "Integrating IT with Business"
Fred is the CEO of the Seriously Good Food Corporation, which is now earning over 500 million dollars a year. Fred explains how his company is successful by integrating technology with his company's goals. Furthermore, he teaches how to choose the right software for a variety of professional purposes.

To:	Fred Bradbury <fbradbury@sgfcorp.com>
From:	Harry Campbell <hcampbell@wfinc.com>
Subject:	Your Lecture
Date:	May 10

Dear Mr. Bradbury,

I really enjoyed your lecture on integrating IT with a business. Since then, I've spoken to my leadership team about getting new software that could help our employees communicate better with each other online. WorldFoods is a global company, so many of our managers work different hours. Therefore, it is difficult to get everyone together to discuss important topics. I am searching for social networking software that would allow everyone to contribute to discussions at any time, regardless of their location or time zone. If you have any recommendations, I would really appreciate them.

Thank you,

Harry Campbell

196. What does Mr. Russo indicate about the convention?

(A) It is an international event.
(B) Employees will receive a discount.
(C) Event volunteers are required.
(D) He will give the keynote speech.

197. What did Ms. Rogers most likely discuss during her lecture?

(A) Uses for artificial intelligence in the workplace
(B) The history of robotics in the manufacturing industry
(C) How to utilize software to maximize profits
(D) The increasing popularity of online social networking

198. What is indicated about Mr. White?

(A) He was unable to attend the event.
(B) He is a former colleague of Mr. Russo's.
(C) He will demonstrate some virtual reality goggles.
(D) He will leave his company soon.

199. What is the purpose of the e-mail?

(A) To express gratitude for a job offer
(B) To ask for software suggestions
(C) To request more information on a lecture
(D) To suggest some social networking strategies

200. What do Mr. Campbell and Mr. Bradbury have in common?

(A) They are doing business with RT Technology.
(B) They spoke at an IT conference before.
(C) They plan to collaborate on a project.
(D) They work in the food industry.

Stop! This is the end of the test. If you finish before time is called, you may go back to Parts 5, 6, and 7 and check your work.

정답 p.474 / 점수 환산표 p.476

실전모의고사
TEST 15

TEST 15 해설

바로 보기

- 시작 시간 _____시 _____분
- 종료 시간 _____시 _____분

▶ 중간에 멈추지 말고 처음부터 끝까지 풀어보세요. 문제를 풀 때는 실전처럼 답안지에 마킹하세요.

READING TEST

In the Reading test, you will read a variety of texts and answer several different types of reading comprehension questions. The entire Reading test will last 75 minutes. There are three parts, and directions are given for each part. You are encouraged to answer as many questions as possible within the time allowed. You must mark your answers on the separate answer sheet. Do not write your answers in your test book.

PART 5

Directions: A word or phrase is missing in each of the sentences below. Four answer choices are given below each sentence. Select the best answer to complete the sentence. Then mark the letter (A), (B), (C), or (D) on your answer sheet.

101. As discussed over the phone this morning, the delivery will be ------- before the date that you requested.
  (A) informed
  (B) contained
  (C) complied
  (D) completed

102. A lot of corporate managers agree that one of their biggest challenges in the workplace is ------- experienced employees.
  (A) retaining
  (B) retain
  (C) retainer
  (D) retained

103. The annual conference was attended by ------- many people that next year we will find a bigger venue.
  (A) very
  (B) such
  (C) so
  (D) large

104. It is always wise to establish ------- relationships with your coworkers because you may need their help sometime in the future.
  (A) cooperate
  (B) cooperated
  (C) cooperative
  (D) cooperatively

105. The new software program will be simpler and more convenient to operate than previous versions, and will also save valuable time for -------.
  (A) users
  (B) use
  (C) used
  (D) using

106. ------- every piece of correspondence will be sent by e-mail, it is important to check for new messages as often as you can.
  (A) So that
  (B) After
  (C) Unless
  (D) Because

107. Please park only in the ------- areas and display your visitor permit in an easily seen location.
  (A) commended
  (B) prohibited
  (C) returned
  (D) designated

108. The sales figures for all of our retail outlets will be ------- at the year-end gathering at Rutgers Hotel next weekend.
  (A) announce
  (B) announced
  (C) announcing
  (D) announces

109. The job fair will be an important opportunity for meeting with prospective ------- and introducing our company to them.

(A) ranges
(B) opponents
(C) purchases
(D) candidates

110. Please be reminded that all reports will be due ------- the end of the day on Friday the 24th.

(A) on
(B) before
(C) after
(D) within

111. All managers should ensure that employees are fully aware of the rules and regulations of our company ------- in the employee manual in detail.

(A) consisted
(B) insisted
(C) outlined
(D) estimated

112. In order to be effective, the process of training new employees should be performed in an ------- fashion.

(A) organize
(B) organization
(C) organized
(D) organizing

113. ------- absence nor tardiness will be tolerated during the coming week, as this time of year will be the most crucial for our business.

(A) Either
(B) Because
(C) Neither
(D) Both

114. During the holiday season, sales representatives will receive a ------- commission for each new customer they attract and retain.

(A) generate
(B) generous
(C) generously
(D) generating

115. Please join us to celebrate the retirement of George Ramos, who ------- with the company for over twenty years.

(A) have been
(B) has been
(C) having been
(D) is being

116. O'Donnell Industries is considering ------- all of its computers in order to install the new award-winning graphics software.

(A) upgrade
(B) has upgraded
(C) to upgrade
(D) upgrading

117. We regret to inform you that the product you ordered is ------- out of stock, but other similar types are still available.

(A) temporarily
(B) sufficiently
(C) approximately
(D) intentionally

118. After only six months of founding her own retail business, Sarah Mullins had successfully ------- a reputation for providing high-quality goods.

(A) earned
(B) attended
(C) defined
(D) presented

119. Once we have relocated to the downtown office, you will not have many options to choose ------- for traveling to and from the workplace.

(A) within
(B) from
(C) in
(D) about

TEST 15

GO ON TO THE NEXT PAGE

120. A majority of residents of Springdale are ------- in favor of renovating the historic City Hall building in the hope that it will boost local tourism.

(A) overwhelmingly
(B) overwhelming
(C) overwhelms
(D) overwhelm

121. The Canadian Lawyer's Guild is an ------- made up of more than 2,500 individuals who currently practice law throughout Canada.

(A) indication
(B) associate
(C) organization
(D) agreement

122. If you want to ------- your flights online, you will need a credit card and your passport information as well as a valid e-mail address.

(A) reserve
(B) depart
(C) board
(D) travel

123. The new budget approved by the committee will finally ------- the cost of fixing the leaking air conditioner on the second floor.

(A) rely
(B) cover
(C) perform
(D) notify

124. Everyone knew that James was ------- to participate, so they were surprised when he volunteered to give a speech at the year-end banquet.

(A) similar
(B) hopeful
(C) reluctant
(D) talented

125. Because of ------- changes in company policy, all the summer interns are now entitled to one weeks' paid vacation.

(A) high
(B) recent
(C) satisfied
(D) usual

126. We accept returns on items within 30 days of purchase ------- you have your original receipt or another proof of purchase.

(A) as long as
(B) prior to
(C) along with
(D) in case of

127. It was impossible to remove the debris that was left by the storm last night without the ------- of heavy machinery.

(A) assist
(B) assists
(C) assistance
(D) assistant

128. According to doctors, regular physical exercise can help people of almost any age ------- most health problems.

(A) avoid
(B) detect
(C) transmit
(D) develop

129. Those employees ------- for participation in an internal survey on workplace safety should contact Nathan Hammond in the Human Resources Department by Monday.

(A) available
(B) willing
(C) interested
(D) renewable

130. Appo Telecommunications was ------- enough to collaborate with the world's leading smartphone manufacturer on its latest project.

(A) promotional
(B) fortunate
(C) convenient
(D) essential

PART 6

Directions: Read the texts that follow. A word, phrase, or sentence is missing in parts of each text. Four answer choices for each question are given below the text. Select the best answer to complete the text. Then mark the letter (A), (B), (C) or (D) on your answer sheet.

Questions 131-134 refer to the following e-mail.

To: Fred Thomas <fthomas@sjw.org>

From: Paul Lee <paullee@rion.org>

Subject: Documents received

Dear Mr. Thomas,

-------. However, I feel that I need some time to consider and check the data you -------. My financial
  131.   **132.**

team is currently evaluating the figures and other details. I am also assessing the potential profitability

of your plan myself, and I will contact you with the results as soon as they are ready.

Hopefully I can meet with you on March 20 to discuss our potential business relationship. Please let

me know ------- this will be convenient for you or not. If everything seems to be in order, this could
       133.

be the beginning of a ------- beneficial partnership.
               134.

Regards,

Paul Lee

Marketing Director

Rion Inc.

131. (A) Congratulations on your promotion.
    (B) I appreciate your understanding and
        cooperation.
    (C) Please consider my suggestions as a
        good starting point.
    (D) Thank you for your business proposal.

132. (A) reserved
    (B) interviewed
    (C) submitted
    (D) occupied

133. (A) who
    (B) what
    (C) that
    (D) whether

134. (A) precisely
    (B) mutually
    (C) separately
    (D) rarely

GO ON TO THE NEXT PAGE

Questions 135-138 refer to the following memo.

To: All Employees

From: Management

Date: November 10

Re: Computer Program Q&A

It has come to my attention that many members of our staff are having trouble using the new scheduling software that was introduced last week. -------. They have also stated that people are
                                                                                          135.
finding it hard to learn ------- to use the various features of the software.
                          136.

To ------- these problems and make sure everyone can get back on track as quickly as possible, we
   137.
will be having a Q&A session this Thursday. Several of our IT staff members will be there to answer questions and demonstrate the use of several key features of Scheduling Now. They will also be distributing a user manual, which many of you will find extremely helpful.

This session will be held in Room 12 on the third floor at 3:00 P.M. All staff members are required to attend. Our weekly staff meeting will be held at 4:00 P.M. as usual. Adjustment to this new software may take some time, but I am confident you will all ------- agree that Scheduling Now is a powerful
                                                                  138.
and highly intuitive program.

Sincerely,

Stephen Larskey, General Manager

---

135. (A) The department managers have informed me about issues with lost data.
(B) We had some problems with the software but these have been resolved.
(C) Please consult your supervisor if you need further training on customer satisfaction.
(D) Be advised that our ordering system will be down for the rest of the day.

136. (A) only
(B) so
(C) how
(D) yet

137. (A) replace
(B) train
(C) address
(D) expand

138. (A) extremely
(B) formerly
(C) soon
(D) enough

Questions 139-142 refer to the following letter.

February 1

Craig Harbin

121 Burke Road

Parkville, Oregon 92040

Dear Mr. Harbin:

It is my pleasure to recommend Ms. Amanda Jones for the position of laboratory technologist. Ms. Jones worked with me in my chemistry lab while she was a student. After observing Amanda's capabilities first-hand, I simply couldn't imagine working with anyone else. She follows -------, isn't
139.
afraid to ask questions, and keeps her workspace organized. Another positive thing to ------- is that
140.
she has a keen desire to learn.

-------. She earned an A+ in my organic chemistry class and had a 4.0 GPA at the end of her studies.
141.
She graduated with first-class honors. In my personal opinion, Ms. Jones has all the necessary
------- to succeed in this challenging position. If you would like additional information, please feel
142.
free to contact me at 555-4563.

Yours truly,

Dr. Hannah Gardiner

139. (A) directs
(B) directing
(C) director
(D) directions

140. (A) search
(B) note
(C) handle
(D) acquire

141. (A) I can also assure you that Ms. Jones has impressive academic experience.
(B) That being said, her grades do leave much to be desired.
(C) Hiring her may be dependent on her last semester's test results.
(D) I'm confident that she has made a significant contribution to you and your organization.

142. (A) demonstrations
(B) attributes
(C) appraisals
(D) estimates

GO ON TO THE NEXT PAGE

Questions 143-146 refer to the following e-mail.

From: Reggie MacDonald <reg.mcdonald@firstuniversity.com>
To: <manager@housingconnection.com>
Subject: Available Apartments
Date: April 23

Dear sir/madam,

I am writing in ------- to your advertisement in last week's edition of our university newspaper.
    143.

I understand that your company specializes in finding affordable housing options for students, and
I'm interested in using your services. ------- .
    144.

First, I need an apartment that is either within walking distance of the campus or on the bus route,
------- I don't currently own a vehicle. Next, I am hoping to share the rent with two of my friends, so
145.
a three-bedroom apartment would be ideal. Finally, I have a cat at my parents' home that I would
love to take back with me next year. I realize pet-friendly buildings are rare, but if you know of any, I
would appreciate hearing about them.

Please send a reply to this address if you think you could help my friends and I find a suitable place.
I would also need to know what type of ------- you typically charge. I look forward to hearing from
    146.
you.

Sincerely,

Reggie MacDonald

---

143. (A) respond
(B) responses
(C) response
(D) responsive

144. (A) I am pleased with the service so far.
(B) I do have a few criteria.
(C) Thank you for sending the article.
(D) The apartment is ready for inspection.

145. (A) as
(B) though
(C) therefore
(D) due to

146. (A) property
(B) device
(C) fee
(D) position

PART 7

Directions: In this part you will read a selection of texts, such as magazine and newspaper articles, e-mails, and instant messages. Each text or set of texts is followed by several questions. Select the best answer for each question and mark the letter (A), (B), (C), or (D) on your answer sheet.

Questions 147-148 refer to the following memo.

To: Sales team
From: Roberto Sanchez
Date: May 5
Subject: Employee manual

Following a recent meeting, the management team decided that our current employee manual is not fit for its intended purpose. Therefore, we have taken steps to publish a new manual. This will outline many important issues, including training obligations, our new dress code, and changes to working hours. Employees should join us in Conference Room C at 15:00 on May 8 to hear our Human Resources manager deliver a presentation on these changes. Please be punctual so that we can begin on time.

147. What is the purpose of the memo?

(A) To detail a recently revised policy
(B) To describe a training schedule
(C) To ask employees for policy suggestions
(D) To announce the alteration of a document

148. What is the course of action suggested in the memo?

(A) Returning old uniforms
(B) Attending a meeting
(C) Contacting Mr. Sanchez in person
(D) Working longer hours

GO ON TO THE NEXT PAGE

Questions 149-150 refer to the following memo.

Memo

To: All staff
From: Simon Topo
Date: July 28

As I'm sure you are aware, next week is our company retreat. I hope you are ready to travel to the Swiss Alps! I spoke to the travel company this morning and now have final confirmation of our flights. Those at our office in Flaton will fly on August 2 from Denver Airport, arriving the same day. The employees in our New Horseville branch will fly a day later and join other employees already there. This works out as the cheapest way of transporting everyone, and I hope it is convenient for you all.

Regards,

Simon Topo

149. What is the purpose of the memo?
(A) To detail some travel plans
(B) To request confirmation of flight reservations
(C) To announce changes to a retreat venue
(D) To seek volunteers to organize an event

150. What is indicated about the employees from the New Horseville office?
(A) They will require a connecting flight.
(B) They will use cheaper transportation.
(C) They will visit several different locations.
(D) They will arrive after the staff from Flaton.

Questions 151-152 refer to the following text-message chain.

ELLIE SPALDING (9:25 P.M.)
Colin… I'm sorry to tell you this, but I think you'll need to oversee the orientation on your own. I just made an urgent doctor's appointment for 10 A.M.

COLIN GULLIVER (9:27 P.M.)
Oh, are you okay? I'm really counting on you. I don't know enough about our company's health and safety policies.

ELLIE SPALDING (9:29 P.M.)
I'm sorry, it's just not possible. I guess I have the flu. There's no way I'd be able to give a talk, and I don't want anyone else to catch this.

COLIN GULLIVER (9:31 P.M.)
I totally understand! I think I can ask Carol in Personnel to cover for you. And, I'll let our manager know about the situation.

ELLIE SPALDING (9:33 P.M.)
That's really kind of you… thanks. I was afraid that my absence would cause a huge problem with the orientation.

COLIN GULLIVER (9:35 P.M.)
Don't mention it. Just focus on getting well, and I'll see you at the office soon.

ELLIE SPALDING (9:36 P.M.)
Okay. And, if you need me anytime tomorrow, feel free to give me a text or a call.

151. What is suggested about Ms. Spalding?

(A) She has recently been transferred to a different location.
(B) She wants to give a presentation.
(C) She is unable to attend an event tomorrow.
(D) She will meet with Mr. Gulliver in the morning.

152. At 9:35 P.M., what does Mr. Gulliver mean when he writes, "Don't mention it"?

(A) He advises Ms. Spalding to keep some information private.
(B) He wants Ms. Spalding not to worry about the event.
(C) He thinks Ms. Spalding will handle the situation very well.
(D) He will discuss a matter with Ms. Spalding later.

GO ON TO THE NEXT PAGE

Questions 153-154 refer to the following letter.

May 24

Rachel Materazzi
Dulce Vita Restaurant
3B Little Venice Road
Chicago, IL 60609

Dear Ms. Materazzi,

Members of our division recently visited your premises to carry out a routine inspection. We regret to inform you that your restaurant was in violation of the city's Health and Sanitation Code, and this is the third time you failed to comply with the code. So, we have no choice but to revoke your operational permit. This means that you are not able to open your restaurant or serve the public until further notice. We will visit again in two months to inspect your property one more time. I hope you will have addressed all the issues that were detected during the recent inspection. As your business has been a part of the local community for over a decade, it would be a shame to have to order the permanent closure of Dulce Vita.

Regards,

NathanOFord

Nathan Ford
Chief Health Inspector

153. What is the main purpose of the letter?
(A) To notify a tenant of lease termination
(B) To organize an upcoming inspection
(C) To order a restaurant closure
(D) To describe renovations at a restaurant

154. What is indicated about Dulce Vita?
(A) It is running a promotion for the next two months.
(B) It operates in several locations throughout Chicago.
(C) It will resume operation in two months.
(D) It has been in business for at least ten years.

Questions 155-157 refer to the following Web page.

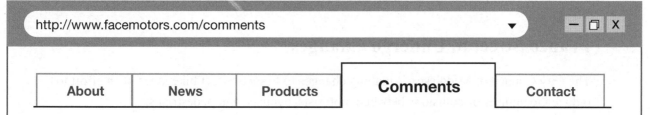

http://www.facemotors.com/comments

| About | News | Products | **Comments** | Contact |

I'm writing to complain about the quality of one of your products, namely the FACE GT-20. My car has been recalled numerous times for things such as poorly-attached seats and poorly designed fuel line couplings, which are both frighteningly dangerous and easily preventable conditions.

As I'm writing this, my car is, once again, at your service center due to a recall. I'm missing yet another day of work so that FACE can correct an EGR valve. This would seem to be a minor thing, but it will take all day to fix, and I must have this corrected and obtain a certificate to renew my car's registration. Once again, I'm faced with paying the penalty for my choice of automobile. Although I explained to the serviceman that it was very important that I get to work and that I was missing work as a result of a defective part, he dismissed me completely with the argument that if they gave everyone a replacement car for the day, they'd have to give out hundreds of cars. As a result, I have no means of transportation and am stuck here in your service center for the duration of the repair work.

John Alfredson

155. What is the purpose of the comment?

(A) To suggest ways to improve a product
(B) To praise a customer service representative
(C) To order replacement automobile parts
(D) To express dissatisfaction with a product

156. What problem does Mr. Alfredson mention?

(A) He cannot afford repair costs.
(B) He must wait several days for parts.
(C) He suffered an injury while driving.
(D) He had to miss a full day of work.

157. According to the comment, what did Mr. Alfredson request from a service center worker?

(A) An apology from an employee
(B) An extended warranty
(C) A temporary vehicle
(D) A discount on repairs

TEST 15

GO ON TO THE NEXT PAGE

Franco Street to Undergo Changes

The City Council of Middlesex is making changes to Franco Street bike lanes in an effort to reduce the number of collisions between motorists, cyclists, and pedestrians.

In the first stage of the plan, Franco Street southbound bike lanes will be painted yellow between the intersection at Richmond Street and the intersection at Lawton Avenue. — [1] —. Also, lines designating the bicycle lanes in both the northbound and southbound directions of Franco Street will be painted thicker, by approximately 15 centimeters, to make the bike lanes more visible to motorists. — [2] —.

The second stage of the plan will see bicycle boxes added to Franco Street at the intersections at Salton Road and Mayfield Street. — [3] —. These will help people riding bikes to make left-hand turns. Bicycle boxes are a fairly new type of on-street marking that enables motorists and cyclists to share the road more safely. The boxes designate a space in front of cars at the red light. Cyclists are permitted to wait in this space and proceed first when the light turns green. — [4] —.

With these changes, the council aims to make bicycle lanes more visible, encourage road users to use extra caution at intersections, and remind turning vehicles to slow down and watch for other road users, including cyclists and pedestrians.

---

158. What is the purpose of the city council's plan?

(A) To alleviate traffic congestion on Franco Street
(B) To reduce the number of bike riders
(C) To decrease the frequency of accidents
(D) To create bicycle-only routes

159. What is mentioned as part of the first stage of the plan?

(A) The addition of bicycle boxes
(B) The widening of road markings
(C) The partial closure of Franco Street
(D) The replacement of old traffic lights

160. In which of the positions marked [1], [2], [3], and [4] does the following sentence best belong?

"Motorists who fail to let cyclists start first will be subject to a fine."

(A) [1]
(B) [2]
(C) [3]
(D) [4]

Questions 161-164 refer to the following online chat discussion.

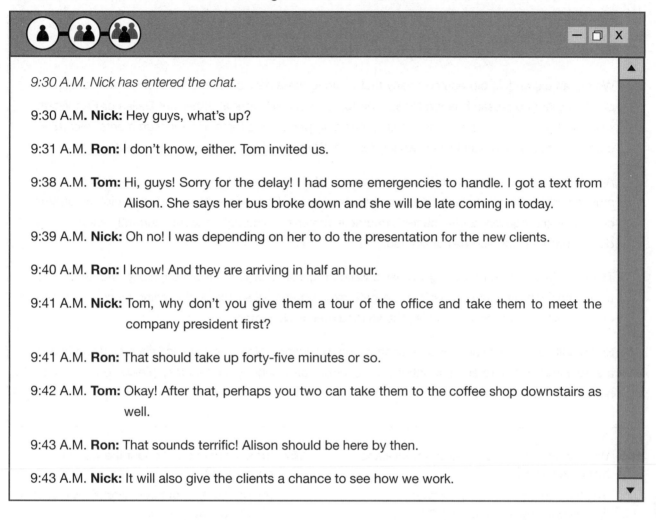

9:30 A.M. *Nick has entered the chat.*

9:30 A.M. **Nick:** Hey guys, what's up?

9:31 A.M. **Ron:** I don't know, either. Tom invited us.

9:38 A.M. **Tom:** Hi, guys! Sorry for the delay! I had some emergencies to handle. I got a text from Alison. She says her bus broke down and she will be late coming in today.

9:39 A.M. **Nick:** Oh no! I was depending on her to do the presentation for the new clients.

9:40 A.M. **Ron:** I know! And they are arriving in half an hour.

9:41 A.M. **Nick:** Tom, why don't you give them a tour of the office and take them to meet the company president first?

9:41 A.M. **Ron:** That should take up forty-five minutes or so.

9:42 A.M. **Tom:** Okay! After that, perhaps you two can take them to the coffee shop downstairs as well.

9:43 A.M. **Ron:** That sounds terrific! Alison should be here by then.

9:43 A.M. **Nick:** It will also give the clients a chance to see how we work.

161. What are the writers mainly discussing?

(A) What to do about a bus route change
(B) Where to have a coffee break
(C) How to handle a schedule delay
(D) When to meet their former coworker

162. When will the clients arrive?

(A) In 15 minutes
(B) In 30 minutes
(C) In 45 minutes
(D) In 60 minutes

163. What does Nick ask Tom to do?

(A) Take the clients to lunch
(B) Give a presentation
(C) Explain a delay
(D) Show the clients around

164. At 9:40 A.M., what does Ron imply when he writes, "I know!"?

(A) He knows how to solve the problem.
(B) He is concerned about a presentation.
(C) He received a text from Alison a moment ago.
(D) He is well prepared for a client meeting.

GO ON TO THE NEXT PAGE

Questions 165-167 refer to the following advertisement.

Lab Techs Required - Vivalabs

We are an expanding biotech company that is hiring three new part-time lab technicians to work in our newly-added research laboratories. The technicians will work at either our Dallas or Fort Worth sites, and will carry out a variety of tasks, including performing tests and measurements, recording data and observation results, and writing reports. Working with animals is not required.

Applicants will be expected to have a minimum of three years of related work experience, which may include medical or chemical laboratory experience. Post-secondary studies in biology and/or chemistry are required, and a master's degree is preferred, although students currently enrolled in a degree program will also be considered.

The work includes some writing, so basic word processing skills are required, along with the ability to use fine instruments and perform delicate experiments. Weekend and evening work is required occasionally and hours are flexible. The starting date is November 4.

Salary will be commensurate with education and experience. Non-compete and secrecy declarations are required. For further information, or to apply and send your résumé, please e-mail us at humanresources@vivalabs.com.

---

165. What is mentioned as a reason for Vivalabs hiring new workers?

(A) Many employees have resigned.
(B) It is opening new facilities.
(C) Sales are expected to increase.
(D) It has recently relocated.

166. What is mentioned as being part of the job?

(A) Transporting lab samples
(B) Leading a field research team
(C) Conducting laboratory tests
(D) Publishing research results

167. What is mentioned about the working conditions?

(A) The number of hours worked will depend on education level.
(B) Successful applicants must work at two different sites.
(C) Research requires various animal tests.
(D) Some overtime work is required.

Questions 168-171 refer to the following letter.

Mr. John Sykes, City Councilor
City Hall,
Farberville, OH 45820

Dear Mr. Sykes,

I would like to inform you of my support for the proposed changes to the traffic flow patterns on Main Street. My restaurant is in the middle of the downtown section and I believe all the businesses there would profit from the changes.

As I understand it, the city is proposing to make the street a one-way street for the four blocks that comprise the downtown. This would include narrowing the street so that angle parking may be instituted, which of course will result in spaces for more cars. The sidewalks may also be widened.

It is my view that there is far too little parking in the downtown area, and anything that can help the situation is to be welcomed. I also believe that encouraging more pedestrian traffic will help boost business. As a mainly tourist town, most of our business depends on casual visitors, and encouraging them to walk around means they notice more and will shop more.

I have several associates in the restaurant industry in the Centennial Square area on the edge of town, and they all report that their business increased when foot traffic was increased. They did this by creating more central parking spaces and instituting pedestrian-only areas. They have also started planting more trees and adding flower boxes.

In view of this, I believe that any changes along these lines would be a good way to spend our property tax dollars, and I ask you to please vote for the proposed changes at the meeting next week.

Thank you for your attention to this matter.

Yours sincerely,

Ronald Green

Ronald Green
Owner, West Side Grill

TEST 15

168. What is suggested about Farberville?

(A) Its parking fees have recently increased.
(B) It attracts a number of visitors.
(C) Many of its businesses are closing.
(D) It has a poor public transportation system.

169. What does Mr. Green think will increase business?

(A) Advertising the town's attractions
(B) Revitalizing all the town parks
(C) Investing in more companies
(D) Encouraging people to walk around

170. What will most likely take place next week?

(A) A city council meeting
(B) Tree and flower planting
(C) Several road modifications
(D) A parking lot development

GO ON TO THE NEXT PAGE

Internship Opportunity

NPP Radio is pleased to announce openings for its fall internship program. NPP interns play an important role in the regular operations in most departments in the company – from music programming to broadcast news. Our interns will assist regular team members while learning new skills in their chosen area. — [1] —.

One of the main features of the NPP internship program is the opportunity for interns to create and produce their own show.

Program Information

Internships occur during the summer, autumn, and winter/spring sessions. Interns work full 40 hours per week during the 12-week summer session and 15 to 40 hours per week during the 18-week autumn and winter/spring sessions. The winter/spring session takes place from January to late March. The summer program begins late May and runs through mid-August. — [2] —. The autumn session takes place from September to December. All programs provide $5.75 per hour. Although interns can obtain academic credit for completing an internship, an agreement between NPP and a participating college is required. — [3] —.

Eligibility

In order to qualify, an applicant must be registered at a recognized post-secondary institute.

How to Apply

Applicants must fill out an internship application form and include a cover letter and résumé with their submission. Depending on the position, additional items such as writing samples may be required. — [4] —.

Application Dates

For the summer session, submissions need to be postmarked by March 1. For the autumn session, submissions need to be postmarked by July 1. For the winter/spring session, submissions must be postmarked by November 1.

171. Who would most likely be interested in the announcement?

(A) Visual arts students
(B) Experienced reporters
(C) Professional musicians
(D) Journalism students

172. What is mentioned about the NPP internship programs?

(A) Every session has the same duration.
(B) Interns will work at various radio stations.
(C) Interns can make their own show.
(D) They have recently won an industry award.

173. What can be asked to include with the application form?

(A) Samples of past work
(B) A letter of recommendation
(C) A copy of a photo ID
(D) A preferred start date

174. What is NOT true about the internship criteria?

(A) Interns receive less money during the fall session.
(B) Interns should attend higher education institutions.
(C) Interns can receive credit recognition from certain colleges.
(D) Interns must work full-time during the summer session.

175. In which of the positions marked [1], [2], [3], and [4] does the following sentence best belong?

"Incomplete application packages will not be considered."

(A) [1]
(B) [2]
(C) [3]
(D) [4]

Memorandum

March 5

Dear Mr. Fielding,

Please make a note that I've scheduled your interview and photo shoot with *Movie Biz* for Wednesday, March 9, at 10:30 A.M. I am amazed at how much media attention your new movie is getting. Last year, *Movie Biz* declined to interview you; this year, they have assigned their top photographer and top writer for the story.

Movie Biz plans to print your article in April, prior to the start of the Star Awards Festival at the end of the month. Alexa Hamilton, the lady who will be interviewing you and writing your story, is likely going to ask you questions about your expectations for the festival. Let's set a time to go over some appropriate responses. I don't want you to tell them how much you want to win that award. We want them to think you're modest.

Johanna Beeson
Publicist for Damien Fielding

Circle of Flames
By Alexa Hamilton

Prior to releasing *Circle of Flames* just last month, Damien Fielding had directed eight films — but none ever received much media attention. Actress Susannah Wallace can be credited with helping to bring Fielding into the spotlight. "I saw *Pieces*, one of his earlier films, and was impressed with his brilliant direction," she said. "I wanted to work with him immediately."

With a well-known actress like Wallace starring in *Circle of Flames*, Fielding has suddenly become famous. According to an entertainment magazine, he is the first choice for the Star Awards Festival's Best Director prize. "I want to be clear that I don't make movies for awards," Fielding comments. "But, of course, I would be honored to receive a Star Award."

Naturally, reviews of *Circle of Flames* have encouraged viewers to re-watch his older films — and they've been pleasantly surprised. Though the films did not do very well at the box office, they exhibit the same high-quality direction as *Circle of Flames*. Fielding is developing a significant following. He is someone from whom we are sure to see great things.

176. Why did Ms. Beeson write a memo to Mr. Fielding?

(A) To inform him that he has won an award
(B) To prepare him for an interview
(C) To advise him on how to pass an audition
(D) To invite him to a film festival

177. When will the article be published?

(A) Before the Star Awards Festival
(B) Before the release of *Circle of Flames*
(C) At the tenth anniversary of *Movie Biz*
(D) During the premiere of *Circle of Flames*

178. What is the purpose of the article?

(A) To celebrate Mr. Fielding's latest film
(B) To explain why Ms. Wallace accepted the role
(C) To promote the Star Awards Festival
(D) To highlight Mr. Fielding's previous films

179. What can be inferred about Mr. Fielding?

(A) He did not feel comfortable during the interview.
(B) He previously worked with Ms. Wallace.
(C) He is already working on a new movie.
(D) He follows the advice of his publicist.

180. In the article, the word "credited" in paragraph 1, line 2, is closest in meaning to

(A) indebted
(B) compensated
(C) recognized
(D) honored

GO ON TO THE NEXT PAGE

Questions 181-185 refer to the following article and letter.

Jarrod Inc. Buys Fluorexco
by Thomas A. Mer

Houston, Texas – Jarrod Inc. today announced that its purchase of Fluorexco, based in Dallas, was being finalized. The sale of the Dallas company has been under discussion for two months, and a final price of $155 million was agreed on.

Jarrod specializes in synthetic fibers used in the manufacturing industry, including those used in furniture, household appliances, automobiles, and plastics for toys and packaging. With its four plants in Texas, it ships a variety of chemicals to manufacturers in both Texas and the northeastern states.

Fluorexco, a privately held company, was founded by Robert McGuinn thirty-five years ago, and has been a leading producer of styrene, ethylene and propylene glycol. The company has been on the market for five years since its founder and owner decided to retire from the business. With no children to take over the company, and no desire to change Fluorexco into a public company, Mr. McGuinn finally decided to sell the company and retire.

Mr. Darryl Hogg, a spokesperson for Jarrod, commented that the acquisition of Fluorexco is a perfect fit for Jarrod since it produces many chemical substances used at various Jarrod sites. In fact, Jarrod was one of Fluorexco's larger customers. "This will streamline our operations, reduce supplier problems, and of course save us money," Mr. Hogg reported.

It is anticipated that there will be little change in staffing at the former Fluorexco sites, with the exception, perhaps, of administrative personnel. Retaining almost all Fluorexco employees was one of the major conditions of the sale agreement. "They have worked hard for me for many years, and I just had to make sure their interests were protected," Mr. McGuinn noted. With this announcement of the sale, the price of Jarrod stock rose by two points today.

Jonathan Dexter, Editor
East Texas Chemical News
4598 Galveston Road
Dallas, TX 88796

Dear Mr. Dexter,

I would like to draw your attention to an article in your latest issue. The reporter is normally very thorough with his research, and I typically enjoy reading his articles, but I'm afraid his latest piece contained a few errors.

In the article, it was stated that Fluorexco makes propylene glycol, among other things. This is not true: we have never sold that product. Please make a correction in a future issue so that our rival companies do not harass our sales force for a chemical we do not produce. The writer also mistook our CEO's name. It was Ronald McGuinn who has headed Fluorexco, not Robert McGuinn. If you have any further questions, please call me at 913-555-0128.

Sincerely,

Maria Aniston

Maria Aniston, Assistant to Ronald McGuinn, Fluorexco

181. What does Jarrod Inc. produce?

(A) Toys made of plastic
(B) Household furniture
(C) Chemical products
(D) Automobile parts

182. Who most likely is Darryl Hogg?

(A) A business merger specialist
(B) A public relations worker
(C) A company president
(D) An independent journalist

183. What is NOT mentioned as an advantage of purchasing Fluorexco?

(A) Cost savings
(B) More secure supplies
(C) Overseas expansion
(D) More effective operations

184. Why did Ms. Aniston write to *East Texas Chemical News*?

(A) To ask for extra issues of the paper
(B) To give them an exclusive press release
(C) To explain Mr. McGuinn's decision to retire
(D) To request that errors be corrected

185. What is indicated about Ms. Aniston?

(A) She writes critical reviews on business pages.
(B) She is familiar with Mr. Mer's past work.
(C) She was interviewed by Mr. Mer.
(D) She is leading a sales team.

GO ON TO THE NEXT PAGE

Top Three Things to See in Loyola City

The Unity Monument

The Unity Monument is a gift of friendship to the United States from Mexico. It is symbolic of the two countries' strong economic relationship. The Unity Monument was dedicated in 1897. It became a national monument in 1931. It is located on Unity Island, so you must take a ferry to get there.

The Wilfred Trust Building

The Wilfred Trust Building is one of the most famous skyscrapers in the world. You can see all of Loyola City from the top of it. This gorgeous skyscraper has been featured in many TV shows and movies, such as *The Great Diamond Heist* in 1977. No trip to Loyola is complete without visiting the Wilfred Trust Building.

SKY Revolving Restaurant

SKY Revolving Restaurant, or SKY 360 for short, is located on the 70th floor of the SKY Media Tower and has incredible views of the Wilfred Trust Building and Mayfield Park. The KBC Studio is located on the ground floor of the SKY Media Tower. TV shows such as *Live Tonight With Matt Fisher* and *The Lisa Riley Show* are recorded there.

E-Mail Message

To:	Cathy Miller <cmiller@regiscorp.com>
From:	Francoise Bruni <fbruni@regiscorp.com>
Subject:	Our Upcoming Trip
Date:	April 17

Hi Cathy,

I am so excited about our trip to Loyola City next week. I know that we need to focus on the presentation we're giving to the potential distributors on the 24th, but I'm hoping we will have time to see some of the local sights the following day before we take our return flight.

I would love to see the Unity Monument, the Wilfred Trust Building, and SKY 360. However, the Unity Monument is located a bit far from the other two. Perhaps we should stick to midtown Loyola for the day. If we stick to midtown, we could do some shopping at Vernon Plaza, grab something to eat, and explore Mayfield Park. We might even be able to catch up with our old coworker, Steve. He moved to Loyola last year, remember? What are your thoughts?

We could also consider joining a small group tour, such as those offered by Happy Bus Tours. It will be more expensive than navigating the city on our own, but at least we can be sure that we will make the most of our short amount of free time there.

Thanks,

Francoise

Happy Bus Tours Review

Customer: Cathy Miller
Date of Tour: April 27
Score: ★★★★★

I was very pleased with the Happy Bus Tour that my colleague and I took of midtown Loyola City. I had never heard of the "Hop On, Hop Off" style of tour until now, and I was so happy to have an easy way to get around the city. Our bus stopped at all the major attractions in the midtown area, and our tour guide was knowledgeable and entertaining. In fact, our tour guide pointed out a celebrity in front of the KBC Studio who was happy to pose for photos. I would never have recognized him without the help of our incredible tour guide. It was such a memorable experience and I highly recommend this company.

186. What is indicated about The Unity Monument?

(A) It became a national monument when it was dedicated.
(B) It is located near midtown Loyola City.
(C) Travelers must take a boat ride to see it.
(D) It was given by the United States in 1897.

187. What is the main purpose of Ms.Bruni and Ms. Miller's trip to Loyola City?

(A) To attend an international convention
(B) To visit a former colleague
(C) To enjoy some sightseeing
(D) To have a business meeting

188. What does Ms. Bruni imply in her e-mail to Ms. Miller?

(A) The Unity Monument is temporarily closed.
(B) They have a limited amount of free time.
(C) Tours are not likely within their travel budget.
(D) An event will take place in Mayfield Park.

189. What did Ms. Bruni and Ms. Miller most likely NOT do during their trip?

(A) Shop at Vernon Plaza
(B) Visit Unity Island
(C) Participate in a bus tour
(D) Visit Mayfield Park

190. Where did Ms. Bruni and Ms. Miller see a celebrity?

(A) Outside the SKY Media Tower
(B) Near the Wilfred Trust Building
(C) In the SKY 360 Revolving Restaurant
(D) In Mayfield Park

GO ON TO THE NEXT PAGE

Questions 191-195 refer to the following advertisement, social media post, and private message.

Joan Rochester Presents . . .
A Ladies Charity Fashion Show
Stoneybrook Hall, White Water Lily Street
Friday, November 19
Doors open 6:30 P.M.

Tickets $15.00
RSVP to Joan Rochester (732) 555-0129

Please join us at our yearly fashion event!

- Fall and winter seasonal trends will be available from local clothing shops.
- Each guest will receive a complimentary glass of wine and a selection of appetizers.
- Live entertainment and photographers will be there to make the night fun and unforgettable.

We look forward to seeing you there!

Katie Mitchell shared Joan Rochester's event.

November 11, 11:09 A.M.

Hi everyone. My dear friend and colleague Joan Rochester is hosting a charity fashion show at Stoneybrook Hall on November 19. Tickets cost only ten dollars, and 100% of proceeds will go towards the Sunday Soup Kitchen, a volunteer organization that helps to support homeless and less fortunate people who are struggling in their journey towards a better life. Personally, I have been volunteering at Sunday Soup Kitchen for six years by handing out food to the homeless on a weekly basis. I have seen many volunteers put an incredible amount of hard work into improving the living conditions of many people in our community.

This event will not only be enjoyable, but it will make a world of difference. 100% of your money will be put to great use. Please join us!

Private Message From: Jessica Smith

November 11, 3:04 P.M.

Hi Katie. I saw your post about the charity fashion show and I am interested in purchasing a ticket. The Sunday Soup Kitchen sounds like a wonderful organization, and I am inspired by your long-term involvement with them. Unfortunately, I do not know anyone else who will be attending the show. Would it be possible to go together? I would be happy to help set up, clean up, or lend a hand in any way that is needed. Please let me know.

In addition to the fashion show, I would like to help out in other ways. I have been extremely busy with my job for a long time, but my schedule has finally opened up in a way that I am available to do volunteer work similar to yours. I would appreciate it if you could introduce me to someone at the show who could arrange this.

Looking forward to hearing from you. Thanks.

— Jessica

191. What is suggested about the fashion show?

(A) It is a contest for local designers.
(B) It will be held by the Sunday Soup Kitchen.
(C) It occurs once per year.
(D) It will be broadcast online.

192. What information does Katie state incorrectly in her social media post?

(A) The location of the event
(B) The date of the event
(C) The identity of the event host
(D) The price of event tickets

193. What will the money collected from ticket sales be used for?

(A) Establishing a charitable foundation
(B) Funding future fashion shows
(C) Repairing Stoneybrook Hall
(D) Helping people in need

194. According to the private message, what would Ms. Smith like to do in her free time?

(A) Assist event staff
(B) Solicit donations
(C) Serve meals
(D) Contribute money

195. In the private message, the word "available" in paragraph 2, line 2, is closest in meaning to

(A) ready
(B) obtainable
(C) vacant
(D) usable

GO ON TO THE NEXT PAGE

Questions 196-200 refer to the following e-mails and task list.

To:	All Staff
From:	Matthew Scott, CEO
Subject:	Employee Announcement
Date:	September 2

Dear Staff:

Please join me in welcoming Tim Solomon. He graduated from Aldershot University in May with degrees in marketing and business. He is enthusiastic about the work we do here at Beyond Veggies, and he is looking forward to coordinating the marketing services for our vegetarian products. In his personal life, he is a vegetarian and environmental activist, so we are excited to see him harness his passions and skills to promote our products to the world.

Tim will be working as a full-time market research assistant in our marketing department and will be reporting directly to Sarah Viggiano. His official mentor will be Aisha Mahmood, so you can find him in the marketing wing right next to Aisha. I have attached Tim's picture to this e-mail so you will be able to recognize and greet him when you see him.

Best wishes,

Matthew Scott

Task List – Monday, September 3

Tim:

Here is a list of your tasks this week. I look forward to our Friday lunch meeting so that I can catch up with you and see how you're doing. Please contact Aisha if you have any questions before then.

Thanks,

Sarah

- Organize Aisha's market research on a daily basis and put it into the database.
- Call clients on our list for promotional events and note whether they plan to attend upcoming events.
- Analyze questionnaires that were completed by New Jersey clients on 5/14.
- Write marketing materials and begin to prepare digital campaigns for social media.

To:	Aisha Mahmood
From:	Tim Solomon
Subject:	Questions and Lunch Meeting
Date:	Monday, September 3

Dear Aisha,

I have some questions regarding one of the tasks recently assigned to me by Sarah, but I haven't seen you at your desk all morning. With this being my first day, I have yet to undergo training on the company's database, so there are several things I'm having difficulty with. Would you be able to give me a quick tutorial on how to use the database, especially about how to add and modify information?

Also, I bumped into the CEO's personal assistant, Ian Jacobs, and he informed me that the CEO would like to take me out for lunch on September 5. I just wanted to consult with you first and make sure you didn't have anything else planned for me on that day. If you could also ask Ms. Viggiano, that would be appreciated.

I hope to hear from you soon. Thank you very much in advance.

Tim Solomon

---

196. What is indicated about Tim Solomon in the first e-mail?

(A) His department supervisor is Aisha Mahmood.
(B) He is passionate about the environment.
(C) He is enjoying Beyond Veggies' products.
(D) He has experience working in the field.

197. What can be inferred about Sarah Viggiano?

(A) She has a supervisory role in the Marketing Department.
(B) She will provide Mr. Solomon with daily feedback during his first week.
(C) She leads staff training sessions on a monthly basis.
(D) She is responsible for recruitment at Beyond Veggies.

198. What is indicated about Mr. Solomon new position?

(A) He will work closely with the owners of health food stores.
(B) He must call clients in order to sell products.
(C) His desk is located next to Ms. Viggiano's office.
(D) He promotes vegetarian products on social media.

199. What task is Mr. Solomon most likely having difficulty with?

(A) Organizing research
(B) Calling clients
(C) Analyzing surveys
(D) Creating marketing materials

200. Who will Mr. Solomon have lunch with on Wednesday?

(A) Ms. Viggiano
(B) Mr. Scott
(C) Ms. Mahmood
(D) Mr. Jacobs

Stop! This is the end of the test. If you finish before time is called, you may go back to Parts 5, 6, and 7 and check your work.

정답 p.475 / 점수 환산표 p.476

TEST 15

정답

TEST 1

PART 5

101. (A) **102.** (A) **103.** (A) **104.** (A) **105.** (C) **106.** (C) **107.** (C) **108.** (A) **109.** (B) **110.** (D) **111.** (A) **112.** (A)
113. (C) **114.** (C) **115.** (C) **116.** (B) **117.** (D) **118.** (C) **119.** (A) **120.** (B) **121.** (D) **122.** (D) **123.** (B) **124.** (D)
125. (B) **126.** (D) **127.** (A) **128.** (A) **129.** (D) **130.** (C)

PART 6

131. (A) **132.** (C) **133.** (B) **134.** (B) **135.** (D) **136.** (B) **137.** (D) **138.** (C) **139.** (C) **140.** (A) **141.** (B) **142.** (D)
143. (B) **144.** (B) **145.** (B) **146.** (D)

PART 7

147. (D) **148.** (C) **149.** (C) **150.** (A) **151.** (D) **152.** (B) **153.** (C) **154.** (B) **155.** (A) **156.** (B) **157.** (C) **158.** (D)
159. (C) **160.** (D) **161.** (A) **162.** (D) **163.** (B) **164.** (C) **165.** (B) **166.** (D) **167.** (D) **168.** (B) **169.** (A) **170.** (D)
171. (C) **172.** (C) **173.** (D) **174.** (B) **175.** (C) **176.** (A) **177.** (D) **178.** (C) **179.** (D) **180.** (D) **181.** (B) **182.** (D)
183. (D) **184.** (C) **185.** (D) **186.** (B) **187.** (A) **188.** (C) **189.** (B) **190.** (D) **191.** (B) **192.** (A) **193.** (C) **194.** (A)
195. (D) **196.** (C) **197.** (C) **198.** (D) **199.** (C) **200.** (A)

TEST 2

PART 5

101. (C) **102.** (C) **103.** (D) **104.** (C) **105.** (A) **106.** (C) **107.** (B) **108.** (C) **109.** (A) **110.** (C) **111.** (B) **112.** (B)
113. (B) **114.** (A) **115.** (B) **116.** (C) **117.** (A) **118.** (D) **119.** (A) **120.** (D) **121.** (D) **122.** (B) **123.** (C) **124.** (C)
125. (D) **126.** (A) **127.** (C) **128.** (C) **129.** (D) **130.** (D)

PART 6

131. (A) **132.** (C) **133.** (B) **134.** (D) **135.** (D) **136.** (B) **137.** (D) **138.** (B) **139.** (D) **140.** (C) **141.** (A) **142.** (B)
143. (B) **144.** (C) **145.** (A) **146.** (D)

PART 7

147. (D) **148.** (D) **149.** (D) **150.** (A) **151.** (D) **152.** (C) **153.** (C) **154.** (A) **155.** (A) **156.** (C) **157.** (B) **158.** (C)
159. (B) **160.** (B) **161.** (B) **162.** (C) **163.** (B) **164.** (B) **165.** (D) **166.** (B) **167.** (C) **168.** (C) **169.** (B) **170.** (B)
171. (D) **172.** (C) **173.** (A) **174.** (B) **175.** (B) **176.** (A) **177.** (B) **178.** (C) **179.** (B) **180.** (A) **181.** (D) **182.** (C)
183. (D) **184.** (B) **185.** (A) **186.** (D) **187.** (A) **188.** (C) **189.** (B) **190.** (C) **191.** (D) **192.** (C) **193.** (B) **194.** (C)
195. (D) **196.** (C) **197.** (C) **198.** (D) **199.** (C) **200.** (D)

TEST 3

PART 5

101. (D) **102.** (B) **103.** (C) **104.** (C) **105.** (A) **106.** (B) **107.** (D) **108.** (B) **109.** (B) **110.** (A) **111.** (B) **112.** (C)
113. (B) **114.** (B) **115.** (A) **116.** (B) **117.** (C) **118.** (A) **119.** (D) **120.** (B) **121.** (A) **122.** (C) **123.** (D) **124.** (A)
125. (B) **126.** (D) **127.** (C) **128.** (D) **129.** (D) **130.** (A)

PART 6

131. (C) **132.** (B) **133.** (A) **134.** (D) **135.** (D) **136.** (B) **137.** (D) **138.** (A) **139.** (C) **140.** (C) **141.** (B) **142.** (D)
143. (A) **144.** (C) **145.** (D) **146.** (D)

PART 7

147. (B) **148.** (C) **149.** (B) **150.** (A) **151.** (D) **152.** (C) **153.** (B) **154.** (A) **155.** (D) **156.** (B) **157.** (D) **158.** (D)
159. (B) **160.** (A) **161.** (C) **162.** (C) **163.** (D) **164.** (B) **165.** (A) **166.** (D) **167.** (B) **168.** (C) **169.** (C) **170.** (B)
171. (A) **172.** (B) **173.** (B) **174.** (B) **175.** (A) **176.** (D) **177.** (A) **178.** (B) **179.** (C) **180.** (D) **181.** (D) **182.** (D)
183. (B) **184.** (D) **185.** (D) **186.** (C) **187.** (B) **188.** (A) **189.** (B) **190.** (C) **191.** (B) **192.** (B) **193.** (D) **194.** (C)
195. (D) **196.** (D) **197.** (C) **198.** (B) **199.** (B) **200.** (C)

TEST 4

PART 5

101. (A) **102.** (A) **103.** (A) **104.** (B) **105.** (B) **106.** (D) **107.** (C) **108.** (D) **109.** (B) **110.** (B) **111.** (C) **112.** (A)
113. (A) **114.** (B) **115.** (C) **116.** (B) **117.** (C) **118.** (C) **119.** (D) **120.** (B) **121.** (A) **122.** (D) **123.** (B) **124.** (A)
125. (C) **126.** (D) **127.** (D) **128.** (B) **129.** (A) **130.** (A)

PART 6

131. (C) **132.** (A) **133.** (D) **134.** (C) **135.** (D) **136.** (C) **137.** (A) **138.** (D) **139.** (B) **140.** (D) **141.** (C) **142.** (A)
143. (B) **144.** (B) **145.** (A) **146.** (A)

PART 7

147. (D) **148.** (B) **149.** (C) **150.** (B) **151.** (C) **152.** (C) **153.** (C) **154.** (A) **155.** (D) **156.** (C) **157.** (B) **158.** (B)
159. (D) **160.** (A) **161.** (D) **162.** (D) **163.** (A) **164.** (D) **165.** (A) **166.** (D) **167.** (A) **168.** (D) **169.** (B) **170.** (B)
171. (A) **172.** (D) **173.** (B) **174.** (A) **175.** (C) **176.** (C) **177.** (D) **178.** (C) **179.** (A) **180.** (C) **181.** (A) **182.** (B)
183. (B) **184.** (C) **185.** (D) **186.** (C) **187.** (D) **188.** (B) **189.** (D) **190.** (A) **191.** (D) **192.** (B) **193.** (B) **194.** (A)
195. (D) **196.** (A) **197.** (C) **198.** (B) **199.** (D) **200.** (C)

TEST 5

PART 5

101. (B) **102.** (D) **103.** (C) **104.** (A) **105.** (D) **106.** (C) **107.** (D) **108.** (A) **109.** (A) **110.** (D) **111.** (A) **112.** (C) **113.** (B) **114.** (D) **115.** (B) **116.** (D) **117.** (A) **118.** (C) **119.** (D) **120.** (A) **121.** (D) **122.** (A) **123.** (A) **124.** (A) **125.** (A) **126.** (C) **127.** (C) **128.** (A) **129.** (A) **130.** (A)

PART 6

131. (A) **132.** (C) **133.** (C) **134.** (C) **135.** (B) **136.** (D) **137.** (A) **138.** (B) **139.** (B) **140.** (D) **141.** (A) **142.** (D) **143.** (D) **144.** (B) **145.** (A) **146.** (D)

PART 7

147. (B) **148.** (D) **149.** (B) **150.** (D) **151.** (D) **152.** (B) **153.** (A) **154.** (C) **155.** (B) **156.** (B) **157.** (B) **158.** (B) **159.** (A) **160.** (C) **161.** (A) **162.** (D) **163.** (D) **164.** (B) **165.** (D) **166.** (B) **167.** (B) **168.** (D) **169.** (B) **170.** (A) **171.** (D) **172.** (A) **173.** (D) **174.** (A) **175.** (C) **176.** (B) **177.** (C) **178.** (A) **179.** (B) **180.** (D) **181.** (B) **182.** (A) **183.** (A) **184.** (C) **185.** (D) **186.** (A) **187.** (B) **188.** (D) **189.** (D) **190.** (B) **191.** (B) **192.** (C) **193.** (B) **194.** (D) **195.** (C) **196.** (C) **197.** (D) **198.** (C) **199.** (B) **200.** (D)

TEST 6

PART 5

101. (A) **102.** (C) **103.** (A) **104.** (B) **105.** (D) **106.** (D) **107.** (D) **108.** (D) **109.** (D) **110.** (B) **111.** (A) **112.** (D) **113.** (A) **114.** (D) **115.** (B) **116.** (D) **117.** (A) **118.** (B) **119.** (D) **120.** (C) **121.** (D) **122.** (C) **123.** (B) **124.** (D) **125.** (D) **126.** (D) **127.** (C) **128.** (C) **129.** (B) **130.** (C)

PART 6

131. (C) **132.** (A) **133.** (A) **134.** (B) **135.** (D) **136.** (A) **137.** (B) **138.** (C) **139.** (D) **140.** (A) **141.** (C) **142.** (D) **143.** (A) **144.** (B) **145.** (B) **146.** (D)

PART 7

147. (D) **148.** (A) **149.** (D) **150.** (A) **151.** (D) **152.** (A) **153.** (C) **154.** (C) **155.** (C) **156.** (C) **157.** (A) **158.** (D) **159.** (B) **160.** (B) **161.** (B) **162.** (D) **163.** (B) **164.** (D) **165.** (C) **166.** (B) **167.** (C) **168.** (A) **169.** (B) **170.** (B) **171.** (A) **172.** (B) **173.** (C) **174.** (B) **175.** (D) **176.** (A) **177.** (B) **178.** (D) **179.** (D) **180.** (C) **181.** (C) **182.** (D) **183.** (D) **184.** (C) **185.** (C) **186.** (D) **187.** (B) **188.** (D) **189.** (B) **190.** (C) **191.** (C) **192.** (B) **193.** (A) **194.** (D) **195.** (B) **196.** (C) **197.** (B) **198.** (B) **199.** (D) **200.** (D)

TEST 7

PART 5

101. (C) **102.** (B) **103.** (C) **104.** (C) **105.** (A) **106.** (A) **107.** (C) **108.** (C) **109.** (C) **110.** (C) **111.** (C) **112.** (D)
113. (B) **114.** (A) **115.** (B) **116.** (B) **117.** (C) **118.** (D) **119.** (D) **120.** (C) **121.** (C) **122.** (D) **123.** (C) **124.** (A)
125. (D) **126.** (A) **127.** (B) **128.** (C) **129.** (D) **130.** (B)

PART 6

131. (B) **132.** (A) **133.** (A) **134.** (D) **135.** (A) **136.** (B) **137.** (C) **138.** (C) **139.** (C) **140.** (B) **141.** (D) **142.** (B)
143. (B) **144.** (D) **145.** (A) **146.** (A)

PART 7

147. (C) **148.** (B) **149.** (B) **150.** (A) **151.** (C) **152.** (B) **153.** (D) **154.** (A) **155.** (B) **156.** (D) **157.** (B) **158.** (C)
159. (B) **160.** (D) **161.** (C) **162.** (A) **163.** (B) **164.** (A) **165.** (B) **166.** (D) **167.** (B) **168.** (B) **169.** (C) **170.** (D)
171. (C) **172.** (C) **173.** (D) **174.** (C) **175.** (B) **176.** (A) **177.** (B) **178.** (D) **179.** (C) **180.** (C) **181.** (C) **182.** (D)
183. (C) **184.** (C) **185.** (A) **186.** (A) **187.** (D) **188.** (C) **189.** (C) **190.** (B) **191.** (C) **192.** (B) **193.** (D) **194.** (C)
195. (A) **196.** (B) **197.** (C) **198.** (D) **199.** (C) **200.** (A)

TEST 8

PART 5

101. (A) **102.** (A) **103.** (D) **104.** (A) **105.** (D) **106.** (A) **107.** (C) **108.** (A) **109.** (A) **110.** (B) **111.** (B) **112.** (D)
113. (A) **114.** (B) **115.** (D) **116.** (D) **117.** (D) **118.** (B) **119.** (D) **120.** (A) **121.** (B) **122.** (D) **123.** (C) **124.** (B)
125. (D) **126.** (D) **127.** (D) **128.** (B) **129.** (D) **130.** (B)

PART 6

131. (D) **132.** (C) **133.** (B) **134.** (B) **135.** (B) **136.** (D) **137.** (C) **138.** (D) **139.** (C) **140.** (A) **141.** (D) **142.** (B)
143. (C) **144.** (D) **145.** (B) **146.** (A)

PART 7

147. (B) **148.** (D) **149.** (A) **150.** (C) **151.** (C) **152.** (B) **153.** (B) **154.** (D) **155.** (D) **156.** (C) **157.** (A) **158.** (C)
159. (B) **160.** (A) **161.** (B) **162.** (D) **163.** (C) **164.** (A) **165.** (C) **166.** (A) **167.** (D) **168.** (D) **169.** (B) **170.** (C)
171. (A) **172.** (B) **173.** (A) **174.** (A) **175.** (B) **176.** (D) **177.** (C) **178.** (B) **179.** (C) **180.** (A) **181.** (B) **182.** (D)
183. (B) **184.** (B) **185.** (C) **186.** (C) **187.** (D) **188.** (A) **189.** (C) **190.** (C) **191.** (A) **192.** (B) **193.** (D) **194.** (C)
195. (D) **196.** (C) **197.** (A) **198.** (B) **199.** (C) **200.** (C)

TEST 9

TEST 10

TEST 11

PART 5

101. (D) **102.** (B) **103.** (B) **104.** (A) **105.** (B) **106.** (C) **107.** (C) **108.** (D) **109.** (D) **110.** (B) **111.** (D) **112.** (C) **113.** (C) **114.** (A) **115.** (B) **116.** (D) **117.** (A) **118.** (A) **119.** (A) **120.** (B) **121.** (C) **122.** (A) **123.** (C) **124.** (D) **125.** (D) **126.** (D) **127.** (D) **128.** (B) **129.** (A) **130.** (C)

PART 6

131. (D) **132.** (C) **133.** (B) **134.** (A) **135.** (A) **136.** (D) **137.** (A) **138.** (D) **139.** (A) **140.** (B) **141.** (A) **142.** (A) **143.** (B) **144.** (D) **145.** (A) **146.** (D)

PART 7

147. (A) **148.** (B) **149.** (D) **150.** (B) **151.** (A) **152.** (D) **153.** (D) **154.** (B) **155.** (C) **156.** (B) **157.** (B) **158.** (D) **159.** (B) **160.** (B) **161.** (D) **162.** (C) **163.** (A) **164.** (B) **165.** (C) **166.** (A) **167.** (B) **168.** (D) **169.** (D) **170.** (D) **171.** (C) **172.** (A) **173.** (C) **174.** (C) **175.** (C) **176.** (A) **177.** (A) **178.** (D) **179.** (B) **180.** (A) **181.** (C) **182.** (A) **183.** (A) **184.** (A) **185.** (A) **186.** (A) **187.** (B) **188.** (C) **189.** (D) **190.** (C) **191.** (B) **192.** (D) **193.** (B) **194.** (C) **195.** (C) **196.** (C) **197.** (D) **198.** (C) **199.** (C) **200.** (B)

TEST 12

PART 5

101. (D) **102.** (A) **103.** (D) **104.** (A) **105.** (C) **106.** (B) **107.** (C) **108.** (D) **109.** (C) **110.** (B) **111.** (A) **112.** (B) **113.** (A) **114.** (C) **115.** (A) **116.** (C) **117.** (B) **118.** (D) **119.** (A) **120.** (B) **121.** (D) **122.** (B) **123.** (C) **124.** (B) **125.** (D) **126.** (A) **127.** (C) **128.** (A) **129.** (C) **130.** (C)

PART 6

131. (B) **132.** (D) **133.** (D) **134.** (D) **135.** (C) **136.** (A) **137.** (C) **138.** (C) **139.** (D) **140.** (D) **141.** (B) **142.** (A) **143.** (D) **144.** (A) **145.** (B) **146.** (C)

PART 7

147. (B) **148.** (B) **149.** (B) **150.** (D) **151.** (D) **152.** (A) **153.** (C) **154.** (C) **155.** (B) **156.** (D) **157.** (C) **158.** (C) **159.** (C) **160.** (D) **161.** (A) **162.** (C) **163.** (D) **164.** (D) **165.** (A) **166.** (B) **167.** (B) **168.** (C) **169.** (D) **170.** (B) **171.** (B) **172.** (B) **173.** (C) **174.** (B) **175.** (B) **176.** (C) **177.** (D) **178.** (C) **179.** (A) **180.** (D) **181.** (C) **182.** (A) **183.** (D) **184.** (C) **185.** (B) **186.** (C) **187.** (C) **188.** (B) **189.** (A) **190.** (D) **191.** (D) **192.** (C) **193.** (C) **194.** (A) **195.** (C) **196.** (D) **197.** (B) **198.** (C) **199.** (A) **200.** (C)

TEST 13

PART 5

101. (C) **102.** (B) **103.** (B) **104.** (B) **105.** (D) **106.** (A) **107.** (B) **108.** (D) **109.** (B) **110.** (A) **111.** (B) **112.** (B) **113.** (D) **114.** (B) **115.** (A) **116.** (B) **117.** (C) **118.** (C) **119.** (D) **120.** (C) **121.** (A) **122.** (B) **123.** (C) **124.** (A) **125.** (D) **126.** (A) **127.** (C) **128.** (D) **129.** (D) **130.** (A)

PART 6

131. (B) **132.** (D) **133.** (B) **134.** (A) **135.** (D) **136.** (D) **137.** (B) **138.** (B) **139.** (B) **140.** (D) **141.** (C) **142.** (D) **143.** (B) **144.** (D) **145.** (B) **146.** (A)

PART 7

147. (B) **148.** (C) **149.** (A) **150.** (A) **151.** (B) **152.** (B) **153.** (A) **154.** (D) **155.** (D) **156.** (B) **157.** (A) **158.** (B) **159.** (D) **160.** (B) **161.** (D) **162.** (C) **163.** (C) **164.** (B) **165.** (D) **166.** (A) **167.** (A) **168.** (B) **169.** (A) **170.** (B) **171.** (C) **172.** (D) **173.** (B) **174.** (C) **175.** (D) **176.** (C) **177.** (A) **178.** (A) **179.** (C) **180.** (D) **181.** (D) **182.** (A) **183.** (B) **184.** (D) **185.** (C) **186.** (D) **187.** (C) **188.** (A) **189.** (B) **190.** (B) **191.** (D) **192.** (C) **193.** (A) **194.** (C) **195.** (B) **196.** (D) **197.** (A) **198.** (D) **199.** (C) **200.** (C)

TEST 14

PART 5

101. (B) **102.** (C) **103.** (D) **104.** (A) **105.** (D) **106.** (B) **107.** (D) **108.** (C) **109.** (D) **110.** (D) **111.** (A) **112.** (B) **113.** (D) **114.** (D) **115.** (A) **116.** (B) **117.** (A) **118.** (A) **119.** (D) **120.** (A) **121.** (A) **122.** (A) **123.** (C) **124.** (A) **125.** (A) **126.** (A) **127.** (B) **128.** (B) **129.** (A) **130.** (B)

PART 6

131. (C) **132.** (A) **133.** (A) **134.** (A) **135.** (B) **136.** (C) **137.** (A) **138.** (D) **139.** (C) **140.** (A) **141.** (C) **142.** (B) **143.** (B) **144.** (C) **145.** (B) **146.** (D)

PART 7

147. (A) **148.** (D) **149.** (C) **150.** (D) **151.** (C) **152.** (B) **153.** (B) **154.** (A) **155.** (B) **156.** (D) **157.** (C) **158.** (D) **159.** (C) **160.** (D) **161.** (D) **162.** (B) **163.** (C) **164.** (D) **165.** (A) **166.** (C) **167.** (A) **168.** (C) **169.** (B) **170.** (B) **171.** (D) **172.** (C) **173.** (B) **174.** (D) **175.** (D) **176.** (B) **177.** (A) **178.** (C) **179.** (A) **180.** (D) **181.** (B) **182.** (D) **183.** (C) **184.** (A) **185.** (B) **186.** (D) **187.** (A) **188.** (A) **189.** (B) **190.** (B) **191.** (B) **192.** (D) **193.** (B) **194.** (C) **195.** (D) **196.** (A) **197.** (D) **198.** (D) **199.** (B) **200.** (D)

TEST 15

PART 5

101. (D) **102.** (A) **103.** (C) **104.** (C) **105.** (A) **106.** (D) **107.** (D) **108.** (B) **109.** (D) **110.** (B) **111.** (C) **112.** (C)
113. (C) **114.** (B) **115.** (B) **116.** (D) **117.** (A) **118.** (A) **119.** (B) **120.** (A) **121.** (C) **122.** (A) **123.** (B) **124.** (C)
125. (B) **126.** (A) **127.** (C) **128.** (A) **129.** (A) **130.** (B)

PART 6

131. (D) **132.** (C) **133.** (D) **134.** (B) **135.** (A) **136.** (C) **137.** (C) **138.** (C) **139.** (D) **140.** (B) **141.** (A) **142.** (B)
143. (C) **144.** (B) **145.** (A) **146.** (C)

PART 7

147. (D) **148.** (B) **149.** (A) **150.** (D) **151.** (C) **152.** (B) **153.** (C) **154.** (D) **155.** (D) **156.** (D) **157.** (C) **158.** (C)
159. (B) **160.** (D) **161.** (C) **162.** (B) **163.** (D) **164.** (B) **165.** (B) **166.** (C) **167.** (D) **168.** (B) **169.** (D) **170.** (A)
171. (D) **172.** (C) **173.** (A) **174.** (A) **175.** (D) **176.** (B) **177.** (A) **178.** (A) **179.** (D) **180.** (C) **181.** (C) **182.** (B)
183. (C) **184.** (D) **185.** (B) **186.** (C) **187.** (D) **188.** (B) **189.** (B) **190.** (A) **191.** (C) **192.** (D) **193.** (D) **194.** (C)
195. (A) **196.** (B) **197.** (A) **198.** (D) **199.** (A) **200.** (B)

TOEIC 점수 환산표 [RC]

맞은 개수 (틀린 개수)	RC 점수	맞은 개수 (틀린 개수)	RC 점수	맞은 개수 (틀린 개수)	RC 점수
100 (0)	495	66 (−34)	275–280	32 (−68)	90–100
99 (−1)	485–495	65 (−35)	270–280	31 (−69)	85–95
98 (−2)	480–490	64 (−36)	265–275	30 (−70)	80–90
97 (−3)	475–485	63 (−37)	260–270	29 (−71)	80–90
96 (−4)	470–480	62 (−38)	255–265	28 (−72)	75–85
95 (−5)	460–470	61 (−39)	245–255	27 (−73)	75–85
94 (−6)	450–460	60 (−40)	240–250	26 (−74)	70–80
93 (−7)	440–450	59 (−41)	235–245	25 (−75)	60–70
92 (−8)	430–440	58 (−42)	230–240	24 (−76)	60–70
91 (−9)	420–430	57 (−43)	225–235	23 (−77)	55–65
90 (−10)	415–425	56 (−44)	215–225	22 (−78)	50–60
89 (−11)	410–420	55 (−45)	210–220	21 (−79)	45–55
88 (−12)	405–415	54 (−46)	205–215	20 (−80)	45–55
87 (−13)	395–405	53 (−47)	200–210	19 (−81)	45–55
86 (−14)	390–400	52 (−48)	195–205	18 (−82)	40–50
85 (−15)	385–395	51 (−49)	185–195	17 (−83)	40–50
84 (−16)	380–390	50 (−50)	180–190	16 (−84)	35–45
83 (−17)	375–385	49 (−51)	175–185	15 (−85)	35–45
82 (−18)	370–380	48 (−52)	170–180	14 (−86)	30–40
81 (−19)	365–375	47 (−53)	165–175	13 (−87)	30–40
80 (−20)	360–370	46 (−54)	160–170	12 (−88)	20–30
79 (−21)	350–360	45 (−55)	155–165	11 (−89)	20–30
78 (−22)	345–355	44 (−56)	150–160	10 (−90)	20–30
77 (−23)	340–350	43 (−57)	145–155	9 (−91)	20–30
76 (−24)	335–345	42 (−58)	140–150	8 (−92)	10–20
75 (−25)	330–340	41 (−59)	130–140	7 (−93)	10–20
74 (−26)	320–330	40 (−60)	125–135	6 (−94)	10–20
73 (−27)	315–325	39 (−61)	120–130	5 (−95)	5–10
72 (−28)	310–320	38 (−62)	115–125	4 (−96)	5–10
71 (−29)	305–315	37 (−63)	110–120	3 (−97)	5
70 (−30)	300–310	36 (−64)	105–115	2 (−98)	5
69 (−31)	290–300	35 (−65)	100–110	1 (−99)	5
68 (−32)	285–295	34 (−66)	95–115	0 (−100)	5
67 (−33)	280–290	33 (−67)	90–100		

ANSWER
SHEET

모의고사 답안지입니다.
절취하여 실제 시험처럼
마킹하면서 풀어보세요.

답안지가 더 필요할 경우
시원스쿨랩(lab.siwonschool.com)
홈페이지의 교재 자료실에서
다운로드 받아 사용하세요.

ANSWER SHEET

시원스쿨 LAB

이름 　　　　 테스트 회차 　　　　 날짜

LISTENING COMPREHENSION (PART 1~4)

NO	ANSWER (A B C D)	NO	ANSWER (A B C D)	NO	ANSWER (A B C D)	NO	ANSWER (A B C D)	NO	ANSWER (A B C D)
1	ⓐ ⓑ ⓒ ⓓ	21	ⓐ ⓑ ⓒ ⓓ	41	ⓐ ⓑ ⓒ ⓓ	61	ⓐ ⓑ ⓒ ⓓ	81	ⓐ ⓑ ⓒ ⓓ
2	ⓐ ⓑ ⓒ ⓓ	22	ⓐ ⓑ ⓒ ⓓ	42	ⓐ ⓑ ⓒ ⓓ	62	ⓐ ⓑ ⓒ ⓓ	82	ⓐ ⓑ ⓒ ⓓ
3	ⓐ ⓑ ⓒ ⓓ	23	ⓐ ⓑ ⓒ ⓓ	43	ⓐ ⓑ ⓒ ⓓ	63	ⓐ ⓑ ⓒ ⓓ	83	ⓐ ⓑ ⓒ ⓓ
4	ⓐ ⓑ ⓒ ⓓ	24	ⓐ ⓑ ⓒ ⓓ	44	ⓐ ⓑ ⓒ ⓓ	64	ⓐ ⓑ ⓒ ⓓ	84	ⓐ ⓑ ⓒ ⓓ
5	ⓐ ⓑ ⓒ ⓓ	25	ⓐ ⓑ ⓒ ⓓ	45	ⓐ ⓑ ⓒ ⓓ	65	ⓐ ⓑ ⓒ ⓓ	85	ⓐ ⓑ ⓒ ⓓ
6	ⓐ ⓑ ⓒ ⓓ	26	ⓐ ⓑ ⓒ ⓓ	46	ⓐ ⓑ ⓒ ⓓ	66	ⓐ ⓑ ⓒ ⓓ	86	ⓐ ⓑ ⓒ ⓓ
7	ⓐ ⓑ ⓒ ⓓ	27	ⓐ ⓑ ⓒ ⓓ	47	ⓐ ⓑ ⓒ ⓓ	67	ⓐ ⓑ ⓒ ⓓ	87	ⓐ ⓑ ⓒ ⓓ
8	ⓐ ⓑ ⓒ ⓓ	28	ⓐ ⓑ ⓒ ⓓ	48	ⓐ ⓑ ⓒ ⓓ	68	ⓐ ⓑ ⓒ ⓓ	88	ⓐ ⓑ ⓒ ⓓ
9	ⓐ ⓑ ⓒ ⓓ	29	ⓐ ⓑ ⓒ ⓓ	49	ⓐ ⓑ ⓒ ⓓ	69	ⓐ ⓑ ⓒ ⓓ	89	ⓐ ⓑ ⓒ ⓓ
10	ⓐ ⓑ ⓒ ⓓ	30	ⓐ ⓑ ⓒ ⓓ	50	ⓐ ⓑ ⓒ ⓓ	70	ⓐ ⓑ ⓒ ⓓ	90	ⓐ ⓑ ⓒ ⓓ
11	ⓐ ⓑ ⓒ ⓓ	31	ⓐ ⓑ ⓒ ⓓ	51	ⓐ ⓑ ⓒ ⓓ	71	ⓐ ⓑ ⓒ ⓓ	91	ⓐ ⓑ ⓒ ⓓ
12	ⓐ ⓑ ⓒ ⓓ	32	ⓐ ⓑ ⓒ ⓓ	52	ⓐ ⓑ ⓒ ⓓ	72	ⓐ ⓑ ⓒ ⓓ	92	ⓐ ⓑ ⓒ ⓓ
13	ⓐ ⓑ ⓒ ⓓ	33	ⓐ ⓑ ⓒ ⓓ	53	ⓐ ⓑ ⓒ ⓓ	73	ⓐ ⓑ ⓒ ⓓ	93	ⓐ ⓑ ⓒ ⓓ
14	ⓐ ⓑ ⓒ ⓓ	34	ⓐ ⓑ ⓒ ⓓ	54	ⓐ ⓑ ⓒ ⓓ	74	ⓐ ⓑ ⓒ ⓓ	94	ⓐ ⓑ ⓒ ⓓ
15	ⓐ ⓑ ⓒ ⓓ	35	ⓐ ⓑ ⓒ ⓓ	55	ⓐ ⓑ ⓒ ⓓ	75	ⓐ ⓑ ⓒ ⓓ	95	ⓐ ⓑ ⓒ ⓓ
16	ⓐ ⓑ ⓒ ⓓ	36	ⓐ ⓑ ⓒ ⓓ	56	ⓐ ⓑ ⓒ ⓓ	76	ⓐ ⓑ ⓒ ⓓ	96	ⓐ ⓑ ⓒ ⓓ
17	ⓐ ⓑ ⓒ ⓓ	37	ⓐ ⓑ ⓒ ⓓ	57	ⓐ ⓑ ⓒ ⓓ	77	ⓐ ⓑ ⓒ ⓓ	97	ⓐ ⓑ ⓒ ⓓ
18	ⓐ ⓑ ⓒ ⓓ	38	ⓐ ⓑ ⓒ ⓓ	58	ⓐ ⓑ ⓒ ⓓ	78	ⓐ ⓑ ⓒ ⓓ	98	ⓐ ⓑ ⓒ ⓓ
19	ⓐ ⓑ ⓒ ⓓ	39	ⓐ ⓑ ⓒ ⓓ	59	ⓐ ⓑ ⓒ ⓓ	79	ⓐ ⓑ ⓒ ⓓ	99	ⓐ ⓑ ⓒ ⓓ
20	ⓐ ⓑ ⓒ ⓓ	40	ⓐ ⓑ ⓒ ⓓ	60	ⓐ ⓑ ⓒ ⓓ	80	ⓐ ⓑ ⓒ ⓓ	100	ⓐ ⓑ ⓒ ⓓ

READING COMPREHENSION (PART 5~7)

NO	ANSWER (A B C D)	NO	ANSWER (A B C D)	NO	ANSWER (A B C D)	NO	ANSWER (A B C D)	NO	ANSWER (A B C D)
101	ⓐ ⓑ ⓒ ⓓ	121	ⓐ ⓑ ⓒ ⓓ	141	ⓐ ⓑ ⓒ ⓓ	161	ⓐ ⓑ ⓒ ⓓ	181	ⓐ ⓑ ⓒ ⓓ
102	ⓐ ⓑ ⓒ ⓓ	122	ⓐ ⓑ ⓒ ⓓ	142	ⓐ ⓑ ⓒ ⓓ	162	ⓐ ⓑ ⓒ ⓓ	182	ⓐ ⓑ ⓒ ⓓ
103	ⓐ ⓑ ⓒ ⓓ	123	ⓐ ⓑ ⓒ ⓓ	143	ⓐ ⓑ ⓒ ⓓ	163	ⓐ ⓑ ⓒ ⓓ	183	ⓐ ⓑ ⓒ ⓓ
104	ⓐ ⓑ ⓒ ⓓ	124	ⓐ ⓑ ⓒ ⓓ	144	ⓐ ⓑ ⓒ ⓓ	164	ⓐ ⓑ ⓒ ⓓ	184	ⓐ ⓑ ⓒ ⓓ
105	ⓐ ⓑ ⓒ ⓓ	125	ⓐ ⓑ ⓒ ⓓ	145	ⓐ ⓑ ⓒ ⓓ	165	ⓐ ⓑ ⓒ ⓓ	185	ⓐ ⓑ ⓒ ⓓ
106	ⓐ ⓑ ⓒ ⓓ	126	ⓐ ⓑ ⓒ ⓓ	146	ⓐ ⓑ ⓒ ⓓ	166	ⓐ ⓑ ⓒ ⓓ	186	ⓐ ⓑ ⓒ ⓓ
107	ⓐ ⓑ ⓒ ⓓ	127	ⓐ ⓑ ⓒ ⓓ	147	ⓐ ⓑ ⓒ ⓓ	167	ⓐ ⓑ ⓒ ⓓ	187	ⓐ ⓑ ⓒ ⓓ
108	ⓐ ⓑ ⓒ ⓓ	128	ⓐ ⓑ ⓒ ⓓ	148	ⓐ ⓑ ⓒ ⓓ	168	ⓐ ⓑ ⓒ ⓓ	188	ⓐ ⓑ ⓒ ⓓ
109	ⓐ ⓑ ⓒ ⓓ	129	ⓐ ⓑ ⓒ ⓓ	149	ⓐ ⓑ ⓒ ⓓ	169	ⓐ ⓑ ⓒ ⓓ	189	ⓐ ⓑ ⓒ ⓓ
110	ⓐ ⓑ ⓒ ⓓ	130	ⓐ ⓑ ⓒ ⓓ	150	ⓐ ⓑ ⓒ ⓓ	170	ⓐ ⓑ ⓒ ⓓ	190	ⓐ ⓑ ⓒ ⓓ
111	ⓐ ⓑ ⓒ ⓓ	131	ⓐ ⓑ ⓒ ⓓ	151	ⓐ ⓑ ⓒ ⓓ	171	ⓐ ⓑ ⓒ ⓓ	191	ⓐ ⓑ ⓒ ⓓ
112	ⓐ ⓑ ⓒ ⓓ	132	ⓐ ⓑ ⓒ ⓓ	152	ⓐ ⓑ ⓒ ⓓ	172	ⓐ ⓑ ⓒ ⓓ	192	ⓐ ⓑ ⓒ ⓓ
113	ⓐ ⓑ ⓒ ⓓ	133	ⓐ ⓑ ⓒ ⓓ	153	ⓐ ⓑ ⓒ ⓓ	173	ⓐ ⓑ ⓒ ⓓ	193	ⓐ ⓑ ⓒ ⓓ
114	ⓐ ⓑ ⓒ ⓓ	134	ⓐ ⓑ ⓒ ⓓ	154	ⓐ ⓑ ⓒ ⓓ	174	ⓐ ⓑ ⓒ ⓓ	194	ⓐ ⓑ ⓒ ⓓ
115	ⓐ ⓑ ⓒ ⓓ	135	ⓐ ⓑ ⓒ ⓓ	155	ⓐ ⓑ ⓒ ⓓ	175	ⓐ ⓑ ⓒ ⓓ	195	ⓐ ⓑ ⓒ ⓓ
116	ⓐ ⓑ ⓒ ⓓ	136	ⓐ ⓑ ⓒ ⓓ	156	ⓐ ⓑ ⓒ ⓓ	176	ⓐ ⓑ ⓒ ⓓ	196	ⓐ ⓑ ⓒ ⓓ
117	ⓐ ⓑ ⓒ ⓓ	137	ⓐ ⓑ ⓒ ⓓ	157	ⓐ ⓑ ⓒ ⓓ	177	ⓐ ⓑ ⓒ ⓓ	197	ⓐ ⓑ ⓒ ⓓ
118	ⓐ ⓑ ⓒ ⓓ	138	ⓐ ⓑ ⓒ ⓓ	158	ⓐ ⓑ ⓒ ⓓ	178	ⓐ ⓑ ⓒ ⓓ	198	ⓐ ⓑ ⓒ ⓓ
119	ⓐ ⓑ ⓒ ⓓ	139	ⓐ ⓑ ⓒ ⓓ	159	ⓐ ⓑ ⓒ ⓓ	179	ⓐ ⓑ ⓒ ⓓ	199	ⓐ ⓑ ⓒ ⓓ
120	ⓐ ⓑ ⓒ ⓓ	140	ⓐ ⓑ ⓒ ⓓ	160	ⓐ ⓑ ⓒ ⓓ	180	ⓐ ⓑ ⓒ ⓓ	200	ⓐ ⓑ ⓒ ⓓ

ANSWER SHEET

시원스쿨 LAB

이름 | 테스트 횟차 | 날짜

LISTENING COMPREHENSION (PART 1~4)

NO	ANSWER A B C D	NO	ANSWER A B C D	NO	ANSWER A B C D	NO	ANSWER A B C D	NO	ANSWER A B C D
1	ⓐ ⓑ ⓒ ⓓ	21	ⓐ ⓑ ⓒ ⓓ	41	ⓐ ⓑ ⓒ ⓓ	61	ⓐ ⓑ ⓒ ⓓ	81	ⓐ ⓑ ⓒ ⓓ
2	ⓐ ⓑ ⓒ ⓓ	22	ⓐ ⓑ ⓒ ⓓ	42	ⓐ ⓑ ⓒ ⓓ	62	ⓐ ⓑ ⓒ ⓓ	82	ⓐ ⓑ ⓒ ⓓ
3	ⓐ ⓑ ⓒ ⓓ	23	ⓐ ⓑ ⓒ ⓓ	43	ⓐ ⓑ ⓒ ⓓ	63	ⓐ ⓑ ⓒ ⓓ	83	ⓐ ⓑ ⓒ ⓓ
4	ⓐ ⓑ ⓒ ⓓ	24	ⓐ ⓑ ⓒ ⓓ	44	ⓐ ⓑ ⓒ ⓓ	64	ⓐ ⓑ ⓒ ⓓ	84	ⓐ ⓑ ⓒ ⓓ
5	ⓐ ⓑ ⓒ ⓓ	25	ⓐ ⓑ ⓒ ⓓ	45	ⓐ ⓑ ⓒ ⓓ	65	ⓐ ⓑ ⓒ ⓓ	85	ⓐ ⓑ ⓒ ⓓ
6	ⓐ ⓑ ⓒ ⓓ	26	ⓐ ⓑ ⓒ ⓓ	46	ⓐ ⓑ ⓒ ⓓ	66	ⓐ ⓑ ⓒ ⓓ	86	ⓐ ⓑ ⓒ ⓓ
7	ⓐ ⓑ ⓒ	27	ⓐ ⓑ ⓒ ⓓ	47	ⓐ ⓑ ⓒ ⓓ	67	ⓐ ⓑ ⓒ ⓓ	87	ⓐ ⓑ ⓒ ⓓ
8	ⓐ ⓑ ⓒ	28	ⓐ ⓑ ⓒ ⓓ	48	ⓐ ⓑ ⓒ ⓓ	68	ⓐ ⓑ ⓒ ⓓ	88	ⓐ ⓑ ⓒ ⓓ
9	ⓐ ⓑ ⓒ	29	ⓐ ⓑ ⓒ ⓓ	49	ⓐ ⓑ ⓒ ⓓ	69	ⓐ ⓑ ⓒ ⓓ	89	ⓐ ⓑ ⓒ ⓓ
10	ⓐ ⓑ ⓒ	30	ⓐ ⓑ ⓒ ⓓ	50	ⓐ ⓑ ⓒ ⓓ	70	ⓐ ⓑ ⓒ ⓓ	90	ⓐ ⓑ ⓒ ⓓ
11	ⓐ ⓑ ⓒ	31	ⓐ ⓑ ⓒ ⓓ	51	ⓐ ⓑ ⓒ ⓓ	71	ⓐ ⓑ ⓒ ⓓ	91	ⓐ ⓑ ⓒ ⓓ
12	ⓐ ⓑ ⓒ	32	ⓐ ⓑ ⓒ ⓓ	52	ⓐ ⓑ ⓒ ⓓ	72	ⓐ ⓑ ⓒ ⓓ	92	ⓐ ⓑ ⓒ ⓓ
13	ⓐ ⓑ ⓒ	33	ⓐ ⓑ ⓒ ⓓ	53	ⓐ ⓑ ⓒ ⓓ	73	ⓐ ⓑ ⓒ ⓓ	93	ⓐ ⓑ ⓒ ⓓ
14	ⓐ ⓑ ⓒ	34	ⓐ ⓑ ⓒ ⓓ	54	ⓐ ⓑ ⓒ ⓓ	74	ⓐ ⓑ ⓒ ⓓ	94	ⓐ ⓑ ⓒ ⓓ
15	ⓐ ⓑ ⓒ	35	ⓐ ⓑ ⓒ ⓓ	55	ⓐ ⓑ ⓒ ⓓ	75	ⓐ ⓑ ⓒ ⓓ	95	ⓐ ⓑ ⓒ ⓓ
16	ⓐ ⓑ ⓒ	36	ⓐ ⓑ ⓒ ⓓ	56	ⓐ ⓑ ⓒ ⓓ	76	ⓐ ⓑ ⓒ ⓓ	96	ⓐ ⓑ ⓒ ⓓ
17	ⓐ ⓑ ⓒ	37	ⓐ ⓑ ⓒ ⓓ	57	ⓐ ⓑ ⓒ ⓓ	77	ⓐ ⓑ ⓒ ⓓ	97	ⓐ ⓑ ⓒ ⓓ
18	ⓐ ⓑ ⓒ	38	ⓐ ⓑ ⓒ ⓓ	58	ⓐ ⓑ ⓒ ⓓ	78	ⓐ ⓑ ⓒ ⓓ	98	ⓐ ⓑ ⓒ ⓓ
19	ⓐ ⓑ ⓒ	39	ⓐ ⓑ ⓒ ⓓ	59	ⓐ ⓑ ⓒ ⓓ	79	ⓐ ⓑ ⓒ ⓓ	99	ⓐ ⓑ ⓒ ⓓ
20	ⓐ ⓑ ⓒ	40	ⓐ ⓑ ⓒ ⓓ	60	ⓐ ⓑ ⓒ ⓓ	80	ⓐ ⓑ ⓒ ⓓ	100	ⓐ ⓑ ⓒ ⓓ

READING COMPREHENSION (PART 5~7)

NO	ANSWER A B C D	NO	ANSWER A B C D	NO	ANSWER A B C D	NO	ANSWER A B C D	NO	ANSWER A B C D
101	ⓐ ⓑ ⓒ ⓓ	121	ⓐ ⓑ ⓒ ⓓ	141	ⓐ ⓑ ⓒ ⓓ	161	ⓐ ⓑ ⓒ ⓓ	181	ⓐ ⓑ ⓒ ⓓ
102	ⓐ ⓑ ⓒ ⓓ	122	ⓐ ⓑ ⓒ ⓓ	142	ⓐ ⓑ ⓒ ⓓ	162	ⓐ ⓑ ⓒ ⓓ	182	ⓐ ⓑ ⓒ ⓓ
103	ⓐ ⓑ ⓒ ⓓ	123	ⓐ ⓑ ⓒ ⓓ	143	ⓐ ⓑ ⓒ ⓓ	163	ⓐ ⓑ ⓒ ⓓ	183	ⓐ ⓑ ⓒ ⓓ
104	ⓐ ⓑ ⓒ ⓓ	124	ⓐ ⓑ ⓒ ⓓ	144	ⓐ ⓑ ⓒ ⓓ	164	ⓐ ⓑ ⓒ ⓓ	184	ⓐ ⓑ ⓒ ⓓ
105	ⓐ ⓑ ⓒ ⓓ	125	ⓐ ⓑ ⓒ ⓓ	145	ⓐ ⓑ ⓒ ⓓ	165	ⓐ ⓑ ⓒ ⓓ	185	ⓐ ⓑ ⓒ ⓓ
106	ⓐ ⓑ ⓒ ⓓ	126	ⓐ ⓑ ⓒ ⓓ	146	ⓐ ⓑ ⓒ ⓓ	166	ⓐ ⓑ ⓒ ⓓ	186	ⓐ ⓑ ⓒ ⓓ
107	ⓐ ⓑ ⓒ ⓓ	127	ⓐ ⓑ ⓒ ⓓ	147	ⓐ ⓑ ⓒ ⓓ	167	ⓐ ⓑ ⓒ ⓓ	187	ⓐ ⓑ ⓒ ⓓ
108	ⓐ ⓑ ⓒ ⓓ	128	ⓐ ⓑ ⓒ ⓓ	148	ⓐ ⓑ ⓒ ⓓ	168	ⓐ ⓑ ⓒ ⓓ	188	ⓐ ⓑ ⓒ ⓓ
109	ⓐ ⓑ ⓒ ⓓ	129	ⓐ ⓑ ⓒ ⓓ	149	ⓐ ⓑ ⓒ ⓓ	169	ⓐ ⓑ ⓒ ⓓ	189	ⓐ ⓑ ⓒ ⓓ
110	ⓐ ⓑ ⓒ ⓓ	130	ⓐ ⓑ ⓒ ⓓ	150	ⓐ ⓑ ⓒ ⓓ	170	ⓐ ⓑ ⓒ ⓓ	190	ⓐ ⓑ ⓒ ⓓ
111	ⓐ ⓑ ⓒ ⓓ	131	ⓐ ⓑ ⓒ ⓓ	151	ⓐ ⓑ ⓒ ⓓ	171	ⓐ ⓑ ⓒ ⓓ	191	ⓐ ⓑ ⓒ ⓓ
112	ⓐ ⓑ ⓒ ⓓ	132	ⓐ ⓑ ⓒ ⓓ	152	ⓐ ⓑ ⓒ ⓓ	172	ⓐ ⓑ ⓒ ⓓ	192	ⓐ ⓑ ⓒ ⓓ
113	ⓐ ⓑ ⓒ ⓓ	133	ⓐ ⓑ ⓒ ⓓ	153	ⓐ ⓑ ⓒ ⓓ	173	ⓐ ⓑ ⓒ ⓓ	193	ⓐ ⓑ ⓒ ⓓ
114	ⓐ ⓑ ⓒ ⓓ	134	ⓐ ⓑ ⓒ ⓓ	154	ⓐ ⓑ ⓒ ⓓ	174	ⓐ ⓑ ⓒ ⓓ	194	ⓐ ⓑ ⓒ ⓓ
115	ⓐ ⓑ ⓒ ⓓ	135	ⓐ ⓑ ⓒ ⓓ	155	ⓐ ⓑ ⓒ ⓓ	175	ⓐ ⓑ ⓒ ⓓ	195	ⓐ ⓑ ⓒ ⓓ
116	ⓐ ⓑ ⓒ ⓓ	136	ⓐ ⓑ ⓒ ⓓ	156	ⓐ ⓑ ⓒ ⓓ	176	ⓐ ⓑ ⓒ ⓓ	196	ⓐ ⓑ ⓒ ⓓ
117	ⓐ ⓑ ⓒ ⓓ	137	ⓐ ⓑ ⓒ ⓓ	157	ⓐ ⓑ ⓒ ⓓ	177	ⓐ ⓑ ⓒ ⓓ	197	ⓐ ⓑ ⓒ ⓓ
118	ⓐ ⓑ ⓒ ⓓ	138	ⓐ ⓑ ⓒ ⓓ	158	ⓐ ⓑ ⓒ ⓓ	178	ⓐ ⓑ ⓒ ⓓ	198	ⓐ ⓑ ⓒ ⓓ
119	ⓐ ⓑ ⓒ ⓓ	139	ⓐ ⓑ ⓒ ⓓ	159	ⓐ ⓑ ⓒ ⓓ	179	ⓐ ⓑ ⓒ ⓓ	199	ⓐ ⓑ ⓒ ⓓ
120	ⓐ ⓑ ⓒ ⓓ	140	ⓐ ⓑ ⓒ ⓓ	160	ⓐ ⓑ ⓒ ⓓ	180	ⓐ ⓑ ⓒ ⓓ	200	ⓐ ⓑ ⓒ ⓓ

ANSWER SHEET

시원스쿨 LAB

이름   테스트 호차   날짜   날짜

LISTENING COMPREHENSION (PART 1~4)

NO	ANSWER (A B C D)	NO	ANSWER (A B C D)	NO	ANSWER (A B C D)	NO	ANSWER (A B C D)
1	ⓐ ⓑ ⓒ ⓓ	21	ⓐ ⓑ ⓒ	41	ⓐ ⓑ ⓒ ⓓ	61	ⓐ ⓑ ⓒ ⓓ
2	ⓐ ⓑ ⓒ ⓓ	22	ⓐ ⓑ ⓒ	42	ⓐ ⓑ ⓒ ⓓ	62	ⓐ ⓑ ⓒ ⓓ
3	ⓐ ⓑ ⓒ ⓓ	23	ⓐ ⓑ ⓒ	43	ⓐ ⓑ ⓒ ⓓ	63	ⓐ ⓑ ⓒ ⓓ
4	ⓐ ⓑ ⓒ ⓓ	24	ⓐ ⓑ ⓒ	44	ⓐ ⓑ ⓒ ⓓ	64	ⓐ ⓑ ⓒ ⓓ
5	ⓐ ⓑ ⓒ ⓓ	25	ⓐ ⓑ ⓒ	45	ⓐ ⓑ ⓒ ⓓ	65	ⓐ ⓑ ⓒ ⓓ
6	ⓐ ⓑ ⓒ ⓓ	26	ⓐ ⓑ ⓒ	46	ⓐ ⓑ ⓒ ⓓ	66	ⓐ ⓑ ⓒ ⓓ
7	ⓐ ⓑ ⓒ ⓓ	27	ⓐ ⓑ ⓒ	47	ⓐ ⓑ ⓒ ⓓ	67	ⓐ ⓑ ⓒ ⓓ
8	ⓐ ⓑ ⓒ ⓓ	28	ⓐ ⓑ ⓒ	48	ⓐ ⓑ ⓒ ⓓ	68	ⓐ ⓑ ⓒ ⓓ
9	ⓐ ⓑ ⓒ ⓓ	29	ⓐ ⓑ ⓒ	49	ⓐ ⓑ ⓒ ⓓ	69	ⓐ ⓑ ⓒ ⓓ
10	ⓐ ⓑ ⓒ ⓓ	30	ⓐ ⓑ ⓒ	50	ⓐ ⓑ ⓒ ⓓ	70	ⓐ ⓑ ⓒ ⓓ
11	ⓐ ⓑ ⓒ ⓓ	31	ⓐ ⓑ ⓒ	51	ⓐ ⓑ ⓒ ⓓ	71	ⓐ ⓑ ⓒ ⓓ
12	ⓐ ⓑ ⓒ ⓓ	32	ⓐ ⓑ ⓒ	52	ⓐ ⓑ ⓒ ⓓ	72	ⓐ ⓑ ⓒ ⓓ
13	ⓐ ⓑ ⓒ ⓓ	33	ⓐ ⓑ ⓒ	53	ⓐ ⓑ ⓒ ⓓ	73	ⓐ ⓑ ⓒ ⓓ
14	ⓐ ⓑ ⓒ ⓓ	34	ⓐ ⓑ ⓒ	54	ⓐ ⓑ ⓒ ⓓ	74	ⓐ ⓑ ⓒ ⓓ
15	ⓐ ⓑ ⓒ ⓓ	35	ⓐ ⓑ ⓒ	55	ⓐ ⓑ ⓒ ⓓ	75	ⓐ ⓑ ⓒ ⓓ
16	ⓐ ⓑ ⓒ ⓓ	36	ⓐ ⓑ ⓒ	56	ⓐ ⓑ ⓒ ⓓ	76	ⓐ ⓑ ⓒ ⓓ
17	ⓐ ⓑ ⓒ ⓓ	37	ⓐ ⓑ ⓒ	57	ⓐ ⓑ ⓒ ⓓ	77	ⓐ ⓑ ⓒ ⓓ
18	ⓐ ⓑ ⓒ ⓓ	38	ⓐ ⓑ ⓒ	58	ⓐ ⓑ ⓒ ⓓ	78	ⓐ ⓑ ⓒ ⓓ
19	ⓐ ⓑ ⓒ ⓓ	39	ⓐ ⓑ ⓒ	59	ⓐ ⓑ ⓒ ⓓ	79	ⓐ ⓑ ⓒ ⓓ
20	ⓐ ⓑ ⓒ ⓓ	40	ⓐ ⓑ ⓒ	60	ⓐ ⓑ ⓒ ⓓ	80	ⓐ ⓑ ⓒ ⓓ

READING COMPREHENSION (PART 5~7)

NO	ANSWER (A B C D)	NO	ANSWER (A B C D)	NO	ANSWER (A B C D)	NO	ANSWER (A B C D)
81	ⓐ ⓑ ⓒ ⓓ	101	ⓐ ⓑ ⓒ ⓓ	121	ⓐ ⓑ ⓒ ⓓ	141	ⓐ ⓑ ⓒ ⓓ
82	ⓐ ⓑ ⓒ ⓓ	102	ⓐ ⓑ ⓒ ⓓ	122	ⓐ ⓑ ⓒ ⓓ	142	ⓐ ⓑ ⓒ ⓓ
83	ⓐ ⓑ ⓒ ⓓ	103	ⓐ ⓑ ⓒ ⓓ	123	ⓐ ⓑ ⓒ ⓓ	143	ⓐ ⓑ ⓒ ⓓ
84	ⓐ ⓑ ⓒ ⓓ	104	ⓐ ⓑ ⓒ ⓓ	124	ⓐ ⓑ ⓒ ⓓ	144	ⓐ ⓑ ⓒ ⓓ
85	ⓐ ⓑ ⓒ ⓓ	105	ⓐ ⓑ ⓒ ⓓ	125	ⓐ ⓑ ⓒ ⓓ	145	ⓐ ⓑ ⓒ ⓓ
86	ⓐ ⓑ ⓒ ⓓ	106	ⓐ ⓑ ⓒ ⓓ	126	ⓐ ⓑ ⓒ ⓓ	146	ⓐ ⓑ ⓒ ⓓ
87	ⓐ ⓑ ⓒ ⓓ	107	ⓐ ⓑ ⓒ ⓓ	127	ⓐ ⓑ ⓒ ⓓ	147	ⓐ ⓑ ⓒ ⓓ
88	ⓐ ⓑ ⓒ ⓓ	108	ⓐ ⓑ ⓒ ⓓ	128	ⓐ ⓑ ⓒ ⓓ	148	ⓐ ⓑ ⓒ ⓓ
89	ⓐ ⓑ ⓒ ⓓ	109	ⓐ ⓑ ⓒ ⓓ	129	ⓐ ⓑ ⓒ ⓓ	149	ⓐ ⓑ ⓒ ⓓ
90	ⓐ ⓑ ⓒ ⓓ	110	ⓐ ⓑ ⓒ ⓓ	130	ⓐ ⓑ ⓒ ⓓ	150	ⓐ ⓑ ⓒ ⓓ
91	ⓐ ⓑ ⓒ ⓓ	111	ⓐ ⓑ ⓒ ⓓ	131	ⓐ ⓑ ⓒ ⓓ	151	ⓐ ⓑ ⓒ ⓓ
92	ⓐ ⓑ ⓒ ⓓ	112	ⓐ ⓑ ⓒ ⓓ	132	ⓐ ⓑ ⓒ ⓓ	152	ⓐ ⓑ ⓒ ⓓ
93	ⓐ ⓑ ⓒ ⓓ	113	ⓐ ⓑ ⓒ ⓓ	133	ⓐ ⓑ ⓒ ⓓ	153	ⓐ ⓑ ⓒ ⓓ
94	ⓐ ⓑ ⓒ ⓓ	114	ⓐ ⓑ ⓒ ⓓ	134	ⓐ ⓑ ⓒ ⓓ	154	ⓐ ⓑ ⓒ ⓓ
95	ⓐ ⓑ ⓒ ⓓ	115	ⓐ ⓑ ⓒ ⓓ	135	ⓐ ⓑ ⓒ ⓓ	155	ⓐ ⓑ ⓒ ⓓ
96	ⓐ ⓑ ⓒ ⓓ	116	ⓐ ⓑ ⓒ ⓓ	136	ⓐ ⓑ ⓒ ⓓ	156	ⓐ ⓑ ⓒ ⓓ
97	ⓐ ⓑ ⓒ ⓓ	117	ⓐ ⓑ ⓒ ⓓ	137	ⓐ ⓑ ⓒ ⓓ	157	ⓐ ⓑ ⓒ ⓓ
98	ⓐ ⓑ ⓒ ⓓ	118	ⓐ ⓑ ⓒ ⓓ	138	ⓐ ⓑ ⓒ ⓓ	158	ⓐ ⓑ ⓒ ⓓ
99	ⓐ ⓑ ⓒ ⓓ	119	ⓐ ⓑ ⓒ ⓓ	139	ⓐ ⓑ ⓒ ⓓ	159	ⓐ ⓑ ⓒ ⓓ
100	ⓐ ⓑ ⓒ ⓓ	120	ⓐ ⓑ ⓒ ⓓ	140	ⓐ ⓑ ⓒ ⓓ	160	ⓐ ⓑ ⓒ ⓓ
		161	ⓐ ⓑ ⓒ ⓓ	181	ⓐ ⓑ ⓒ ⓓ		
		162	ⓐ ⓑ ⓒ ⓓ	182	ⓐ ⓑ ⓒ ⓓ		
		163	ⓐ ⓑ ⓒ ⓓ	183	ⓐ ⓑ ⓒ ⓓ		
		164	ⓐ ⓑ ⓒ ⓓ	184	ⓐ ⓑ ⓒ ⓓ		
		165	ⓐ ⓑ ⓒ ⓓ	185	ⓐ ⓑ ⓒ ⓓ		
		166	ⓐ ⓑ ⓒ ⓓ	186	ⓐ ⓑ ⓒ ⓓ		
		167	ⓐ ⓑ ⓒ ⓓ	187	ⓐ ⓑ ⓒ ⓓ		
		168	ⓐ ⓑ ⓒ ⓓ	188	ⓐ ⓑ ⓒ ⓓ		
		169	ⓐ ⓑ ⓒ ⓓ	189	ⓐ ⓑ ⓒ ⓓ		
		170	ⓐ ⓑ ⓒ ⓓ	190	ⓐ ⓑ ⓒ ⓓ		
		171	ⓐ ⓑ ⓒ ⓓ	191	ⓐ ⓑ ⓒ ⓓ		
		172	ⓐ ⓑ ⓒ ⓓ	192	ⓐ ⓑ ⓒ ⓓ		
		173	ⓐ ⓑ ⓒ ⓓ	193	ⓐ ⓑ ⓒ ⓓ		
		174	ⓐ ⓑ ⓒ ⓓ	194	ⓐ ⓑ ⓒ ⓓ		
		175	ⓐ ⓑ ⓒ ⓓ	195	ⓐ ⓑ ⓒ ⓓ		
		176	ⓐ ⓑ ⓒ ⓓ	196	ⓐ ⓑ ⓒ ⓓ		
		177	ⓐ ⓑ ⓒ ⓓ	197	ⓐ ⓑ ⓒ ⓓ		
		178	ⓐ ⓑ ⓒ ⓓ	198	ⓐ ⓑ ⓒ ⓓ		
		179	ⓐ ⓑ ⓒ ⓓ	199	ⓐ ⓑ ⓒ ⓓ		
		180	ⓐ ⓑ ⓒ ⓓ	200	ⓐ ⓑ ⓒ ⓓ		

ANSWER SHEET

시원스쿨 LAB

이름 | 테스트 회차 | 날짜

LISTENING COMPREHENSION (PART 1~4)

NO	ANSWER A B C D	NO	ANSWER A B C D	NO	ANSWER A B C D	NO	ANSWER A B C D	NO	ANSWER A B C D
1	ⓐ ⓑ ⓒ ⓓ	21	ⓐ ⓑ ⓒ ⓓ	41	ⓐ ⓑ ⓒ ⓓ	61	ⓐ ⓑ ⓒ ⓓ	81	ⓐ ⓑ ⓒ ⓓ
2	ⓐ ⓑ ⓒ ⓓ	22	ⓐ ⓑ ⓒ ⓓ	42	ⓐ ⓑ ⓒ ⓓ	62	ⓐ ⓑ ⓒ ⓓ	82	ⓐ ⓑ ⓒ ⓓ
3	ⓐ ⓑ ⓒ ⓓ	23	ⓐ ⓑ ⓒ ⓓ	43	ⓐ ⓑ ⓒ ⓓ	63	ⓐ ⓑ ⓒ ⓓ	83	ⓐ ⓑ ⓒ ⓓ
4	ⓐ ⓑ ⓒ ⓓ	24	ⓐ ⓑ ⓒ ⓓ	44	ⓐ ⓑ ⓒ ⓓ	64	ⓐ ⓑ ⓒ ⓓ	84	ⓐ ⓑ ⓒ ⓓ
5	ⓐ ⓑ ⓒ ⓓ	25	ⓐ ⓑ ⓒ ⓓ	45	ⓐ ⓑ ⓒ ⓓ	65	ⓐ ⓑ ⓒ ⓓ	85	ⓐ ⓑ ⓒ ⓓ
6	ⓐ ⓑ ⓒ ⓓ	26	ⓐ ⓑ ⓒ ⓓ	46	ⓐ ⓑ ⓒ ⓓ	66	ⓐ ⓑ ⓒ ⓓ	86	ⓐ ⓑ ⓒ ⓓ
7	ⓐ ⓑ ⓒ ⓓ	27	ⓐ ⓑ ⓒ ⓓ	47	ⓐ ⓑ ⓒ ⓓ	67	ⓐ ⓑ ⓒ ⓓ	87	ⓐ ⓑ ⓒ ⓓ
8	ⓐ ⓑ ⓒ ⓓ	28	ⓐ ⓑ ⓒ ⓓ	48	ⓐ ⓑ ⓒ ⓓ	68	ⓐ ⓑ ⓒ ⓓ	88	ⓐ ⓑ ⓒ ⓓ
9	ⓐ ⓑ ⓒ ⓓ	29	ⓐ ⓑ ⓒ ⓓ	49	ⓐ ⓑ ⓒ ⓓ	69	ⓐ ⓑ ⓒ ⓓ	89	ⓐ ⓑ ⓒ ⓓ
10	ⓐ ⓑ ⓒ ⓓ	30	ⓐ ⓑ ⓒ ⓓ	50	ⓐ ⓑ ⓒ ⓓ	70	ⓐ ⓑ ⓒ ⓓ	90	ⓐ ⓑ ⓒ ⓓ
11	ⓐ ⓑ ⓒ ⓓ	31	ⓐ ⓑ ⓒ ⓓ	51	ⓐ ⓑ ⓒ ⓓ	71	ⓐ ⓑ ⓒ ⓓ	91	ⓐ ⓑ ⓒ ⓓ
12	ⓐ ⓑ ⓒ ⓓ	32	ⓐ ⓑ ⓒ ⓓ	52	ⓐ ⓑ ⓒ ⓓ	72	ⓐ ⓑ ⓒ ⓓ	92	ⓐ ⓑ ⓒ ⓓ
13	ⓐ ⓑ ⓒ ⓓ	33	ⓐ ⓑ ⓒ ⓓ	53	ⓐ ⓑ ⓒ ⓓ	73	ⓐ ⓑ ⓒ ⓓ	93	ⓐ ⓑ ⓒ ⓓ
14	ⓐ ⓑ ⓒ ⓓ	34	ⓐ ⓑ ⓒ ⓓ	54	ⓐ ⓑ ⓒ ⓓ	74	ⓐ ⓑ ⓒ ⓓ	94	ⓐ ⓑ ⓒ ⓓ
15	ⓐ ⓑ ⓒ ⓓ	35	ⓐ ⓑ ⓒ ⓓ	55	ⓐ ⓑ ⓒ ⓓ	75	ⓐ ⓑ ⓒ ⓓ	95	ⓐ ⓑ ⓒ ⓓ
16	ⓐ ⓑ ⓒ ⓓ	36	ⓐ ⓑ ⓒ ⓓ	56	ⓐ ⓑ ⓒ ⓓ	76	ⓐ ⓑ ⓒ ⓓ	96	ⓐ ⓑ ⓒ ⓓ
17	ⓐ ⓑ ⓒ ⓓ	37	ⓐ ⓑ ⓒ ⓓ	57	ⓐ ⓑ ⓒ ⓓ	77	ⓐ ⓑ ⓒ ⓓ	97	ⓐ ⓑ ⓒ ⓓ
18	ⓐ ⓑ ⓒ ⓓ	38	ⓐ ⓑ ⓒ ⓓ	58	ⓐ ⓑ ⓒ ⓓ	78	ⓐ ⓑ ⓒ ⓓ	98	ⓐ ⓑ ⓒ ⓓ
19	ⓐ ⓑ ⓒ ⓓ	39	ⓐ ⓑ ⓒ ⓓ	59	ⓐ ⓑ ⓒ ⓓ	79	ⓐ ⓑ ⓒ ⓓ	99	ⓐ ⓑ ⓒ ⓓ
20	ⓐ ⓑ ⓒ ⓓ	40	ⓐ ⓑ ⓒ ⓓ	60	ⓐ ⓑ ⓒ ⓓ	80	ⓐ ⓑ ⓒ ⓓ	100	ⓐ ⓑ ⓒ ⓓ

READING COMPREHENSION (PART 5~7)

NO	ANSWER A B C D	NO	ANSWER A B C D	NO	ANSWER A B C D	NO	ANSWER A B C D	NO	ANSWER A B C D
101	ⓐ ⓑ ⓒ ⓓ	121	ⓐ ⓑ ⓒ ⓓ	141	ⓐ ⓑ ⓒ ⓓ	161	ⓐ ⓑ ⓒ ⓓ	181	ⓐ ⓑ ⓒ ⓓ
102	ⓐ ⓑ ⓒ ⓓ	122	ⓐ ⓑ ⓒ ⓓ	142	ⓐ ⓑ ⓒ ⓓ	162	ⓐ ⓑ ⓒ ⓓ	182	ⓐ ⓑ ⓒ ⓓ
103	ⓐ ⓑ ⓒ ⓓ	123	ⓐ ⓑ ⓒ ⓓ	143	ⓐ ⓑ ⓒ ⓓ	163	ⓐ ⓑ ⓒ ⓓ	183	ⓐ ⓑ ⓒ ⓓ
104	ⓐ ⓑ ⓒ ⓓ	124	ⓐ ⓑ ⓒ ⓓ	144	ⓐ ⓑ ⓒ ⓓ	164	ⓐ ⓑ ⓒ ⓓ	184	ⓐ ⓑ ⓒ ⓓ
105	ⓐ ⓑ ⓒ ⓓ	125	ⓐ ⓑ ⓒ ⓓ	145	ⓐ ⓑ ⓒ ⓓ	165	ⓐ ⓑ ⓒ ⓓ	185	ⓐ ⓑ ⓒ ⓓ
106	ⓐ ⓑ ⓒ ⓓ	126	ⓐ ⓑ ⓒ ⓓ	146	ⓐ ⓑ ⓒ ⓓ	166	ⓐ ⓑ ⓒ ⓓ	186	ⓐ ⓑ ⓒ ⓓ
107	ⓐ ⓑ ⓒ ⓓ	127	ⓐ ⓑ ⓒ ⓓ	147	ⓐ ⓑ ⓒ ⓓ	167	ⓐ ⓑ ⓒ ⓓ	187	ⓐ ⓑ ⓒ ⓓ
108	ⓐ ⓑ ⓒ ⓓ	128	ⓐ ⓑ ⓒ ⓓ	148	ⓐ ⓑ ⓒ ⓓ	168	ⓐ ⓑ ⓒ ⓓ	188	ⓐ ⓑ ⓒ ⓓ
109	ⓐ ⓑ ⓒ ⓓ	129	ⓐ ⓑ ⓒ ⓓ	149	ⓐ ⓑ ⓒ ⓓ	169	ⓐ ⓑ ⓒ ⓓ	189	ⓐ ⓑ ⓒ ⓓ
110	ⓐ ⓑ ⓒ ⓓ	130	ⓐ ⓑ ⓒ ⓓ	150	ⓐ ⓑ ⓒ ⓓ	170	ⓐ ⓑ ⓒ ⓓ	190	ⓐ ⓑ ⓒ ⓓ
111	ⓐ ⓑ ⓒ ⓓ	131	ⓐ ⓑ ⓒ ⓓ	151	ⓐ ⓑ ⓒ ⓓ	171	ⓐ ⓑ ⓒ ⓓ	191	ⓐ ⓑ ⓒ ⓓ
112	ⓐ ⓑ ⓒ ⓓ	132	ⓐ ⓑ ⓒ ⓓ	152	ⓐ ⓑ ⓒ ⓓ	172	ⓐ ⓑ ⓒ ⓓ	192	ⓐ ⓑ ⓒ ⓓ
113	ⓐ ⓑ ⓒ ⓓ	133	ⓐ ⓑ ⓒ ⓓ	153	ⓐ ⓑ ⓒ ⓓ	173	ⓐ ⓑ ⓒ ⓓ	193	ⓐ ⓑ ⓒ ⓓ
114	ⓐ ⓑ ⓒ ⓓ	134	ⓐ ⓑ ⓒ ⓓ	154	ⓐ ⓑ ⓒ ⓓ	174	ⓐ ⓑ ⓒ ⓓ	194	ⓐ ⓑ ⓒ ⓓ
115	ⓐ ⓑ ⓒ ⓓ	135	ⓐ ⓑ ⓒ ⓓ	155	ⓐ ⓑ ⓒ ⓓ	175	ⓐ ⓑ ⓒ ⓓ	195	ⓐ ⓑ ⓒ ⓓ
116	ⓐ ⓑ ⓒ ⓓ	136	ⓐ ⓑ ⓒ ⓓ	156	ⓐ ⓑ ⓒ ⓓ	176	ⓐ ⓑ ⓒ ⓓ	196	ⓐ ⓑ ⓒ ⓓ
117	ⓐ ⓑ ⓒ ⓓ	137	ⓐ ⓑ ⓒ ⓓ	157	ⓐ ⓑ ⓒ ⓓ	177	ⓐ ⓑ ⓒ ⓓ	197	ⓐ ⓑ ⓒ ⓓ
118	ⓐ ⓑ ⓒ ⓓ	138	ⓐ ⓑ ⓒ ⓓ	158	ⓐ ⓑ ⓒ ⓓ	178	ⓐ ⓑ ⓒ ⓓ	198	ⓐ ⓑ ⓒ ⓓ
119	ⓐ ⓑ ⓒ ⓓ	139	ⓐ ⓑ ⓒ ⓓ	159	ⓐ ⓑ ⓒ ⓓ	179	ⓐ ⓑ ⓒ ⓓ	199	ⓐ ⓑ ⓒ ⓓ
120	ⓐ ⓑ ⓒ ⓓ	140	ⓐ ⓑ ⓒ ⓓ	160	ⓐ ⓑ ⓒ ⓓ	180	ⓐ ⓑ ⓒ ⓓ	200	ⓐ ⓑ ⓒ ⓓ

ANSWER SHEET

시원스쿨 LAB

이름　　테스트 회차　　날짜

LISTENING COMPREHENSION (PART 1~4)

NO	ANSWER A B C D	NO	ANSWER A B C D	NO	ANSWER A B C D	NO	ANSWER A B C D	NO	ANSWER A B C D
1	ⓐ ⓑ ⓒ ⓓ	21	ⓐ ⓑ ⓒ	41	ⓐ ⓑ ⓒ ⓓ	61	ⓐ ⓑ ⓒ ⓓ	81	ⓐ ⓑ ⓒ ⓓ
2	ⓐ ⓑ ⓒ ⓓ	22	ⓐ ⓑ ⓒ	42	ⓐ ⓑ ⓒ ⓓ	62	ⓐ ⓑ ⓒ ⓓ	82	ⓐ ⓑ ⓒ ⓓ
3	ⓐ ⓑ ⓒ ⓓ	23	ⓐ ⓑ ⓒ	43	ⓐ ⓑ ⓒ ⓓ	63	ⓐ ⓑ ⓒ ⓓ	83	ⓐ ⓑ ⓒ ⓓ
4	ⓐ ⓑ ⓒ ⓓ	24	ⓐ ⓑ ⓒ	44	ⓐ ⓑ ⓒ ⓓ	64	ⓐ ⓑ ⓒ ⓓ	84	ⓐ ⓑ ⓒ ⓓ
5	ⓐ ⓑ ⓒ ⓓ	25	ⓐ ⓑ ⓒ	45	ⓐ ⓑ ⓒ ⓓ	65	ⓐ ⓑ ⓒ ⓓ	85	ⓐ ⓑ ⓒ ⓓ
6	ⓐ ⓑ ⓒ ⓓ	26	ⓐ ⓑ ⓒ	46	ⓐ ⓑ ⓒ ⓓ	66	ⓐ ⓑ ⓒ ⓓ	86	ⓐ ⓑ ⓒ ⓓ
7	ⓐ ⓑ ⓒ	27	ⓐ ⓑ ⓒ	47	ⓐ ⓑ ⓒ ⓓ	67	ⓐ ⓑ ⓒ ⓓ	87	ⓐ ⓑ ⓒ ⓓ
8	ⓐ ⓑ ⓒ	28	ⓐ ⓑ ⓒ	48	ⓐ ⓑ ⓒ ⓓ	68	ⓐ ⓑ ⓒ ⓓ	88	ⓐ ⓑ ⓒ ⓓ
9	ⓐ ⓑ ⓒ	29	ⓐ ⓑ ⓒ	49	ⓐ ⓑ ⓒ ⓓ	69	ⓐ ⓑ ⓒ ⓓ	89	ⓐ ⓑ ⓒ ⓓ
10	ⓐ ⓑ ⓒ	30	ⓐ ⓑ ⓒ	50	ⓐ ⓑ ⓒ ⓓ	70	ⓐ ⓑ ⓒ ⓓ	90	ⓐ ⓑ ⓒ ⓓ
11	ⓐ ⓑ ⓒ	31	ⓐ ⓑ ⓒ ⓓ	51	ⓐ ⓑ ⓒ ⓓ	71	ⓐ ⓑ ⓒ ⓓ	91	ⓐ ⓑ ⓒ ⓓ
12	ⓐ ⓑ ⓒ	32	ⓐ ⓑ ⓒ ⓓ	52	ⓐ ⓑ ⓒ ⓓ	72	ⓐ ⓑ ⓒ ⓓ	92	ⓐ ⓑ ⓒ ⓓ
13	ⓐ ⓑ ⓒ	33	ⓐ ⓑ ⓒ ⓓ	53	ⓐ ⓑ ⓒ ⓓ	73	ⓐ ⓑ ⓒ ⓓ	93	ⓐ ⓑ ⓒ ⓓ
14	ⓐ ⓑ ⓒ	34	ⓐ ⓑ ⓒ ⓓ	54	ⓐ ⓑ ⓒ ⓓ	74	ⓐ ⓑ ⓒ ⓓ	94	ⓐ ⓑ ⓒ ⓓ
15	ⓐ ⓑ ⓒ	35	ⓐ ⓑ ⓒ ⓓ	55	ⓐ ⓑ ⓒ ⓓ	75	ⓐ ⓑ ⓒ ⓓ	95	ⓐ ⓑ ⓒ ⓓ
16	ⓐ ⓑ ⓒ	36	ⓐ ⓑ ⓒ ⓓ	56	ⓐ ⓑ ⓒ ⓓ	76	ⓐ ⓑ ⓒ ⓓ	96	ⓐ ⓑ ⓒ ⓓ
17	ⓐ ⓑ ⓒ	37	ⓐ ⓑ ⓒ ⓓ	57	ⓐ ⓑ ⓒ ⓓ	77	ⓐ ⓑ ⓒ ⓓ	97	ⓐ ⓑ ⓒ ⓓ
18	ⓐ ⓑ ⓒ	38	ⓐ ⓑ ⓒ ⓓ	58	ⓐ ⓑ ⓒ ⓓ	78	ⓐ ⓑ ⓒ ⓓ	98	ⓐ ⓑ ⓒ ⓓ
19	ⓐ ⓑ ⓒ	39	ⓐ ⓑ ⓒ ⓓ	59	ⓐ ⓑ ⓒ ⓓ	79	ⓐ ⓑ ⓒ ⓓ	99	ⓐ ⓑ ⓒ ⓓ
20	ⓐ ⓑ ⓒ	40	ⓐ ⓑ ⓒ ⓓ	60	ⓐ ⓑ ⓒ ⓓ	80	ⓐ ⓑ ⓒ ⓓ	100	ⓐ ⓑ ⓒ ⓓ

READING COMPREHENSION (PART 5~7)

NO	ANSWER A B C D	NO	ANSWER A B C D	NO	ANSWER A B C D	NO	ANSWER A B C D	NO	ANSWER A B C D
101	ⓐ ⓑ ⓒ ⓓ	121	ⓐ ⓑ ⓒ ⓓ	141	ⓐ ⓑ ⓒ ⓓ	161	ⓐ ⓑ ⓒ ⓓ	181	ⓐ ⓑ ⓒ ⓓ
102	ⓐ ⓑ ⓒ ⓓ	122	ⓐ ⓑ ⓒ ⓓ	142	ⓐ ⓑ ⓒ ⓓ	162	ⓐ ⓑ ⓒ ⓓ	182	ⓐ ⓑ ⓒ ⓓ
103	ⓐ ⓑ ⓒ ⓓ	123	ⓐ ⓑ ⓒ ⓓ	143	ⓐ ⓑ ⓒ ⓓ	163	ⓐ ⓑ ⓒ ⓓ	183	ⓐ ⓑ ⓒ ⓓ
104	ⓐ ⓑ ⓒ ⓓ	124	ⓐ ⓑ ⓒ ⓓ	144	ⓐ ⓑ ⓒ ⓓ	164	ⓐ ⓑ ⓒ ⓓ	184	ⓐ ⓑ ⓒ ⓓ
105	ⓐ ⓑ ⓒ ⓓ	125	ⓐ ⓑ ⓒ ⓓ	145	ⓐ ⓑ ⓒ ⓓ	165	ⓐ ⓑ ⓒ ⓓ	185	ⓐ ⓑ ⓒ ⓓ
106	ⓐ ⓑ ⓒ ⓓ	126	ⓐ ⓑ ⓒ ⓓ	146	ⓐ ⓑ ⓒ ⓓ	166	ⓐ ⓑ ⓒ ⓓ	186	ⓐ ⓑ ⓒ ⓓ
107	ⓐ ⓑ ⓒ ⓓ	127	ⓐ ⓑ ⓒ ⓓ	147	ⓐ ⓑ ⓒ ⓓ	167	ⓐ ⓑ ⓒ ⓓ	187	ⓐ ⓑ ⓒ ⓓ
108	ⓐ ⓑ ⓒ ⓓ	128	ⓐ ⓑ ⓒ ⓓ	148	ⓐ ⓑ ⓒ ⓓ	168	ⓐ ⓑ ⓒ ⓓ	188	ⓐ ⓑ ⓒ ⓓ
109	ⓐ ⓑ ⓒ ⓓ	129	ⓐ ⓑ ⓒ ⓓ	149	ⓐ ⓑ ⓒ ⓓ	169	ⓐ ⓑ ⓒ ⓓ	189	ⓐ ⓑ ⓒ ⓓ
110	ⓐ ⓑ ⓒ ⓓ	130	ⓐ ⓑ ⓒ ⓓ	150	ⓐ ⓑ ⓒ ⓓ	170	ⓐ ⓑ ⓒ ⓓ	190	ⓐ ⓑ ⓒ ⓓ
111	ⓐ ⓑ ⓒ ⓓ	131	ⓐ ⓑ ⓒ ⓓ	151	ⓐ ⓑ ⓒ ⓓ	171	ⓐ ⓑ ⓒ ⓓ	191	ⓐ ⓑ ⓒ ⓓ
112	ⓐ ⓑ ⓒ ⓓ	132	ⓐ ⓑ ⓒ ⓓ	152	ⓐ ⓑ ⓒ ⓓ	172	ⓐ ⓑ ⓒ ⓓ	192	ⓐ ⓑ ⓒ ⓓ
113	ⓐ ⓑ ⓒ ⓓ	133	ⓐ ⓑ ⓒ ⓓ	153	ⓐ ⓑ ⓒ ⓓ	173	ⓐ ⓑ ⓒ ⓓ	193	ⓐ ⓑ ⓒ ⓓ
114	ⓐ ⓑ ⓒ ⓓ	134	ⓐ ⓑ ⓒ ⓓ	154	ⓐ ⓑ ⓒ ⓓ	174	ⓐ ⓑ ⓒ ⓓ	194	ⓐ ⓑ ⓒ ⓓ
115	ⓐ ⓑ ⓒ ⓓ	135	ⓐ ⓑ ⓒ ⓓ	155	ⓐ ⓑ ⓒ ⓓ	175	ⓐ ⓑ ⓒ ⓓ	195	ⓐ ⓑ ⓒ ⓓ
116	ⓐ ⓑ ⓒ ⓓ	136	ⓐ ⓑ ⓒ ⓓ	156	ⓐ ⓑ ⓒ ⓓ	176	ⓐ ⓑ ⓒ ⓓ	196	ⓐ ⓑ ⓒ ⓓ
117	ⓐ ⓑ ⓒ ⓓ	137	ⓐ ⓑ ⓒ ⓓ	157	ⓐ ⓑ ⓒ ⓓ	177	ⓐ ⓑ ⓒ ⓓ	197	ⓐ ⓑ ⓒ ⓓ
118	ⓐ ⓑ ⓒ ⓓ	138	ⓐ ⓑ ⓒ ⓓ	158	ⓐ ⓑ ⓒ ⓓ	178	ⓐ ⓑ ⓒ ⓓ	198	ⓐ ⓑ ⓒ ⓓ
119	ⓐ ⓑ ⓒ ⓓ	139	ⓐ ⓑ ⓒ ⓓ	159	ⓐ ⓑ ⓒ ⓓ	179	ⓐ ⓑ ⓒ ⓓ	199	ⓐ ⓑ ⓒ ⓓ
120	ⓐ ⓑ ⓒ ⓓ	140	ⓐ ⓑ ⓒ ⓓ	160	ⓐ ⓑ ⓒ ⓓ	180	ⓐ ⓑ ⓒ ⓓ	200	ⓐ ⓑ ⓒ ⓓ

ANSWER SHEET

시원스쿨 LAB

| 이름 | | 테스트 회차 | | 날짜 | |

LISTENING COMPREHENSION (PART 1~4)

NO	ANSWER A B C D	NO	ANSWER A B C D	NO	ANSWER A B C D	NO	ANSWER A B C D	NO	ANSWER A B C D
1	ⓐ ⓑ ⓒ ⓓ	21	ⓐ ⓑ ⓒ ⓓ	41	ⓐ ⓑ ⓒ ⓓ	61	ⓐ ⓑ ⓒ ⓓ	81	ⓐ ⓑ ⓒ ⓓ
2	ⓐ ⓑ ⓒ ⓓ	22	ⓐ ⓑ ⓒ ⓓ	42	ⓐ ⓑ ⓒ ⓓ	62	ⓐ ⓑ ⓒ ⓓ	82	ⓐ ⓑ ⓒ ⓓ
3	ⓐ ⓑ ⓒ ⓓ	23	ⓐ ⓑ ⓒ ⓓ	43	ⓐ ⓑ ⓒ ⓓ	63	ⓐ ⓑ ⓒ ⓓ	83	ⓐ ⓑ ⓒ ⓓ
4	ⓐ ⓑ ⓒ ⓓ	24	ⓐ ⓑ ⓒ ⓓ	44	ⓐ ⓑ ⓒ ⓓ	64	ⓐ ⓑ ⓒ ⓓ	84	ⓐ ⓑ ⓒ ⓓ
5	ⓐ ⓑ ⓒ	25	ⓐ ⓑ ⓒ ⓓ	45	ⓐ ⓑ ⓒ ⓓ	65	ⓐ ⓑ ⓒ ⓓ	85	ⓐ ⓑ ⓒ ⓓ
6	ⓐ ⓑ ⓒ	26	ⓐ ⓑ ⓒ ⓓ	46	ⓐ ⓑ ⓒ ⓓ	66	ⓐ ⓑ ⓒ ⓓ	86	ⓐ ⓑ ⓒ ⓓ
7	ⓐ ⓑ ⓒ	27	ⓐ ⓑ ⓒ ⓓ	47	ⓐ ⓑ ⓒ ⓓ	67	ⓐ ⓑ ⓒ ⓓ	87	ⓐ ⓑ ⓒ ⓓ
8	ⓐ ⓑ ⓒ	28	ⓐ ⓑ ⓒ ⓓ	48	ⓐ ⓑ ⓒ ⓓ	68	ⓐ ⓑ ⓒ ⓓ	88	ⓐ ⓑ ⓒ ⓓ
9	ⓐ ⓑ ⓒ	29	ⓐ ⓑ ⓒ ⓓ	49	ⓐ ⓑ ⓒ ⓓ	69	ⓐ ⓑ ⓒ ⓓ	89	ⓐ ⓑ ⓒ ⓓ
10	ⓐ ⓑ ⓒ	30	ⓐ ⓑ ⓒ ⓓ	50	ⓐ ⓑ ⓒ ⓓ	70	ⓐ ⓑ ⓒ ⓓ	90	ⓐ ⓑ ⓒ ⓓ
11	ⓐ ⓑ ⓒ	31	ⓐ ⓑ ⓒ ⓓ	51	ⓐ ⓑ ⓒ ⓓ	71	ⓐ ⓑ ⓒ ⓓ	91	ⓐ ⓑ ⓒ ⓓ
12	ⓐ ⓑ ⓒ	32	ⓐ ⓑ ⓒ ⓓ	52	ⓐ ⓑ ⓒ ⓓ	72	ⓐ ⓑ ⓒ ⓓ	92	ⓐ ⓑ ⓒ ⓓ
13	ⓐ ⓑ ⓒ	33	ⓐ ⓑ ⓒ ⓓ	53	ⓐ ⓑ ⓒ ⓓ	73	ⓐ ⓑ ⓒ ⓓ	93	ⓐ ⓑ ⓒ ⓓ
14	ⓐ ⓑ ⓒ	34	ⓐ ⓑ ⓒ ⓓ	54	ⓐ ⓑ ⓒ ⓓ	74	ⓐ ⓑ ⓒ ⓓ	94	ⓐ ⓑ ⓒ ⓓ
15	ⓐ ⓑ ⓒ	35	ⓐ ⓑ ⓒ ⓓ	55	ⓐ ⓑ ⓒ ⓓ	75	ⓐ ⓑ ⓒ ⓓ	95	ⓐ ⓑ ⓒ ⓓ
16	ⓐ ⓑ ⓒ	36	ⓐ ⓑ ⓒ ⓓ	56	ⓐ ⓑ ⓒ ⓓ	76	ⓐ ⓑ ⓒ ⓓ	96	ⓐ ⓑ ⓒ ⓓ
17	ⓐ ⓑ ⓒ	37	ⓐ ⓑ ⓒ ⓓ	57	ⓐ ⓑ ⓒ ⓓ	77	ⓐ ⓑ ⓒ ⓓ	97	ⓐ ⓑ ⓒ ⓓ
18	ⓐ ⓑ ⓒ	38	ⓐ ⓑ ⓒ ⓓ	58	ⓐ ⓑ ⓒ ⓓ	78	ⓐ ⓑ ⓒ ⓓ	98	ⓐ ⓑ ⓒ ⓓ
19	ⓐ ⓑ ⓒ	39	ⓐ ⓑ ⓒ ⓓ	59	ⓐ ⓑ ⓒ ⓓ	79	ⓐ ⓑ ⓒ ⓓ	99	ⓐ ⓑ ⓒ ⓓ
20	ⓐ ⓑ ⓒ	40	ⓐ ⓑ ⓒ ⓓ	60	ⓐ ⓑ ⓒ ⓓ	80	ⓐ ⓑ ⓒ ⓓ	100	ⓐ ⓑ ⓒ ⓓ

READING COMPREHENSION (PART 5~7)

NO	ANSWER A B C D	NO	ANSWER A B C D	NO	ANSWER A B C D	NO	ANSWER A B C D	NO	ANSWER A B C D
101	ⓐ ⓑ ⓒ ⓓ	121	ⓐ ⓑ ⓒ ⓓ	141	ⓐ ⓑ ⓒ ⓓ	161	ⓐ ⓑ ⓒ ⓓ	181	ⓐ ⓑ ⓒ ⓓ
102	ⓐ ⓑ ⓒ ⓓ	122	ⓐ ⓑ ⓒ ⓓ	142	ⓐ ⓑ ⓒ ⓓ	162	ⓐ ⓑ ⓒ ⓓ	182	ⓐ ⓑ ⓒ ⓓ
103	ⓐ ⓑ ⓒ ⓓ	123	ⓐ ⓑ ⓒ ⓓ	143	ⓐ ⓑ ⓒ ⓓ	163	ⓐ ⓑ ⓒ ⓓ	183	ⓐ ⓑ ⓒ ⓓ
104	ⓐ ⓑ ⓒ ⓓ	124	ⓐ ⓑ ⓒ ⓓ	144	ⓐ ⓑ ⓒ ⓓ	164	ⓐ ⓑ ⓒ ⓓ	184	ⓐ ⓑ ⓒ ⓓ
105	ⓐ ⓑ ⓒ ⓓ	125	ⓐ ⓑ ⓒ ⓓ	145	ⓐ ⓑ ⓒ ⓓ	165	ⓐ ⓑ ⓒ ⓓ	185	ⓐ ⓑ ⓒ ⓓ
106	ⓐ ⓑ ⓒ ⓓ	126	ⓐ ⓑ ⓒ ⓓ	146	ⓐ ⓑ ⓒ ⓓ	166	ⓐ ⓑ ⓒ ⓓ	186	ⓐ ⓑ ⓒ ⓓ
107	ⓐ ⓑ ⓒ ⓓ	127	ⓐ ⓑ ⓒ ⓓ	147	ⓐ ⓑ ⓒ ⓓ	167	ⓐ ⓑ ⓒ ⓓ	187	ⓐ ⓑ ⓒ ⓓ
108	ⓐ ⓑ ⓒ ⓓ	128	ⓐ ⓑ ⓒ ⓓ	148	ⓐ ⓑ ⓒ ⓓ	168	ⓐ ⓑ ⓒ ⓓ	188	ⓐ ⓑ ⓒ ⓓ
109	ⓐ ⓑ ⓒ ⓓ	129	ⓐ ⓑ ⓒ ⓓ	149	ⓐ ⓑ ⓒ ⓓ	169	ⓐ ⓑ ⓒ ⓓ	189	ⓐ ⓑ ⓒ ⓓ
110	ⓐ ⓑ ⓒ ⓓ	130	ⓐ ⓑ ⓒ ⓓ	150	ⓐ ⓑ ⓒ ⓓ	170	ⓐ ⓑ ⓒ ⓓ	190	ⓐ ⓑ ⓒ ⓓ
111	ⓐ ⓑ ⓒ ⓓ	131	ⓐ ⓑ ⓒ ⓓ	151	ⓐ ⓑ ⓒ ⓓ	171	ⓐ ⓑ ⓒ ⓓ	191	ⓐ ⓑ ⓒ ⓓ
112	ⓐ ⓑ ⓒ ⓓ	132	ⓐ ⓑ ⓒ ⓓ	152	ⓐ ⓑ ⓒ ⓓ	172	ⓐ ⓑ ⓒ ⓓ	192	ⓐ ⓑ ⓒ ⓓ
113	ⓐ ⓑ ⓒ ⓓ	133	ⓐ ⓑ ⓒ ⓓ	153	ⓐ ⓑ ⓒ ⓓ	173	ⓐ ⓑ ⓒ ⓓ	193	ⓐ ⓑ ⓒ ⓓ
114	ⓐ ⓑ ⓒ ⓓ	134	ⓐ ⓑ ⓒ ⓓ	154	ⓐ ⓑ ⓒ ⓓ	174	ⓐ ⓑ ⓒ ⓓ	194	ⓐ ⓑ ⓒ ⓓ
115	ⓐ ⓑ ⓒ ⓓ	135	ⓐ ⓑ ⓒ ⓓ	155	ⓐ ⓑ ⓒ ⓓ	175	ⓐ ⓑ ⓒ ⓓ	195	ⓐ ⓑ ⓒ ⓓ
116	ⓐ ⓑ ⓒ ⓓ	136	ⓐ ⓑ ⓒ ⓓ	156	ⓐ ⓑ ⓒ ⓓ	176	ⓐ ⓑ ⓒ ⓓ	196	ⓐ ⓑ ⓒ ⓓ
117	ⓐ ⓑ ⓒ ⓓ	137	ⓐ ⓑ ⓒ ⓓ	157	ⓐ ⓑ ⓒ ⓓ	177	ⓐ ⓑ ⓒ ⓓ	197	ⓐ ⓑ ⓒ ⓓ
118	ⓐ ⓑ ⓒ ⓓ	138	ⓐ ⓑ ⓒ ⓓ	158	ⓐ ⓑ ⓒ ⓓ	178	ⓐ ⓑ ⓒ ⓓ	198	ⓐ ⓑ ⓒ ⓓ
119	ⓐ ⓑ ⓒ ⓓ	139	ⓐ ⓑ ⓒ ⓓ	159	ⓐ ⓑ ⓒ ⓓ	179	ⓐ ⓑ ⓒ ⓓ	199	ⓐ ⓑ ⓒ ⓓ
120	ⓐ ⓑ ⓒ ⓓ	140	ⓐ ⓑ ⓒ ⓓ	160	ⓐ ⓑ ⓒ ⓓ	180	ⓐ ⓑ ⓒ ⓓ	200	ⓐ ⓑ ⓒ ⓓ

ANSWER SHEET

시원스쿨 LAB

이름   테스트 횟차   날짜

LISTENING COMPREHENSION (PART 1~4)

READING COMPREHENSION (PART 5~7)

ANSWER SHEET

시원스쿨LAB

이름 | 테스트 회차 | 날짜

LISTENING COMPREHENSION (PART 1~4)

NO	ANSWER A B C D	NO	ANSWER A B C D	NO	ANSWER A B C D	NO	ANSWER A B C D	NO	ANSWER A B C D
1	ⓐⓑⓒⓓ	21	ⓐⓑⓒⓓ	41	ⓐⓑⓒⓓ	61	ⓐⓑⓒⓓ	81	ⓐⓑⓒⓓ
2	ⓐⓑⓒⓓ	22	ⓐⓑⓒⓓ	42	ⓐⓑⓒⓓ	62	ⓐⓑⓒⓓ	82	ⓐⓑⓒⓓ
3	ⓐⓑⓒⓓ	23	ⓐⓑⓒⓓ	43	ⓐⓑⓒⓓ	63	ⓐⓑⓒⓓ	83	ⓐⓑⓒⓓ
4	ⓐⓑⓒⓓ	24	ⓐⓑⓒⓓ	44	ⓐⓑⓒⓓ	64	ⓐⓑⓒⓓ	84	ⓐⓑⓒⓓ
5	ⓐⓑⓒⓓ	25	ⓐⓑⓒⓓ	45	ⓐⓑⓒⓓ	65	ⓐⓑⓒⓓ	85	ⓐⓑⓒⓓ
6	ⓐⓑⓒⓓ	26	ⓐⓑⓒⓓ	46	ⓐⓑⓒⓓ	66	ⓐⓑⓒⓓ	86	ⓐⓑⓒⓓ
7	ⓐⓑⓒⓓ	27	ⓐⓑⓒⓓ	47	ⓐⓑⓒⓓ	67	ⓐⓑⓒⓓ	87	ⓐⓑⓒⓓ
8	ⓐⓑⓒⓓ	28	ⓐⓑⓒⓓ	48	ⓐⓑⓒⓓ	68	ⓐⓑⓒⓓ	88	ⓐⓑⓒⓓ
9	ⓐⓑⓒⓓ	29	ⓐⓑⓒⓓ	49	ⓐⓑⓒⓓ	69	ⓐⓑⓒⓓ	89	ⓐⓑⓒⓓ
10	ⓐⓑⓒⓓ	30	ⓐⓑⓒⓓ	50	ⓐⓑⓒⓓ	70	ⓐⓑⓒⓓ	90	ⓐⓑⓒⓓ
11	ⓐⓑⓒⓓ	31	ⓐⓑⓒⓓ	51	ⓐⓑⓒⓓ	71	ⓐⓑⓒⓓ	91	ⓐⓑⓒⓓ
12	ⓐⓑⓒⓓ	32	ⓐⓑⓒⓓ	52	ⓐⓑⓒⓓ	72	ⓐⓑⓒⓓ	92	ⓐⓑⓒⓓ
13	ⓐⓑⓒⓓ	33	ⓐⓑⓒⓓ	53	ⓐⓑⓒⓓ	73	ⓐⓑⓒⓓ	93	ⓐⓑⓒⓓ
14	ⓐⓑⓒⓓ	34	ⓐⓑⓒⓓ	54	ⓐⓑⓒⓓ	74	ⓐⓑⓒⓓ	94	ⓐⓑⓒⓓ
15	ⓐⓑⓒⓓ	35	ⓐⓑⓒⓓ	55	ⓐⓑⓒⓓ	75	ⓐⓑⓒⓓ	95	ⓐⓑⓒⓓ
16	ⓐⓑⓒⓓ	36	ⓐⓑⓒⓓ	56	ⓐⓑⓒⓓ	76	ⓐⓑⓒⓓ	96	ⓐⓑⓒⓓ
17	ⓐⓑⓒⓓ	37	ⓐⓑⓒⓓ	57	ⓐⓑⓒⓓ	77	ⓐⓑⓒⓓ	97	ⓐⓑⓒⓓ
18	ⓐⓑⓒⓓ	38	ⓐⓑⓒⓓ	58	ⓐⓑⓒⓓ	78	ⓐⓑⓒⓓ	98	ⓐⓑⓒⓓ
19	ⓐⓑⓒⓓ	39	ⓐⓑⓒⓓ	59	ⓐⓑⓒⓓ	79	ⓐⓑⓒⓓ	99	ⓐⓑⓒⓓ
20	ⓐⓑⓒⓓ	40	ⓐⓑⓒⓓ	60	ⓐⓑⓒⓓ	80	ⓐⓑⓒⓓ	100	ⓐⓑⓒⓓ

READING COMPREHENSION (PART 5~7)

NO	ANSWER A B C D	NO	ANSWER A B C D	NO	ANSWER A B C D	NO	ANSWER A B C D	NO	ANSWER A B C D
101	ⓐⓑⓒⓓ	121	ⓐⓑⓒⓓ	141	ⓐⓑⓒⓓ	161	ⓐⓑⓒⓓ	181	ⓐⓑⓒⓓ
102	ⓐⓑⓒⓓ	122	ⓐⓑⓒⓓ	142	ⓐⓑⓒⓓ	162	ⓐⓑⓒⓓ	182	ⓐⓑⓒⓓ
103	ⓐⓑⓒⓓ	123	ⓐⓑⓒⓓ	143	ⓐⓑⓒⓓ	163	ⓐⓑⓒⓓ	183	ⓐⓑⓒⓓ
104	ⓐⓑⓒⓓ	124	ⓐⓑⓒⓓ	144	ⓐⓑⓒⓓ	164	ⓐⓑⓒⓓ	184	ⓐⓑⓒⓓ
105	ⓐⓑⓒⓓ	125	ⓐⓑⓒⓓ	145	ⓐⓑⓒⓓ	165	ⓐⓑⓒⓓ	185	ⓐⓑⓒⓓ
106	ⓐⓑⓒⓓ	126	ⓐⓑⓒⓓ	146	ⓐⓑⓒⓓ	166	ⓐⓑⓒⓓ	186	ⓐⓑⓒⓓ
107	ⓐⓑⓒⓓ	127	ⓐⓑⓒⓓ	147	ⓐⓑⓒⓓ	167	ⓐⓑⓒⓓ	187	ⓐⓑⓒⓓ
108	ⓐⓑⓒⓓ	128	ⓐⓑⓒⓓ	148	ⓐⓑⓒⓓ	168	ⓐⓑⓒⓓ	188	ⓐⓑⓒⓓ
109	ⓐⓑⓒⓓ	129	ⓐⓑⓒⓓ	149	ⓐⓑⓒⓓ	169	ⓐⓑⓒⓓ	189	ⓐⓑⓒⓓ
110	ⓐⓑⓒⓓ	130	ⓐⓑⓒⓓ	150	ⓐⓑⓒⓓ	170	ⓐⓑⓒⓓ	190	ⓐⓑⓒⓓ
111	ⓐⓑⓒⓓ	131	ⓐⓑⓒⓓ	151	ⓐⓑⓒⓓ	171	ⓐⓑⓒⓓ	191	ⓐⓑⓒⓓ
112	ⓐⓑⓒⓓ	132	ⓐⓑⓒⓓ	152	ⓐⓑⓒⓓ	172	ⓐⓑⓒⓓ	192	ⓐⓑⓒⓓ
113	ⓐⓑⓒⓓ	133	ⓐⓑⓒⓓ	153	ⓐⓑⓒⓓ	173	ⓐⓑⓒⓓ	193	ⓐⓑⓒⓓ
114	ⓐⓑⓒⓓ	134	ⓐⓑⓒⓓ	154	ⓐⓑⓒⓓ	174	ⓐⓑⓒⓓ	194	ⓐⓑⓒⓓ
115	ⓐⓑⓒⓓ	135	ⓐⓑⓒⓓ	155	ⓐⓑⓒⓓ	175	ⓐⓑⓒⓓ	195	ⓐⓑⓒⓓ
116	ⓐⓑⓒⓓ	136	ⓐⓑⓒⓓ	156	ⓐⓑⓒⓓ	176	ⓐⓑⓒⓓ	196	ⓐⓑⓒⓓ
117	ⓐⓑⓒⓓ	137	ⓐⓑⓒⓓ	157	ⓐⓑⓒⓓ	177	ⓐⓑⓒⓓ	197	ⓐⓑⓒⓓ
118	ⓐⓑⓒⓓ	138	ⓐⓑⓒⓓ	158	ⓐⓑⓒⓓ	178	ⓐⓑⓒⓓ	198	ⓐⓑⓒⓓ
119	ⓐⓑⓒⓓ	139	ⓐⓑⓒⓓ	159	ⓐⓑⓒⓓ	179	ⓐⓑⓒⓓ	199	ⓐⓑⓒⓓ
120	ⓐⓑⓒⓓ	140	ⓐⓑⓒⓓ	160	ⓐⓑⓒⓓ	180	ⓐⓑⓒⓓ	200	ⓐⓑⓒⓓ

ANSWER SHEET

시원스쿨 LAB

이름	테스트 회차	날짜

LISTENING COMPREHENSION (PART 1~4)

NO	A B C D	NO	A B C D	NO	A B C D	NO	A B C D
1	ⓐ ⓑ ⓒ ⓓ	21	ⓐ ⓑ ⓒ ⓓ	41	ⓐ ⓑ ⓒ ⓓ	61	ⓐ ⓑ ⓒ ⓓ
2	ⓐ ⓑ ⓒ ⓓ	22	ⓐ ⓑ ⓒ ⓓ	42	ⓐ ⓑ ⓒ ⓓ	62	ⓐ ⓑ ⓒ ⓓ
3	ⓐ ⓑ ⓒ ⓓ	23	ⓐ ⓑ ⓒ ⓓ	43	ⓐ ⓑ ⓒ ⓓ	63	ⓐ ⓑ ⓒ ⓓ
4	ⓐ ⓑ ⓒ ⓓ	24	ⓐ ⓑ ⓒ ⓓ	44	ⓐ ⓑ ⓒ ⓓ	64	ⓐ ⓑ ⓒ ⓓ
5	ⓐ ⓑ ⓒ ⓓ	25	ⓐ ⓑ ⓒ ⓓ	45	ⓐ ⓑ ⓒ ⓓ	65	ⓐ ⓑ ⓒ ⓓ
6	ⓐ ⓑ ⓒ ⓓ	26	ⓐ ⓑ ⓒ ⓓ	46	ⓐ ⓑ ⓒ ⓓ	66	ⓐ ⓑ ⓒ ⓓ
7	ⓐ ⓑ ⓒ	27	ⓐ ⓑ ⓒ ⓓ	47	ⓐ ⓑ ⓒ ⓓ	67	ⓐ ⓑ ⓒ ⓓ
8	ⓐ ⓑ ⓒ	28	ⓐ ⓑ ⓒ ⓓ	48	ⓐ ⓑ ⓒ ⓓ	68	ⓐ ⓑ ⓒ ⓓ
9	ⓐ ⓑ ⓒ	29	ⓐ ⓑ ⓒ ⓓ	49	ⓐ ⓑ ⓒ ⓓ	69	ⓐ ⓑ ⓒ ⓓ
10	ⓐ ⓑ ⓒ	30	ⓐ ⓑ ⓒ ⓓ	50	ⓐ ⓑ ⓒ ⓓ	70	ⓐ ⓑ ⓒ ⓓ
11	ⓐ ⓑ ⓒ	31	ⓐ ⓑ ⓒ ⓓ	51	ⓐ ⓑ ⓒ ⓓ	71	ⓐ ⓑ ⓒ ⓓ
12	ⓐ ⓑ ⓒ	32	ⓐ ⓑ ⓒ ⓓ	52	ⓐ ⓑ ⓒ ⓓ	72	ⓐ ⓑ ⓒ ⓓ
13	ⓐ ⓑ ⓒ	33	ⓐ ⓑ ⓒ ⓓ	53	ⓐ ⓑ ⓒ ⓓ	73	ⓐ ⓑ ⓒ ⓓ
14	ⓐ ⓑ ⓒ	34	ⓐ ⓑ ⓒ ⓓ	54	ⓐ ⓑ ⓒ ⓓ	74	ⓐ ⓑ ⓒ ⓓ
15	ⓐ ⓑ ⓒ	35	ⓐ ⓑ ⓒ ⓓ	55	ⓐ ⓑ ⓒ ⓓ	75	ⓐ ⓑ ⓒ ⓓ
16	ⓐ ⓑ ⓒ	36	ⓐ ⓑ ⓒ ⓓ	56	ⓐ ⓑ ⓒ ⓓ	76	ⓐ ⓑ ⓒ ⓓ
17	ⓐ ⓑ ⓒ	37	ⓐ ⓑ ⓒ ⓓ	57	ⓐ ⓑ ⓒ ⓓ	77	ⓐ ⓑ ⓒ ⓓ
18	ⓐ ⓑ ⓒ	38	ⓐ ⓑ ⓒ ⓓ	58	ⓐ ⓑ ⓒ ⓓ	78	ⓐ ⓑ ⓒ ⓓ
19	ⓐ ⓑ ⓒ	39	ⓐ ⓑ ⓒ ⓓ	59	ⓐ ⓑ ⓒ ⓓ	79	ⓐ ⓑ ⓒ ⓓ
20	ⓐ ⓑ ⓒ	40	ⓐ ⓑ ⓒ ⓓ	60	ⓐ ⓑ ⓒ ⓓ	80	ⓐ ⓑ ⓒ ⓓ

READING COMPREHENSION (PART 5~7)

NO	A B C D	NO	A B C D	NO	A B C D	NO	A B C D
81	ⓐ ⓑ ⓒ ⓓ	101	ⓐ ⓑ ⓒ ⓓ	121	ⓐ ⓑ ⓒ ⓓ	141	ⓐ ⓑ ⓒ ⓓ
82	ⓐ ⓑ ⓒ ⓓ	102	ⓐ ⓑ ⓒ ⓓ	122	ⓐ ⓑ ⓒ ⓓ	142	ⓐ ⓑ ⓒ ⓓ
83	ⓐ ⓑ ⓒ ⓓ	103	ⓐ ⓑ ⓒ ⓓ	123	ⓐ ⓑ ⓒ ⓓ	143	ⓐ ⓑ ⓒ ⓓ
84	ⓐ ⓑ ⓒ ⓓ	104	ⓐ ⓑ ⓒ ⓓ	124	ⓐ ⓑ ⓒ ⓓ	144	ⓐ ⓑ ⓒ ⓓ
85	ⓐ ⓑ ⓒ ⓓ	105	ⓐ ⓑ ⓒ ⓓ	125	ⓐ ⓑ ⓒ ⓓ	145	ⓐ ⓑ ⓒ ⓓ
86	ⓐ ⓑ ⓒ ⓓ	106	ⓐ ⓑ ⓒ ⓓ	126	ⓐ ⓑ ⓒ ⓓ	146	ⓐ ⓑ ⓒ ⓓ
87	ⓐ ⓑ ⓒ ⓓ	107	ⓐ ⓑ ⓒ ⓓ	127	ⓐ ⓑ ⓒ ⓓ	147	ⓐ ⓑ ⓒ ⓓ
88	ⓐ ⓑ ⓒ ⓓ	108	ⓐ ⓑ ⓒ ⓓ	128	ⓐ ⓑ ⓒ ⓓ	148	ⓐ ⓑ ⓒ ⓓ
89	ⓐ ⓑ ⓒ ⓓ	109	ⓐ ⓑ ⓒ ⓓ	129	ⓐ ⓑ ⓒ ⓓ	149	ⓐ ⓑ ⓒ ⓓ
90	ⓐ ⓑ ⓒ ⓓ	110	ⓐ ⓑ ⓒ ⓓ	130	ⓐ ⓑ ⓒ ⓓ	150	ⓐ ⓑ ⓒ ⓓ
91	ⓐ ⓑ ⓒ ⓓ	111	ⓐ ⓑ ⓒ ⓓ	131	ⓐ ⓑ ⓒ ⓓ	151	ⓐ ⓑ ⓒ ⓓ
92	ⓐ ⓑ ⓒ ⓓ	112	ⓐ ⓑ ⓒ ⓓ	132	ⓐ ⓑ ⓒ ⓓ	152	ⓐ ⓑ ⓒ ⓓ
93	ⓐ ⓑ ⓒ ⓓ	113	ⓐ ⓑ ⓒ ⓓ	133	ⓐ ⓑ ⓒ ⓓ	153	ⓐ ⓑ ⓒ ⓓ
94	ⓐ ⓑ ⓒ ⓓ	114	ⓐ ⓑ ⓒ ⓓ	134	ⓐ ⓑ ⓒ ⓓ	154	ⓐ ⓑ ⓒ ⓓ
95	ⓐ ⓑ ⓒ ⓓ	115	ⓐ ⓑ ⓒ ⓓ	135	ⓐ ⓑ ⓒ ⓓ	155	ⓐ ⓑ ⓒ ⓓ
96	ⓐ ⓑ ⓒ ⓓ	116	ⓐ ⓑ ⓒ ⓓ	136	ⓐ ⓑ ⓒ ⓓ	156	ⓐ ⓑ ⓒ ⓓ
97	ⓐ ⓑ ⓒ ⓓ	117	ⓐ ⓑ ⓒ ⓓ	137	ⓐ ⓑ ⓒ ⓓ	157	ⓐ ⓑ ⓒ ⓓ
98	ⓐ ⓑ ⓒ ⓓ	118	ⓐ ⓑ ⓒ ⓓ	138	ⓐ ⓑ ⓒ ⓓ	158	ⓐ ⓑ ⓒ ⓓ
99	ⓐ ⓑ ⓒ ⓓ	119	ⓐ ⓑ ⓒ ⓓ	139	ⓐ ⓑ ⓒ ⓓ	159	ⓐ ⓑ ⓒ ⓓ
100	ⓐ ⓑ ⓒ ⓓ	120	ⓐ ⓑ ⓒ ⓓ	140	ⓐ ⓑ ⓒ ⓓ	160	ⓐ ⓑ ⓒ ⓓ

NO	A B C D	NO	A B C D
161	ⓐ ⓑ ⓒ ⓓ	181	ⓐ ⓑ ⓒ ⓓ
162	ⓐ ⓑ ⓒ ⓓ	182	ⓐ ⓑ ⓒ ⓓ
163	ⓐ ⓑ ⓒ ⓓ	183	ⓐ ⓑ ⓒ ⓓ
164	ⓐ ⓑ ⓒ ⓓ	184	ⓐ ⓑ ⓒ ⓓ
165	ⓐ ⓑ ⓒ ⓓ	185	ⓐ ⓑ ⓒ ⓓ
166	ⓐ ⓑ ⓒ ⓓ	186	ⓐ ⓑ ⓒ ⓓ
167	ⓐ ⓑ ⓒ ⓓ	187	ⓐ ⓑ ⓒ ⓓ
168	ⓐ ⓑ ⓒ ⓓ	188	ⓐ ⓑ ⓒ ⓓ
169	ⓐ ⓑ ⓒ ⓓ	189	ⓐ ⓑ ⓒ ⓓ
170	ⓐ ⓑ ⓒ ⓓ	190	ⓐ ⓑ ⓒ ⓓ
171	ⓐ ⓑ ⓒ ⓓ	191	ⓐ ⓑ ⓒ ⓓ
172	ⓐ ⓑ ⓒ ⓓ	192	ⓐ ⓑ ⓒ ⓓ
173	ⓐ ⓑ ⓒ ⓓ	193	ⓐ ⓑ ⓒ ⓓ
174	ⓐ ⓑ ⓒ ⓓ	194	ⓐ ⓑ ⓒ ⓓ
175	ⓐ ⓑ ⓒ ⓓ	195	ⓐ ⓑ ⓒ ⓓ
176	ⓐ ⓑ ⓒ ⓓ	196	ⓐ ⓑ ⓒ ⓓ
177	ⓐ ⓑ ⓒ ⓓ	197	ⓐ ⓑ ⓒ ⓓ
178	ⓐ ⓑ ⓒ ⓓ	198	ⓐ ⓑ ⓒ ⓓ
179	ⓐ ⓑ ⓒ ⓓ	199	ⓐ ⓑ ⓒ ⓓ
180	ⓐ ⓑ ⓒ ⓓ	200	ⓐ ⓑ ⓒ ⓓ

ANSWER SHEET

시원스쿨 LAB

이름

테스트 회차

날짜

LISTENING COMPREHENSION (PART 1~4)

NO	ANSWER A B C D	NO	ANSWER A B C D	NO	ANSWER A B C D	NO	ANSWER A B C D	NO	ANSWER A B C D
1	ⓐ ⓑ ⓒ ⓓ	21	ⓐ ⓑ ⓒ ⓓ	41	ⓐ ⓑ ⓒ ⓓ	61	ⓐ ⓑ ⓒ ⓓ	81	ⓐ ⓑ ⓒ ⓓ
2	ⓐ ⓑ ⓒ ⓓ	22	ⓐ ⓑ ⓒ ⓓ	42	ⓐ ⓑ ⓒ ⓓ	62	ⓐ ⓑ ⓒ ⓓ	82	ⓐ ⓑ ⓒ ⓓ
3	ⓐ ⓑ ⓒ ⓓ	23	ⓐ ⓑ ⓒ ⓓ	43	ⓐ ⓑ ⓒ ⓓ	63	ⓐ ⓑ ⓒ ⓓ	83	ⓐ ⓑ ⓒ ⓓ
4	ⓐ ⓑ ⓒ ⓓ	24	ⓐ ⓑ ⓒ ⓓ	44	ⓐ ⓑ ⓒ ⓓ	64	ⓐ ⓑ ⓒ ⓓ	84	ⓐ ⓑ ⓒ ⓓ
5	ⓐ ⓑ ⓒ	25	ⓐ ⓑ ⓒ ⓓ	45	ⓐ ⓑ ⓒ ⓓ	65	ⓐ ⓑ ⓒ ⓓ	85	ⓐ ⓑ ⓒ ⓓ
6	ⓐ ⓑ ⓒ	26	ⓐ ⓑ ⓒ ⓓ	46	ⓐ ⓑ ⓒ ⓓ	66	ⓐ ⓑ ⓒ ⓓ	86	ⓐ ⓑ ⓒ ⓓ
7	ⓐ ⓑ ⓒ	27	ⓐ ⓑ ⓒ ⓓ	47	ⓐ ⓑ ⓒ ⓓ	67	ⓐ ⓑ ⓒ ⓓ	87	ⓐ ⓑ ⓒ ⓓ
8	ⓐ ⓑ ⓒ	28	ⓐ ⓑ ⓒ ⓓ	48	ⓐ ⓑ ⓒ ⓓ	68	ⓐ ⓑ ⓒ ⓓ	88	ⓐ ⓑ ⓒ ⓓ
9	ⓐ ⓑ ⓒ	29	ⓐ ⓑ ⓒ ⓓ	49	ⓐ ⓑ ⓒ ⓓ	69	ⓐ ⓑ ⓒ ⓓ	89	ⓐ ⓑ ⓒ ⓓ
10	ⓐ ⓑ ⓒ	30	ⓐ ⓑ ⓒ ⓓ	50	ⓐ ⓑ ⓒ ⓓ	70	ⓐ ⓑ ⓒ ⓓ	90	ⓐ ⓑ ⓒ ⓓ
11	ⓐ ⓑ ⓒ	31	ⓐ ⓑ ⓒ	51	ⓐ ⓑ ⓒ ⓓ	71	ⓐ ⓑ ⓒ ⓓ	91	ⓐ ⓑ ⓒ ⓓ
12	ⓐ ⓑ ⓒ	32	ⓐ ⓑ ⓒ ⓓ	52	ⓐ ⓑ ⓒ ⓓ	72	ⓐ ⓑ ⓒ ⓓ	92	ⓐ ⓑ ⓒ ⓓ
13	ⓐ ⓑ ⓒ	33	ⓐ ⓑ ⓒ ⓓ	53	ⓐ ⓑ ⓒ ⓓ	73	ⓐ ⓑ ⓒ ⓓ	93	ⓐ ⓑ ⓒ ⓓ
14	ⓐ ⓑ ⓒ	34	ⓐ ⓑ ⓒ ⓓ	54	ⓐ ⓑ ⓒ ⓓ	74	ⓐ ⓑ ⓒ ⓓ	94	ⓐ ⓑ ⓒ ⓓ
15	ⓐ ⓑ ⓒ	35	ⓐ ⓑ ⓒ ⓓ	55	ⓐ ⓑ ⓒ ⓓ	75	ⓐ ⓑ ⓒ ⓓ	95	ⓐ ⓑ ⓒ ⓓ
16	ⓐ ⓑ ⓒ	36	ⓐ ⓑ ⓒ ⓓ	56	ⓐ ⓑ ⓒ ⓓ	76	ⓐ ⓑ ⓒ ⓓ	96	ⓐ ⓑ ⓒ ⓓ
17	ⓐ ⓑ ⓒ	37	ⓐ ⓑ ⓒ ⓓ	57	ⓐ ⓑ ⓒ ⓓ	77	ⓐ ⓑ ⓒ ⓓ	97	ⓐ ⓑ ⓒ ⓓ
18	ⓐ ⓑ ⓒ	38	ⓐ ⓑ ⓒ ⓓ	58	ⓐ ⓑ ⓒ ⓓ	78	ⓐ ⓑ ⓒ ⓓ	98	ⓐ ⓑ ⓒ ⓓ
19	ⓐ ⓑ ⓒ	39	ⓐ ⓑ ⓒ ⓓ	59	ⓐ ⓑ ⓒ ⓓ	79	ⓐ ⓑ ⓒ ⓓ	99	ⓐ ⓑ ⓒ ⓓ
20	ⓐ ⓑ ⓒ	40	ⓐ ⓑ ⓒ ⓓ	60	ⓐ ⓑ ⓒ ⓓ	80	ⓐ ⓑ ⓒ ⓓ	100	ⓐ ⓑ ⓒ ⓓ

READING COMPREHENSION (PART 5~7)

NO	ANSWER A B C D	NO	ANSWER A B C D	NO	ANSWER A B C D	NO	ANSWER A B C D	NO	ANSWER A B C D
101	ⓐ ⓑ ⓒ ⓓ	121	ⓐ ⓑ ⓒ ⓓ	141	ⓐ ⓑ ⓒ ⓓ	161	ⓐ ⓑ ⓒ ⓓ	181	ⓐ ⓑ ⓒ ⓓ
102	ⓐ ⓑ ⓒ ⓓ	122	ⓐ ⓑ ⓒ ⓓ	142	ⓐ ⓑ ⓒ ⓓ	162	ⓐ ⓑ ⓒ ⓓ	182	ⓐ ⓑ ⓒ ⓓ
103	ⓐ ⓑ ⓒ ⓓ	123	ⓐ ⓑ ⓒ ⓓ	143	ⓐ ⓑ ⓒ ⓓ	163	ⓐ ⓑ ⓒ ⓓ	183	ⓐ ⓑ ⓒ ⓓ
104	ⓐ ⓑ ⓒ ⓓ	124	ⓐ ⓑ ⓒ ⓓ	144	ⓐ ⓑ ⓒ ⓓ	164	ⓐ ⓑ ⓒ ⓓ	184	ⓐ ⓑ ⓒ ⓓ
105	ⓐ ⓑ ⓒ ⓓ	125	ⓐ ⓑ ⓒ ⓓ	145	ⓐ ⓑ ⓒ ⓓ	165	ⓐ ⓑ ⓒ ⓓ	185	ⓐ ⓑ ⓒ ⓓ
106	ⓐ ⓑ ⓒ ⓓ	126	ⓐ ⓑ ⓒ ⓓ	146	ⓐ ⓑ ⓒ ⓓ	166	ⓐ ⓑ ⓒ ⓓ	186	ⓐ ⓑ ⓒ ⓓ
107	ⓐ ⓑ ⓒ ⓓ	127	ⓐ ⓑ ⓒ ⓓ	147	ⓐ ⓑ ⓒ ⓓ	167	ⓐ ⓑ ⓒ ⓓ	187	ⓐ ⓑ ⓒ ⓓ
108	ⓐ ⓑ ⓒ ⓓ	128	ⓐ ⓑ ⓒ ⓓ	148	ⓐ ⓑ ⓒ ⓓ	168	ⓐ ⓑ ⓒ ⓓ	188	ⓐ ⓑ ⓒ ⓓ
109	ⓐ ⓑ ⓒ ⓓ	129	ⓐ ⓑ ⓒ ⓓ	149	ⓐ ⓑ ⓒ ⓓ	169	ⓐ ⓑ ⓒ ⓓ	189	ⓐ ⓑ ⓒ ⓓ
110	ⓐ ⓑ ⓒ ⓓ	130	ⓐ ⓑ ⓒ ⓓ	150	ⓐ ⓑ ⓒ ⓓ	170	ⓐ ⓑ ⓒ ⓓ	190	ⓐ ⓑ ⓒ ⓓ
111	ⓐ ⓑ ⓒ ⓓ	131	ⓐ ⓑ ⓒ ⓓ	151	ⓐ ⓑ ⓒ ⓓ	171	ⓐ ⓑ ⓒ ⓓ	191	ⓐ ⓑ ⓒ ⓓ
112	ⓐ ⓑ ⓒ ⓓ	132	ⓐ ⓑ ⓒ ⓓ	152	ⓐ ⓑ ⓒ ⓓ	172	ⓐ ⓑ ⓒ ⓓ	192	ⓐ ⓑ ⓒ ⓓ
113	ⓐ ⓑ ⓒ ⓓ	133	ⓐ ⓑ ⓒ ⓓ	153	ⓐ ⓑ ⓒ ⓓ	173	ⓐ ⓑ ⓒ ⓓ	193	ⓐ ⓑ ⓒ ⓓ
114	ⓐ ⓑ ⓒ ⓓ	134	ⓐ ⓑ ⓒ ⓓ	154	ⓐ ⓑ ⓒ ⓓ	174	ⓐ ⓑ ⓒ ⓓ	194	ⓐ ⓑ ⓒ ⓓ
115	ⓐ ⓑ ⓒ ⓓ	135	ⓐ ⓑ ⓒ ⓓ	155	ⓐ ⓑ ⓒ ⓓ	175	ⓐ ⓑ ⓒ ⓓ	195	ⓐ ⓑ ⓒ ⓓ
116	ⓐ ⓑ ⓒ ⓓ	136	ⓐ ⓑ ⓒ ⓓ	156	ⓐ ⓑ ⓒ ⓓ	176	ⓐ ⓑ ⓒ ⓓ	196	ⓐ ⓑ ⓒ ⓓ
117	ⓐ ⓑ ⓒ ⓓ	137	ⓐ ⓑ ⓒ ⓓ	157	ⓐ ⓑ ⓒ ⓓ	177	ⓐ ⓑ ⓒ ⓓ	197	ⓐ ⓑ ⓒ ⓓ
118	ⓐ ⓑ ⓒ ⓓ	138	ⓐ ⓑ ⓒ ⓓ	158	ⓐ ⓑ ⓒ ⓓ	178	ⓐ ⓑ ⓒ ⓓ	198	ⓐ ⓑ ⓒ ⓓ
119	ⓐ ⓑ ⓒ ⓓ	139	ⓐ ⓑ ⓒ ⓓ	159	ⓐ ⓑ ⓒ ⓓ	179	ⓐ ⓑ ⓒ ⓓ	199	ⓐ ⓑ ⓒ ⓓ
120	ⓐ ⓑ ⓒ ⓓ	140	ⓐ ⓑ ⓒ ⓓ	160	ⓐ ⓑ ⓒ ⓓ	180	ⓐ ⓑ ⓒ ⓓ	200	ⓐ ⓑ ⓒ ⓓ

ANSWER SHEET

시원스쿨 LAB

| 이름 | | 테스트 회차 | | 날짜 | |

LISTENING COMPREHENSION (PART 1~4)

NO	ANSWER A B C D	NO	ANSWER A B C D	NO	ANSWER A B C D	NO	ANSWER A B C D
1	ⓐⓑⓒⓓ	21	ⓐⓑⓒⓓ	41	ⓐⓑⓒⓓ	61	ⓐⓑⓒⓓ
2	ⓐⓑⓒⓓ	22	ⓐⓑⓒⓓ	42	ⓐⓑⓒⓓ	62	ⓐⓑⓒⓓ
3	ⓐⓑⓒⓓ	23	ⓐⓑⓒⓓ	43	ⓐⓑⓒⓓ	63	ⓐⓑⓒⓓ
4	ⓐⓑⓒⓓ	24	ⓐⓑⓒⓓ	44	ⓐⓑⓒⓓ	64	ⓐⓑⓒⓓ
5	ⓐⓑⓒⓓ	25	ⓐⓑⓒⓓ	45	ⓐⓑⓒⓓ	65	ⓐⓑⓒⓓ
6	ⓐⓑⓒⓓ	26	ⓐⓑⓒⓓ	46	ⓐⓑⓒⓓ	66	ⓐⓑⓒⓓ
7	ⓐⓑⓒⓓ	27	ⓐⓑⓒⓓ	47	ⓐⓑⓒⓓ	67	ⓐⓑⓒⓓ
8	ⓐⓑⓒⓓ	28	ⓐⓑⓒⓓ	48	ⓐⓑⓒⓓ	68	ⓐⓑⓒⓓ
9	ⓐⓑⓒⓓ	29	ⓐⓑⓒⓓ	49	ⓐⓑⓒⓓ	69	ⓐⓑⓒⓓ
10	ⓐⓑⓒⓓ	30	ⓐⓑⓒⓓ	50	ⓐⓑⓒⓓ	70	ⓐⓑⓒⓓ
11	ⓐⓑⓒⓓ	31	ⓐⓑⓒⓓ	51	ⓐⓑⓒⓓ	71	ⓐⓑⓒⓓ
12	ⓐⓑⓒⓓ	32	ⓐⓑⓒⓓ	52	ⓐⓑⓒⓓ	72	ⓐⓑⓒⓓ
13	ⓐⓑⓒⓓ	33	ⓐⓑⓒⓓ	53	ⓐⓑⓒⓓ	73	ⓐⓑⓒⓓ
14	ⓐⓑⓒⓓ	34	ⓐⓑⓒⓓ	54	ⓐⓑⓒⓓ	74	ⓐⓑⓒⓓ
15	ⓐⓑⓒⓓ	35	ⓐⓑⓒⓓ	55	ⓐⓑⓒⓓ	75	ⓐⓑⓒⓓ
16	ⓐⓑⓒⓓ	36	ⓐⓑⓒⓓ	56	ⓐⓑⓒⓓ	76	ⓐⓑⓒⓓ
17	ⓐⓑⓒⓓ	37	ⓐⓑⓒⓓ	57	ⓐⓑⓒⓓ	77	ⓐⓑⓒⓓ
18	ⓐⓑⓒⓓ	38	ⓐⓑⓒⓓ	58	ⓐⓑⓒⓓ	78	ⓐⓑⓒⓓ
19	ⓐⓑⓒⓓ	39	ⓐⓑⓒⓓ	59	ⓐⓑⓒⓓ	79	ⓐⓑⓒⓓ
20	ⓐⓑⓒⓓ	40	ⓐⓑⓒⓓ	60	ⓐⓑⓒⓓ	80	ⓐⓑⓒⓓ

NO	ANSWER A B C D
81	ⓐⓑⓒⓓ
82	ⓐⓑⓒⓓ
83	ⓐⓑⓒⓓ
84	ⓐⓑⓒⓓ
85	ⓐⓑⓒⓓ
86	ⓐⓑⓒⓓ
87	ⓐⓑⓒⓓ
88	ⓐⓑⓒⓓ
89	ⓐⓑⓒⓓ
90	ⓐⓑⓒⓓ
91	ⓐⓑⓒⓓ
92	ⓐⓑⓒⓓ
93	ⓐⓑⓒⓓ
94	ⓐⓑⓒⓓ
95	ⓐⓑⓒⓓ
96	ⓐⓑⓒⓓ
97	ⓐⓑⓒⓓ
98	ⓐⓑⓒⓓ
99	ⓐⓑⓒⓓ
100	ⓐⓑⓒⓓ

READING COMPREHENSION (PART 5~7)

NO	ANSWER A B C D	NO	ANSWER A B C D	NO	ANSWER A B C D	NO	ANSWER A B C D	NO	ANSWER A B C D
101	ⓐⓑⓒⓓ	121	ⓐⓑⓒⓓ	141	ⓐⓑⓒⓓ	161	ⓐⓑⓒⓓ	181	ⓐⓑⓒⓓ
102	ⓐⓑⓒⓓ	122	ⓐⓑⓒⓓ	142	ⓐⓑⓒⓓ	162	ⓐⓑⓒⓓ	182	ⓐⓑⓒⓓ
103	ⓐⓑⓒⓓ	123	ⓐⓑⓒⓓ	143	ⓐⓑⓒⓓ	163	ⓐⓑⓒⓓ	183	ⓐⓑⓒⓓ
104	ⓐⓑⓒⓓ	124	ⓐⓑⓒⓓ	144	ⓐⓑⓒⓓ	164	ⓐⓑⓒⓓ	184	ⓐⓑⓒⓓ
105	ⓐⓑⓒⓓ	125	ⓐⓑⓒⓓ	145	ⓐⓑⓒⓓ	165	ⓐⓑⓒⓓ	185	ⓐⓑⓒⓓ
106	ⓐⓑⓒⓓ	126	ⓐⓑⓒⓓ	146	ⓐⓑⓒⓓ	166	ⓐⓑⓒⓓ	186	ⓐⓑⓒⓓ
107	ⓐⓑⓒⓓ	127	ⓐⓑⓒⓓ	147	ⓐⓑⓒⓓ	167	ⓐⓑⓒⓓ	187	ⓐⓑⓒⓓ
108	ⓐⓑⓒⓓ	128	ⓐⓑⓒⓓ	148	ⓐⓑⓒⓓ	168	ⓐⓑⓒⓓ	188	ⓐⓑⓒⓓ
109	ⓐⓑⓒⓓ	129	ⓐⓑⓒⓓ	149	ⓐⓑⓒⓓ	169	ⓐⓑⓒⓓ	189	ⓐⓑⓒⓓ
110	ⓐⓑⓒⓓ	130	ⓐⓑⓒⓓ	150	ⓐⓑⓒⓓ	170	ⓐⓑⓒⓓ	190	ⓐⓑⓒⓓ
111	ⓐⓑⓒⓓ	131	ⓐⓑⓒⓓ	151	ⓐⓑⓒⓓ	171	ⓐⓑⓒⓓ	191	ⓐⓑⓒⓓ
112	ⓐⓑⓒⓓ	132	ⓐⓑⓒⓓ	152	ⓐⓑⓒⓓ	172	ⓐⓑⓒⓓ	192	ⓐⓑⓒⓓ
113	ⓐⓑⓒⓓ	133	ⓐⓑⓒⓓ	153	ⓐⓑⓒⓓ	173	ⓐⓑⓒⓓ	193	ⓐⓑⓒⓓ
114	ⓐⓑⓒⓓ	134	ⓐⓑⓒⓓ	154	ⓐⓑⓒⓓ	174	ⓐⓑⓒⓓ	194	ⓐⓑⓒⓓ
115	ⓐⓑⓒⓓ	135	ⓐⓑⓒⓓ	155	ⓐⓑⓒⓓ	175	ⓐⓑⓒⓓ	195	ⓐⓑⓒⓓ
116	ⓐⓑⓒⓓ	136	ⓐⓑⓒⓓ	156	ⓐⓑⓒⓓ	176	ⓐⓑⓒⓓ	196	ⓐⓑⓒⓓ
117	ⓐⓑⓒⓓ	137	ⓐⓑⓒⓓ	157	ⓐⓑⓒⓓ	177	ⓐⓑⓒⓓ	197	ⓐⓑⓒⓓ
118	ⓐⓑⓒⓓ	138	ⓐⓑⓒⓓ	158	ⓐⓑⓒⓓ	178	ⓐⓑⓒⓓ	198	ⓐⓑⓒⓓ
119	ⓐⓑⓒⓓ	139	ⓐⓑⓒⓓ	159	ⓐⓑⓒⓓ	179	ⓐⓑⓒⓓ	199	ⓐⓑⓒⓓ
120	ⓐⓑⓒⓓ	140	ⓐⓑⓒⓓ	160	ⓐⓑⓒⓓ	180	ⓐⓑⓒⓓ	200	ⓐⓑⓒⓓ

ANSWER SHEET

시원스쿨 LAB

이름 | 테스트 회차 | 날짜

LISTENING COMPREHENSION (PART 1~4)

NO	ANSWER A B C D	NO	ANSWER A B C D	NO	ANSWER A B C D	NO	ANSWER A B C D	NO	ANSWER A B C D
1	ⓐ ⓑ ⓒ ⓓ	21	ⓐ ⓑ ⓒ	41	ⓐ ⓑ ⓒ ⓓ	61	ⓐ ⓑ ⓒ ⓓ	81	ⓐ ⓑ ⓒ ⓓ
2	ⓐ ⓑ ⓒ ⓓ	22	ⓐ ⓑ ⓒ	42	ⓐ ⓑ ⓒ ⓓ	62	ⓐ ⓑ ⓒ ⓓ	82	ⓐ ⓑ ⓒ ⓓ
3	ⓐ ⓑ ⓒ ⓓ	23	ⓐ ⓑ ⓒ	43	ⓐ ⓑ ⓒ ⓓ	63	ⓐ ⓑ ⓒ ⓓ	83	ⓐ ⓑ ⓒ ⓓ
4	ⓐ ⓑ ⓒ ⓓ	24	ⓐ ⓑ ⓒ	44	ⓐ ⓑ ⓒ ⓓ	64	ⓐ ⓑ ⓒ ⓓ	84	ⓐ ⓑ ⓒ ⓓ
5	ⓐ ⓑ ⓒ ⓓ	25	ⓐ ⓑ ⓒ	45	ⓐ ⓑ ⓒ ⓓ	65	ⓐ ⓑ ⓒ ⓓ	85	ⓐ ⓑ ⓒ ⓓ
6	ⓐ ⓑ ⓒ ⓓ	26	ⓐ ⓑ ⓒ	46	ⓐ ⓑ ⓒ ⓓ	66	ⓐ ⓑ ⓒ ⓓ	86	ⓐ ⓑ ⓒ ⓓ
7	ⓐ ⓑ ⓒ	27	ⓐ ⓑ ⓒ	47	ⓐ ⓑ ⓒ ⓓ	67	ⓐ ⓑ ⓒ ⓓ	87	ⓐ ⓑ ⓒ ⓓ
8	ⓐ ⓑ ⓒ	28	ⓐ ⓑ ⓒ	48	ⓐ ⓑ ⓒ ⓓ	68	ⓐ ⓑ ⓒ ⓓ	88	ⓐ ⓑ ⓒ ⓓ
9	ⓐ ⓑ ⓒ	29	ⓐ ⓑ ⓒ	49	ⓐ ⓑ ⓒ ⓓ	69	ⓐ ⓑ ⓒ ⓓ	89	ⓐ ⓑ ⓒ ⓓ
10	ⓐ ⓑ ⓒ	30	ⓐ ⓑ ⓒ	50	ⓐ ⓑ ⓒ ⓓ	70	ⓐ ⓑ ⓒ ⓓ	90	ⓐ ⓑ ⓒ ⓓ
11	ⓐ ⓑ ⓒ	31	ⓐ ⓑ ⓒ	51	ⓐ ⓑ ⓒ ⓓ	71	ⓐ ⓑ ⓒ ⓓ	91	ⓐ ⓑ ⓒ ⓓ
12	ⓐ ⓑ ⓒ	32	ⓐ ⓑ ⓒ	52	ⓐ ⓑ ⓒ ⓓ	72	ⓐ ⓑ ⓒ ⓓ	92	ⓐ ⓑ ⓒ ⓓ
13	ⓐ ⓑ ⓒ	33	ⓐ ⓑ ⓒ	53	ⓐ ⓑ ⓒ ⓓ	73	ⓐ ⓑ ⓒ ⓓ	93	ⓐ ⓑ ⓒ ⓓ
14	ⓐ ⓑ ⓒ	34	ⓐ ⓑ ⓒ	54	ⓐ ⓑ ⓒ ⓓ	74	ⓐ ⓑ ⓒ ⓓ	94	ⓐ ⓑ ⓒ ⓓ
15	ⓐ ⓑ ⓒ	35	ⓐ ⓑ ⓒ	55	ⓐ ⓑ ⓒ ⓓ	75	ⓐ ⓑ ⓒ ⓓ	95	ⓐ ⓑ ⓒ ⓓ
16	ⓐ ⓑ ⓒ	36	ⓐ ⓑ ⓒ	56	ⓐ ⓑ ⓒ ⓓ	76	ⓐ ⓑ ⓒ ⓓ	96	ⓐ ⓑ ⓒ ⓓ
17	ⓐ ⓑ ⓒ	37	ⓐ ⓑ ⓒ	57	ⓐ ⓑ ⓒ ⓓ	77	ⓐ ⓑ ⓒ ⓓ	97	ⓐ ⓑ ⓒ ⓓ
18	ⓐ ⓑ ⓒ	38	ⓐ ⓑ ⓒ	58	ⓐ ⓑ ⓒ ⓓ	78	ⓐ ⓑ ⓒ ⓓ	98	ⓐ ⓑ ⓒ ⓓ
19	ⓐ ⓑ ⓒ	39	ⓐ ⓑ ⓒ	59	ⓐ ⓑ ⓒ ⓓ	79	ⓐ ⓑ ⓒ ⓓ	99	ⓐ ⓑ ⓒ ⓓ
20	ⓐ ⓑ ⓒ	40	ⓐ ⓑ ⓒ	60	ⓐ ⓑ ⓒ ⓓ	80	ⓐ ⓑ ⓒ ⓓ	100	ⓐ ⓑ ⓒ ⓓ

READING COMPREHENSION (PART 5~7)

NO	ANSWER A B C D	NO	ANSWER A B C D	NO	ANSWER A B C D	NO	ANSWER A B C D	NO	ANSWER A B C D
101	ⓐ ⓑ ⓒ ⓓ	121	ⓐ ⓑ ⓒ ⓓ	141	ⓐ ⓑ ⓒ ⓓ	161	ⓐ ⓑ ⓒ ⓓ	181	ⓐ ⓑ ⓒ ⓓ
102	ⓐ ⓑ ⓒ ⓓ	122	ⓐ ⓑ ⓒ ⓓ	142	ⓐ ⓑ ⓒ ⓓ	162	ⓐ ⓑ ⓒ ⓓ	182	ⓐ ⓑ ⓒ ⓓ
103	ⓐ ⓑ ⓒ ⓓ	123	ⓐ ⓑ ⓒ ⓓ	143	ⓐ ⓑ ⓒ ⓓ	163	ⓐ ⓑ ⓒ ⓓ	183	ⓐ ⓑ ⓒ ⓓ
104	ⓐ ⓑ ⓒ ⓓ	124	ⓐ ⓑ ⓒ ⓓ	144	ⓐ ⓑ ⓒ ⓓ	164	ⓐ ⓑ ⓒ ⓓ	184	ⓐ ⓑ ⓒ ⓓ
105	ⓐ ⓑ ⓒ ⓓ	125	ⓐ ⓑ ⓒ ⓓ	145	ⓐ ⓑ ⓒ ⓓ	165	ⓐ ⓑ ⓒ ⓓ	185	ⓐ ⓑ ⓒ ⓓ
106	ⓐ ⓑ ⓒ ⓓ	126	ⓐ ⓑ ⓒ ⓓ	146	ⓐ ⓑ ⓒ ⓓ	166	ⓐ ⓑ ⓒ ⓓ	186	ⓐ ⓑ ⓒ ⓓ
107	ⓐ ⓑ ⓒ ⓓ	127	ⓐ ⓑ ⓒ ⓓ	147	ⓐ ⓑ ⓒ ⓓ	167	ⓐ ⓑ ⓒ ⓓ	187	ⓐ ⓑ ⓒ ⓓ
108	ⓐ ⓑ ⓒ ⓓ	128	ⓐ ⓑ ⓒ ⓓ	148	ⓐ ⓑ ⓒ ⓓ	168	ⓐ ⓑ ⓒ ⓓ	188	ⓐ ⓑ ⓒ ⓓ
109	ⓐ ⓑ ⓒ ⓓ	129	ⓐ ⓑ ⓒ ⓓ	149	ⓐ ⓑ ⓒ ⓓ	169	ⓐ ⓑ ⓒ ⓓ	189	ⓐ ⓑ ⓒ ⓓ
110	ⓐ ⓑ ⓒ ⓓ	130	ⓐ ⓑ ⓒ ⓓ	150	ⓐ ⓑ ⓒ ⓓ	170	ⓐ ⓑ ⓒ ⓓ	190	ⓐ ⓑ ⓒ ⓓ
111	ⓐ ⓑ ⓒ ⓓ	131	ⓐ ⓑ ⓒ ⓓ	151	ⓐ ⓑ ⓒ ⓓ	171	ⓐ ⓑ ⓒ ⓓ	191	ⓐ ⓑ ⓒ ⓓ
112	ⓐ ⓑ ⓒ ⓓ	132	ⓐ ⓑ ⓒ ⓓ	152	ⓐ ⓑ ⓒ ⓓ	172	ⓐ ⓑ ⓒ ⓓ	192	ⓐ ⓑ ⓒ ⓓ
113	ⓐ ⓑ ⓒ ⓓ	133	ⓐ ⓑ ⓒ ⓓ	153	ⓐ ⓑ ⓒ ⓓ	173	ⓐ ⓑ ⓒ ⓓ	193	ⓐ ⓑ ⓒ ⓓ
114	ⓐ ⓑ ⓒ ⓓ	134	ⓐ ⓑ ⓒ ⓓ	154	ⓐ ⓑ ⓒ ⓓ	174	ⓐ ⓑ ⓒ ⓓ	194	ⓐ ⓑ ⓒ ⓓ
115	ⓐ ⓑ ⓒ ⓓ	135	ⓐ ⓑ ⓒ ⓓ	155	ⓐ ⓑ ⓒ ⓓ	175	ⓐ ⓑ ⓒ ⓓ	195	ⓐ ⓑ ⓒ ⓓ
116	ⓐ ⓑ ⓒ ⓓ	136	ⓐ ⓑ ⓒ ⓓ	156	ⓐ ⓑ ⓒ ⓓ	176	ⓐ ⓑ ⓒ ⓓ	196	ⓐ ⓑ ⓒ ⓓ
117	ⓐ ⓑ ⓒ ⓓ	137	ⓐ ⓑ ⓒ ⓓ	157	ⓐ ⓑ ⓒ ⓓ	177	ⓐ ⓑ ⓒ ⓓ	197	ⓐ ⓑ ⓒ ⓓ
118	ⓐ ⓑ ⓒ ⓓ	138	ⓐ ⓑ ⓒ ⓓ	158	ⓐ ⓑ ⓒ ⓓ	178	ⓐ ⓑ ⓒ ⓓ	198	ⓐ ⓑ ⓒ ⓓ
119	ⓐ ⓑ ⓒ ⓓ	139	ⓐ ⓑ ⓒ ⓓ	159	ⓐ ⓑ ⓒ ⓓ	179	ⓐ ⓑ ⓒ ⓓ	199	ⓐ ⓑ ⓒ ⓓ
120	ⓐ ⓑ ⓒ ⓓ	140	ⓐ ⓑ ⓒ ⓓ	160	ⓐ ⓑ ⓒ ⓓ	180	ⓐ ⓑ ⓒ ⓓ	200	ⓐ ⓑ ⓒ ⓓ

ANSWER SHEET

시원스쿨 LAB

이름	테스트 회차	날짜

LISTENING COMPREHENSION (PART 1~4)

NO	ANSWER A B C D	NO	ANSWER A B C D	NO	ANSWER A B C D	NO	ANSWER A B C D
1	ⓐ ⓑ ⓒ ⓓ	21	ⓐ ⓑ ⓒ ⓓ	41	ⓐ ⓑ ⓒ ⓓ	61	ⓐ ⓑ ⓒ ⓓ
2	ⓐ ⓑ ⓒ ⓓ	22	ⓐ ⓑ ⓒ ⓓ	42	ⓐ ⓑ ⓒ ⓓ	62	ⓐ ⓑ ⓒ ⓓ
3	ⓐ ⓑ ⓒ ⓓ	23	ⓐ ⓑ ⓒ ⓓ	43	ⓐ ⓑ ⓒ ⓓ	63	ⓐ ⓑ ⓒ ⓓ
4	ⓐ ⓑ ⓒ ⓓ	24	ⓐ ⓑ ⓒ ⓓ	44	ⓐ ⓑ ⓒ ⓓ	64	ⓐ ⓑ ⓒ ⓓ
5	ⓐ ⓑ ⓒ ⓓ	25	ⓐ ⓑ ⓒ ⓓ	45	ⓐ ⓑ ⓒ ⓓ	65	ⓐ ⓑ ⓒ ⓓ
6	ⓐ ⓑ ⓒ ⓓ	26	ⓐ ⓑ ⓒ ⓓ	46	ⓐ ⓑ ⓒ ⓓ	66	ⓐ ⓑ ⓒ ⓓ
7	ⓐ ⓑ ⓒ	27	ⓐ ⓑ ⓒ ⓓ	47	ⓐ ⓑ ⓒ ⓓ	67	ⓐ ⓑ ⓒ ⓓ
8	ⓐ ⓑ ⓒ	28	ⓐ ⓑ ⓒ ⓓ	48	ⓐ ⓑ ⓒ ⓓ	68	ⓐ ⓑ ⓒ ⓓ
9	ⓐ ⓑ ⓒ	29	ⓐ ⓑ ⓒ	49	ⓐ ⓑ ⓒ ⓓ	69	ⓐ ⓑ ⓒ ⓓ
10	ⓐ ⓑ ⓒ	30	ⓐ ⓑ ⓒ	50	ⓐ ⓑ ⓒ ⓓ	70	ⓐ ⓑ ⓒ ⓓ
11	ⓐ ⓑ ⓒ	31	ⓐ ⓑ ⓒ	51	ⓐ ⓑ ⓒ ⓓ	71	ⓐ ⓑ ⓒ ⓓ
12	ⓐ ⓑ ⓒ	32	ⓐ ⓑ ⓒ ⓓ	52	ⓐ ⓑ ⓒ ⓓ	72	ⓐ ⓑ ⓒ ⓓ
13	ⓐ ⓑ ⓒ	33	ⓐ ⓑ ⓒ ⓓ	53	ⓐ ⓑ ⓒ ⓓ	73	ⓐ ⓑ ⓒ ⓓ
14	ⓐ ⓑ ⓒ	34	ⓐ ⓑ ⓒ ⓓ	54	ⓐ ⓑ ⓒ ⓓ	74	ⓐ ⓑ ⓒ ⓓ
15	ⓐ ⓑ ⓒ	35	ⓐ ⓑ ⓒ ⓓ	55	ⓐ ⓑ ⓒ ⓓ	75	ⓐ ⓑ ⓒ ⓓ
16	ⓐ ⓑ ⓒ	36	ⓐ ⓑ ⓒ ⓓ	56	ⓐ ⓑ ⓒ ⓓ	76	ⓐ ⓑ ⓒ ⓓ
17	ⓐ ⓑ ⓒ	37	ⓐ ⓑ ⓒ ⓓ	57	ⓐ ⓑ ⓒ ⓓ	77	ⓐ ⓑ ⓒ ⓓ
18	ⓐ ⓑ ⓒ	38	ⓐ ⓑ ⓒ ⓓ	58	ⓐ ⓑ ⓒ ⓓ	78	ⓐ ⓑ ⓒ ⓓ
19	ⓐ ⓑ ⓒ	39	ⓐ ⓑ ⓒ ⓓ	59	ⓐ ⓑ ⓒ ⓓ	79	ⓐ ⓑ ⓒ ⓓ
20	ⓐ ⓑ ⓒ	40	ⓐ ⓑ ⓒ ⓓ	60	ⓐ ⓑ ⓒ ⓓ	80	ⓐ ⓑ ⓒ ⓓ
						81	ⓐ ⓑ ⓒ ⓓ
						82	ⓐ ⓑ ⓒ ⓓ
						83	ⓐ ⓑ ⓒ ⓓ
						84	ⓐ ⓑ ⓒ ⓓ
						85	ⓐ ⓑ ⓒ ⓓ
						86	ⓐ ⓑ ⓒ ⓓ
						87	ⓐ ⓑ ⓒ ⓓ
						88	ⓐ ⓑ ⓒ ⓓ
						89	ⓐ ⓑ ⓒ ⓓ
						90	ⓐ ⓑ ⓒ ⓓ
						91	ⓐ ⓑ ⓒ ⓓ
						92	ⓐ ⓑ ⓒ ⓓ
						93	ⓐ ⓑ ⓒ ⓓ
						94	ⓐ ⓑ ⓒ ⓓ
						95	ⓐ ⓑ ⓒ ⓓ
						96	ⓐ ⓑ ⓒ ⓓ
						97	ⓐ ⓑ ⓒ ⓓ
						98	ⓐ ⓑ ⓒ ⓓ
						99	ⓐ ⓑ ⓒ ⓓ
						100	ⓐ ⓑ ⓒ ⓓ

READING COMPREHENSION (PART 5~7)

NO	ANSWER A B C D	NO	ANSWER A B C D	NO	ANSWER A B C D	NO	ANSWER A B C D
101	ⓐ ⓑ ⓒ ⓓ	121	ⓐ ⓑ ⓒ ⓓ	141	ⓐ ⓑ ⓒ ⓓ	161	ⓐ ⓑ ⓒ ⓓ
102	ⓐ ⓑ ⓒ ⓓ	122	ⓐ ⓑ ⓒ ⓓ	142	ⓐ ⓑ ⓒ ⓓ	162	ⓐ ⓑ ⓒ ⓓ
103	ⓐ ⓑ ⓒ ⓓ	123	ⓐ ⓑ ⓒ ⓓ	143	ⓐ ⓑ ⓒ ⓓ	163	ⓐ ⓑ ⓒ ⓓ
104	ⓐ ⓑ ⓒ ⓓ	124	ⓐ ⓑ ⓒ ⓓ	144	ⓐ ⓑ ⓒ ⓓ	164	ⓐ ⓑ ⓒ ⓓ
105	ⓐ ⓑ ⓒ ⓓ	125	ⓐ ⓑ ⓒ ⓓ	145	ⓐ ⓑ ⓒ ⓓ	165	ⓐ ⓑ ⓒ ⓓ
106	ⓐ ⓑ ⓒ ⓓ	126	ⓐ ⓑ ⓒ ⓓ	146	ⓐ ⓑ ⓒ ⓓ	166	ⓐ ⓑ ⓒ ⓓ
107	ⓐ ⓑ ⓒ ⓓ	127	ⓐ ⓑ ⓒ ⓓ	147	ⓐ ⓑ ⓒ ⓓ	167	ⓐ ⓑ ⓒ ⓓ
108	ⓐ ⓑ ⓒ ⓓ	128	ⓐ ⓑ ⓒ ⓓ	148	ⓐ ⓑ ⓒ ⓓ	168	ⓐ ⓑ ⓒ ⓓ
109	ⓐ ⓑ ⓒ ⓓ	129	ⓐ ⓑ ⓒ ⓓ	149	ⓐ ⓑ ⓒ ⓓ	169	ⓐ ⓑ ⓒ ⓓ
110	ⓐ ⓑ ⓒ ⓓ	130	ⓐ ⓑ ⓒ ⓓ	150	ⓐ ⓑ ⓒ ⓓ	170	ⓐ ⓑ ⓒ ⓓ
111	ⓐ ⓑ ⓒ ⓓ	131	ⓐ ⓑ ⓒ ⓓ	151	ⓐ ⓑ ⓒ ⓓ	171	ⓐ ⓑ ⓒ ⓓ
112	ⓐ ⓑ ⓒ ⓓ	132	ⓐ ⓑ ⓒ ⓓ	152	ⓐ ⓑ ⓒ ⓓ	172	ⓐ ⓑ ⓒ ⓓ
113	ⓐ ⓑ ⓒ ⓓ	133	ⓐ ⓑ ⓒ ⓓ	153	ⓐ ⓑ ⓒ ⓓ	173	ⓐ ⓑ ⓒ ⓓ
114	ⓐ ⓑ ⓒ ⓓ	134	ⓐ ⓑ ⓒ ⓓ	154	ⓐ ⓑ ⓒ ⓓ	174	ⓐ ⓑ ⓒ ⓓ
115	ⓐ ⓑ ⓒ ⓓ	135	ⓐ ⓑ ⓒ ⓓ	155	ⓐ ⓑ ⓒ ⓓ	175	ⓐ ⓑ ⓒ ⓓ
116	ⓐ ⓑ ⓒ ⓓ	136	ⓐ ⓑ ⓒ ⓓ	156	ⓐ ⓑ ⓒ ⓓ	176	ⓐ ⓑ ⓒ ⓓ
117	ⓐ ⓑ ⓒ ⓓ	137	ⓐ ⓑ ⓒ ⓓ	157	ⓐ ⓑ ⓒ ⓓ	177	ⓐ ⓑ ⓒ ⓓ
118	ⓐ ⓑ ⓒ ⓓ	138	ⓐ ⓑ ⓒ ⓓ	158	ⓐ ⓑ ⓒ ⓓ	178	ⓐ ⓑ ⓒ ⓓ
119	ⓐ ⓑ ⓒ ⓓ	139	ⓐ ⓑ ⓒ ⓓ	159	ⓐ ⓑ ⓒ ⓓ	179	ⓐ ⓑ ⓒ ⓓ
120	ⓐ ⓑ ⓒ ⓓ	140	ⓐ ⓑ ⓒ ⓓ	160	ⓐ ⓑ ⓒ ⓓ	180	ⓐ ⓑ ⓒ ⓓ
						181	ⓐ ⓑ ⓒ ⓓ
						182	ⓐ ⓑ ⓒ ⓓ
						183	ⓐ ⓑ ⓒ ⓓ
						184	ⓐ ⓑ ⓒ ⓓ
						185	ⓐ ⓑ ⓒ ⓓ
						186	ⓐ ⓑ ⓒ ⓓ
						187	ⓐ ⓑ ⓒ ⓓ
						188	ⓐ ⓑ ⓒ ⓓ
						189	ⓐ ⓑ ⓒ ⓓ
						190	ⓐ ⓑ ⓒ ⓓ
						191	ⓐ ⓑ ⓒ ⓓ
						192	ⓐ ⓑ ⓒ ⓓ
						193	ⓐ ⓑ ⓒ ⓓ
						194	ⓐ ⓑ ⓒ ⓓ
						195	ⓐ ⓑ ⓒ ⓓ
						196	ⓐ ⓑ ⓒ ⓓ
						197	ⓐ ⓑ ⓒ ⓓ
						198	ⓐ ⓑ ⓒ ⓓ
						199	ⓐ ⓑ ⓒ ⓓ
						200	ⓐ ⓑ ⓒ ⓓ

ANSWER SHEET

시원스쿨 LAB

이름

테스트 회차

날짜

LISTENING COMPREHENSION (PART 1~4)

NO	ANSWER A B C D	NO	ANSWER A B C D	NO	ANSWER A B C D	NO	ANSWER A B C D	NO	ANSWER A B C D
1	ⓐ ⓑ ⓒ	21	ⓐ ⓑ ⓒ ⓓ	41	ⓐ ⓑ ⓒ ⓓ	61	ⓐ ⓑ ⓒ ⓓ	81	ⓐ ⓑ ⓒ ⓓ
2	ⓐ ⓑ ⓒ	22	ⓐ ⓑ ⓒ ⓓ	42	ⓐ ⓑ ⓒ ⓓ	62	ⓐ ⓑ ⓒ ⓓ	82	ⓐ ⓑ ⓒ ⓓ
3	ⓐ ⓑ ⓒ	23	ⓐ ⓑ ⓒ ⓓ	43	ⓐ ⓑ ⓒ ⓓ	63	ⓐ ⓑ ⓒ ⓓ	83	ⓐ ⓑ ⓒ ⓓ
4	ⓐ ⓑ ⓒ ⓓ	24	ⓐ ⓑ ⓒ ⓓ	44	ⓐ ⓑ ⓒ ⓓ	64	ⓐ ⓑ ⓒ ⓓ	84	ⓐ ⓑ ⓒ ⓓ
5	ⓐ ⓑ ⓒ ⓓ	25	ⓐ ⓑ ⓒ ⓓ	45	ⓐ ⓑ ⓒ ⓓ	65	ⓐ ⓑ ⓒ ⓓ	85	ⓐ ⓑ ⓒ ⓓ
6	ⓐ ⓑ ⓒ ⓓ	26	ⓐ ⓑ ⓒ ⓓ	46	ⓐ ⓑ ⓒ ⓓ	66	ⓐ ⓑ ⓒ ⓓ	86	ⓐ ⓑ ⓒ ⓓ
7	ⓐ ⓑ ⓒ	27	ⓐ ⓑ ⓒ ⓓ	47	ⓐ ⓑ ⓒ ⓓ	67	ⓐ ⓑ ⓒ ⓓ	87	ⓐ ⓑ ⓒ ⓓ
8	ⓐ ⓑ ⓒ	28	ⓐ ⓑ ⓒ ⓓ	48	ⓐ ⓑ ⓒ ⓓ	68	ⓐ ⓑ ⓒ ⓓ	88	ⓐ ⓑ ⓒ ⓓ
9	ⓐ ⓑ ⓒ	29	ⓐ ⓑ ⓒ ⓓ	49	ⓐ ⓑ ⓒ ⓓ	69	ⓐ ⓑ ⓒ ⓓ	89	ⓐ ⓑ ⓒ ⓓ
10	ⓐ ⓑ ⓒ	30	ⓐ ⓑ ⓒ ⓓ	50	ⓐ ⓑ ⓒ ⓓ	70	ⓐ ⓑ ⓒ ⓓ	90	ⓐ ⓑ ⓒ ⓓ
11	ⓐ ⓑ ⓒ	31	ⓐ ⓑ ⓒ	51	ⓐ ⓑ ⓒ ⓓ	71	ⓐ ⓑ ⓒ ⓓ	91	ⓐ ⓑ ⓒ ⓓ
12	ⓐ ⓑ ⓒ	32	ⓐ ⓑ ⓒ	52	ⓐ ⓑ ⓒ ⓓ	72	ⓐ ⓑ ⓒ ⓓ	92	ⓐ ⓑ ⓒ ⓓ
13	ⓐ ⓑ ⓒ	33	ⓐ ⓑ ⓒ	53	ⓐ ⓑ ⓒ ⓓ	73	ⓐ ⓑ ⓒ ⓓ	93	ⓐ ⓑ ⓒ ⓓ
14	ⓐ ⓑ ⓒ	34	ⓐ ⓑ ⓒ	54	ⓐ ⓑ ⓒ ⓓ	74	ⓐ ⓑ ⓒ ⓓ	94	ⓐ ⓑ ⓒ ⓓ
15	ⓐ ⓑ ⓒ	35	ⓐ ⓑ ⓒ	55	ⓐ ⓑ ⓒ ⓓ	75	ⓐ ⓑ ⓒ ⓓ	95	ⓐ ⓑ ⓒ ⓓ
16	ⓐ ⓑ ⓒ	36	ⓐ ⓑ ⓒ	56	ⓐ ⓑ ⓒ ⓓ	76	ⓐ ⓑ ⓒ ⓓ	96	ⓐ ⓑ ⓒ ⓓ
17	ⓐ ⓑ ⓒ	37	ⓐ ⓑ ⓒ	57	ⓐ ⓑ ⓒ ⓓ	77	ⓐ ⓑ ⓒ ⓓ	97	ⓐ ⓑ ⓒ ⓓ
18	ⓐ ⓑ ⓒ	38	ⓐ ⓑ ⓒ	58	ⓐ ⓑ ⓒ ⓓ	78	ⓐ ⓑ ⓒ ⓓ	98	ⓐ ⓑ ⓒ ⓓ
19	ⓐ ⓑ ⓒ	39	ⓐ ⓑ ⓒ	59	ⓐ ⓑ ⓒ ⓓ	79	ⓐ ⓑ ⓒ ⓓ	99	ⓐ ⓑ ⓒ ⓓ
20	ⓐ ⓑ ⓒ	40	ⓐ ⓑ ⓒ	60	ⓐ ⓑ ⓒ ⓓ	80	ⓐ ⓑ ⓒ ⓓ	100	ⓐ ⓑ ⓒ ⓓ

READING COMPREHENSION (PART 5~7)

NO	ANSWER A B C D	NO	ANSWER A B C D	NO	ANSWER A B C D	NO	ANSWER A B C D	NO	ANSWER A B C D
101	ⓐ ⓑ ⓒ ⓓ	121	ⓐ ⓑ ⓒ ⓓ	141	ⓐ ⓑ ⓒ ⓓ	161	ⓐ ⓑ ⓒ ⓓ	181	ⓐ ⓑ ⓒ ⓓ
102	ⓐ ⓑ ⓒ ⓓ	122	ⓐ ⓑ ⓒ ⓓ	142	ⓐ ⓑ ⓒ ⓓ	162	ⓐ ⓑ ⓒ ⓓ	182	ⓐ ⓑ ⓒ ⓓ
103	ⓐ ⓑ ⓒ ⓓ	123	ⓐ ⓑ ⓒ ⓓ	143	ⓐ ⓑ ⓒ ⓓ	163	ⓐ ⓑ ⓒ ⓓ	183	ⓐ ⓑ ⓒ ⓓ
104	ⓐ ⓑ ⓒ ⓓ	124	ⓐ ⓑ ⓒ ⓓ	144	ⓐ ⓑ ⓒ ⓓ	164	ⓐ ⓑ ⓒ ⓓ	184	ⓐ ⓑ ⓒ ⓓ
105	ⓐ ⓑ ⓒ ⓓ	125	ⓐ ⓑ ⓒ ⓓ	145	ⓐ ⓑ ⓒ ⓓ	165	ⓐ ⓑ ⓒ ⓓ	185	ⓐ ⓑ ⓒ ⓓ
106	ⓐ ⓑ ⓒ ⓓ	126	ⓐ ⓑ ⓒ ⓓ	146	ⓐ ⓑ ⓒ ⓓ	166	ⓐ ⓑ ⓒ ⓓ	186	ⓐ ⓑ ⓒ ⓓ
107	ⓐ ⓑ ⓒ ⓓ	127	ⓐ ⓑ ⓒ ⓓ	147	ⓐ ⓑ ⓒ ⓓ	167	ⓐ ⓑ ⓒ ⓓ	187	ⓐ ⓑ ⓒ ⓓ
108	ⓐ ⓑ ⓒ ⓓ	128	ⓐ ⓑ ⓒ ⓓ	148	ⓐ ⓑ ⓒ ⓓ	168	ⓐ ⓑ ⓒ ⓓ	188	ⓐ ⓑ ⓒ ⓓ
109	ⓐ ⓑ ⓒ ⓓ	129	ⓐ ⓑ ⓒ ⓓ	149	ⓐ ⓑ ⓒ ⓓ	169	ⓐ ⓑ ⓒ ⓓ	189	ⓐ ⓑ ⓒ ⓓ
110	ⓐ ⓑ ⓒ ⓓ	130	ⓐ ⓑ ⓒ ⓓ	150	ⓐ ⓑ ⓒ ⓓ	170	ⓐ ⓑ ⓒ ⓓ	190	ⓐ ⓑ ⓒ ⓓ
111	ⓐ ⓑ ⓒ ⓓ	131	ⓐ ⓑ ⓒ ⓓ	151	ⓐ ⓑ ⓒ ⓓ	171	ⓐ ⓑ ⓒ ⓓ	191	ⓐ ⓑ ⓒ ⓓ
112	ⓐ ⓑ ⓒ ⓓ	132	ⓐ ⓑ ⓒ ⓓ	152	ⓐ ⓑ ⓒ ⓓ	172	ⓐ ⓑ ⓒ ⓓ	192	ⓐ ⓑ ⓒ ⓓ
113	ⓐ ⓑ ⓒ ⓓ	133	ⓐ ⓑ ⓒ ⓓ	153	ⓐ ⓑ ⓒ ⓓ	173	ⓐ ⓑ ⓒ ⓓ	193	ⓐ ⓑ ⓒ ⓓ
114	ⓐ ⓑ ⓒ ⓓ	134	ⓐ ⓑ ⓒ ⓓ	154	ⓐ ⓑ ⓒ ⓓ	174	ⓐ ⓑ ⓒ ⓓ	194	ⓐ ⓑ ⓒ ⓓ
115	ⓐ ⓑ ⓒ ⓓ	135	ⓐ ⓑ ⓒ ⓓ	155	ⓐ ⓑ ⓒ ⓓ	175	ⓐ ⓑ ⓒ ⓓ	195	ⓐ ⓑ ⓒ ⓓ
116	ⓐ ⓑ ⓒ ⓓ	136	ⓐ ⓑ ⓒ ⓓ	156	ⓐ ⓑ ⓒ ⓓ	176	ⓐ ⓑ ⓒ ⓓ	196	ⓐ ⓑ ⓒ ⓓ
117	ⓐ ⓑ ⓒ ⓓ	137	ⓐ ⓑ ⓒ ⓓ	157	ⓐ ⓑ ⓒ ⓓ	177	ⓐ ⓑ ⓒ ⓓ	197	ⓐ ⓑ ⓒ ⓓ
118	ⓐ ⓑ ⓒ ⓓ	138	ⓐ ⓑ ⓒ ⓓ	158	ⓐ ⓑ ⓒ ⓓ	178	ⓐ ⓑ ⓒ ⓓ	198	ⓐ ⓑ ⓒ ⓓ
119	ⓐ ⓑ ⓒ ⓓ	139	ⓐ ⓑ ⓒ ⓓ	159	ⓐ ⓑ ⓒ ⓓ	179	ⓐ ⓑ ⓒ ⓓ	199	ⓐ ⓑ ⓒ ⓓ
120	ⓐ ⓑ ⓒ ⓓ	140	ⓐ ⓑ ⓒ ⓓ	160	ⓐ ⓑ ⓒ ⓓ	180	ⓐ ⓑ ⓒ ⓓ	200	ⓐ ⓑ ⓒ ⓓ

ANSWER SHEET

시원스쿨 LAB

이름   테스트 회차   날짜

LISTENING COMPREHENSION (PART 1~4)

NO	ANSWER A B C D	NO	ANSWER A B C D	NO	ANSWER A B C D	NO	ANSWER A B C D
1	ⓐ ⓑ ⓒ ⓓ	21	ⓐ ⓑ ⓒ ⓓ	41	ⓐ ⓑ ⓒ ⓓ	61	ⓐ ⓑ ⓒ ⓓ
2	ⓐ ⓑ ⓒ ⓓ	22	ⓐ ⓑ ⓒ ⓓ	42	ⓐ ⓑ ⓒ ⓓ	62	ⓐ ⓑ ⓒ ⓓ
3	ⓐ ⓑ ⓒ ⓓ	23	ⓐ ⓑ ⓒ ⓓ	43	ⓐ ⓑ ⓒ ⓓ	63	ⓐ ⓑ ⓒ ⓓ
4	ⓐ ⓑ ⓒ ⓓ	24	ⓐ ⓑ ⓒ ⓓ	44	ⓐ ⓑ ⓒ ⓓ	64	ⓐ ⓑ ⓒ ⓓ
5	ⓐ ⓑ ⓒ ⓓ	25	ⓐ ⓑ ⓒ ⓓ	45	ⓐ ⓑ ⓒ ⓓ	65	ⓐ ⓑ ⓒ ⓓ
6	ⓐ ⓑ ⓒ ⓓ	26	ⓐ ⓑ ⓒ ⓓ	46	ⓐ ⓑ ⓒ ⓓ	66	ⓐ ⓑ ⓒ ⓓ
7	ⓐ ⓑ ⓒ	27	ⓐ ⓑ ⓒ ⓓ	47	ⓐ ⓑ ⓒ ⓓ	67	ⓐ ⓑ ⓒ ⓓ
8	ⓐ ⓑ ⓒ	28	ⓐ ⓑ ⓒ ⓓ	48	ⓐ ⓑ ⓒ ⓓ	68	ⓐ ⓑ ⓒ ⓓ
9	ⓐ ⓑ ⓒ	29	ⓐ ⓑ ⓒ ⓓ	49	ⓐ ⓑ ⓒ ⓓ	69	ⓐ ⓑ ⓒ ⓓ
10	ⓐ ⓑ ⓒ	30	ⓐ ⓑ ⓒ ⓓ	50	ⓐ ⓑ ⓒ ⓓ	70	ⓐ ⓑ ⓒ ⓓ
11	ⓐ ⓑ ⓒ	31	ⓐ ⓑ ⓒ ⓓ	51	ⓐ ⓑ ⓒ ⓓ	71	ⓐ ⓑ ⓒ ⓓ
12	ⓐ ⓑ ⓒ	32	ⓐ ⓑ ⓒ ⓓ	52	ⓐ ⓑ ⓒ ⓓ	72	ⓐ ⓑ ⓒ ⓓ
13	ⓐ ⓑ ⓒ	33	ⓐ ⓑ ⓒ ⓓ	53	ⓐ ⓑ ⓒ ⓓ	73	ⓐ ⓑ ⓒ ⓓ
14	ⓐ ⓑ ⓒ	34	ⓐ ⓑ ⓒ ⓓ	54	ⓐ ⓑ ⓒ ⓓ	74	ⓐ ⓑ ⓒ ⓓ
15	ⓐ ⓑ ⓒ	35	ⓐ ⓑ ⓒ ⓓ	55	ⓐ ⓑ ⓒ ⓓ	75	ⓐ ⓑ ⓒ ⓓ
16	ⓐ ⓑ ⓒ	36	ⓐ ⓑ ⓒ ⓓ	56	ⓐ ⓑ ⓒ ⓓ	76	ⓐ ⓑ ⓒ ⓓ
17	ⓐ ⓑ ⓒ	37	ⓐ ⓑ ⓒ ⓓ	57	ⓐ ⓑ ⓒ ⓓ	77	ⓐ ⓑ ⓒ ⓓ
18	ⓐ ⓑ ⓒ	38	ⓐ ⓑ ⓒ ⓓ	58	ⓐ ⓑ ⓒ ⓓ	78	ⓐ ⓑ ⓒ ⓓ
19	ⓐ ⓑ ⓒ	39	ⓐ ⓑ ⓒ ⓓ	59	ⓐ ⓑ ⓒ ⓓ	79	ⓐ ⓑ ⓒ ⓓ
20	ⓐ ⓑ ⓒ	40	ⓐ ⓑ ⓒ ⓓ	60	ⓐ ⓑ ⓒ ⓓ	80	ⓐ ⓑ ⓒ ⓓ

READING COMPREHENSION (PART 5~7)

NO	ANSWER A B C D	NO	ANSWER A B C D	NO	ANSWER A B C D	NO	ANSWER A B C D	NO	ANSWER A B C D	NO	ANSWER A B C D
81	ⓐ ⓑ ⓒ ⓓ	101	ⓐ ⓑ ⓒ ⓓ	121	ⓐ ⓑ ⓒ ⓓ	141	ⓐ ⓑ ⓒ ⓓ	161	ⓐ ⓑ ⓒ ⓓ	181	ⓐ ⓑ ⓒ ⓓ
82	ⓐ ⓑ ⓒ ⓓ	102	ⓐ ⓑ ⓒ ⓓ	122	ⓐ ⓑ ⓒ ⓓ	142	ⓐ ⓑ ⓒ ⓓ	162	ⓐ ⓑ ⓒ ⓓ	182	ⓐ ⓑ ⓒ ⓓ
83	ⓐ ⓑ ⓒ ⓓ	103	ⓐ ⓑ ⓒ ⓓ	123	ⓐ ⓑ ⓒ ⓓ	143	ⓐ ⓑ ⓒ ⓓ	163	ⓐ ⓑ ⓒ ⓓ	183	ⓐ ⓑ ⓒ ⓓ
84	ⓐ ⓑ ⓒ ⓓ	104	ⓐ ⓑ ⓒ ⓓ	124	ⓐ ⓑ ⓒ ⓓ	144	ⓐ ⓑ ⓒ ⓓ	164	ⓐ ⓑ ⓒ ⓓ	184	ⓐ ⓑ ⓒ ⓓ
85	ⓐ ⓑ ⓒ ⓓ	105	ⓐ ⓑ ⓒ ⓓ	125	ⓐ ⓑ ⓒ ⓓ	145	ⓐ ⓑ ⓒ ⓓ	165	ⓐ ⓑ ⓒ ⓓ	185	ⓐ ⓑ ⓒ ⓓ
86	ⓐ ⓑ ⓒ ⓓ	106	ⓐ ⓑ ⓒ ⓓ	126	ⓐ ⓑ ⓒ ⓓ	146	ⓐ ⓑ ⓒ ⓓ	166	ⓐ ⓑ ⓒ ⓓ	186	ⓐ ⓑ ⓒ ⓓ
87	ⓐ ⓑ ⓒ ⓓ	107	ⓐ ⓑ ⓒ ⓓ	127	ⓐ ⓑ ⓒ ⓓ	147	ⓐ ⓑ ⓒ ⓓ	167	ⓐ ⓑ ⓒ ⓓ	187	ⓐ ⓑ ⓒ ⓓ
88	ⓐ ⓑ ⓒ ⓓ	108	ⓐ ⓑ ⓒ ⓓ	128	ⓐ ⓑ ⓒ ⓓ	148	ⓐ ⓑ ⓒ ⓓ	168	ⓐ ⓑ ⓒ ⓓ	188	ⓐ ⓑ ⓒ ⓓ
89	ⓐ ⓑ ⓒ ⓓ	109	ⓐ ⓑ ⓒ ⓓ	129	ⓐ ⓑ ⓒ ⓓ	149	ⓐ ⓑ ⓒ ⓓ	169	ⓐ ⓑ ⓒ ⓓ	189	ⓐ ⓑ ⓒ ⓓ
90	ⓐ ⓑ ⓒ ⓓ	110	ⓐ ⓑ ⓒ ⓓ	130	ⓐ ⓑ ⓒ ⓓ	150	ⓐ ⓑ ⓒ ⓓ	170	ⓐ ⓑ ⓒ ⓓ	190	ⓐ ⓑ ⓒ ⓓ
91	ⓐ ⓑ ⓒ ⓓ	111	ⓐ ⓑ ⓒ ⓓ	131	ⓐ ⓑ ⓒ ⓓ	151	ⓐ ⓑ ⓒ ⓓ	171	ⓐ ⓑ ⓒ ⓓ	191	ⓐ ⓑ ⓒ ⓓ
92	ⓐ ⓑ ⓒ ⓓ	112	ⓐ ⓑ ⓒ ⓓ	132	ⓐ ⓑ ⓒ ⓓ	152	ⓐ ⓑ ⓒ ⓓ	172	ⓐ ⓑ ⓒ ⓓ	192	ⓐ ⓑ ⓒ ⓓ
93	ⓐ ⓑ ⓒ ⓓ	113	ⓐ ⓑ ⓒ ⓓ	133	ⓐ ⓑ ⓒ ⓓ	153	ⓐ ⓑ ⓒ ⓓ	173	ⓐ ⓑ ⓒ ⓓ	193	ⓐ ⓑ ⓒ ⓓ
94	ⓐ ⓑ ⓒ ⓓ	114	ⓐ ⓑ ⓒ ⓓ	134	ⓐ ⓑ ⓒ ⓓ	154	ⓐ ⓑ ⓒ ⓓ	174	ⓐ ⓑ ⓒ ⓓ	194	ⓐ ⓑ ⓒ ⓓ
95	ⓐ ⓑ ⓒ ⓓ	115	ⓐ ⓑ ⓒ ⓓ	135	ⓐ ⓑ ⓒ ⓓ	155	ⓐ ⓑ ⓒ ⓓ	175	ⓐ ⓑ ⓒ ⓓ	195	ⓐ ⓑ ⓒ ⓓ
96	ⓐ ⓑ ⓒ ⓓ	116	ⓐ ⓑ ⓒ ⓓ	136	ⓐ ⓑ ⓒ ⓓ	156	ⓐ ⓑ ⓒ ⓓ	176	ⓐ ⓑ ⓒ ⓓ	196	ⓐ ⓑ ⓒ ⓓ
97	ⓐ ⓑ ⓒ ⓓ	117	ⓐ ⓑ ⓒ ⓓ	137	ⓐ ⓑ ⓒ ⓓ	157	ⓐ ⓑ ⓒ ⓓ	177	ⓐ ⓑ ⓒ ⓓ	197	ⓐ ⓑ ⓒ ⓓ
98	ⓐ ⓑ ⓒ ⓓ	118	ⓐ ⓑ ⓒ ⓓ	138	ⓐ ⓑ ⓒ ⓓ	158	ⓐ ⓑ ⓒ ⓓ	178	ⓐ ⓑ ⓒ ⓓ	198	ⓐ ⓑ ⓒ ⓓ
99	ⓐ ⓑ ⓒ ⓓ	119	ⓐ ⓑ ⓒ ⓓ	139	ⓐ ⓑ ⓒ ⓓ	159	ⓐ ⓑ ⓒ ⓓ	179	ⓐ ⓑ ⓒ ⓓ	199	ⓐ ⓑ ⓒ ⓓ
100	ⓐ ⓑ ⓒ ⓓ	120	ⓐ ⓑ ⓒ ⓓ	140	ⓐ ⓑ ⓒ ⓓ	160	ⓐ ⓑ ⓒ ⓓ	180	ⓐ ⓑ ⓒ ⓓ	200	ⓐ ⓑ ⓒ ⓓ

ANSWER SHEET

시원스쿨 LAB

이름 | 테스트 회차 | 날짜

LISTENING COMPREHENSION (PART 1~4)

NO	ANSWER A B C D	NO	ANSWER A B C D	NO	ANSWER A B C D	NO	ANSWER A B C D	NO	ANSWER A B C D
1	ⓐⓑⓒⓓ	21	ⓐⓑⓒⓓ	41	ⓐⓑⓒⓓ	61	ⓐⓑⓒⓓ	81	ⓐⓑⓒⓓ
2	ⓐⓑⓒⓓ	22	ⓐⓑⓒⓓ	42	ⓐⓑⓒⓓ	62	ⓐⓑⓒⓓ	82	ⓐⓑⓒⓓ
3	ⓐⓑⓒⓓ	23	ⓐⓑⓒⓓ	43	ⓐⓑⓒⓓ	63	ⓐⓑⓒⓓ	83	ⓐⓑⓒⓓ
4	ⓐⓑⓒⓓ	24	ⓐⓑⓒⓓ	44	ⓐⓑⓒⓓ	64	ⓐⓑⓒⓓ	84	ⓐⓑⓒⓓ
5	ⓐⓑⓒⓓ	25	ⓐⓑⓒⓓ	45	ⓐⓑⓒⓓ	65	ⓐⓑⓒⓓ	85	ⓐⓑⓒⓓ
6	ⓐⓑⓒⓓ	26	ⓐⓑⓒⓓ	46	ⓐⓑⓒⓓ	66	ⓐⓑⓒⓓ	86	ⓐⓑⓒⓓ
7	ⓐⓑⓒⓓ	27	ⓐⓑⓒⓓ	47	ⓐⓑⓒⓓ	67	ⓐⓑⓒⓓ	87	ⓐⓑⓒⓓ
8	ⓐⓑⓒⓓ	28	ⓐⓑⓒⓓ	48	ⓐⓑⓒⓓ	68	ⓐⓑⓒⓓ	88	ⓐⓑⓒⓓ
9	ⓐⓑⓒⓓ	29	ⓐⓑⓒⓓ	49	ⓐⓑⓒⓓ	69	ⓐⓑⓒⓓ	89	ⓐⓑⓒⓓ
10	ⓐⓑⓒⓓ	30	ⓐⓑⓒⓓ	50	ⓐⓑⓒⓓ	70	ⓐⓑⓒⓓ	90	ⓐⓑⓒⓓ
11	ⓐⓑⓒⓓ	31	ⓐⓑⓒⓓ	51	ⓐⓑⓒⓓ	71	ⓐⓑⓒⓓ	91	ⓐⓑⓒⓓ
12	ⓐⓑⓒⓓ	32	ⓐⓑⓒⓓ	52	ⓐⓑⓒⓓ	72	ⓐⓑⓒⓓ	92	ⓐⓑⓒⓓ
13	ⓐⓑⓒⓓ	33	ⓐⓑⓒⓓ	53	ⓐⓑⓒⓓ	73	ⓐⓑⓒⓓ	93	ⓐⓑⓒⓓ
14	ⓐⓑⓒⓓ	34	ⓐⓑⓒⓓ	54	ⓐⓑⓒⓓ	74	ⓐⓑⓒⓓ	94	ⓐⓑⓒⓓ
15	ⓐⓑⓒⓓ	35	ⓐⓑⓒⓓ	55	ⓐⓑⓒⓓ	75	ⓐⓑⓒⓓ	95	ⓐⓑⓒⓓ
16	ⓐⓑⓒⓓ	36	ⓐⓑⓒⓓ	56	ⓐⓑⓒⓓ	76	ⓐⓑⓒⓓ	96	ⓐⓑⓒⓓ
17	ⓐⓑⓒⓓ	37	ⓐⓑⓒⓓ	57	ⓐⓑⓒⓓ	77	ⓐⓑⓒⓓ	97	ⓐⓑⓒⓓ
18	ⓐⓑⓒⓓ	38	ⓐⓑⓒⓓ	58	ⓐⓑⓒⓓ	78	ⓐⓑⓒⓓ	98	ⓐⓑⓒⓓ
19	ⓐⓑⓒⓓ	39	ⓐⓑⓒⓓ	59	ⓐⓑⓒⓓ	79	ⓐⓑⓒⓓ	99	ⓐⓑⓒⓓ
20	ⓐⓑⓒⓓ	40	ⓐⓑⓒⓓ	60	ⓐⓑⓒⓓ	80	ⓐⓑⓒⓓ	100	ⓐⓑⓒⓓ

READING COMPREHENSION (PART 5~7)

NO	ANSWER A B C D	NO	ANSWER A B C D	NO	ANSWER A B C D	NO	ANSWER A B C D	NO	ANSWER A B C D
101	ⓐⓑⓒⓓ	121	ⓐⓑⓒⓓ	141	ⓐⓑⓒⓓ	161	ⓐⓑⓒⓓ	181	ⓐⓑⓒⓓ
102	ⓐⓑⓒⓓ	122	ⓐⓑⓒⓓ	142	ⓐⓑⓒⓓ	162	ⓐⓑⓒⓓ	182	ⓐⓑⓒⓓ
103	ⓐⓑⓒⓓ	123	ⓐⓑⓒⓓ	143	ⓐⓑⓒⓓ	163	ⓐⓑⓒⓓ	183	ⓐⓑⓒⓓ
104	ⓐⓑⓒⓓ	124	ⓐⓑⓒⓓ	144	ⓐⓑⓒⓓ	164	ⓐⓑⓒⓓ	184	ⓐⓑⓒⓓ
105	ⓐⓑⓒⓓ	125	ⓐⓑⓒⓓ	145	ⓐⓑⓒⓓ	165	ⓐⓑⓒⓓ	185	ⓐⓑⓒⓓ
106	ⓐⓑⓒⓓ	126	ⓐⓑⓒⓓ	146	ⓐⓑⓒⓓ	166	ⓐⓑⓒⓓ	186	ⓐⓑⓒⓓ
107	ⓐⓑⓒⓓ	127	ⓐⓑⓒⓓ	147	ⓐⓑⓒⓓ	167	ⓐⓑⓒⓓ	187	ⓐⓑⓒⓓ
108	ⓐⓑⓒⓓ	128	ⓐⓑⓒⓓ	148	ⓐⓑⓒⓓ	168	ⓐⓑⓒⓓ	188	ⓐⓑⓒⓓ
109	ⓐⓑⓒⓓ	129	ⓐⓑⓒⓓ	149	ⓐⓑⓒⓓ	169	ⓐⓑⓒⓓ	189	ⓐⓑⓒⓓ
110	ⓐⓑⓒⓓ	130	ⓐⓑⓒⓓ	150	ⓐⓑⓒⓓ	170	ⓐⓑⓒⓓ	190	ⓐⓑⓒⓓ
111	ⓐⓑⓒⓓ	131	ⓐⓑⓒⓓ	151	ⓐⓑⓒⓓ	171	ⓐⓑⓒⓓ	191	ⓐⓑⓒⓓ
112	ⓐⓑⓒⓓ	132	ⓐⓑⓒⓓ	152	ⓐⓑⓒⓓ	172	ⓐⓑⓒⓓ	192	ⓐⓑⓒⓓ
113	ⓐⓑⓒⓓ	133	ⓐⓑⓒⓓ	153	ⓐⓑⓒⓓ	173	ⓐⓑⓒⓓ	193	ⓐⓑⓒⓓ
114	ⓐⓑⓒⓓ	134	ⓐⓑⓒⓓ	154	ⓐⓑⓒⓓ	174	ⓐⓑⓒⓓ	194	ⓐⓑⓒⓓ
115	ⓐⓑⓒⓓ	135	ⓐⓑⓒⓓ	155	ⓐⓑⓒⓓ	175	ⓐⓑⓒⓓ	195	ⓐⓑⓒⓓ
116	ⓐⓑⓒⓓ	136	ⓐⓑⓒⓓ	156	ⓐⓑⓒⓓ	176	ⓐⓑⓒⓓ	196	ⓐⓑⓒⓓ
117	ⓐⓑⓒⓓ	137	ⓐⓑⓒⓓ	157	ⓐⓑⓒⓓ	177	ⓐⓑⓒⓓ	197	ⓐⓑⓒⓓ
118	ⓐⓑⓒⓓ	138	ⓐⓑⓒⓓ	158	ⓐⓑⓒⓓ	178	ⓐⓑⓒⓓ	198	ⓐⓑⓒⓓ
119	ⓐⓑⓒⓓ	139	ⓐⓑⓒⓓ	159	ⓐⓑⓒⓓ	179	ⓐⓑⓒⓓ	199	ⓐⓑⓒⓓ
120	ⓐⓑⓒⓓ	140	ⓐⓑⓒⓓ	160	ⓐⓑⓒⓓ	180	ⓐⓑⓒⓓ	200	ⓐⓑⓒⓓ

ANSWER SHEET

시원스쿨 LAB

이름		테스트 호차		날짜			

LISTENING COMPREHENSION (PART 1~4)

NO	ANSWER	NO	ANSWER	NO	ANSWER	NO	ANSWER
	A B C D		A B C D		A B C D		A B C D
1	ⓐ ⓑ ⓒ	21	ⓐ ⓑ ⓒ	41	ⓐ ⓑ ⓒ ⓓ	61	ⓐ ⓑ ⓒ ⓓ
2	ⓐ ⓑ ⓒ	22	ⓐ ⓑ ⓒ	42	ⓐ ⓑ ⓒ ⓓ	62	ⓐ ⓑ ⓒ ⓓ
3	ⓐ ⓑ ⓒ	23	ⓐ ⓑ ⓒ	43	ⓐ ⓑ ⓒ ⓓ	63	ⓐ ⓑ ⓒ ⓓ
4	ⓐ ⓑ ⓒ ⓓ	24	ⓐ ⓑ ⓒ	44	ⓐ ⓑ ⓒ ⓓ	64	ⓐ ⓑ ⓒ ⓓ
5	ⓐ ⓑ ⓒ ⓓ	25	ⓐ ⓑ ⓒ	45	ⓐ ⓑ ⓒ ⓓ	65	ⓐ ⓑ ⓒ ⓓ
6	ⓐ ⓑ ⓒ ⓓ	26	ⓐ ⓑ ⓒ	46	ⓐ ⓑ ⓒ ⓓ	66	ⓐ ⓑ ⓒ ⓓ
7	ⓐ ⓑ ⓒ	27	ⓐ ⓑ ⓒ	47	ⓐ ⓑ ⓒ ⓓ	67	ⓐ ⓑ ⓒ ⓓ
8	ⓐ ⓑ ⓒ	28	ⓐ ⓑ ⓒ	48	ⓐ ⓑ ⓒ ⓓ	68	ⓐ ⓑ ⓒ ⓓ
9	ⓐ ⓑ ⓒ	29	ⓐ ⓑ ⓒ	49	ⓐ ⓑ ⓒ ⓓ	69	ⓐ ⓑ ⓒ ⓓ
10	ⓐ ⓑ ⓒ	30	ⓐ ⓑ ⓒ	50	ⓐ ⓑ ⓒ ⓓ	70	ⓐ ⓑ ⓒ ⓓ
11	ⓐ ⓑ ⓒ	31	ⓐ ⓑ ⓒ	51	ⓐ ⓑ ⓒ ⓓ	71	ⓐ ⓑ ⓒ ⓓ
12	ⓐ ⓑ ⓒ	32	ⓐ ⓑ ⓒ ⓓ	52	ⓐ ⓑ ⓒ ⓓ	72	ⓐ ⓑ ⓒ ⓓ
13	ⓐ ⓑ ⓒ	33	ⓐ ⓑ ⓒ ⓓ	53	ⓐ ⓑ ⓒ ⓓ	73	ⓐ ⓑ ⓒ ⓓ
14	ⓐ ⓑ ⓒ	34	ⓐ ⓑ ⓒ ⓓ	54	ⓐ ⓑ ⓒ ⓓ	74	ⓐ ⓑ ⓒ ⓓ
15	ⓐ ⓑ ⓒ	35	ⓐ ⓑ ⓒ ⓓ	55	ⓐ ⓑ ⓒ ⓓ	75	ⓐ ⓑ ⓒ ⓓ
16	ⓐ ⓑ ⓒ	36	ⓐ ⓑ ⓒ ⓓ	56	ⓐ ⓑ ⓒ ⓓ	76	ⓐ ⓑ ⓒ ⓓ
17	ⓐ ⓑ ⓒ	37	ⓐ ⓑ ⓒ ⓓ	57	ⓐ ⓑ ⓒ ⓓ	77	ⓐ ⓑ ⓒ ⓓ
18	ⓐ ⓑ ⓒ	38	ⓐ ⓑ ⓒ ⓓ	58	ⓐ ⓑ ⓒ ⓓ	78	ⓐ ⓑ ⓒ ⓓ
19	ⓐ ⓑ ⓒ	39	ⓐ ⓑ ⓒ ⓓ	59	ⓐ ⓑ ⓒ ⓓ	79	ⓐ ⓑ ⓒ ⓓ
20	ⓐ ⓑ ⓒ	40	ⓐ ⓑ ⓒ ⓓ	60	ⓐ ⓑ ⓒ ⓓ	80	ⓐ ⓑ ⓒ ⓓ

READING COMPREHENSION (PART 5~7)

NO	ANSWER	NO	ANSWER	NO	ANSWER	NO	ANSWER	NO	ANSWER
	A B C D		A B C D		A B C D		A B C D		A B C D
81	ⓐ ⓑ ⓒ ⓓ	101	ⓐ ⓑ ⓒ ⓓ	121	ⓐ ⓑ ⓒ ⓓ	141	ⓐ ⓑ ⓒ ⓓ	161	ⓐ ⓑ ⓒ ⓓ	181	ⓐ ⓑ ⓒ ⓓ
82	ⓐ ⓑ ⓒ ⓓ	102	ⓐ ⓑ ⓒ ⓓ	122	ⓐ ⓑ ⓒ ⓓ	142	ⓐ ⓑ ⓒ ⓓ	162	ⓐ ⓑ ⓒ ⓓ	182	ⓐ ⓑ ⓒ ⓓ
83	ⓐ ⓑ ⓒ ⓓ	103	ⓐ ⓑ ⓒ ⓓ	123	ⓐ ⓑ ⓒ ⓓ	143	ⓐ ⓑ ⓒ ⓓ	163	ⓐ ⓑ ⓒ ⓓ	183	ⓐ ⓑ ⓒ ⓓ
84	ⓐ ⓑ ⓒ ⓓ	104	ⓐ ⓑ ⓒ ⓓ	124	ⓐ ⓑ ⓒ ⓓ	144	ⓐ ⓑ ⓒ ⓓ	164	ⓐ ⓑ ⓒ ⓓ	184	ⓐ ⓑ ⓒ ⓓ
85	ⓐ ⓑ ⓒ ⓓ	105	ⓐ ⓑ ⓒ ⓓ	125	ⓐ ⓑ ⓒ ⓓ	145	ⓐ ⓑ ⓒ ⓓ	165	ⓐ ⓑ ⓒ ⓓ	185	ⓐ ⓑ ⓒ ⓓ
86	ⓐ ⓑ ⓒ ⓓ	106	ⓐ ⓑ ⓒ ⓓ	126	ⓐ ⓑ ⓒ ⓓ	146	ⓐ ⓑ ⓒ ⓓ	166	ⓐ ⓑ ⓒ ⓓ	186	ⓐ ⓑ ⓒ ⓓ
87	ⓐ ⓑ ⓒ ⓓ	107	ⓐ ⓑ ⓒ ⓓ	127	ⓐ ⓑ ⓒ ⓓ	147	ⓐ ⓑ ⓒ ⓓ	167	ⓐ ⓑ ⓒ ⓓ	187	ⓐ ⓑ ⓒ ⓓ
88	ⓐ ⓑ ⓒ ⓓ	108	ⓐ ⓑ ⓒ ⓓ	128	ⓐ ⓑ ⓒ ⓓ	148	ⓐ ⓑ ⓒ ⓓ	168	ⓐ ⓑ ⓒ ⓓ	188	ⓐ ⓑ ⓒ ⓓ
89	ⓐ ⓑ ⓒ ⓓ	109	ⓐ ⓑ ⓒ ⓓ	129	ⓐ ⓑ ⓒ ⓓ	149	ⓐ ⓑ ⓒ ⓓ	169	ⓐ ⓑ ⓒ ⓓ	189	ⓐ ⓑ ⓒ ⓓ
90	ⓐ ⓑ ⓒ ⓓ	110	ⓐ ⓑ ⓒ ⓓ	130	ⓐ ⓑ ⓒ ⓓ	150	ⓐ ⓑ ⓒ ⓓ	170	ⓐ ⓑ ⓒ ⓓ	190	ⓐ ⓑ ⓒ ⓓ
91	ⓐ ⓑ ⓒ ⓓ	111	ⓐ ⓑ ⓒ ⓓ	131	ⓐ ⓑ ⓒ ⓓ	151	ⓐ ⓑ ⓒ ⓓ	171	ⓐ ⓑ ⓒ ⓓ	191	ⓐ ⓑ ⓒ ⓓ
92	ⓐ ⓑ ⓒ ⓓ	112	ⓐ ⓑ ⓒ ⓓ	132	ⓐ ⓑ ⓒ ⓓ	152	ⓐ ⓑ ⓒ ⓓ	172	ⓐ ⓑ ⓒ ⓓ	192	ⓐ ⓑ ⓒ ⓓ
93	ⓐ ⓑ ⓒ ⓓ	113	ⓐ ⓑ ⓒ ⓓ	133	ⓐ ⓑ ⓒ ⓓ	153	ⓐ ⓑ ⓒ ⓓ	173	ⓐ ⓑ ⓒ ⓓ	193	ⓐ ⓑ ⓒ ⓓ
94	ⓐ ⓑ ⓒ ⓓ	114	ⓐ ⓑ ⓒ ⓓ	134	ⓐ ⓑ ⓒ ⓓ	154	ⓐ ⓑ ⓒ ⓓ	174	ⓐ ⓑ ⓒ ⓓ	194	ⓐ ⓑ ⓒ ⓓ
95	ⓐ ⓑ ⓒ ⓓ	115	ⓐ ⓑ ⓒ ⓓ	135	ⓐ ⓑ ⓒ ⓓ	155	ⓐ ⓑ ⓒ ⓓ	175	ⓐ ⓑ ⓒ ⓓ	195	ⓐ ⓑ ⓒ ⓓ
96	ⓐ ⓑ ⓒ ⓓ	116	ⓐ ⓑ ⓒ ⓓ	136	ⓐ ⓑ ⓒ ⓓ	156	ⓐ ⓑ ⓒ ⓓ	176	ⓐ ⓑ ⓒ ⓓ	196	ⓐ ⓑ ⓒ ⓓ
97	ⓐ ⓑ ⓒ ⓓ	117	ⓐ ⓑ ⓒ ⓓ	137	ⓐ ⓑ ⓒ ⓓ	157	ⓐ ⓑ ⓒ ⓓ	177	ⓐ ⓑ ⓒ ⓓ	197	ⓐ ⓑ ⓒ ⓓ
98	ⓐ ⓑ ⓒ ⓓ	118	ⓐ ⓑ ⓒ ⓓ	138	ⓐ ⓑ ⓒ ⓓ	158	ⓐ ⓑ ⓒ ⓓ	178	ⓐ ⓑ ⓒ ⓓ	198	ⓐ ⓑ ⓒ ⓓ
99	ⓐ ⓑ ⓒ ⓓ	119	ⓐ ⓑ ⓒ ⓓ	139	ⓐ ⓑ ⓒ ⓓ	159	ⓐ ⓑ ⓒ ⓓ	179	ⓐ ⓑ ⓒ ⓓ	199	ⓐ ⓑ ⓒ ⓓ
100	ⓐ ⓑ ⓒ ⓓ	120	ⓐ ⓑ ⓒ ⓓ	140	ⓐ ⓑ ⓒ ⓓ	160	ⓐ ⓑ ⓒ ⓓ	180	ⓐ ⓑ ⓒ ⓓ	200	ⓐ ⓑ ⓒ ⓓ